# FORGOTTEN
# SHRINES

CW00677351

Harrington Hall.

# FORGOTTEN SHRINES

AN ACCOUNT OF SOME OLD CATHOLIC
HALLS AND FAMILIES IN ENGLAND
AND OF RELICS AND MEMORIALS
OF THE ENGLISH MARTYRS

*By* DOM BEDE CAMM, O.S.B., B.A. Oxon.
AUTHOR OF 'LIVES OF THE ENGLISH MARTYRS' ETC.
EDITOR OF 'THE ST. NICHOLAS SERIES OF BEAUTIFUL BOOKS'

GRACEWING

First published in 1910 by Macdonald & Evans, London
This edition published in 2004

Gracewing
2 Southern Avenue, Leominster
Herefordshire HR6 0QF

All rights reserved. No part of this publication may be reproduced, stored
in a retrieval system, or transmitted in any form, or by any means, elec-
tronic, mechanical, photocopying, recording or otherwise, without the
written permission of the publisher.

Introduction to the Gracewing edition © Aidan Bellenger, OSB 2004

This edition © Gracewing Publishing 2004


ISBN 0 85244 615 2


Additional typesetting by
Action Publishing Technology Ltd
Gloucester GL1 5SR


Printed in England by
Antony Rowe Ltd
Eastbourne BN23 6QT

# INTRODUCTION

*Forgotten Shrines* was first published in 1910 by Macdonald and Evans in London and by Herder in St Louis. It was a lavishly illustrated presentation volume, almost a coffee-table book, of some four hundred generously margined pages with a stamped cover and numerous illustrations, many of them evocative full-plate photographs. It was both expensive and appealing. It was also epoch making. In evoking a lost Catholic England of 'ancient manor houses' which provided 'the last refuges of the ancient faith' it presented the reading public with a portrait of an alternative pre-industrial England, another country, concealed for centuries by the implications of the great disruption of the Reformation. This other Catholic England, of priests' hiding places, martyrs executed for treason who espoused a truer nationalism, and of relics and times rather than more tangible remains, was to leave a permanent mark on the popular perception of the Catholic past and helped to construct a recusant ideal and identity which remains potent.

The book was compiled by a Benedictine, Dom Bede Camm, an industrious monk resident at Erdington Abbey in the sprawling suburbs of Birmingham whose adult life and considerable scholarly energies were dedicated to the English Catholic martyrs of the Reformation and their lost world. He was a pioneer in his field combining nostalgia with critical scholarship, modern research tools (including the motor car and the camera) with traditional antiquarianism, imagination and analysis. His book may contain some slips and not a few optimistic conclusions and assertions but it is always based on sound research and 'on site' visits. His careful historical notes preserved at Downside are an impressive monument to both his energy and his skill at transcription and analysis.

Reginald Bede Camm, born at Sunbury Park, Middlesex, on 26 December 1864, was the son of John Camm, late of the Twelfth Lancers. He was educated at Westminster School and at Keble College, Oxford, where he graduated in 1887. A ritualist from childhood, Camm served a curacy as a Church of England clergyman at the church of St Agnes in Kennington South London (having completed his theological training at Cuddesdon College in rural Oxfordshire) before his reception into the Catholic Church in 1890. He joined the Benedictine community at Maredsous in Belgium, established in 1872 as a daughter house of Beuron in Germany, a monastery celebrated for its liturgical splendour and strict observance. It was attracting a number of English subjects not least since the establishment of the English Beuronese monastery at Erdington in 1876. Professed in 1891, Camm was ordained in 1895 and was resident at Erdington continuously from 1896–1912. In 1913 he was closely

# INTRODUCTION

involved with the reception into the Catholic Church of the Anglican communities of monks on Caldey Island and nuns at Milford Haven, and in the same year he was affiliated to the English Benedictine abbey of Downside in Somerset. Anti-German feeling was gathering in the run-up to the Great War and Camm's 'Englishness' seemed more appropriately settled at Downside. The Somerset monastery had changed greatly since Camm's conversion. The old English Benedictine ideal of the mission was being replaced by an observant, conventual life. Downside had been elevated to abbatial status, accepted more 'monastic' constitutions and begun to rebuild its church on even higher Gothic principles than Maredsous.

Camm's monastic life at Downside was not one of quiet stability. He spent most of the war as a chaplain to the Forces in the Middle East and the years 1919–31 at Cambridge where he was master of Benet House, the Downside house of studies for the university. Elected a Fellow of the Society of Antiquaries in 1922 his later scholarly interests moved backwards to the Middle Ages — and especially to Devonshire rood screens — but he was always best remembered for his association with the martyrs and recusancy. He died on 8 September 1942, after a long decline, and is buried at Downside.

Camm was heir to the English Benedictine tradition of historical writing which sought a revisionist interpretation of the English past and he was to some extent, too, the natural successor to the English Jesuit martyrologists like John Hungerford Pollen (1858–1925) whose *Acts of the English Martyrs* was published in 1896. Overall, however, he had no master, peer or historical disciple, ploughing his own historical furrow. His first major work, *A Benedictine Martyr in England* (1897) was a life of John Roberts, one of the founders of the English Benedictine Congregation of the Seventeenth Century, and it was followed in quick succession by *In the Brave Days of Old* and *Blessed Sebastian Newdigate* (both 1900) and the two-volume *Lives of the English Martyrs* (1904). *A Birthday Book of English Martyrs* (1908), published by Washbourne's approaches *Forgotten Shrines* in its quality of production.

*Forgotten Shrines* does not pretend to be an encyclopedia of recusant sites or Catholic houses. Many important locations, notably East Anglian ones like Oxburgh and Sawston receive at most a passing attention. The highly important symbolic Catholic buildings of Thomas Tresham (1534–1605) in Northamptonshire are not mentioned. The rich Catholic tradition of Scotland celebrated in Dom Odo Blundell's *Ancient Catholic Houses of Scotland* (1907) is ignored. He has a special liking for moated manor houses in the Midlands, especially Harvington Hall and Baddesley Clinton, which sum up his ideal of the Catholic home. He has an

# INTRODUCTION

antiquary's appetite for monumental inscriptions and pleasing decay and an enthusiasm for the hidden and the forgotten. Camm probably thought he was recording a world which was on the brink of extinction and that many of the sites he visited would soon fall into terminal decay. What makes Camm's work so attractive today is that so many of his 'shrines' are still recognisable and much more accessible than a century ago.

Harvington Hall, sold by its recusant owners in the 1920s, was saved by the Archdiocese of Birmingham in the 1970s and Baddesley Clinton is in the hands of the National Trust. Both are open regularly. Some 'forgotten shrines' are still at risk (2003), including Rectory Farm at Lower Brailes in Warwick, Snore Hall in Norfolk and most important of all Sawston Hall near Cambridge, with its classic Nicholas Owen hide of 1592–3, recently on the market for £5 million.

Camm was a significant figure in the late Victorian and Edwardian rediscovery of 'heritage' which showed itself in many similar books to Camm's and in the foundation of both the National Trust (1895) and *Country Life* (1897) magazine. J.H. Shorthouses's Anglo-Catholic romance, *John Inglesant* (1896) redolent of country houses, was a pioneer in its genre. His telling of the story of the skull of Wardley Hall may have owed something to the writings of the Cambridge scholar M.R. James (1862–1936) whose first collection of *Ghost Stories of an Antiquary*, with their erudition and imaginative reconstruction resembling Camm's approach, was published in 1904. Macmillan's county guides under the series title 'Highways and Byways' were being published at the same time as *Forgotten Shrines* and share its whimsicality and good use of illustrations. Camm's work may have had its influence, too, on the writings of R.H. Benson (1871–1914) and on the extraordinary volume of stories by Dom Roger Huddleston (1874–1936), of Downside, writing as Roger Pater, *Mystic Voices* (1933) recollecting the fictional experiences of a squire who was also a priest. In the longer term, too, Evelyn Waugh in his 'Catholic novel' *Brideshead Revisited* (1945) writes in the same tradition to say nothing of Chesterton or Belloc.

*Forgotten Shrines* can be looked at on many levels. Like H.V. Morton (1892–1979), who began his journalistic career at Birmingham in 1910, in his *In Search of England* (1927) it is a journey to a land of lost content although in Camm's work peopled by ghosts rather than living men and women. Camm's panorama is a pilgrimage, suffused with a strong sense of *genius loci*, and a healthy devotion. It has a picturesque feel, too, and a profound Englishness seeking an English Catholicism sympathetic to a convert from Anglicanism. It has an elegiac tone which wishes farewell to an increasingly struggling identity soon to be swept away by the Great

# INTRODUCTION

War. Above all else, however, it is a celebration of Catholic life and witness in England intended to educate and hearten.

Dom Aidan Bellenger
Downside Abbey
6 August 2003

# PREFACE

CARDINAL NEWMAN, in the most wonderful of all his sermons, has treated with matchless eloquence the theme of the decay and death of the ancient Church in this land, and of its miraculous resurrection in that "Second Spring" which came so unexpectedly to close the long winter of persecution.

"All seemed to be lost," he says; "there was a struggle for a time, and then its priests were cast out or martyred. There were sacrileges innumerable. Its temples were profaned or destroyed; its revenues seized by covetous nobles, or squandered upon the ministers of a new faith. The presence of Catholicism was at length simply removed,—its grace disowned—its power despised—its name, except as a matter of history, at length almost unknown. . . .

"No longer the Catholic Church in the country; nay, no longer, I may say a Catholic community; but a few adherents of the Old Religion, moving silently and sorrowfully about, as memorials of what had been. . . . There, perhaps, an elderly person, seen walking in the streets, grave and solitary, and strange, though noble in bearing, and said to be of good family and a 'Roman Catholic.' An old-fashioned house of gloomy appearance, closed in with high walls, with an iron gate and yews, and the report attaching to it that 'Roman Catholics' lived there; but who they were, or what was meant by calling them Roman Catholics, no one could tell; though it had an unpleasant sound and told of form and superstition."

I have attempted in this book to tell the story of some of those ancient manor houses which became the last refuges of the ancient faith, when it was proscribed and persecuted throughout the land. The air of mystery and romance which seems to exhale from the crumbling walls of these old houses, irresistibly moves those who come across them to curiosity if not to reverence. And this is an attempt to satisfy such legitimate curiosity.

Englishmen of all creeds have grown more sympathetic of late, as they have come to know something of the true story of that long persecution which made their Catholic fellow countrymen outlaws in their own land, and turned their most treasured religious convictions into crime against the State. We are beginning to understand the extraordinary loyalty of these Recusants, so faithful to the sovereign who persecuted them just because they were so true to the religion of their

PREFACE

fathers, and with Gairdner, Jessopp, Cox, Frere and many another Anglican writer, can give our tribute of admiration to those heroic men who bore the horrors of Tyburn without flinching rather than betray their conscience or deny their faith.

It is hoped, therefore, that this book, which deals with some of the most romantic of these ancient homes, and with the lives of some of those who dwelt there, may have an interest for a far wider circle of readers than can be looked for among the small body of English Catholics.

I have attempted also to give some account of the principal relics and memorials of the martyrs of those sad days, relics which are cherished, for the most part, by the older religious communities, or by the families which have clung to the faith all through the penal times.

There are so many friends to whom my gratitude is due for their kind assistance, that it is really impossible to name them all. But I cannot omit to mention Mr. George Buchannan of Whitby, Mr. R. Trappes-Lomax, Miss Louise Imogen Guiney, Mr. Fitzherbert of Swynnerton, the Lady Stafford, Mr. W. Fitzherbert-Brockholes of Claughton Hall, Colonel Hart-Davis of Wardley Hall, Mr. Joseph Gillow, Mr. James Watts of Abney Hall, Sir Benjamin Stone of Erdington, Mr. Stafford H. Jerningham, Mr. John Eyston of Hendred House, Mr. John Foster of Horton-in-Ribblesdale, Sir Henry Ingilby of Ripley Castle, the Rev. Father Storey of Egton Bridge, Mr. R. H. Murray of Worcester, Mr. John Humphreys of Birmingham, Miss Capel Miers of Eastbach Court, Mr. William Bolton and Miss A. Jackson of Chorley, Mr. George Hull of Gregson Lane, Mr. Peter Worden, and Mr. Joseph F. Carter of Kimbolton, who have all given generous help in various ways.

To my friends Miss Gunning and Miss Jewitt of Erdington, we owe the excellent index, which adds so much to the value of a book of this kind.

I have to thank, too, her Grace the Duchess of Norfolk for leave to reproduce the unique "Badge of the Pilgrimage of Grace," which is appropriately stamped on the cover of this volume ; Mr. Fletcher Moss, author of *Pilgrimages to Old Homes*, for the loan of several blocks, chiefly illustrating the section on Father Barlow ; Mr. James Britten, K.S.G., and the Committee of the Catholic Truth Society for leave to reprint part of the life of Father Barlow, which I had already published under their auspices ; the Rev. J. J. Wynne, S.J., and the Editors of the *Dublin Review*, the *Catholic Fireside* and the *Catholic World* for leave to reproduce portions of the text and, in some cases, illustrations, which had already appeared in their pages. I have also to thank Sir Benjamin

xii

# PREFACE

Stone and Mr. Bate of Bromsgrove, for permission to reproduce some of their beautiful photographs of Harvington Hall.

Most of the photographs illustrating the text are my own work, and I trust that I have not infringed any copyright in reproducing the others. I have to thank Mr. Miller of Christchurch, Hants., Messrs. Stott of Ripley, Mr. Frank Sutcliffe of Whitby, and Mr. Bateson of Gregson Lane, who have kindly placed their photographs at my disposal.

But I feel a very special debt of gratitude to my artist, Mr. Joseph Pike, for the very beautiful drawings with which he has illustrated and adorned the text. Mr. Pike is still a young man, and there can be no doubt as to his great talent. It is, however, unnecessary for me to praise work of which my readers can judge the merit for themselves.

And in conclusion I feel I must thank the many kind friends, known and unknown, who so generously subscribed to this work while it was yet unprinted; nor can I refrain from expressing my deep gratitude for the kind and gracious encouragement with which his Grace the Archbishop of Westminster and almost every member of the Catholic Hierarchy in England have been pleased to welcome and to bless my scheme.

Though I cannot but fear that manifold imperfections in carrying it out may cause disappointment to some of my readers, I venture to hope that, on the whole, this work may prove useful, and that it may help in some small degree to spread a deeper understanding and a wider sympathy for the old Religion of our country, and for those who clung to it so faithfully in the dark days that are past.

D. B. C.

Erdington Abbey,
 Feast of the Nativity of Our Lady.
  *September* 8, 1910.

# CONTENTS

xv

# CONTENTS

xvi

# ILLUSTRATIONS

# ILLUSTRATIONS

# ILLUSTRATIONS

# ILLUSTRATIONS

THE CHANCEL OF NORBURY CHURCH
*The brass of Sir Anthony Fitzherbert lies on the floor
between the two altar tombs. Photo by the author*

*To face page* 1

# THE TRAGEDY OF THE FITZHERBERTS

## THE ORIGIN OF THE FAMILY

THERE are but few families still flourishing in England that are able to prove a lineal male descent from an ancestor who took part in the Norman Conquest, and still fewer able to establish their pedigree from authentic documents remaining in their own possession. This distinction, however, belongs to the Fitzherberts of Norbury and Swynnerton. For over seven hundred years the Manor of Norbury, with its ancient Hall, was in possession of the family, and though it has unhappily passed out of the hands of the present head of the house, Swynnerton still remains to the Fitzherberts, as well as other estates which have belonged to them for centuries.

But to the Catholic, the Fitzherberts possess a title to fame far more glorious than that of ancient lineage or wide possessions. In spite of centuries of fierce persecution they have been ever loyal to the ancient faith, ever true to their grand device, *Ung je serviray;* shrinking not from poverty or exile, imprisonment or death, so that they might remain the true servants of their King.

It is principally with the story of these Fitzherberts, who were loyal even under the supreme test of martyrdom, that we are here concerned. Other more competent writers have traced the family history and recounted its fortunes, yet it may not be out of place to give here some account of the origin of a house that is thus doubly illustrious.

Fortunately, the materials for the family history are as voluminous as they are interesting. The great MS. " Family Book " preserved at Swynnerton, a huge folio drawn up by Michael Jones, F.S.A., under the direction of Thomas Fitzherbert, Esquire, Twenty-fifth Lord of Norbury (1789–1857), and since continued up to date, is a storehouse of records, pedigrees, biographies, and copies of documents, together with drawings, prints, and facsimiles of grants, monuments, brasses, portraits, the illuminated shields of the families with which the Fitzherberts have contracted alliances, and everything that the most patient care and wide learning have been able to gather together about the family. It is true that here and there later investigation has been able to correct some of the conclusions arrived at by the author. More than one Derbyshire antiquary of note has laboured at the Fitzherbert history with learned enthusiasm, and their discoveries have not been neglected here.

A

# FORGOTTEN SHRINES

The present writer has been given free access to the original documents preserved at Swynnerton, as well as to the Family Book. One of his pilgrimages to Norbury was made in company with the present head of the family, without whose kind and generous co-operation this record could not have seen the light.*

The ancestor of the Fitzherberts was a Norman, who seems to have been a retainer of one of the Conqueror's most powerful barons, Henry de Ferrers. This ancestor, Herbert by name, had a son named William, who, according to a custom prevalent among the Normans, was known as Fils or Fitz Herbert, and thus Fitzherbert became the family patronymic.

His feudal lord, Henry de Ferrers, had a vast share of the spoil when the Conqueror began to apportion it out among his followers. He received no less than 113 manors in Derbyshire alone. He thus laid the foundation of a great family, which has survived to our own day, and in one of its elder branches (the Ferrers of Baddesley Clinton) has had, like the Fitzherberts themselves, the grace to preserve the faith intact throughout all the vicissitudes of fortune.

The Norman conquerors were devout Catholics, and gave the Church a generous share of their spoil. In 1080 Henry de Ferrers founded the Benedictine Priory of the Blessed Virgin Mary of Tutbury, though the first charter of foundation was not granted until the succeeding reign (1087–1100) by Robert, first Earl Ferrers. Among the numerous manors with which he endowed the monastery was that of Norbury.

Norbury is situated on the Dove, close to the south-western border of Derbyshire, and about four miles from Ashbourne. It belonged in the reign of the Confessor to a great Saxon thane named Siward. There was even then a priest and a church, besides a mill, twenty-four acres of meadow land, and a wood, one mile in length and breadth, for pasturing swine.

But the monks of Tutbury did not long retain possession of the manor. In 1125 (no doubt at the instance of Robert de Ferrers)

* The writer must also express his obligations to the writings of Dr. J. Charles Cox, who has made this subject peculiarly his own. See *Churches of Derbyshire* (Bemrose, 1877), vols. iii. and v. ; *Three Centuries of Derbyshire Annals*, vol. i. (Bemrose, 1890) ; the *Journal of the Derbyshire Archæological Society*, vols. vii. and xxv. He also is indebted to various papers by Sir Ernest Clarke, as well as to Mr. St. John Hope, *Journal*, vol. iv. ; Mr. J. Bailey, *Journal*, vols. iv. and v. ; the Rev. Reginald H. C. Fitzherbert, *Journal*, xix. and xx. ; Mr. J. Tilley, *Old Halls, Manors and Families of Derbyshire*, by J.T. (1893) ; also to Mr. R. Trappes-Lomax, who has put his transcripts from the Fitzherbert records and many valuable notes at the author's disposition. The *Journal of the Derbyshire Archæological Society* is quoted in these notes simply as the *Journal*.

2

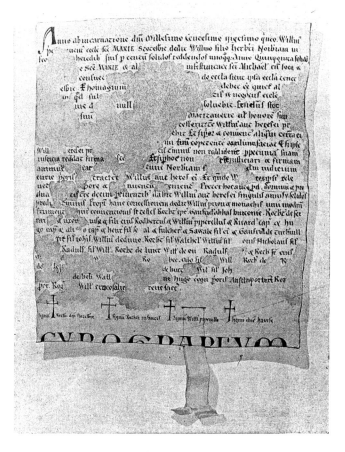

## THE ORIGINAL DEED GRANTING NORBURY TO THE FITZHERBERTS
*From the facsimile in the Family Book at Swynnerton*
*Photo by the author*

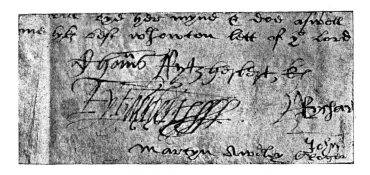

## SIGNATURES OF SIR THOMAS FITZHERBERT, KT., THOMAS FITZHERBERT, ESQ., AND MARTIN AUDLEY
*From a deed at Swynnerton.* *Photo by the author* *To face page 2*

William the Prior granted it by charter to William Fitz Herbert and to his heirs, to be holden in fee of the Priory of Tutbury, subject to the yearly fee-farm rent of one hundred shillings, and of five shillings annually in lieu of tithes for the lands in demesne and two bovates, and subject also to the usual feudal burdens.

From this date the Fitzherberts held Norbury as tenants of Tutbury Priory. However, in the fifteenth century, the then lord of Norbury, Nicholas Fitzherbert, with Ralph, his son, enfranchised the manor from these rents and services, giving in exchange to Thomas Gedney, then Prior of Tutbury, various lands, tenements, and rents in Osmaston, Foston, and Church Broughton, Derbyshire.

The precious charter which granted Norbury to William Fitzherbert is still in the possession of his twenty-seventh lineal descendent, Basil Fitzherbert, Esquire, of Swynnerton, County Stafford, as is the later document by which the manor was enfranchised. We give an illustration of the former taken from a *facsimile* made by Willemart for the Family Book, as the original charter has been so injured by chemicals in the attempt to make it legible, that it is almost impossible to photograph it.

We give a translation of a copy of this deed in the Chartulary of Tutbury, now in the College of Arms—(The copy is not a complete transcript) : " In the year from the Incarnation of our Lord 1125 William the Prior and the Convent of the Church of St. Mary of Tutbury, Granted to William the son of Herbert, Norbury in fee to him and his heirs, rendering 100 shillings every year, 50 shillings at the Annunciation of St. Mary and other 50 shillings at the feast of St. Michael for his homage . . . and if he shall be summoned by the Prior he shall . . . in the province of Tutbury—and if the Lord of Tutbury should redeem his body from captivity or should marry his eldest daughter or should repurchase his honour [? pay a relief] and the Prior of Tutbury should grant to him an aid for these purposes, then the said William or his heirs shall contribute to the said Prior a competent aid according to his fee. And if the Prior and Convent should purchase any land, the said William or his heir shall make a competent aid according to his fee. And if the said William or his heir shall not pay the said rent at the appointed times, he shall be brought to justice, and if he cannot be brought to justice and shall retain the rents the Prior shall then cause Norbury to be seized and afterwards the said William or his heir shall be justly dealt with according to the judgment of the Court of the Prior, and when the said William shall die his heir shall relieve his fee given from the Prior and Convent. Moreover also the said William or his heir shall give

3

every year on the aforesaid times five shillings for the tythes of the Demesne and for two bovates of land liable to tythe. For this grant the said William gave to the said Prior and monks a measure of wheat. And of this convention are witnesses Robert the Bishop, Gaufrid Abbot of Burton, Robert de Ferrers and his wife Avise and his sons, &c. &c."

During the centuries that they held Norbury the Fitzherberts invariably intermarried with families of their own knightly rank and as a rule with heiresses. Thus they can boast of being able to make the proof, so much prized on the Continent, of "sixteen quarterings without a window," for all their alliances have been with armigerous families. Indeed, their shield at Swynnerton is emblazoned with no fewer than 121 quarterings. This shield of arms occurs at the foot of the great pedigree, compiled by Francis Townsend, Windsor Herald, for Basil Fitzherbert in 1796. The original arms of the family are taken from those of their feudal lords, as was so frequently the custom among vassals as a mark of subinfeudation.

William de Ferrers, third Earl of Derby (who was living in 1167), married Margaret, heiress of William de Peverel, Earl of Nottingham, and adopted her father's arms, *Vairé or and gules*, as his own. This coat henceforth became the arms of the Earls Ferrers, and the Fitzherberts of Norbury adopted part of them as their own.

The shield is thus blazoned : *Argent, a chief Vairé or and gules surtout a bend sable*. There is a very ancient deed preserved in the family records bearing this shield. We give a photograph of it, since it is one of the earliest known instances of the seal of arms of a private gentleman. It is attached to a deed executed by John Fitzherbert, the grandson of William, the first grantee of Norbury, and its date is probably late in the reign of Henry II., who died in 1189.

It grants to William the Chaplain, son of Robert, and to whomsoever he shall assign them for his homage and service, one culture of land between the land of Robert de Wyvile and Depedale and between the ditches of the said William the Chaplain and the road. Also an acre of meadow in the moor, namely between the meadow which Obverdes [?] held and the meadow which Rondulfus Peket held, and an acre of land in the wood along the boundary of Snelliston [in Norbury]. To be holden of him and his heirs in fee and inheritance truly, quietly, honourably, with all liberties and free Commons and all Easements to the town of Norbury or Rossington belonging. Rendering thence annually to me and my heirs after me xii pence before the Nativity of Our Lord for all service and secular demand. And that this my Concession and grant shall be ratified and

4

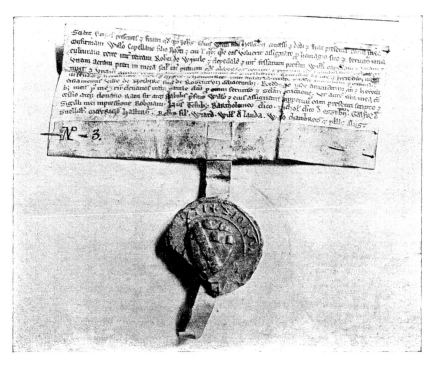

THE OLDEST SEAL WITH THE FITZHERBERT ARMS

GRANT BY KING EDWARD I. TO SIR HENRY FITZHERBERT
TO DIVERT THE HIGH ROAD WHICH RAN THROUGH THE
COURT OF NORBURY MANOR HOUSE

*Photo by the author from the original deeds preserved at Swynnerton*     *To face page* 4

stable to the said William and his assigns for ever, I have fortified the same by the impression of my seal to this present writing—Witnesses &c.

Three centuries later, as we shall see, Sir Anthony Fitzherbert, the famous judge, adopted the arms of Fitzherbert of Deane, quartered with the ancient arms, and this coat (*Gules* 3 *Lions rampant Or*) was used by the family indiscriminately with the ancient arms, till quite recently, and is still used exclusively by the Fitzherberts of Somersall and Tissington.

It is not easy to conjecture why Sir Anthony adopted this coat, but it is probable that it had a reference to the noble house of Herbert, Earls of Pembroke, who bear *Party per Pale azure and gules,* 3 *lions rampant argent.* Sir Anthony may have believed that he was himself descended from their Ancestor, Herbert the Chamberlain to Henry II., though that was not the fact. In any case the family have now given up these arms.

Their crest is a dexter arm from the elbow, the hand within a gauntlet proper. The motto is : *Ung je serviray*. This is the same as that of the Earls of Pembroke, so that it was probably adopted by the Fitzherberts of Norbury at the same time as the shield of the three Lions. If so, although adopted in error, it was a very happy choice, a truly *felix culpa*. For no motto could be more appropriate to a family who were loyal to the death to the one Lord and the one Faith.


## NORBURY HALL

IT would be difficult to imagine a spot more delightful than the ancient house of the Fitzherberts. The charms of a church of extraordinary dignity and beauty, filled with ancient glass and historic monuments, would be themselves sufficient to make Norbury a place of delight, but the rarer glories of a mediæval Manor House, inhabited for centuries by the family that built it seven hundred years ago, and redolent of the romance that is exhaled by the heroic deeds and sufferings of a race of Christian heroes, make it a very shrine of pilgrimage.

The surroundings are very beautiful. Standing on a high cliff above the river Dove, the Church and Manor House are embowered in splendid trees which enhance their architectural charms.

The Manor House is now untenanted, but is carefully preserved by its new owners, who take the greatest pride in its possession. The garden is filled with beautiful flowers and shrubs, and a few pieces of good old furniture are placed in the panelled rooms. The Great Hall is still used as a barn and is un-restored.

This Hall was built by Sir Henry Fitzherbert, Sixth Lord of Norbury, at the beginning of the fourteenth century. In the old Pedigrees he is styled a Knight Banneret (8 Edward II., 1314). Up to this time the Manor House Court was a public thoroughfare, for the road from Yeaveley (where the Knights of St. John had a Preceptory) to Ellaston passed right through it, crossing the Dove just below the house. Before rebuilding his house Sir Henry sought to divert this public road, and eventually obtained leave to do so, on payment of a fee of forty shillings, and on condition of making another road through his own land equally convenient for travellers. This Licence was granted by Letters Patent of 8 May, 33 Edward I. (1305), and is still preserved at Swynnerton.* We give a reproduction.

It is curious that Sir Henry, while he was about it, did not divert the road still further, for it passes, at present, inconveniently near the south side of the house. He cannot have moved it more than 68 paces. The Great Hall and State apartments built at this time are well seen in our illustration, which is taken from the west. As Dr. Cox remarks, "There is but very little domestic work left in England of so early a date." The building consists of a parallelogram some 55 feet long by 25 feet broad, and divided internally by a wall, which cuts off about 14 feet at the south end to form an ante-room.†

The building was divided, originally as now, into two stories, the exterior string-course marking the floor-level. It will be observed that the door is of the fifteenth-century date, the original entrance to both stories was at the south end. The Great Hall was lighted by three square-headed windows on the west side, which were equi-distant between the buttresses. The two original windows of the state-room above remain, but are blocked up. The chimney is on the east side; there is a rude stone chimney-piece within the state-room which was 37 feet 9 inches in length and only 9 feet 10 inches high to the moulded oak beams, some of which remain, though the ceiling has been removed and the space is open to the modern roof of red tile. Originally it would appear that this apartment was lighted by three windows in the west and two in the east wall, and these windows were, no doubt, emblazoned with many of the coats of arms in stained glass, which were enumerated by Laurence Bostock, the herald, on his journey from London to Cheshire in October 1581. At the northern end is an arched doorway

---

* No. 7 of the Norbury deeds. It is printed in Rymer's *Foedera*.

† Cox, *Journal*, vol. vii., gives a good description of the house, with a plan and several illustrations. We are indebted to this account for much of the detail of our description.

6

ROYDON MANOR HOUSE
THE GREAT HALL

which, it is conjectured, opened upon a wooden gallery communicating with the west wall of the church, in which a closed doorway with the diagonal line of a penthouse roof above used to be distinctly visible.

Nicholas Fitzherbert, Eleventh Lord of Norbury, who did so much for the Church, has also left his mark on the fabric of the Hall. The beautiful west doorway, of which we give an illustration,* was, no doubt, his work, though the door which is now hung in it is believed by Dr. Cox to be of earlier date, and to have been moved here from some inner doorway, as is indicated by the traceried openings with which it is pierced. These circular openings are of Decorated design, and are, therefore, probably Sir Henry's work. Sir Nicholas is, no doubt, also responsible for the moulded beams of the flat roofs of the rooms of both stories at the south end of the Great Hall building. A very narrow staircase of oak, about 2 feet 6 inches only in the width, leads from the lower room to the upper, and thus gives access to the state apartment. The ceiling of this upper room has fine foliated bosses at the intersection of the beams, similar in character to those on the roof of the Church.

At right angles to the Great Hall stands the only other portion of the once extensive buildings of the Manor House. This block forms the southern side of what was originally the inner Court. But both fronts were refaced with red brick in the eighteenth century, and few who pass it on the road would guess the real antiquity of the building. The date of this portion is not quite certain. It is probably to be attributed to Nicholas Fitzherbert (who died in 1473), or at least to his son Ralph, who mentions the "new hall at Norbury" in his will, January 21, 1484. Dr. Cox, however, believes that Sir Anthony Fitzherbert, the famous judge, Fourteenth Lord of Norbury (1531–1538) rebuilt or at any rate refitted this block. "Undisputed tradition has assigned to an upper apartment . . ." at the north-west corner of this building . . . "the name of 'Sir Anthony's Study,' and a private letter of the family, written in 1703, records the then belief that he wrote with his own hand the various texts with which the panels are in many places covered. We believe that the panelled oak wainscoting of this upper study, as well as of the oak parlour on the ground floor, were put in by the judge." He admits, however, that this panelling may be of the fifteenth-century date and be the work of Nicholas. We give a photograph of Sir Anthony's study, and a drawing of the oak parlour which occupies the south-west corner of the ground floor. Unfortunately the photograph does not show the text painted in black letter on so many of the panels of Sir Anthony's study. One

* Facing page 50.

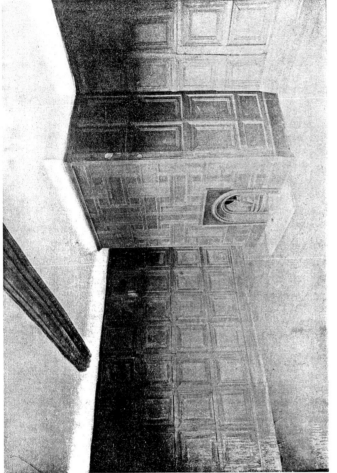

SIR ANTHONY FITZHERBERT'S STUDY,
NORBURY MANOR HOUSE
*Photo by the author*

*To face page 8*

panel bears a death's head and the device, *Memento mori*.   On another is the text, *Omnes stabimus ante tribunal Christi unusquisque nostrum pro se racionem redet Deo. Ro. 14.* (We shall all stand before the judgment-seat of Christ . . . each one of us shall render account for himself to God.)   On another is painted, *Principium sapientiæ timor dni, Pro. 9.* (The fear of the Lord is the beginning of wisdom.)

If the old judge inscribed these texts upon the walls of his room to help him in his preparation for death, he was also, unconsciously,

Oak Parlour
NORBVRY MANOR
HOVSE

affording strength and consolation to his children and descendants in the dark days that were coming on them.

It is instructive to linger in this room and think of the effect these stern reminders of eternal truths had on those who dwelt within these walls, urging them to constancy and endurance, placing ever before their eyes the visions of death and judgment, helping them to weigh in the balance of the sanctuary the fleeting honours and pleasures of this world against the eternal weight of glory reserved for those who remain faithful unto death.

*Memento novissima tua et nunquam peccabis.*   "Remember thy latter end and thou shalt never sin," had been the device of Blessed Thomas More, the thought that supported him in his hour of trial; and it was this same truth which came home to the heart of the old judge who had

B

himself, alas ! helped to condemn the martyr to death, as he in his turn faced his last passage with penitence and hope.

He died in 1538, and according to the family tradition, as he lay on his death-bed, he solemnly enjoined his children under no pretext to stain their souls with the possession of Church-lands. And three of the sons who knelt by that bed-side were to be faithful not merely to their father's dying admonition, but to truth and conscience and religion, till after weary sufferings and long imprisonment they gained themselves the martyr's crown. This is what makes Norbury so dear and so wonderful : it is the home of martyrs.

The remarkable reticulated panelling of the oak parlour is seen in Mr. Pike's beautiful sketch.

There is not much else of interest in the building, save the ancient stained glass, poor fragments of the magnificent display which must once have filled the windows of the Manor House. These have additional value because it would seem that they were inserted by the martyr, Sir Thomas Fitzherbert, Fifteenth Lord of the Manor. In a circle in the entrance hall is a splendid shield containing the arms of Sir Thomas himself, impaled with those of his wife, Anne Eyre, heiress of Padley. Another circle represents the scourging of our Blessed Lord, and is pronounced by Mr. George Bailey to be Dutch work of the middle of the sixteenth century. There is also a mutilated Nativity of Christ, and six circles representing the first six months of the year.*

## NORBURY CHURCH

The gallery that connected the Manor House with the Church has now disappeared, as we have seen, though much of it was still standing at the beginning of the nineteenth century.

It will be unnecessary here to give an elaborate description of this very beautiful and remarkable Church, as this has already been done by an expert.† That it is of rare beauty will be acknowledged by all who examine our illustrations. Its ground-plan is quite unusual, and Dr. Cox has explained how this came about. Originally an aisleless Norman Church, it was entirely rebuilt in the fourteenth and fifteenth centuries. Some large fragments of pre-Norman crosses, finely sculptured, were found at the last restoration, so that an earlier Church even than the Norman one must have once existed here.

* Mr. Bailey has given an elaborate description and careful coloured drawings of all these fragments of stained glass in the fourth and fifth volumes of the *Journal* (1882–1883).

† Dr. J. L. Cox, F.S.A., in his *Churches of Derbyshire*, and the *Journal* of the Derbyshire Archæological Society.

THE TOMB OF NICHOLAS FITZHERBERT
*Photo by James Watts*

NORBURY.

NORBURY CHURCH FROM THE SOUTH

The Dedication to St. Burlok (or Barlac), an utterly unknown Saxon Abbot, also speaks of the early foundation of the Church.

There is a representation of this Saint in one of the windows, but only guesses can be made as to his identity. Though St. Burlok is mentioned in pre-Reformation Fitzherbert wills as patron of the Church, in later days it has often been described as dedicated to Our Lady.

The chancel is by far the most striking part of the Church, indeed its beauty takes away the breath of those who visit it for the first time. It was probably built, according to Dr. Cox, in 1360, though Mickle-thwaite ascribed it to an earlier date, just before the outbreak of the Black Death in 1349. But the former's opinion is no doubt correct, and he shows that the building of this magnificent chancel is probably due to the rector, Henry Kniveton, a man of wealth, to whom there was formerly a slab in the floor, stating that he was, in fact, the builder of the chancel. This slab, apparently, disappeared during the disastrous "restoration" of 1842. Kniveton was presented to the rectory by Sir John Fitzherbert in the year of the Black Death, 1349, and his successor, another Henry Kniveton, was not instituted till 1395. Between these dates the chancel was probably built. The general effect of this chancel is one of extreme lightness and elegance. The magnificent windows, four on either side, are filled with the original fourteenth-century glass in grisaille, covered with interlacing scrollwork and floriated designs, relieved here and there with colour, and having the shield of arms of a noble Lancastrian family inserted in each light. Some beautiful specimens of these windows appear in Lysons' *Magna Britannia*, and in Bournan's *Specimens of the Ecclesiastical Architecture of Great Britain*.

Dr. Cox says with truth that "there certainly are not six parish churches in the kingdom that have so fine and extensive a display." Unhappily, the glass of the great east window, said to have been the finest of all, was sold about 1824 by the parson, the Rev. Thomas Bingham, to some Catholic family in Yorkshire. This window was blocked up with lath and plaster till the "restoration" of 1842, when it was filled with fifteenth-century glass taken from the nave and chapels.

This was far from being a fortunate expedient. The glass was naturally damaged in removal, the original plan of the glazing of the Church was destroyed, and the beautiful colour-scheme of the fourteenth-century glass injured by the juxtaposition of much later work. Still, it is difficult now to suggest a better plan, for modern glass would have been still more out of harmony with the old.

The figures of the twelve apostles were taken from the west and three north windows of the north aisle, and the representation of the

12

NORBURY CHURCH FROM THE EAST

*Photo by James Watts*

*To face page 12*

Blessed Trinity now in the centre light, as well as the figures of SS. Chad and Fabian, from the south-west chapel. The apostles had each a scroll bearing an article of the Creed, according to the ancient tradition of its composing, but these have got confused in the transfer. The east window of the north aisle, we may add, contained three virgin saints, one of them St. Margaret, probably that now in the east window. The clerestory windows were filled with the heraldic bearings of the Fitzherberts.

Below the windows of the chancel runs a series of cinquefoil-headed blind arches, and a low stone seat extending along the whole of the wall. A considerable portion of good fifteenth-century oak stall-work still remains to enhance the beauty of this exquisite chancel. Unfortunately, the screen is modern and poor.

The Fitzherbert tombs, which form the great glory of the chancel at present, are not in their original position, but come from the nave ; and before describing them, we had better give some account of the Church as a whole. The ground-plan is peculiar, the position of the tower in the centre of the south aisle being all but unique. There is indeed a striking dissimilarity between the chancel and the nave of the Church, the latter dating nearly a hundred years later than the former, and being of a much more commonplace design. The present nave was built by Nicholas Fitzherbert, Eleventh Lord of Norbury, who, as we have said, died in 1473. In his epitaph occur the lines :

> " This Church he made of his own expence
> In the joy of Heaven be his recompence."

The north aisle is separated from the nave by an arcade of four bays, while the south aisle consists of the tower (the lowest story of which forms the porch), and a chapel to the east and west. The length of the nave is about 50 ft., that of the chancel about 47 ft. 10 in.

Dr. Cox thinks that the tower was built before the present nave, in the first half of the fifteenth century, and that when the nave was rebuilt with clerestory and north aisle, somewhat later in the century, the chapels east and west of the tower were designed " to produce as near an approach to an aisle as possible, without removing the tower."

John Fitzherbert, Thirteenth Lord of Norbury, grandson of Nicholas, built the south-west chapel, in which his tomb is placed, and from his will, dated September 21, 1517, we find that this work was then " newe made."

The rebuilding of the nave made it necessary to change the pitch of the chancel roof, which was lowered, and the chancel arch probably disappeared at the same time. The rector, Henry Prince (1466–1500), is said upon his tomb (an alabaster slab in the chancel) to have done this work, at least as regards the roof. The roof was lowered and the walls slightly raised, while the quaint battlements with pointed edge, which it has been fancied may have been suggested by the heraldic bearing, *vaire*, borne in the chief of the Fitzherbert shield, were added as a finish. The initials N. F. constantly repeated in the quarries of the glass now in the east window, together with the *rose en soleil* of Edward IV., show that the nave was completed about 1450. Other quarries bear J. F., and come from the south-west chapel, which is now used as a vestry. The east window of the south-east chapel has a window, representing St. Anne teaching Our Lady to read, with St. Winefrid on the right and St. Syth on the left. Below are the arms of Fitzherbert impaling Bothe, and figures of Nicholas Fitzherbert with his eight sons (in blue) and Alice Bothe, his first wife, with her five daughters, kneeling on either side. In the south window are found the enigmatical St. Burlok with St. John Baptist and St. Anthony. *Sanctus Burlok Abbas* is depicted in a red cope, with crozier and book. Below, on either side of the shield of arms, are Nicholas with his two sons, and his second wife, Isabel Ludlow, with two daughters. This window commemorates the second marriage and its offspring.

In the account of the Church written by Michael Jones in the Family Book, we get a valuable description of the glass then remaining in the Church, before it was removed from its original position.

The following paragraph also makes us regret the ill-starred " restoration" of 1842 :

"The screen of curiously carved oak, with much curvilinear tracery, which has been painted in red, blue and gold, separates the chancel from the nave. Similar screens and canopies occupy the spaces between the arches both on the south and north aisles forming chapels in which are placed the tomb of Nicholas Fitzherbert on the south, and the tomb of Ralph Fitzherbert and his wife Elizabeth Marshall on the north."

The most ancient Fitzherbert monument is that of Sir Henry, builder of the Hall. This is a stone effigy representing the good knight clad in chain armour and surcoat, and cross-legged. When Michael Jones wrote in 1828, this figure was on the north side of the chancel near the east end. In the seventies it was put in the middle of the chancel, it has now been removed to the archway leading into the south-east chapel of the nave, where the monument of Nicholas Fitzherbert formerly stood.

The Fitzherbert monuments have been moved over and over again, in the most reckless way imaginable. In 1842 they were removed to the eastern extremity of the chancel, by the then rector, the Rev. Clement F. Broughton. The Communion table was brought forward into the chancel, and the space behind railed off to hold the monuments.

We now come to the two tombs, which make the chief glory of Norbury

Church, and which are now placed on either side of the chancel. There are few parish churches in England that possess two such tombs as these. Our illustrations give an excellent idea of their beauty. They are precisely similar in treatment and appear to be of the same date. Dr. Cox has shown that they were probably erected by John Fitzherbert, Thirteenth Lord of Norbury, to the memory of his grandfather, Nicholas, and his father, Ralph, towards the end of the fifteenth century. They are "obviously the work of the same sculptor or school of Nottingham sculptors in Chellaston alabaster," and must have been made after 1483, which is the date of Ralph's death.

Nicholas, the great builder, lies on the south side. His effigy, delicately carved in alabaster, is in plate armour, the hands are joined as in prayer, the hair is straight, the head resting on a helmet, the vizor punctured with round holes. The helmet is surmounted by a wreath from which rises the Fitzherbert crest, the clenched left hand within a gauntlet. He wears the collar of suns and roses with a lion pendant, which also occurs on the brass of his brother-in-law, Roger Bothe, in Sawley Church.* The sword-belt is beautifully ornamented with rosettes, and from it are suspended the long sword and the dagger, both perfect. The feet rest upon the figure of a lion. A tiny angel holding a shield sits on the lion's back and supports the tip of the right foot. The two figures at the west end of the tomb represent the two wives of the squire. Names were originally painted beneath these and all the figures on the sides of the tomb. Some are yet fairly decipherable. Very exquisite are these little figures under their crocketed canopies. On the south side are the eight sons by the first wife, Alice Bothe. One is in armour, with a cross upon his shoulder, one a monk, another a lawyer, and so on.

The five daughters, with the two sons and two daughters of the second marriage, find their places on the north side of the tomb. One is a nun with veil and rosary.

On an alabaster slab in the chancel floor is an incised effigy of Alice Bothe, the mother of thirteen of these children. The tomb of Ralph Fitzherbert is wider than that of his father, for with him is represented his wife Elizabeth, the heiress of John Marshall, of Upton. In her will, which (as well as that of her husband) still exists at Swynnerton, she directs that her body should be "buried in the Churche of Seint Barloke by fore the ymage of Seint Nicholas by syde the body of Rauffe ffitzherbert late my husband.†

The figure of the squire is nearly an exact counterpart of that of his

* Cox, *Journal*, xxv.
† Printed by Rev. R. H. C. Fitzherbert in the *Journal*, vol. xx. An abstract of Ralph's will is in vol. xix.

father, but the hand in the crest is a right hand, and he has no dagger. He too wears the collar of Edward IV., but the pendant is a boar, the cognizance of Richard III. The lady is dressed in a close bodice and gown which has been painted green, and a mantle painted red. She has a reticulated cap, gilt, with high double-peaked head-dress. Round her neck is a chain from which hangs a pendant representing Our Lady and the Holy Child. Ralph's feet rest on a lion, but instead of the angel there is a curious crouching figure of a little monk or bedesman supporting the right foot. At the lady's feet are two small dogs. Two angels support the cushion at her head. At the west end of this tomb are three angels holding large shields. On the north side are six niches ; the first contains the figure of a Knight of St. John ; in the sixth are two boys. Each of these figures has a shield.

According to Sir Ernest Clarke, F.S.A., the seven sons here represented were John the eldest, Henry, Thomas, Richard, William, Anthony, and one who died in infancy. This is the order in which they are named in their mother's will, and it is no doubt the order of their birth. But they are not represented in that order on the tomb. First comes the Knight of Rhodes, Richard, the fourth son ; then an ecclesiastic, probably Thomas, the third son ; he became Rector of Norbury (1500–1518) and Precentor of Lichfield Cathedral. Next is a pilgrim, who is possibly meant for John, the heir ; then a civilian with purse at his side, no doubt Henry, the second son, a mercer of London ; * the next three are boys of whom (if we are correct) one will be William, the fifth son, who became a distinguished ecclesiastic, Prebendary of Hereford and Lincoln, Chancellor of Lichfield and Rector of Wrington, Somerset ; while another will be the sixth surviving son, Anthony, the most famous of all.

William and Anthony were minors at the time of their mother's death (her will is dated 20 October, 1490), and John is directed to pay to the latter the sum of five marks per annum "towards his exhibition at Court" (*i.e.* his studies at Gray's Inn) "upon condition that he continue his learning at the same." He did so to some purpose, for he became one of the most learned of English judges.†

The great blue stone slab with brasses that now lies between the tombs of Nicholas and Ralph Fitzherbert, is the monument of Sir Anthony and his second wife, Dame Maud Cotton. It has been moved from the gangway of the nave. Unhappily it is incomplete : the judge's

---

* He was admitted a member of the Mercers Company in 1483, after an apprenticeship to John Matthew Alderman.

† It will be noticed that the eastern ends of the tombs of both Nicholas and Ralph Fitzherbert are bare of ornament. This would not have been seen had they been left in their original positions, built against the eastern pillar on either side of the nave.

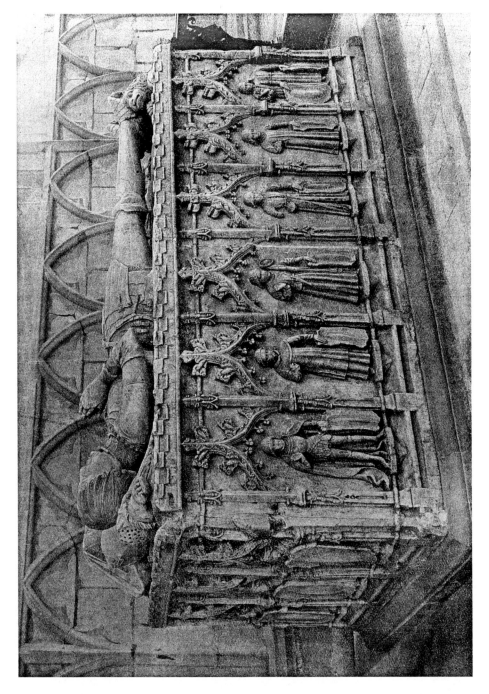

THE TOMB OF RALPH FITZHERBERT
*Photo by the author*

head is missing, as well as a great part of the marginal inscription. In 1871 Dr. Cox made the discovery that fragments of the brass, then loose, were "palimpsests" or re-used fragments of older brasses from some religious house. At the time of Sir Anthony's death such memorials must have been drugs in the market, owing to the destruction of the monastic churches.*

The Latin verses below were composed, it is said, by Sir Anthony himself. Some think that the two pieces of brass on which these verses are inscribed have been wrongly placed in recent years, and that the inscription should begin with the line,

*Ille ego qui quondam fuerat dum vita superstes,*

which is now the seventh line.

Dr. Cox gives an English translation by Mr. Sankey, then of Marlborough College, from which we quote some lines :

> " A lifetime's deeds are all that here I have
> Who by my words am followed to the grave ;
> Though erst a judge, now at the bar I stand,
> And wait the judgment of a juster hand.
> But, holy Christ, hear !—for thyself dost pray—
> My pardon grant and wash my sins away."

His five daughters are represented kneeling below, with their names, and the text, *Misericordias Domini in eternum cantabo*, but the corresponding piece with the figures of the five sons, three of whom were such glorious champions of the faith, has unhappily disappeared.

These sons were Thomas, John, Richard, who married Mary Westcott, and William, who married Elizabeth Swynnerton of Swynnerton, and brought that property to the Fitzherberts. The eldest son, whose name is unknown, died young. (According to some writers, there were two who died young.)

Of the daughters, two died young ; and of those who survived, Dorothy married Sir Ralph Longford, and secondly, Sir John Port ; Elizabeth became the wife of William Bassett of Blore ; and Katherine, of John Sacheverell. They were all counted worthy to suffer much for the faith.

The marginal legend, when complete, read as follows :—

" Of your charitie pray for the soule of Sir Anthony Fitzherbert Knight one of the King's Justices of the Commen benche and sometyme lorde and patrone of this Town and Dorothie his wyfe Daughter of Sir Henry Willoughby, Knight and Dame Maude his last wife one of the

---

* Mr. St. John Hope has described this brass and its inscriptions in the *Journal*, vol. iv. He gives a good illustration.

Daughters and heirs of Richard Coton of Hampstall Rydware Esq. by whom he had five sonnes and five daughters which Sir Antony deceased the 27 May A° Dni 1538 & the said Dame Maude . . ."

The only other monument we need mention is that of John Fitzherbert, Sir Anthony's eldest brother. While he provided such splendid sepulchres for his father and grandfather, he was himself contented with a very simple monument. It is a plain altar-tomb, with alabaster sides, in the south-west chapel. A brass plate on the upper slab bears his name and the date of his death, the Vigil of St. James, 1531.

There is very much more that it would be interesting to describe in and about Norbury Church, but we are compelled to pass it over in order to tell something of the history of the family and of its sufferings for the faith.*

Here, too, we must pass over much that is interesting. The story of John Fitzherbert and his quarrel with his brother, Sir Anthony, his unhappy marriage, his authorship of the famous *Boke of Husbandrie* and the *Boke of Surveying and Improvements* (London, 1523), so long attributed to his "brother justice," but now vindicated for their true author by Sir Ernest Clarke,† besides much that is interesting about Nicholas and Ralph Fitzherbert must be perforce passed over here for lack of space.

The piety and charity displayed in the Fitzherbert wills are not, indeed, extraordinary for the period, but are sufficiently interesting to be briefly noted here. Thus Ralph Fitzherbert, in his will (dated December 20, 1483), commends his soul to God the Father Almighty, to Blessed Mary and All His Saints, and leaves seven pounds of wax to be burnt round his body at his obsequies, bequests to every priest (4*d.*) and every clerk (2*d.*) assisting at his funeral, and legacies to the fabrics of the Cathedrals of Coventry and Lichfield, to the Church, priests, and poor of Norbury, Snelleston, and Cubley, to the Abbot and Convent of Rocester and Croxden, the Prior and Canons of Colwich, the Vicar of Ellaston, and to the churches and the poor of these places. Also to the Prior of the Friars' House in the villa of Derby, 10*s.* to celebrate a trental (*i.e.* the thirty Gregorian masses) for his soul, and a like bequest to the Abbot and Convent of Croxden, and to Sir Thomas Harding, priest.‡

His widow, Elizabeth, makes much the same provisions, bequeathing

* Here again we must express our obligations to Dr. J. Charles Cox, F.S.A., who has made a special study of this history.

† Dr. J. M. Rigg, in the *Dictionary of National Biography*, argues for Sir Anthony's authorship, but he has been refuted by Sir Ernest Clarke.

‡ The original Probate copy is at Swynnerton. See *Journal*, vol. xix., abstract by Rev. R. H. C. Fitzherbert.

besides sums to the fabrics of the churches of Sibbesdon, Yoxall, Duffield, Colwich, and Rocester :

"Item, I bequeath to the Abbot and Convent of the abbey of Darley to pray for my soul for a trental to be said for my soul 10s. Also I bequeath to the finding of a priest to pray for the soul of Ralph Fitzherbert late my husband, and for my soul £10 of money beside the rent of Calton. Also I bequeath to seven priests at the trust and disposition of mine executors to pray for my soul 46s. 8d., that is to wit to every priest 6s. 8d. to say Placebo and Dirige every night and mass on the morrow during that year, and every Priest to be assigned to his day by mine executors. . . . Also I will that my said feoffees retain and keep in their hands lands and tenements to the yearly value of 20s. to find an obit yearly at Norbury for my said husband's soul, my soul, our fathers' and mothers' and all Christian souls. And that the said 20s. be disposed in this wise :—first, to every Priest there being at Dirige and mass 4ᵈ ; and to every clerk there being 1ᵈ. And that that remaineth over at any time to be laid out in purchase of bread and divided among the poor parishioners of Norbury, by the discretion of my said son and heir, and curate of the church for the time there being."*

John "leaves thirteen pounds of wax to be used in as many tapers 'abowte my herse,' two tapers to burn night and day upon the herse till the seventh day was past. Every man, woman, and child at the burying to have a farthing white loaf and a penny of silver. On the seventh day after, both priests and clergy to have on the same manner, and the poor folk as before." He leaves bequests for masses to a great many religious houses, among others to every house of Austin Friars and to every Charterhouse in England. He does not forget even the ringers of the bells, and he leaves "to Norbury Church 20 marks to buy a cope of velvet, and a vestment branched of one colour." The list of heirlooms appended to this will is exceedingly interesting. It forms an inventory of all the better furniture in the Manor House ; as well as "for husbandry and other things necessary," oxen, pigs, horses, sheep, ploughs, tools, wheat, barley, rye, &c. Never was there such a curious list of "heirlooms"! Among other things we find "a pair of wafer yrons," for making and stamping hosts for the altar.†

Dr. Cox points out that this was done by John Fitzherbert, no doubt at Sir Anthony's suggestion, to outwit his wife "Bennet," or "Benedicta," with whom he had quarrelled. He thus made almost all his

---

* Original Probate copy at Swynnerton. See *Journal*, vol. xx.

† This will is not at Swynnerton. We owe the above details to Dr. Cox. *Journal*, vol. vii. pp. 226–239.

chattels heirlooms, giving them in his lifetime to Richard Cotton, "one of his executors, and then resuming the use of them on loan."

Before leaving this beautiful church, it is only right to say that it is now excellently cared for by its present patrons, who have spent much money in repairing it and in re-leading the old glass.


## CONFESSORS OF THE FAITH

SIR ANTHONY FITZHERBERT forms the link between the old order and the new. He lived through some of the most troublous days of Henry VIII., saw the religious houses dissolved, the martyrs slain, and England torn from the unity of Christendom. He was born in 1470, and succeeded his brother John as Fourteenth Lord of Norbury in 1531. He had been knighted in 1516, and in 1522 was made a Justice of the Common Pleas. His biography has often been written. His fame of learning as a lawyer was surpassed only by the renown of his probity, for he was known far and wide as an upright judge.

"Though he never attained to the position of Chief Justice, Fitzherbert possessed a profound knowledge of English law, combined with a strong logical faculty and remarkable power of lucid exposition. His *Grand Abridgement of the Common Law*, first printed in 1514, was the first serious attempt to reduce the entire law of England to systematic shape. As such it served as a model to later writers." *

Nevertheless we have to own with regret that, as a Catholic, he did not take that firm position which brought such immortal glory on Sir Thomas More. Though he never acquired monastic lands, and cautioned his children against doing so, he took a prominent part in the suppression of the monasteries, and his name is on the list of Commissioners to take the surrender of Abbeys, dated 29 Henry VIII. 1537. He was one of those who received the surrender of the Abbeys of Whalley and Furness, only a year before his death. Worse than this, he was on the Commission which tried the most illustrious of our Blessed Martyrs; on April 29, 1535, he assisted at the trial of the Blessed Carthusian Priors, Blessed Richard Reynolds of Syon,† and Blessed John Hale; and he was also a member of the tribunals that tried Blessed John Fisher and Blessed Thomas More in the following June and July.

As to this, Mr. Gillow remarks that "notwithstanding the

* Dr. J. M. Rigg in the *Dictionary of National Biography*.
† In 1503 he had been appointed feoffee in trust for the Abbess and Convent of Syon.

20

disgust which the conviction of those two Martyrs universally excited, Fitzherbert's reputation sustained no blemish, the world knowing that his being on the Commission was an act that he could not prevent, and that his interference with the will of the arbitrary despot would have been both useless and dangerous. His judicial character had been raised whilst on the circuit at York by his having allowed bills for extortion to be found against Wolsey, then at the height of his power. For this he was rebuked by the Cardinal. He also disapproved of the Cardinal's alienating the Church lands."

This is quite true; and that the family tradition as to his Catholic faith and piety is really correct is best proved by the magnificent constancy of his children and descendants.

Sir Anthony died, as his tomb tells us, on May 27, 1538; his widow survived him thirteen years, dying September 29, 1551.

The old judge passed his last days in retirement at Norbury, meditating, as we have seen, on death and judgment to come, and we cannot doubt that in his case the last prayer of Blessed Thomas More was fulfilled, when he said to his judges, after his condemnation in Westminster Hall, that he hoped in the Divine goodness and mercy, that, as St. Paul and St. Stephen, whom he persecuted, were now friends in Paradise, so he and they, though differing in this world, might be united in perfect charity in the other.

Dodd, in his *Church History*, has placed Sir Anthony Fitzherbert among his Catholic heroes, and though we may grieve that the judge did not rise to that sublimity of self-sacrifice to which his own sons attained, yet we feel that his name is not unworthy of our veneration.

But if Sir Anthony was not himself heroic, his eldest son, Sir Thomas, who succeeded him as Fifteenth Lord of Norbury, was one of the most glorious of our Catholic confessors, and died a martyr in chains.

Sir Thomas Fitzherbert was born in 1517 or 1518, and succeeded his father at the age of 21.* His mother was Sir Anthony's second wife, Maud or Matilda Cotton. The mansion, demesne-lands and advowson of Hampstall Ridware, County Stafford, came to him at her death in 1551. Shaw gives a description of Sir Thomas' great house at Hampstall Ridware, as it was in 1792: Two octagonal porters' lodges in stone flanked the gateway, from which a paved way ran across the court to the main entrance. This was protected by a porch 20 feet in length supported on pillars, and a massive front door. The great hall had an immense dining-table running down one side, with a bench fixed against the wall, a high arched fireplace with cast metal fire-back embossed with

---

* According to Topcliffe's pedigree he was the third son of Sir Anthony, two elder brothers having died in infancy. But it is more probable that he was the second son.

armorial bearings, iron dogs, &c., a very lofty roof, and a musician's gallery at mid-height. Circular windows lighted it at one end. A watch-tower, fifty feet high, had a staircase which communicated with the principal apartments.

It is interesting to know that one of the bells in the church tower bore (and doubtless still bears) the inscription :

> " Syr Thomas Fiharbor Knight
> God presarve him in all right."

To the Fitzherbert and Cotton Manors, Sir Thomas added the wide estates of Padley and Hathersage in the Peak of Derbyshire, by his marriage with Anne, sole daughter and heiress of Sir Arthur Eyre of Over Padley. The marriage settlement is dated October 20, 1535. It is still preserved at Swynnerton. Among the stained glass still left in the Manor House of Norbury is a splendid shield bearing the arms of Sir Thomas Fitzherbert, impaled with those of his wife (quarterly, Padley and Eyre), and with another shield (quarterly *argent* and *sable*, over all a bend *gules* charged with three annulets *or*), which it seems impossible to identify. This would seem to suggest that Sir Thomas had a second wife, but there is no mention of this in any family record, and it seems more probable that these arms belong to some alliance of the Eyres, and that it is simply a piece of bad sixteenth-century heraldry.* In any case, he was childless. His wife, Dame Anne Fitzherbert, died in 1576.

It was Sir Thomas who adorned the windows of the Manor House with the heraldic glass, which excited the admiration of Laurence Bostock in 1581. It must, indeed, have been a splendid display. Sir Thomas' shield, which we here give from the Fitzherbert Pedigree at Swynnerton, displays the Eyre arms on an escutcheon of pretence.

In 1546 Sir Thomas was appointed Sheriff of Staffordshire (the original Letters Patent of November 23, 1546, are at Swynnerton), and he again filled that office under Philip and Mary in 1554. It is not certain when he was knighted, but he is styled knight in a deed of April 4, 1552. He was appointed in this year (6 Edward VI.) one of the Commissioners to take survey and inventory of Church goods and ornaments in the Hundreds of Offley and Pirehill ; † and in the Lichfield Chapter Acts we find recorded (January 27, 1552-3) that he was one of

---

* Mr. George Bailey has given a coloured reproduction of this shield. *Journal*, vol. v. p. 65.

† W. Salt Library, Stafford, vol. vi. pt. i. p. 176.

the Commissioners who took from the ministers of that church an inventory of the jewels, vestments, &c., and sold them *pro vilissimo pretio*, placing the best jewels and vestments under seal for the King.

This act of sacrilege must have been exceedingly repugnant to Sir Thomas, who for the remainder of his life was to prove himself an ardent, open, and inflexible adherent to the faith of his fathers.

From a letter among the Lansdowne MSS. in the British Museum, written by Sir Thomas to Sir William Cecil (afterwards Lord Burghley) it would appear that Sir Thomas acted as agent or auditor for Cecil's estates at Wootton-under-Weever, near Norbury. This letter is dated January 8, 1556–7. Its tone is that of an equal, though Sir Thomas calls himself an "officer" of Cecil's. At this time, it will be remembered, Cecil feigned to be an excellent Catholic. It was not long, however, before he was to throw off the mask.

In the first year of Elizabeth (1559) an Act of Parliament was passed for "restoring to the Crown the antient jurisdiction over the estate ecclesiastical and spiritual," that is to say, for abolishing once more the Papal Supremacy, and restoring to the Crown the jurisdiction over the Church usurped by Henry VIII. Though Elizabeth shrank from proclaiming herself "Supreme Head," she arrogated to herself all the spiritual pretensions of her father, with the title of "Supreme Governor."

By this Act the Queen was authorised to name, by Letters Patent, under the Great Seal of England, Commissioners to exercise ecclesiastical jurisdiction, "and to visit, reform, redress, order, and correct all such errors, heresies, schisms, abuses, offences, contempts, and enormities whatsoever," which by any manner of spiritual authority could lawfully be reformed, &c., within the realm.

The oath of supremacy, acknowledging the Queen's new title, and renouncing any other spiritual or ecclesiastical authority, was to be taken by all ecclesiastical persons, all and every judge, justice, mayor, and every other lay or temporal officer employed by the Crown, and the penalty for refusing to take it was loss of all offices and all civil rights. At the same time the Act of Uniformity made the Book of Common Prayer the only authorised manual of worship, prohibited any other rites, and enforced, under severe penalties, the attendance of every person at the new services. In a word, the Holy Sacrifice of the Mass had become a crime in England.

Thus began, somewhat mildly at first, but with ever-increasing severity, the persecution of those who clung to the old religion, and whose consciences would not permit them to assent to the Queen's proceedings.

23

# FORGOTTEN SHRINES

Dr. Cox, himself an Anglican clergyman, speaks of it as follows : " A general policy of outrageous and long-continued oppression, before which the short-lived and fierce Marian persecution absolutely pales in comparison. . . . This page of our national history has been generally slurred over, through ignorance or wilful suppression of the truth, by most of our historians. The facts are beyond dispute ; . . . almost every persecution short of death (which was soon added to the other penalties by the legislation of 1571 and 1584) was resorted to immediately after Elizabeth's accession ; the Recusants were everywhere harassed by fines, forfeitures, and imprisonment, in order to compel their attendance at church. Where the local magistrates were lax in their efforts, Special Commissioners, armed with the fullest powers immediately from the Crown—powers, which in their full use of torture, as well as in other respects, more closely resembled the Inquisition than anything hitherto established in England—visited the disaffected districts, or had the delinquents summoned before them in London. This phase of the persecution was specially severe between 1561 and 1563, particularly in Derbyshire and Staffordshire." *

Another Anglican clergyman, Dr. Jessopp,† writes : " At the accession of Elizabeth there were not wanting many men of conscientious convictions, who would have boldly faced the scaffold rather than acknowledge the claim of the spiritual supremacy of the sovereign. . . . The oath in its new form became the cause of deep and widespread offence. A very large proportion of English gentry refused to swear allegiance in the terms prescribed. These men were from this time known as Recusants,‡ or refusers of the oath, and the stigma and inconvenience attaching to the term began then first to be felt in its odious force.

" But the Act of Uniformity was one which touched the Catholics in a different way. The re-establishment of the Mass in Queen Mary's reign had caused immense joy throughout the land . . . now it was enacted that the Book of Common Prayer alone should be used, and ' to sing or say any common or open prayer, or to administer any sacrament otherwise . . . than is mentioned in the said book . . . in any cathedral or parish church or chapel, *or in any other place*' subjected the offender to forfeiture of his goods, and on a repetition of his offence, to imprisonment for life. The Mass was felt to be, and known to be, the one great and precious mystery which every devout Catholic clung

* *Journal,* vol. vii. pp. 243–4.
† *One Generation of a Norfolk House* (1879), p. 63.
‡ It is more usually stated that the term " Recusant" arose from the refusal to go to church, and this seems more correct.

24

to with unspeakable awe and fervour, and to rob him of that was to rob him of the one thing on which his religious life depended ; that gone, it was imagined that all else would go with it. . . .

"But there was yet another clause in this Act, which was even more galling and hateful than the others. The fourteenth clause enacted that any person not resorting to his parish church on Sundays and holy days was to forfeit twelve pence for every offence, the money to go to the poor of the parish. The Churchwardens were bound to present offenders to the Ordinary." * So far Dr. Jessopp.

Sir Thomas Fitzherbert had the honour to be one of the first victims of these detestable laws. Already in 1561 the good knight was sent up to London by the Queen's Commissioners and imprisoned in the Fleet, where he had as fellow captives the last Catholic Bishop of Chester and the last Catholic Dean of St. Paul's. "For thirty years," says Dr. Cox,† "Sir Thomas Fitzherbert, with only three brief intervals of freedom, was dragged about from prison to prison, now in the Fleet, now in the county gaol at Derby, now at Lambeth, and now in the Tower, in which State prison he finally died in·1591 at the age of seventy-four. At any moment he could have obtained his release by consenting to attend church."

We can trace his name through State papers and Privy Council Acts, and get glimpses now and again of the weary imprisonment endured to the end with so much heroic fortitude.

On July 12, 1563, Grindal, Bishop of London, writes to Cecil : "Your second letter was for Sir Thomas Fitzherbert. He is a very stiff man. We had a solemn assembly of Commissioners in the end of the term only for his case, where Mr. Chancellor of the duchy was present, and there concluded to let Mr. Fitzherbert be abroad upon sureties, if he would be bound in the mean time to go orderly to the Church, without binding him to receive the Communion. That Sir Thomas refused. We will have a new conference upon occasion of your letter, and consider the circumstances of his case and after certify you of the same."

Sir Thomas was still a prisoner in the Fleet in 1565, when Sir Thomas Chaloner made an unsuccessful suit for him to the same Bishop of London,‡ and he was still there in 1570.§

* By an Act of 1581, in addition to this, those who absented themselves from church for over a month had to pay to the Exchequer a fine of £20 for each lunar month of four Sundays (i.e. £260 a year) as long as they remained Recusants or had anything left to lose. If they kept in their house any inmate guilty of such absence they were to forfeit £10 for every such month.

† Three Centuries of Derbyshire Annals (Bemrose, 1890), vol. i. p. 252.
‡ S. P. Dom. Eliz. xxxvii, 1.  § Ibid. lxvii. 86.

D

In 1568 we get a glimpse of him in connection with a fellow prisoner, the Venerable Bishop of Peterborough, Dr. David Pole. This good Bishop died in the Fleet Prison probably in May 1568.

In his will, dated May 17, he appoints Sir Thomas as his executor-in-chief, and stipulates that, in case he should not be able himself to take action, the others should in all things defer to him. With Sir Thomas, the Bishop named, as co-executor to his will, " Mr. John Wilkinson, citizen of London." Foreseeing, however, that it might not be possible for Sir Thomas to execute the will " in his own person," he appoints in that case, Martin Audley, his servant, " to do all things therein as the said Sir Thomas shall appoint him, as his deputy, and to make reckoning to the said Sir Thomas of all things that he doth." The Bishop also states " that the said Sir Thomas shall not need to appear before any judge about the execution " of the will, and in case of this being required he wills him " utterly to be discharged thereof and that the said Martin be full executor with Mr. Wilkinson to do all things." Yet even in this case he desires Sir Thomas to confer with Mr. Wilkinson about the due execution of his wishes.

To each of his executors, the Bishop leaves " seven pounds in money," " a gilt goblet " and a ring ; a ring also is left to Lady Fitzherbert.

The will was sworn to on the following July 6 by John Lewis, public notary, on behalf of Sir Thomas Fitzherbert ; and by John Wilkinson and Martin Audley.*

A knight imprisoned in the Fleet had to pay the sum of 18s. 6d. for his weekly commons and wine, besides 2s. 4d. a week for his room ; charges equivalent to £10 a week in modern money.

The weary imprisonment had its natural effect on his health. At a meeting of the Privy Council, May 2, 1574, a letter was sent to the Archbishop of Canterbury (the same Edmund Grindal) to use his discretion upon a suit made for the enlargement of Sir Thomas Fitzherbert for two months, in respect of his sickness, and disposing of his lands and goods.†

The latter motive was probably the more effective with the Council. The prisoner had still to pay the crushing fines levied on Recusants, and if he was " enlarged " from time to time, it was chiefly that he might find the means of raising this money by the sale of lands or goods.

In a list of " Evil-disposed persons of whom complaint hath been made, which lurk so secretly that process cannot be served upon them," printed by Strype, is mentioned " Robert Grey, priest, who hath been

* Phillips, *Extinction of the Ancient Hierarchy*, pp. 285–91.
† *Privy Council Acts*, vol. viii. p. 234.

much supported at Sir Thomas Fitzherbert's. . . ." "Then, we are informed, that through the example of Sir Thomas Fitzherbert . . . and others . . . by us committed to prison, . . . and through the bearing and succouring of their wives, friends, &c., a great part of the shires of Stafford and Derby are generally ill-inclined towards Religion."

The Privy Council, July 26, 1581, wrote to the Bishop of London " to licence Sir Thomas Fitzherbert for this summer time to repair to his house, upon good bonds and sureties in a round sum to her Majesty's use, that he shall not admit into his house any person not conformable in Religion, nor repair to the houses or company of any which refuse to come to the church and conform themselves, and that he shall at Michaelmas next either return to his Lordship and the place from whence he is released, or bring him a testimonial from his Ordinary of his conformity." *

Whether he was willing at this time to give these bonds, does not appear, but the summer of the next year found him at his dear Norbury, but very sick. How grievous it must have been to him no longer to be able to hear Mass in his beautiful parish church among the tombs of his Catholic ancestors! Still we may be sure that the Holy Sacrifice was offered secretly in some garret of the old Manor House, for Norbury is constantly denounced at this period as being a lurking-place for Popish priests.

As to Padley, it was inhabited by Sir Thomas' next brother, John Fitzherbert and his family, who were equally devoted to the old Religion.

The Council wrote, June 18, 1582, to Sir Walter Aston and Sir Thomas Cockayne of Ashbourne, as follows : " Whereas Sir Thomas Fitzherbert, knight, of late prisoner for matters of Religion, and at his humble suit, and the ordering of his private affairs, hath been permitted upon bonds and sureties to repair to his own house for a time, and to return his body to the prison of the Fleet at the latter end of this term ; forasmuch as their Lordships are given to understand by letters from Sir Thomas Cockayne and other of the Justices of the Peace in that county, that the said Sir Thomas is at this present in so feeble state by sickness as he may not, without apparent danger of his life, travel hither to yield himself prisoner according to his bond, their Lordships have thought good to pray and require the aforenamed Sir Walter Aston and Sir Thomas Cockayne forthwith to think upon some gentleman of good and sound Religion, residing within the county where Sir Thomas is now remaining, who will be contented to receive him into his house and take charge of him as of a prisoner, until he may recover his health, or our pleasures shall be further signified, and thereupon to cause the said Sir Thomas imme-

* *Acts*, vol. xiii. p. 139.

27

diately to be conveyed unto him, giving him charge by authority hereof that he suffer not any Recusant to frequent the company of the said Sir Thomas, or to have conference with him, unless it shall be on necessary occasions, at which time the said Sir Thomas shall have speech with any such Recusant only in the presence and hearing of his guardian ; and further, that like regard be had that the said Sir Thomas be not suffered to infect or corrupt others that are already good subjects and well persuaded in Religion, which we hope shall be prevented by your care in the choice of the gentleman to whom you shall commit him.

"Their Lordships also send herewith the copy of a condition for a bond their Lordships think fit that they should take of him for his remaining true prisoner in the place where they shall place him, permitting him to have such liberty as in the said condition is mentioned, and to send unto their Lordships the bond that they shall take of him, to the end his other bond whereupon he remaineth may be cancelled." *

Unhappily the Register of the Privy Council is missing from June 26, 1582, to February 19, 1585-6, so that we lose sight of the valiant confessor of Christ during some of the fiercest years of the persecution.

An undated paper in the Record Office,† calendared under July 1582, but perhaps of earlier date, gives an inventory of Catholic books found in the prison cells of some of the principal Recusants. It is extremely interesting to see the kind of books which nourished the piety and sustained the constancy of these good laymen.

Mr. George Cotton (of Warblington) had a long list under his name :

> *Expositio Canonis Missæ, Gabriel Biel,* 4to. ‡
> *Testimonia Sacræ Scripturæ Patrum.*
> *Concordantiæ, etc. per Konygstein Minoritam,* 8vo.
> *Catechismus Romanus.*
> *Joannis Vitæ Speculum,* 15°.

* *Acts,* vol. xiii. pp. 449–450.　　　　　　　　† *S. P. Dom. Eliz.* cliv. 75.

‡ Dom Cuthbert Almond, O.S.B., has very kindly helped me to identify most of these books :

*Expositio Canonis Missæ* is *Sacri canonis missæ expositio brevis et interlinearis, sc. Expositio eximii viri Magistri Gabrielis* (Biel of Spires). Strasburg.

*Concordantiæ, etc.* per Konygstein, is the *Monotessaron evangeliorum* of Konygstein, otherwise Antonius Broickwy.

The *Catechismus Romanus* is perhaps that of B. Canisius, S.J.

*Joannis Vitæ Speculum* is one of the first monuments of typography probably printed by Gutenburg. *Explicit humaneque salutis summula plane a me fratie Johanne tui pater ordinis alme vir b'ndicte puto quasi minimo monacho.* There are editions of 1476, 1492, &c.

*Syntaxis Historiæ Evangelicæ* is the *Historiæ Evangelicæ Veritas* of Alan Cope (*i.e.* Archdeacon Nicholas Harpsfield, a confessor of the faith). Louvain, 1572.

*Chronographia Christianæ Ecclesiæ* may be "Chronographia" : a description of time . . . collected out of sundrie authors, but for the most part abridged and translated out

# THE TRAGEDY OF THE FITZHERBERTS

*Syntaxis Historiæ Evangelicæ Alani Copi*, 4to.
*Chronographia Christianæ Ecclesiæ.*
*Martyrologium Usuardi*, 8vo.
*Surii Cartusiani Historia*—5 volum. leaft behind.

A paper w^t a red hart &c.
A crucifix pictured set on a burd.
A written treatise of divinite beginning
*In cæteris* etc. and endeth *Laus Deo.*

In the same chamber,
Sir Thomas Fitzherbert had :

*Antidotarium Anto : Sariceti.*
*Diurnale Romanum.*
*Manuale confessariorum.*
*Pharetra divini amoris.*

Other prisoners mentioned are Mr. Erasmus Sanders who had Blessed Thomas More's *Dialogue of Comfort in Tribulation,* Thomas à Kempis, *Our Ladye's Psalter,* &c., and Mr. Anstey who had only one, viz. " *Certayne devout and godly petitions called Jesus Psalter.*"
We only know from this casual circumstance that Sir Thomas shared his cell in the Fleet with a like-minded friend, that stout old confessor George Cotton, of whom we shall hear more in the course of this book.

Among the deeds relating to Norbury preserved in the family archives at Swynnerton, are several connected with Sir Thomas Fitz-herbert. Of these the most important, from the point of view of the family pedigree, is No. 25, being an Exemplification of Letters Patent of

of Codomannus his Annales Sacræ Scripturæ . . . London by Richard Field for Robert, 1590.

*Martyrologium Usuardi,* possibly the edition of Florence, 1486.

*Surii Cartusiani Historia,* will probably be the Cologne edition, 1570, or 1581, in six volumes.

The *Antidotarium* is *Antidotarius Animæ* by Nicolaus de Saliceto, printed at Antwerp by Gerard Leen, 1490 (and at Louvain, 1490).

*Manuale Confessariorum* by Johannes Nyder. The best known edition is that of John of Westphalia (c. 1481), or that of 1485. There is a Paris edition, 1473, folio.

*Pharetra Divini Amoris,* probably St. Bonaventura's treatise generally entitled *Liber Salutaris Pharetra Vocatus,* printed at Paris by Rembolt, 1518.

*Our Ladye's Psalter* may be St. Bonaventure's *Psalterium b'tæ Virginis,* imprinted at London in Flete Aley the XXI daye of October by Simon Uoter (c. 1520), or perhaps a translation of this work.

The *Certayne devout and godly petitions called Jesus Psalter,* is probably the edition *Antwerpiæ Johan. Foulerum,* 1575.

Sir Thomas More's *Dialogue of Comfort in Tribulation* (written in the Tower of London) and Thomas à Kempis are too well known to need comment.

28 November, 23 Elizabeth 1580, of the pleadings in a suit of the Court of Arches in which Sir Thomas was plaintiff against Nicholas Browne, farmer of the tithes of Norbury. The record recites the original charter of the Prior of Tutbury granting the Manor and two bovates of land in Norbury to William the son of Herbert, subject to the payment of 5s. in lieu of tithes; and enumerates by name the successive Lords of the Manor in their descent from the said William down to the plaintiff. Sir Thomas established his claim to exemption from tithes upon payment of the said annual sum of 5s. The genealogy of the family is thus legally authenticated.

## THE GATHERING OF THE STORM

WE now come to the year 1585. Dangers on all sides threatened the Government, and its agents were more on the alert than ever. Spain was overcoming the resistance of her rebellious subjects in the Low Countries, and the fall of Antwerp in July 1585 caused a feverish anxiety among the English Protestants.

War with Spain was inevitable, and eventually an English force under the Earl of Leicester was sent to support the rebels. France, or rather the Duke of Guise, threatened invasion on behalf of the captive Queen of Scots. Walsingham's toils were closing round that hapless princess, and the last act of her long-drawn tragedy was at hand. But the true heir to the throne had many faithful adherents in the country, and the plots to release her from captivity were a constant anxiety to the Government, though not, perhaps, to Walsingham, whose spies acted as *agents provocateurs* in fomenting the conspiracies which he used to involve the Queen of Scots and her friends in a common ruin.

Here, as ever, the Catholics had to suffer. Special Commissioners were appointed to " deal with the said Recusants to deliver the true state of their livings, revenues and livelihoods, that thereby a proportion might be made to allow them that which might be thought convenient for their maintenance, and the rest to be answered for the penalties they incur by breach and offence against the lawes." *

A little later they were assessed to provide money " towards the providing of horses and furniture for her Majesty's present services in the Low Countries," *i.e.* towards the war now being waged, under the incompetent Leicester, in support of the Protestant rebels against Spain. It was stated that " her Majesty seeth so much the less cause to spare them in this and the like charges, as that she daily findeth them to bestow no

* *Acts Privy Council,* vol. xiv. p. 8.

small contributions, both within and without the Realm, towards the feeding and maintaining of such her evil affected subjects as are sent and continued within the Realm to practice the overthrow of her Majesty's quiet Government." *

The State papers still preserved give abundant evidence how searching and universal this new exaction became. In October 1585, we have catalogues of the names of the Popish Recusants in each diocese, with the number of lances and light horses to be assessed upon each. At the same time we get quantities of letters from the unhappy Recusants to Walsingham protesting their inability to meet the demand, as they are either in prison, or their whole living has been already exhausted by the fines for recusancy.

Some, indeed, were able to fulfil the demand, others offered sums of money instead.

On October 26, Sir Thomas wrote from Hampstead to Walsingham explaining that the Earl of Shrewsbury, Lord Lieutenant of Derbyshire, and the Sheriff and Justices of Staffordshire, had already seized his armour and horses, and requesting a warrant of discharge. It was, in fact, the usual thing to disarm all Catholic gentlemen.

This letter seems to have been without effect. Accordingly, on November 19, Anthony Radcliffe, Sheriff of London, wrote the following letter to the all-powerful secretary, explaining the situation.

Sir Thomas had provided as many as four light horse, quite an unusual number. But he now sought to compound with a sum of money.

The letter runs as follows :

" Right honourable, my duty remembered, &c.
" Whereas, by your former letter Sir Thomas Fitzherbert was nominated amongst the rest without any number of horses appointed in the schedule, yet notwithstanding, by persuasion, he yielded unto the service of four light horse, and sent for them from his houses out of the counties of Derby and Stafford. Sithence which time one of them hath miscarried, and findeth the rest not serviceable as he would wish, as also he allegeth his armour to be in the hands of the justices of these two Shires. Wherefore he hath required me to write unto your Honour to accept of £50 (the which he hath paid unto me), and that it would please you that he might have your Honour's letter unto the Sheriff of the two Shires before written for his discharge there." †

This is followed by a letter from Sir Thomas himself to the Secretary (a facsimile of the original being appended) :

* *Acts Privy Council*, vol. xiv. pp. 15, 87.  † *S. P. Dom. Eliz.* clxxxiv. 34.

" I do think myself bound so to thank your Honour for that great goodness I have found in you, even at your first sight and acquaintance with me, and since in your tending my poor estate, which would to God it were simply laid before your Honour as in truth it is, and as my good Lord Treasurer hath an abstract thereof. My annual rents are under three hundred pounds, and I pay largely thereof yearly above two hundred pounds. In truth and in my conscience, the meanest Esquire in Derby and Stafford Shires (the counties where my poor living lieth) are better able to abide exactions, and to live in their callings than I am, and yet not one more willing (though I say it) to serve her Majesty. Good Sir, I humbly require you to pity me, as you have mercifully begun with me, but even as the truth and equity of my estate shall deserve.

" I do find in your Honour (as I have often heard of you) a courteous nature and mild disposition. Therefore I dare boldly yield me to your Honour's prescript and determination in all things present and to come ; with this my most humble request that if your Honour do not credit sufficiently this my sincere and free report of my very estate, that it may like you to make a trial of it, and so to credit and use me as your Honour shall then try me.

" The Almighty preserve you in honour and long happy life.

" Hampstead, this 20th of November, 1584."

Then follows a postscript, written in hastily, and somewhat hard to decipher :—

" I would fain carry this old mortified body of mine whence I brought him of late, if it might so like her Majesty and your Honours all. Howbeit, I never dare or will ask anything further [?] than shall seem good unto you, save only mercy and pity towards my old age."

It would seem that this pathetic letter had some effect, for on January 15, 1585–6, he was released on bond, and though we find him apparently still in Middlesex in March, it seems that a little later he was allowed to retire, broken in health, and half-ruined in fortune, for a few months' repose to his beloved Norbury.

Though a prisoner, Sir Thomas had, of course, to pay the exorbitant fines levied on Recusants who refused to attend the Anglican services. In March he and some other of the wealthier Catholics attempted to purchase a dispensation from Elizabeth. It is computed that the Queen made no less than £20,000 a year by such dispensations.* It was, probably, in reply to a question from the authorities as to how much

* Charles Butler, *Historical Memoirs of the English Catholics*, vol. i. p. 292.

HOLOGRAPH LETTER OF SIR THOMAS FITZHERBERT
TO SECRETARY WALSINGHAM

*To face page 32*

they would be willing to pay to compound for the recusancy fines, that we get the following letter.

On March 14, 1585–6, Sir Gilbert Gerard, Master of the Rolls, and Sir Owen Hopton, Lieutenant of the Tower, sent to the Council, " an abstract of the offers made by the Recusants remaining in London and Middlesex tò be paid yearly unto her Majesty to be freed from the penalty of the Statute." *

The name of Sir Thomas Fitzherbert heads the list of twenty-four names. He writes as follows :—

"Sir Thomas Fitzherbert, Knight, in respect that there is a great charge going out of his living which he saith is not above £263 5s. 3d., and the charge going out thereof to divers persons is above £203, yet notwithstanding he is content to offer of his own free will yearly the sum of £40.

"(Signed)   Thoms Ffytzherbt."

Some of the other " offers " may be added. Lord Vaux offered £80, Sir John Arundell, Sir Thomas Tresham, and Dame Elizabeth Poulet, £100 each, Katherine Bellamy, widow, £10, John Gifford, of Chillington, £66.

It does not appear whether these offers were considered satisfactory. It is noteworthy that Sir Thomas Fitzherbert, with scrupulous honour, actually valued his " living " higher than the official valuation, which was only £200 a year. It could not have been found easy to extract £260 a year in fines out of this estate, already so greatly burdened, so that, perhaps, her Majesty was graciously pleased to be satisfied with the offer of £40. At least we may hope that the old knight was allowed a few months of peace at Norbury, before the greater trials that were coming burst on him.

In August, 1586, we find him at Norbury, very sick. The horrors of a long imprisonment in Elizabethan days are better imagined than described. No wonder that the poor old man, now nearing three score years and ten, should have been " very weak and indisposed in bodie, not able to travel as yet without further danger of his person." He was therefore graciously permitted by my Lords of the Council to remain " at any of his houses either in Derbyshire or Staffordshire for the space of three months . . . without breach of his bond wherein he standeth bound to the Queen's Majesty." †

This bond had been dated January 17, 1585–6, and he was at last able to present himself again before the Council on February 4, 1586–7.

* *S. P. Dom. Eliz.* clxxxvii. 48.          † *Acts*, vol. xiv. p. 212.

E

He was enjoined not to depart until he should be dismissed by their Lordships.* He had had just a year of comparative liberty.

But now the great tragedy of his life was about to overwhelm him. The story is a very terrible one. " Have I not chosen you twelve and one of you is a devil ? "—these words of our Blessed Lord seem to ring in one's ears, as one studies the story of the Fitzherberts.

The children of John Fitzherbert, like their father and uncle, were to suffer many things for the love of Christ and to be faithful unto death, but one of them was a traitor, nay, a devil. Thomas, the eldest surviving son (really the third, for two older boys had died in childhood) was his uncle's acknowledged heir. The deed of entail made by Sir Thomas, after his wife's death, had secured his wide estates on this nephew and namesake. He had married in 1578, Elizabeth, daughter of John Westby of Mowbrick,† County Lancaster, the staunchest of Catholics, who suffered imprisonment for the hospitality he showed to Blessed Edmund Campion. It was on the occasion of this marriage that Sir Thomas entailed his property on his nephew. Fortunately the marriage was childless, so that no future Fitzherbert was to have the traitor's blood in his veins.

Thomas Fitzherbert, we do not know when or how, but probably at the time he was imprisoned in Derby gaol for recusancy, about 1583, fell into the hands of one of the greatest villains who ever lived, Richard Topcliffe, the priest-catcher. This detestable scoundrel persuaded him to plot against the life of his father and uncle in order that he might inherit their estates. He persuaded him that if he did not take speedy steps the whole property would be forfeited for recusancy so that he would never enjoy it. As a matter of fact, before Sir Thomas Fitzherbert's death in the Tower, he had been mulcted of two-thirds of his property.

The treachery was the more horrible, as Sir Thomas had brought up his nephew from childhood as his heir, and loaded him with every kindness. But Topcliffe knew how to terrify by his threats as well as to fawn and cajole, and no doubt the wretched young man had somehow put himself in the villain's power : Topcliffe was the prince of villains. At any rate, we know by the miserable young man's own avowal that he " entered into a bond to give £3000 unto Topcliffe

---

* *Acts*, vol. xiv. p. 318. During the time he was waiting on the Council's commands he stayed at Hampstead, as we learn from the *Interrogatory* cited below.

† The marriage settlement is at Swynnerton. It should be noted that a deed of 20 January, 9 Eliz. 1567, stipulates that if Sir Thomas and Dame Anne Fitzherbert should die without heirs of the body of the said Anne, Padley should go to the use of the right heirs of the said Sir Thomas.

if he would persecute his father and uncle to death together with Mr. Basset."*

Mr. William Basset was his uncle by marriage, having espoused Elizabeth, daughter of Sir Anthony Fitzherbert. His estates were at Langley, County Derby, and Blore, County Stafford, and he was a man of means, besides being a good Catholic who suffered fines and imprisonment for the faith.

In any case, Topcliffe busied himself to fulfil his part of the bargain. In the Privy Council Acts is a letter (dated March 26, 1587), "to Mr. Rookeby and Mr. Herbert, Masters of the Requestes, that whereas Sir Thomas Fitzherbert is charged with sundry things contained in certain articles which this bearer, Edmund Brown, shall deliver, their Lordships have thought good to require them to send for the same Sir Thomas to come before them, and to examine him upon the said articles." One of the Councillors who signs this letter is the Earl of Shrewsbury.†

This attempt to bring the confessor to a traitor's end proved unsuccessful, but the conspirators, foiled in this, turned their attention elsewhere. Thomas Fitzherbert's one thought was how best to secure for himself the family estates. To gain these he stuck at nothing. Topcliffe aided him, in order to secure his own ends, for to the older villain Fitzherbert was but a tool, to be thrown aside when no longer useful. Padley was to be his own prize, "a delightful solitary place" where he intended to end his days.

We find the next move in a letter from the Council (September 6, 1587) to the Lord Chief Baron and Justice Wyndham, which declares that they are informed "that there are divers suits and controversies depending between Sir Thomas Fitzherbert, knight, and Thomas Fitzherbert, his nephew, concerning certain fraudulent estates pretended to be made of all the inheritance of the said Sir Thomas, only to defeat the said Thomas, who ought to have the same by way of remainder, and that there is extraordinary proceeding against him for that purpose by Privy Sessions held in Staffordshire and otherwise." Their lordships therefore "*thought her Majesty would take it well, if they* (the Judges) *took due regard and care at the Assizes next to be holden at Stafford, and at all other times hereafter, that he were dealt withall in every of his causes according to conscience and the equity thereof.*" ‡

It is difficult to know whether to admire more the hypocrisy or the

---

* Jessopp, *op. cit.* p. 71.

† It is just possible that the *Interrogatory* quoted below belongs to this period, but there are substantial reasons for referring it to a later date.

‡ *Acts*, vol. xv. p. 226. The italics are our own.

effrontery of this admonition to the Judges to favour the cause of this unnatural traitor, her Majesty's *protégé*.

A careful study of the Fitzherbert deeds preserved at Swynnerton shows the steps that Sir Thomas took in attempting to save the family estates from falling into the hands of the traitor and his accomplice. The process is very complicated, and it would need a somewhat profound knowledge of the law at this period to understand properly all its details. But we think we can give the story with at least fair accuracy in such a way that it may be understood by the general reader.*

On April 1, 1578, Sir Thomas, being then a childless widower, made settlement of the manors of Norbury, Hamstall Ridware, and his other property, upon the marriage of his nephew, Thomas Fitzherbert. The lands were settled to the use of Sir Thomas for life ; remainder to his brother John Fitzherbert for life ; remainder to Thomas and his heirs male by Elizabeth Westby ; remainder to his younger brother, Richard Fitzherbert of Hartsmere, County Stafford, in tail male ; remainder to Humphrey Fitzherbert of Uphall, County Herts.†

So it remained, until October, 1583, when Sir Thomas must have received clear proofs of the worthlessness of his unhappy nephew. There are deeds of October 1, October 10, October 17, and October 19 of this year. The general effect of these is that Sir Thomas combined with his brother, John Fitzherbert, to pass over Thomas the traitor as far as they could, and convey the lands to Richard Fitzherbert. This appears to have been effected by the doctrine of collateral warranties, as we see both from the deeds themselves and from the petition of Thomas the younger hereafter quoted.

On October 1, Sir Thomas and John Fitzherbert leased Norbury, Padley, and the other estates, to Erasmus Wolsley of Wolsley, Esquire, and Richard Ensor of Abbots Bromley for one hundred years.

This was a trust term. Perhaps the form of lease was used to evade the Statute of Uses.

On October 10, Erasmus Wolsley and his fellow trustee granted the same properties in fee to Richard Fitzherbert of Hartsmere.

On October 17, Sir Thomas conveyed the said manors and lands to

---

* For help in this legal tangle I have to thank Francis de Zulueta, Esq., M.A., Fellow of New College, Oxford.

† Marriage Settlement at Swynnerton, No. 4. This is a very voluminous and interesting document. It bears the autographs and seals of Sir Thomas, his brother John, and his nephew, Thomas Fitzherbert. Also (as witnesses) those of Richard Fitzherbert, Anthony Fitzherbert, and Thomas Fitzherbert of Swynnerton, the future Jesuit, besides that of Martin Audley and others whose names come prominently into this history. Sir Thomas' seal bears an antique head, which is the seal he generally uses ; John Fitzherbert's has a death's-head, and Thomas the younger has the crest of the family.

# THE TRAGEDY OF THE FITZHERBERTS

Richard Fitzherbert in fee simple, *i.e.* to his heirs and assigns for ever. On October 19, John Fitzherbert did the same.

Then on February 17, 1583–4, Richard Fitzherbert made a re-settlement conveying the said manors and lands to trustees, John Harpur of Swarkeston and others, to hold to the following uses :

First to the use of Sir Thomas Fitzherbert for seventy years, if he should so long live, after his decease to the use of John Fitzherbert for sixty years, or the term of his natural life, then to trustees for Thomas Fitzherbert, nephew, either for life, or as tenant at will (it is not clear which, for the statements in the deeds are contradictory). Remainder to Nicholas, younger son of John Fitzherbert, in tail male ; remainder to Anthony, another younger son of the said John Fitzherbert in tail male ; remainder to the heirs male of the body of Sir Anthony Fitzherbert, knight, deceased, father of the said Sir Thomas ; remainder to the right heirs of the said Anthony Fitzherbert for ever.*

It was apparently impossible to cut the younger Thomas Fitzherbert out of all enjoyment of the property, but by putting it thus into the hands of trustees and making him their tenant at will, he would be prevented, it was hoped, from doing much harm. Apparently, however, all these elaborate safeguards were swept away by the judges at Stafford in obedience to the orders of the Council, and when Thomas finally came into the property he did so in virtue of the original settlement of 1578.

He failed, however, in securing Padley, owing to the greater cunning of his accomplice. In Trinity term, 1590, he was induced to levy a fine, *i.e.* to make a conveyance of that manor and other lands to Topcliffe, as it would seem, in trust for his own benefit. This he did in order to defeat if possible Sir Thomas' attempts to disinherit him " by means of collateral warranties."

An exemplification of the fine, granted in the Court of Common Pleas, dated Trinity Term, 1590, is preserved at Swynnerton. It bears Topcliffe's endorsement and signature. This exemplification is three years later than the fine itself, being dated November 6, anno 35 Elizabeth, *i.e.* 1593, and we append a reproduction of this most interesting document, with Topcliffe's extraordinary signature attached.

We give a transcript of the fine in the Appendix, as Elizabethan court-hand is far from easy to read, so it will be sufficient here to summarise the document.

The deforciant, Thomas Fitzherbert, Esquire, grants to the plaintiff, Richard Topcliffe, Esquire, and to his heirs for ever, the manors of Over Padley and Nether Padley, on the Derwent, with six messuages, two cottages, ten gardens, ten orchards, a thousand acres of land, five

* All the deeds quoted are preserved at Swynnerton.

hundred acres of meadow-land, six hundred acres of pasture, three hundred acres of wood, a thousand acres of furze and heath (*jampnorum et bruere*), etc., in Padley, Grindelford and Lyham, in the Parish of Hathersage, in consideration of eight hundred marks of silver. Four proclamations had been made of this fine according to statute, and the royal seal had been affixed on November 6, of the thirty-fifth year of Elizabeth, 1593. There is no mention of any trust in the deed, but, in any case, it would probably have been a secret one.

Topcliffe, however, represented the transaction as a conveyance of the property for his own benefit, so that Fitzherbert was obliged to institute a suit in Chancery to compel him to disgorge. But this suit does not seem to have been successful.*

The letter of the Privy Council quoted above, also informs us that Edward Browne, the informer, was bound for his appearance at the Stafford Assizes, but that he was wanted in London " to prosecute certain informations by him exhibited before their Lordships," and so that neither he nor his surety were to be " dampnyfyed " for his absence, as to the persons who were prosecuting him, they might do so in the King's Bench next term, if the Judges thought it convenient. Evidently the troubles of Sir Thomas were not yet over. This Browne must have been another tool of Topcliffe's.

But to understand the proceedings taken against the Fitzherberts, it will be necessary to have some idea of the state of the law at this time, as it regarded Catholics.

The penal statutes had gradually increased in ferocity, especially after the excommunication of the Queen by St. Pius V., and had been crowned in 1585 (27 Elizabeth, cap. 2) by a law which banished all priests from the kingdom, and enacted that if any priest ordained by authority of the See of Rome since the first year of Elizabeth, or any religious or ecclesiastical person should come into or remain in the Queen's dominions he should be adjudged a traitor and suffer accordingly. Furthermore, every person who should receive, relieve, or maintain any such priest should be adjudged a felon and suffer death and forfeiture as in cases of felony. Moreover, whoever should know of any such ecclesiastic being in the realm and should not disclose it to a Justice within twelve days, should be fined and imprisoned at her Majesty's pleasure, &c. &c.

The great majority of our martyrs suffered under this infamous statute which immensely simplified the methods of the persecution. Nor was this the worst. " The truth is," writes the Rev. Dr. Jessopp, " a

* This suit is recorded in the printed calendar of Proceedings in Chancery in the reign of Elizabeth, p. 320. F.f.9.

THE FITZHERBERT-TOPCLIFFE FINE. Photo by the author
From the original deed at Swynnerton.

detestable system had now begun to spring up, under which no one with any conscience or any religious scruples could hold himself safe for an hour. An army of spies and common informers were prowling about the length and breadth of the land, living by their wits, and feeding partly upon the terrors of others and partly upon the letter of the law as laid down in the recent Acts—wretches who had everything to gain by straining the penalties to the uttermost, for they claimed their share of the spoil. Armed with warrants from weak magistrates, who themselves were afraid of suspicion, or failing these, armed with an order from the Privy Council, which was only too easily to be obtained, they sallied forth on their mission of treachery. They were nothing but bandits protected by the law, let loose upon that portion of the community which might be harried and robbed with impunity. In some cases the pursuivants, after arresting their victims and appropriating their money, were content to let them alone, and save themselves further trouble ; in others they kept them till a ransom might come from friends ; in any case there was always the fun of half-scuttling a big house and living at free quarters during a search, and the chance of securing a handsome bribe in consideration of being left unmolested for the future. Chief among these miscreants was one Richard Topcliffe. The cruelties of this monster would fill a volume." *

## THE MARTYRS OF PADLEY

Before continuing our story, it will be well to make a pilgrimage to Padley, the home of Mr. John Fitzherbert, though the property of Sir Thomas. Situated in the parish of Hathersage, in the fairest part of the High Peak of Derbyshire, Padley (or Over Padley, as it is more correctly styled) lies at the very opposite extremity of the county to Norbury, close to the Yorkshire border.

The immediate neighbourhood of the old Hall has been greatly spoilt in recent years by a railway line and station, but even now the surroundings are of rare beauty. Hathersage stands on the slope of a range of hills, an offshoot of the noted Stanage Edge, and the road from the village to Padley is a very beautiful one of some three miles, for the most part following the course of the river Derwent, which hurries down the valley through magnificent woods of giant chestnuts and oaks. All that is now left of the once splendid Manor House of the Eyres is the ancient Domestic Chapel built over the Great Hall. This Chapel, utterly neglected—desecrated, indeed—as it now is, almost a ruin, is

* *One Generation of a Norfolk House*, pp. 69-70.

nevertheless one of the most sacred of those Forgotten Shrines which this book attempts to make known.

Not, indeed, that Padley is altogether forgotten. The secluded parish of Hathersage has ever been a stronghold of the faith, and there has never been a time when holy Mass has not been said in some secret corner of the district. To the little flock, hidden away in the heart of the Peak, Padley Chapel has always been a sacred shrine, and of late

PADLEY
CHAPEL.

years it has become the goal of an annual pilgrimage under the auspices of the Guild of Our Lady of Ransom. On these occasions a Mass is usually sung in the old Catholic Church of Hathersage, a procession with crucifix, lights and banners is formed, and the faithful who have come from far and wide, pass with rosary and hymn and litany to pray at the sacred spot which sheltered the martyrs of Christ. At Padley the voice of a Catholic priest is once more uplifted in prayer and blessing, and the story of the martyrs who lived here is told again for the consolation of their children's children. The present writer had once the privilege of preaching at this pilgrimage.

The following description of Padley Chapel is given by Dr. Cox, in his *Churches of Derbyshire*: * " The old chapel, with the offices below it,

* Vol. ii. pp. 252–3.

is the only part of Padley Hall now standing, with the exception of certain barns and outbuildings. It seems that the principal part of the old Hall, or Manor House, consisted of an enclosed quadrangle, the south side of which was formed by the chapel. Access to this court or quadrangle was gained by an arched passage through the lower story or ground floor of the building containing the chapel.* . . . The chapel occupies the upper part of the building, the floor-level being indicated by the base of

Padley Hall Chapel
S.W.
Pike 1910

THIS DRAWING SHOWS THE CHIMNEY IN WHICH THE MARTYRS ARE SAID TO HAVE
BEEN HIDDEN

the two narrow doorways closely adjoining each other, just over the archway. Access to these doorways must have been gained by stairways (perhaps of wood) that have now been removed. We see from the interior of the chapel that a substantial screen divided the building between these two doorways, and it seems probable that the one nearest the east end was the entrance for the family, and the other for the household retainers or neighbours. There was a third entrance" (scarcely shown in the drawing) " at the extreme east of this north side, into that part of the Hall which there adjoined it, and there can be no doubt that this was the private door for the priest, communicating directly with his chamber.

"There was also an external entrance to this angle of the chapel on

* Our illustration on page 40 shows the north or inner side of the chapel, with the arched entrance to the courtyard built up.

the east side, now hidden by a modern lean-to, which would enable the priest to quit the hall or chapel without going into any other part of the building."

We also give a drawing of the south side of this most interesting shrine.

" On the south side there is no entrance to the chapel, but the full size of the arched passage to the court can there be seen, and the two large buttresses, one on each side, which were ingeniously contrived by the architect to serve as chimneys. The offices on the ground floor are now used as a cow-house and stables, and the upper story or chapel as a barn for hay and other farm produce. The whole is much dilapidated. The main timbers of the roof are in fair preservation. There are four finely-carved hammer-beams, with wall pieces rising from stone corbels ; the two at the west end bear simple shields, but those towards the east end have well-designed shield-bearing angels."

Mr. S. O. Addy, in his *Evolution of the English House*, mentions Padley as "being as good an example as can be found now of an ancient Manor House." He gives a ground-plan and two illustrations. He considers that the arched way divided on the ground floor the hall from the buttery, and was, in fact, the passage known in ancient houses as the " screens." On entering from the south, the hall was on the right—*i.e.* at the eastern end of the building. The room on the left was the buttery or store-room. A buttress dying into the wall of this buttery has inside an opening of some size, probably used as a chimney. Mr. Addy thinks that the western end of the upper storey may have been the ladies' bower, but it seems probable that Dr. Cox is right, and that it was part of the chapel, screened off for the domestics and retainers.

The old floor has been removed, and the present one is three feet lower than the old level. The east window is square-headed, of two lights ; it has been walled up, but the tracery is still intact. The piscina remains on the south side of the window. Here then John Fitzherbert and his family gained strength for the conflict before them, for he and his were almost as obnoxious to the authorities as Sir Thomas, and for the same reason : their steadfast adherence to the Faith.

On January 29, 1587–8, the Lord-Lieutenant of Derbyshire, the Earl of Shrewsbury, a cruel persecutor of the faithful under his jurisdiction, wrote to John Manners, his brother-in-law and Deputy-Lieutenant, and Roger Columbell of Derby, ordering them to search for all Seminarists and other Papists lurking in the hundred of the High Peak, and to apprehend them. Also immediately to apprehend John Fitzherbert of Padley, his neighbour Richard Fenton of North Lees (another ancient mansion of the Eyres, near Hathersage), and two other gentlemen, and commit them as Queen's prisoners. Their destination was already decided on ; as to Mr. Fitzherbert, Dr. Cox prints from the Belvoir MSS. a letter of Shrewsbury's to one " Mr. Walton of Derbie, Preacher," dated Sheffield, January 29, 1586–7, in which he requires him " forthwith to receave into your charge and custodie the bodie of Jno. Fitzherbert of Padley gent. recusant and him safely to kepe as hir Maties prisoner upon his owne cost and charge untill furder order shal be given you in that behalf, Whereof faill you not as you tender hir Maj. service and will answer the contrary." *

When, however, on Candlemas Day (1587–8), Roger Columbell, with a score of men, proceeded to Padley, he " made diligent search for Mr. John Fitzherbert, but could not find him."

But this was only a brief respite, for to John Fitzherbert, as well as to his elder brother, the crown of martyrdom was destined by divine Providence. Meanwhile Anthony, his seventh son, was carried off to the pestiferous gaol at Derby, where he was soon at death's door from gaol fever, though not destined to succumb to it.

Lord Shrewsbury seems to have suspected the fidelity of his agents, or the thoroughness of their search. Another raid was determined on, though a few months were allowed to elapse, perhaps in order to lull the victims into a fancied security.

Behind the dignified figures of the Lords of the Privy Council and the County Magistrates, we discern the hateful form of Topcliffe, thirsting for his blood-money. The destruction of John Fitzherbert was, he knew well, only a question of time and patience. The son was in his toils, only too eager to betray his father. Once it could be proved that he had harboured a priest in his house, his condemnation was secured. And priests were constantly at Padley.

At last, one summer morning, the Holy Sacrifice of the Mass was celebrated in Padley Chapel by two priests, who with the Divine Victim offered the sacrifice of their blood. It was July 12, 1588, a notable day, perhaps the last day when Holy Mass was said in Padley Chapel.

For on that day the long-expected blow fell on the fated house. " Padley," as Shrewsbury had written, " may be doubted much to be a house of evil resort," but up to this time the hunters had failed to find their prey. Now they had a Judas to aid them. Thomas Fitzherbert actually sent word to Lord Shrewsbury as to the day and hour when he would find his father at home. The Lord-Lieutenant came in person, and this time the raid was entirely successful. Not only did he capture John Fitzherbert, but he found even richer prey in the persons of the two holy priests who were concealed in the house. It is said

* *Three Centuries of Derbyshire Annals*, vol. i. p. 259.

that they were found in a hiding-place in the great chimney of the hall.

These priests were the Venerable Servants of God, Nicholas Garlick and Robert Ludlam. Both were Derbyshire men by birth.

John Fitzherbert, ten of his retainers, and the priests, were carried off in triumph and lodged first at Sheffield and then in Derby gaol. They had not long to wait for their trial. The priests were indicted, on July 23, of high treason, and their host of felony for harbouring them. Mr. Fitzherbert was condemned to death as well as his guests. It was, indeed, asserted that, as a matter of fact, he did not know of their presence in the house at the time ; but this did not save him. Nor, indeed, does it seem very likely.

However this may be, John Fitzherbert's life was saved by his son-in-law, Thomas Eyre, of Holme Hall, who had married his daughter Jane. He sold his manor of Whittington, and with the help of other friends, raised the then enormous sum of £10,000, with which he purchased a reprieve. " It is said," adds Dr. Cox, " that it was also stipulated that John Fitzherbert should be set at liberty, but, as this was a secret transaction, the recipients of the money could not be brought to task, and he died in prison." *

He remained for about two years in " that foul hole Derby Gaol, that always stank and bred corruption in the prisoners," according to Topcliffe's own testimony, and was then sent to London to the Fleet Prison, where he died in great destitution, November 9, 1590, having faithfully followed his brother along the Royal Way of the Holy Cross, but reaching the goal before him.

Dr. Cox says that he died of gaol-fever,† and this point is important, as usually Rome will not afford to a confessor who dies in chains the honours reserved to martyrs, unless it can be shown that his imprisonment shortened his life.

The priests had not to wait so long to gain their crown. In the prison they found a third priest, by name Richard Sympson, who had been condemned at the Lent Assizes, but whose life had been spared on his promise to go to church. But the influence of the newcomers was sufficient to make him repent of his weakness, and to make atonement by giving his blood. The Summer Assizes were held on July 23, and both priests were condemned. Two days later they won their crown. An eye-witness says that they met death " with much constancy and Christian magnanimity, without the least sign of fear or dismay."

The Venerable Nicholas Garlick had been the master of Bishop Pursglove's Grammar School at Tideswell, in the Peak. He was an

* _Journal_, vol. vii. p. 247.    † _Derbyshire Annals_, i. p. 263.

44

Oxford man. Among his pupils at Tideswell were several future priests, and with them a martyr, the Venerable Christopher Buxton. Ordained at Rheims in 1582, Garlick was sent on the English Mission in January, 1583. Next year he was arrested and banished, but returned immediately to England. At his trial he was very bold. "I am not come to seduce," he told the judge, "but to induce men to the Catholic faith. For this end have I come to the country, and for this will I work as long as I live."

"I thought," he exclaimed, as the three left the dock, "that Cain would never be satisfied till he had the blood of his brother Abel." Was the martyr thinking of the wretched young Thomas Fitzherbert?

The three priests were drawn on hurdles to the place of execution, by St. Mary's Bridge at Derby, close to the spot where Pugin's beautiful Catholic Church now stands.

Garlick was merry and bright to the last. On the way to execution he was met by one of his friends who told him they had "shot off together."

"True," said he, "but I am now to shoot off such a shot as I never shot in all my life."

The martyrdom followed, with all the usual atrocities. It is said that Sympson showed signs of fear, but Garlick went before him up the ladder, kissing it, and, as the fire was not ready, he spoke to the people stirring words about the salvation of their souls. He closed his speech by casting among them a number of loose papers written in prison, which he declared would prove what he affirmed. It is said that every one into whose hands these papers fell was subsequently reconciled to the Church.

When Venerable Richard Sympson was stripped for the quartering they found that he wore a shirt of hair, no doubt in penance for his fall. The third martyr looked on at the horrible butchery unmoved, even smiling. When he was upon the ladder, and just ready to be cast off, looking up to heaven with a smiling countenance, he uttered these his last words, as if speaking to saints or angels appearing to him, "*Venite benedicti Dei*" ("Come, ye blessed of God.")

So died for Christ the martyr priests of Padley.* Their quarters were afterwards rescued from the bridge and reverently buried. According to tradition the head of Fr. Garlick was interred in the churchyard of Tideswell.

The following verses of an old ballad have often been printed,

* For further details see *Nicholas Garlick, Martyr*, by Edward King, S.J. (Burns & Oates, 1904); also *Padley Chapel and Padley Martyrs*, by the Rev. F. M. Hayward, of Derwent (1905).

but we cannot refrain from quoting them here. They are given by Bishop Challoner :

" When Garlick did the ladder kiss,
And Sympson after hie,
Methought that there St. Andrew was,
Desirous for to die—

" When Ludlam looked on smilingly,
And joyful did remain,
It seemed St. Stephen was standing by,
For to be stoned again.

" And what if Sympson seemed to yield,
For doubt and dread to die ;
He rose again, and won the field,
And died most constantly.

" His watching, fasting, shirt of hair,
His speech, his death, and all,
Do record give, do witness bear,
He wailed his former fall."

Meanwhile the time-serving Shrewsbury was making the most of his achievement. On August 9, 1588, a few days after the martyrdom, he wrote from Sheffield to his " deare Soveraigne " to report to her the state of the counties under his lieutenancy. All is well, for the most part. " As for the others, recusants and bad members, order is given whereby they shall be more straitly looked unto. On Sunday last I was in those parts of Derbyshire, where I lately took John Fitzherbert and the other Seminaries, of purpose only to reduce into some good order the multitude of ignorant people heretofore by them seduced. Where at one sermon before me came above two hundred persons, whereof many had not comed to church twenty years before, and as many not since the beginning of your Majesty's reign. Beside them be two hundred and twenty which came not as yet, but I hope ere long, seeing their Captain is caught they will generally become more obedient subjects." He goes on to protest his loyalty : " Though I be old, yet shall your quarrel make me young again, though lame in body, yet lusty in heart to lend your greatest enemy one blow and to stand so near your defence every way wherein your Majesty shall employ me." *

* *S. P. Dom. Eliz.*, ccxiv. No. 51.

46

# THE TRAGEDY OF THE FITZHERBERTS

## THE CROWN

Meanwhile the traitor was straining every nerve to get his reward. On Sunday, July 21, the Privy Council wrote to Mr. Solicitor informing him that the young man claimed that his uncle, Sir Thomas, had conveyed unto him "long sithence" one half of the manor of Padley, and two parts of another manor. Mr. Solicitor was "to peruse the said evidence" and report.*

He evidently feared that Padley would be forfeited to the Crown, as the possession of convicted felons. He also tried to prevent his uncle selling the timber on his estates, and obtained on July 24 a letter from the Council "to stay the felling or sale of such woods as Sir Thomas Fitzherbert hath growing on any of his manors," or, if already felled, to stay them there on the ground till further disposition were made.† However, it would appear that here he over-reached himself. Sir Thomas informed their Lordships that, "being indebted to her Majesty, he purposed to make sale of certain woods for the discharge of the said debt," and the Council were not going to stop such praiseworthy proceedings for any nephew's sake; they therefore "thought meet the said Sir Thomas should be permitted to make sale, cut down, and fell such woods . . . of his own as the laws of the Realm doth permit him to do."

Padley had been seized by Lord Shrewsbury, not, as it would appear, for the Crown. Sir Thomas wrote to him "from London, this 28th day of May, 1589," as follows :

"Very good Lord,

"With all humble duty I crave leave in lowly wise to open my grief unto you. I suppose your Honour hath known me above fifty years and my wife, that was daughter and heir unto Sir Arthur Eyre. I trust I have been dutiful unto my Lords your grandfather, your father, and your Honour, and I have found your Honours all my good Lords, till now of late your Lordship entering into the house of Padley, found two Seminaries there all unknown to my brother, as was confessed at their death, and is since well approved by good testimony. Sithence which time your Lordship also hath entered upon my house at Padley, and the demesne thereof, seized all the goods of my brother's and mine that was in that house, amongst which I had certain evidences of a wood and meadow under Levin House called Fawltcliff, which as I am informed your Honour

---

* *Acts Privy Council*, xvi. p. 169.  † *Ibid.* p. 177.

47

hath entered upon and occupied, wholly to your use, though I had been possessed, and my wife's ancestors time out of mind.

"Very good Lord, these things are greater than my present poor estate can suffer, or in anywise bear, I paying to Her Majesty the statute of recusancy, being £260 by year, which is more than all my rents yearly rise unto. Loath am I to complain of your Honour any way, wherefore I complain me first unto your Lordship, hoping you will deal so nobly and charitably with me as I shall be restored to my house, lands, and goods by your Honour, so I shall be fully satisfied and be able to pay her Majesty, and for ever bound to pray for your Lordship's life in all honour long to continue."

On June 29, 1589, Sir Thomas, with other Recusants, was released on bail, "to return at or before the first day of the next term." *

Sir Thomas had been able to get no redress from Lord Shrewsbury. He therefore petitioned the Lords of the Council, and on July 7, they wrote to Lord Shrewsbury to restore to him "his farm called Padley, with his evidences and such things as appertained unto him." † Lord Shrewsbury was indignant at this and wrote on August 17 to explain that he or his tenants at Padley would pay the recusancy fines, and as this was all the Council cared for, on September 22 they approved of his proposal. But Sir Thomas still protested, and at last the Council gave him some redress. They wrote to Shrewsbury, December 28, "Signifying unto his Lordship that he would do well to let a house of Sir Thomas Fitzherbert called Padley, that heretofore served for a receptacle and harbourer to Seminaries and Jesuits, to be tenanted by such as Sir Thomas should name, being known to his Lordship to be of no bad disposition. And if he should make choice of none such, then his Lordship to appoint with his consent some honest person to inhabit the same and occupy the ground, that might answer such rent to the said Sir Thomas that might conveniently be raised of the same, whereby he should have no occasion to complain of any wrong done unto him, and that inconvenience avoided that was not to be tolerated in these doubtful times." ‡

It was easy (as Dasent remarks in the Preface to this volume of the Acts) to make a show of justice over a transaction, the real purpose of which was to secure the recusancy fines.

The Spanish Armada had been destroyed at the very time that the martyrs of Padley were being executed at Derby. But there were fears of a renewal of hostilities, and this was now made a pretext for confining

* *Acts Privy Council*, xvii. p. 319.     † *Ibid.* p. 357.
‡ *Acts*, vol. xviii. p. 286.

Broughton Castle.                                                    J.Pike 1910.

the principal Recusants in prisons distant from London.   It was therefore
arranged (March 13, 1589–90) that Sir Thomas Fitzherbert with fifteen
other Catholic gentlemen of importance (the names include those of
Sir William Catesby, Gervase Pierpoint, John Towneley, Thomas

G                                                                    49

Newdigate, John Talbot of Grafton, and Thomas Throckmorton) should be committed to the charge of Richard Fiennes of Broughton Castle near Banbury. Those of the diocese of Winchester were sent to Farnham Castle, while others were incarcerated at Wisbech or in the Bishop's Palace at Ely. Yet, as Dr. Cox points out, Sir Thomas Fitzherbert was "so loyal to Elizabeth in matters temporal, that notwithstanding the heavy and repeated fines to which he had been subjected, he had volunteered to supply double the contribution demanded of his estate on the approach of the Armada."

At Broughton, the Keeper was instructed to remove his wife and family from the house, not to allow his prisoners or their servants to carry swords, and only to take his prisoners out for exercise one at a time, and not more than a mile from the Castle. Their beds, chests, trunks, and apparel were to be carefully searched for papers. It adds a new interest to the beautiful old Castle at Broughton to know that these valiant confessors of Christ were, for a time, confined within its walls.

Mr. Dasent remarks, "Amongst all the entries relating to Recusancy (in the Privy Council Acts) it is remarkable that we find only one which indicates a possible conversion," * surely a very wonderful testimony to the constancy of hundreds of Catholics.

Sir Thomas remained a prisoner at Broughton about seven months, he was then sent back to London to endure the last and cruellest trial of his long martyrdom. But before recounting it, we must turn back for a while to Norbury.

When Sir Thomas was first imprisoned by the Commissioners, his younger brother Richard (old Sir Anthony's third surviving son) escaped to the Continent. (He is called "the fugitive" in the Privy Council Acts.†) After a time, however, he returned, and lived for a while peaceably at Norbury. As we have seen, Sir Thomas, in 1583, conveyed to him his manors in trust. He is there called "of Hartsmere," which was an estate in Staffordshire belonging to Sir Thomas, which the Knight had let to him for a term of years.

The spies reported the fugitive's return in 1590, and the Privy Council despatched a man named Thorne, a notorious pursuivant of the roughest character, to effect his capture. The story is given from a manuscript of Father Christopher Grene's now preserved at Oscott College.‡ "Thorne practising to apprehend Mr. Richard Fitzherbert used this policy. To Norbury, where he knew this gentleman lay, came three lame supposed beggars, one man, two women, among divers others that there had alms. And when all were served as accustomed, these

---

* *Acts*, vol. xix. p. 24.          † Vol. xviii. p. 140.
‡ Printed by Morris, *Troubles of our Catholic Forefathers*, third series, pp. 15–16.

THE DOOR OF THE GREAT HALL,
NORBURY MANOR HOUSE
*Photo by James Watts*

*To face page* 50

three continued still crying and craving more alms, as seeming more needy. The good gentleman, going down himself at their pitiful cry, to give them some money, the man beggar arrested him, laying hands on him to carry him to an officer and threw the gentleman down. With this noise his friends within came out to rescue him. The beggar, seeing that, having a dagg [pistol] ready charged at his girdle, offered to discharge it at Mr. Fitzherbert's breast, but it went not off. Thereupon the beggar, beaten, let fall his dagg and went a little way off, where Thorne expected his return with hope of prey. The dagg then taken up by one of that house, went off itself without hurting anybody, albeit there were many present."

We find from the Privy Council papers that Thorne was no stranger to Richard Fitzherbert. He had already dispossessed him of the estates of Hartsmere and Bancroft, in spite of Sir Thomas' protests. He had carried off all his cattle, and was in fact a veritable pest to all the faithful in Staffordshire.*

Now he wrote furiously to complain to the Privy Council of his ill-success in his attempt at Norbury. Their Lordships were much horrified. They wrote to Lord Shrewsbury ordering him to arrest Richard Fitzherbert, and detailing the injuries which Thorne pretended his agents had received in the attempt at Norbury. "By virtue of our warrant, the said Thorne, having by means of one Thomas Elkin and others apprehended the said Richard, he was never the less by divers like evil disposed persons inhabiting the said house and town of Norbury presently rescued, and with strong hand taken away . . . and in the same affair have grievously wounded and hurt Elkin and others, whereof they are at this present in great peril of life. Forasmuch as this notable outrage ought speedily to be redressed, and that your Lordship by reason of other your occasions and dispositions of body cannot so conveniently travel yourself, we have therefore thought it expedient to pray your Lordship to appoint your son, the Lord Talbot, calling to him the bearer hereof, Mr. Richard Topcliffe, purposely sent down to attend your Lordship about this matter, and such others as his Lordship shall think fit to make his present repair unto Norbury above said . . . and by virtue hereof to search all houses, apprehend and send up hither the principal and chief of the men so offending under safe custody, to be proceeded with here according to law." †

It is pretty clear that the Council mistrusted Gilbert, Lord Talbot (we find among the State Papers denunciations of this nobleman, after he had succeeded to his father's title and jurisdiction, as a friend and

---

* Morris, *Troubles of our Catholic Forefathers*, third series, p. 23.
† *Acts*, vol. xix. p. 141. Letter dated May 20, 1590.

harbourer of Papists), and so sent the redoubtable Topcliffe himself to see that nothing went wrong this time. It is moving to think of this inhuman monster at beautiful Norbury. Did he bring with him, we wonder, his wretched tool, Thomas Fitzherbert? The miserable man was to take a part two years later, in arresting, at Topcliffe's command, the holy martyr, Father Robert Southwell, though even that villainy seems small beside his parricidal exploits.*

This time, under such a leader, the expedition to Norbury was, of course, successful. The Council wrote to Shrewsbury on September 21, thanking him for his "great care and diligence in apprehending Fitzherbert, Martin Audley,† Richard Twyford, and the rest"; and begging him to authorise Thorne to arrest "Alice Royston, keeper of Sir Thomas Fitzherbert's house at Norbury, and also one Thomas Coxon, keeper of the said Sir Thomas his park at Ridwaye, and other such persons from time to time as the said Thorne shall give notice of to your Lordship."

It seems that all this was done at the instigation of Topcliffe and his accomplice Thomas the traitor. The old document at Oscott, already quoted, says: "Mr. John Fitzherbert molested and troubled by his own son, imprisoned and there dead. This imp also, Thomas Fitzherbert, hath sought by all means to take away the life of old Sir Thomas Fitzherbert, who made him his heir and brought him up from a child. He hath caused him to be suspected of statute treason, and to be committed to the Tower where he continueth. He hath procured also divers of his uncle's tenants to be imprisoned in Stafford, and there some of them are dead."‡

Poor Richard Fitzherbert fell ill in prison after his arrest, but on August 6 the Council ordered him to be sent up to London "as soon as might be without endangering of his life in respect of his infirmity."§

---

* It is certain, at any rate, that Thorne knew Fitzherbert well. We find the following in an old manuscript :—

"Nicholas Thornes, the pursuivant, a most bad persecutor, lying on his deathbed, said : 'Now Queen Elizabeth cannot answer for me, nor Topcliffe, nor Thomas Fitzherbert do me any good. He wished he might speak with a priest specially, whom he had sought much for, and that he should both come and go safely. In the end, he said he was condemned for persecuting the Church of God.' "—From Fr. Grene's MS. " F," printed by Foley, *Records*, vol. iii. p. 227.

"As to Father Southwell, Thomas Fitzherbert was not only with Topcliffe when he arrested the holy martyr at Mr. Bellamy's house at Harrow, but was the chosen messenger dispatched by Topcliffe to the Court to announce the good news and 'tell what good service he had done.' "—Father H. Garnet's letter, Foley, vol. i. pp. 352-3.

† Martin Audley was the faithful body-servant of Sir Thomas. He seems to have been a native of Hamstall Ridware, and to have had a son who was a priest.

‡ In the margin is written : " Old Sir Thomas now dead in the Tower."

§ *Acts*, xix. p. 368.

# THE TRAGEDY OF THE FITZHERBERTS

The same letter orders that John Fitzherbert be also sent up to London, since they understood that by his "'lewd disposition' he did great hurt in Derby gaol." Evidently his two years' imprisonment in that pestiferous place had not shaken his constancy or dimmed his zeal.

The two brothers were accordingly sent up to London, where the prison doors closed on them, and we hear of them no more.*

It was ordered by the Council† that Richard Fitzherbert and his friends should be "severely and strictly examined" by Topcliffe, a fearful ordeal in which torture had, no doubt, a predominant place. For Topcliffe was as one possessed with diabolical hatred of Catholics, and to recount his cruelties would, as Dr. Jessopp says, fill a volume.

In October, 1590, the Council seem to have come to the conclusion that their Catholic prisoners were not likely, after all, to aid a foreign invader, should he come. They therefore graciously permitted that those confined at Broughton and Ely should be released on giving security and satisfying the Archbishop of Canterbury as to certain conditions to be observed after their liberation.

Before this release could be obtained, however, the keeper's charges had to be met, for in those days one paid heavily for the privilege of being imprisoned.‡ At Broughton, the keeper expected "over and above their ordinary charges of diet . . . some reasonable allowance towards the use and spoil of his linen and other his household stuff used and employed in their service."§ Their Lordships politely hoped the prisoners would not refuse this, "being all persons of quality and behaviour," who could "well consider what appertaineth thereto." The situation certainly has its humorous side!

Sir Thomas Fitzherbert was sent up to the Archbishop with his fellow prisoners, but in his case special measures were taken. Topcliff and young Fitzherbert were determined that he should not escape them. The Archbishop was desired on October 28, "to make stay of him in his house until her Majesty's pleasure may be known,"‖ and after this the good old knight was confined in the Lord Mayor's house for a time, during which the Attorney General was consulted as to his offence "and how far he might be charged therewith by law."

The Council wrote ¶ (November 30, 1590) to Mr. Rookeby, Master

* The fact of Richard Fitzherbert's death in prison is not absolutely certain, but there can be little doubt that, like his brothers, he won the martyr's crown.

† *Acts*, xix. p. 370.

‡ At the Fleet, as at Wisbech, *an entrance fee of fifty-three shillings and fourpence* was actually demanded! If these fees were refused the keeper was authorised to seize the prisoner's goods.

§ *Acts*, vol. xx. p. 18. Dated October 5, 1590.

‖ *Ibid.* p. 62.          ¶ *Ibid.* p. 100.

of St. Katherine's, and others that, "Whereas Sir Thomas Fitzherbert, Knight, stood charged with certain matters of great importance that concerned her Majesty and the State . . . because Mr. Topcliffe was acquainted with those causes, there were certain interrogations which he should exhibit unto him under the hand of Mr. Attorney General, whereupon her Majesty's pleasure was the said Sir Thomas Fitzherbert should be by him examined."

They were therefore to repair to the house of the said Sir John Hart, Lord Mayor, and take the examination with "discretion and care" as well of Sir Thomas as of "such others as Mr. Topcliffe should give them notice of that were privy or able to disclose any of his dealings." It is to this date that we assign the *Interrogatories* drawn up by Topcliffe, which Dr. Cox has printed as an appendix to his "Norbury Manor House." *

It was evidently desired to bring the old man to a traitor's death at Tyburn. Dr. Cox says that Sir Thomas was examined under torture. It is very probable that it was so, if not on this occasion, at least during the following months which he was to spend in the gloomy dungeons of the Tower. To inflict the extremity of torture on a Catholic was Topcliffe's highest joy. His fiendish cruelty to the Venerable martyrs, Robert Southwell, Henry Walpole and Eustace White, are instances in point.

In his exultation at seeing his prey at last within his grasp Topcliffe wrote to Lord Shrewsbury on December 8, as follows : "Neither will God suffer the practises of the wicked to be hidden, as lately hath burst out the lewd dispositions of that dangerous family the Fitzherberts in the country, in whose three houses hath been moulded and tempered the most dangerous and loathsome Treasons." †

The Interrogatories contain the most absurd charges. They seek to involve the good old knight in the Rising of the North, so far back as 1569, as well as in Babington's conspiracy of 1586.‡ We see now the reason for the arrest of his housekeeper, the keeper of his park at Hamstall Ridware, his bailiff and tenants. They, as well as Richard Fitzherbert himself, are to be cited as witnesses against him. In fact, the name of Richard Fitzherbert heads the list of witnesses "to prove these to be true." Among others are the very men who were arrested with Richard at Norbury—Martin Audley, Richard Twyford, and the rest. There are about

---

* *Journal*, pp. 256–9.

† Quoted from the Talbot MSS., Lodge, *Illustrations of British History*, vol. ii. p. 402. Shrewsbury died December 18, 1590.

‡ He was connected with the Babingtons by marriage, his aunt, Edith Fitzherbert, having married Thomas Babington, of Dethick, grandfather of Anthony the conspirator. Their arms, impaled, are still to be seen on the roodscreen in Ashover Church, where Thomas Babington has a beautiful tomb.

twenty witnesses named, all of whom were relatives or tenants of Sir Thomas, and all prosecuted for recusancy. "It is not likely," as Dr. Cox remarks, "that much could have been got from them unless torture was applied." Even then, it would appear that the charges completely broke down, for Sir Thomas was never brought to trial. Not that many of these changes (*i.e.* those of harbouring priests and favouring religion) were untrue, but that it was found impossible to prove them. Nothing is said about Padley, so probably Mr. Attorney General pointed out that no charge could be substantiated against Sir Thomas on this head, since he could not have known of the presence of the priests there in July 1588.

The first of these Interrogatories inquired whether he were not with Blessed Thomas Percy at his house at Topcliffe a month before the Rebellion in the North. If this is true, it is an interesting fact; but there is no proof of it. We may quote here some of the questions which probably have a good deal of truth in their suggestions.

"Item, whether he hath not for the space of these sixteen years and more, kept in his house at Norbury massing priests and now doth, to say service there daily.

"Item, whether he doth not keep in his house at this instant four priests, viz. Sir Richard Arnold, Abraham Sutton, Robert Gray, and one Francis, besides daily Recusants and all sorts of Papists.

"Item, whether he doth not relieve daily, and ever hath done, both Jesuits, seminaries, and massing priests, and now doth keep house only for the maintenance of such persons, and ever hath done.

"Item, whether all his servants both men and women be not Recusants as also reconciled and vowed Papists so to continue.

"Item, whether Father Persons the Jesuit did not preach and say mass at his house at Norbury, and whether that all his household people both men and women, did not receive at the same time with divers others . . .

"Item, whether he hath had the Pope's pardons brought him at any time, and whether he and his household have received the Communion upon the same pardons, and how often and how long since."

The name of Abraham Sutton brings us into connection with another martyr. He was the brother of Venerable Robert Sutton, who suffered at Stafford for his priesthood, July 27, 1588, and whose incorrupt thumb is kept as a relic at Stonyhurst. There were three brothers priests, natives of Burton-on-Trent. Abraham Sutton was for years tutor to the young Fitzherberts.

The other priests are identified by Dr. Cox. Robert Gray was also tutor to the Fitzherberts; he was imprisoned both in London and Derby,

and was tortured by Topcliffe. Eventually he escaped to France.*
John Francis was a friar, a native of Repton. Richard Arnold (alias
Audley) was a young priest, son of one of the tenants at Hamstall
Ridware.

No doubt many other priests had found a shelter at Norbury and at
Hamstall, during Sir Thomas' long imprisonment, and doubtless it was
hoped that Alice Royston, the housekeeper at Norbury, would give
valuable evidence on this head. But these humble Catholics were as
faithful as their master.

On December 29, 1590, the Council ordered Mr. Attorney to
confer with Mr. Topcliffe on the examinations and confessions of
Sir Thomas Fitzherbert, "and of his brethren, servants, tenants and
others," who had been examined, and after due deliberation on the
results obtained, to certify their Lordships with speed his opinion as to
the dangerous nature of Sir Thomas' offence, and how far he might be
charged therewith by law.†

The result of this report appears in a letter of January 10, 1590–1,
" to the Lieutenant of the Tower in the nature of a warrant : " " These
shall be to require you to receive into your safe custody the persons of
Sir Thomas Fitzherbert, knight, and John Gage, to be kept close
prisoners in such strict sort as no manner [of] person be suffered to
have access unto either of them without special direction from us ;
and touching the charges of the diet and otherwise of Sir Thomas
Fitzherbert during his being with you, you shall take order with the
said knight and John Gage for the defraying thereof themselves. And
so requiring you to have due care in the performance hereof, we bid you
farewell."

And so the last act of the tragedy begins. We hear the heavy portals
of Traitors' Gate clash behind the brave old knight, and then there is
silence.  He was now in his 74th year, and he had been thirty years in
bonds for Christ.

The unbroken solitude and complete isolation of a close prisoner in
the Tower made it a very severe punishment even for young and healthy
men. It is no wonder that the old knight's health broke down under the
strain, and that he died in less than nine months.

In June 1591, the Council was informed that from want of exercise
and close confinement in his dungeon the old man had become diseased
in his legs and would shortly lose the use of them altogether if some
relief were not granted him.  They therefore ordered the Lieutenant to
permit his prisoner " to walk at some convenient time and place within
the Tower in his company, or in the company of some trusty person

* Foley, *Records, S.J.*, vol. vi. p. 167.　　† *Acts*, vol. xx. p. 175.

whom he should appoint, so that no manner of person had access to him or conferred with him by any means." *

But the remedy came too late. Topcliffe and the traitor had achieved their end at last. On October 3, 1591, the old knight died in the Tower, and, at last released from the prison of the body, entered into the joy of his Lord. He must have died without any of the consolations of the religion for which he had suffered so much, but even for this last sacrifice must have merited an eternal weight of glory. *Euge serve bone et fidelis.*†

Dr. Cox tells us that shortly before his death, Sir Thomas made a will by which he disinherited his nephew, the traitor, "but Topcliffe was on the look out, obtained access to his cell, found the will, carried it off to Archbishop Whitgift, and with his sanction it was destroyed."

"In the oldest Act Book of the Probate Court of Lichfield is an entry for administering the goods of Sir Thomas Fitzherbert (treated as an intestate) taken out by his nephew Thomas as next of kin, under date October 10, 1591." ‡

And so the iniquity was consummated for which Topcliffe tells us he had toiled and laboured with Thomas Fitzherbert for seven years.

## THE FATE OF THE ACCOMPLICES

Now that the old lion was dead the jackals began to divide the spoil.§ Thomas Fitzherbert having had his uncle's will destroyed, claimed as heir-at-law, in virtue of the marriage settlement, executed April 1, 1578.

* *Acts.* vol. xxi. p. 187.

† The Venerable Eustace White, one of Topcliffe's most illustrious victims, writing from his prison to Father Henry Garnet, S.J., November 23, 1591, sent his letter by the hands of one who had been Sir Thomas' faithful servant in the Tower.

He writes : "This bearer, Mr. ———, *late and last servant unto the good Sir Thomas Fitzherbert ( for he attended on him . . . his death in the Tower)* can partly relate unto you mine estate from the mouth of *his good . . .* in prison by me, my dearest friend in bonds. For he hath spared from himself to relieve me with victuals as he could through a little hole, and with other such necessaries as he could by that means do, whom truly I did never see in my life but through a hole. Nothing was too dear unto him that he could convey unto me, for whom as I am bound so will I daily pray while I live.

"I have been close prisoner since the 18th day of September, where of forty-six days together I lay upon a little straw in my boots, my hands continually manacled in irons, for one month together never once taken off," &c.

The words in italics were erased by the prudence of Father Garnet, but owing to the ink drying in different colours they can now be read, though part of the original is still illegible.

‡ *Journal,* vii. p. 248.

§ The Commissions to the escheators of Derbyshire and Staffordshire, issued on the death of Sir Thomas, are dated December 1, 1591. This has led to the erroneous state-

H

The young man was a spendthrift and a profligate, and probably already heavily burdened with debt. He soon began to dissipate his inheritance and to raise mortgages on the property.

On June 9, 1592, the Council ordered that certain parcels of plate belonging to the deceased should be handed over to Thomas Fitzherbert, Esquire, his administrator, under bond to pay within eight days the true value of the plate equally unto Sir Michael Blount, Lieutenant of the Tower, and to Richard Pickering, Keeper of the Gatehouse in Westminster, "for the charges of the diet and other duties grown due unto them during his (Sir Thomas') imprisonment severally with them." * This is the only mention we have found of the fact that Sir Thomas had been imprisoned in the Gatehouse where so many valiant confessors suffered the cruellest hardships. He was, no doubt, transferred from that prison to the Tower in January, 1591.

Though Sir Thomas was dead, and his murderers now hoped to enjoy the spoils, they did not relax their cruel persecution of his relatives and friends. Topcliffe now felt that he had the whole family in his power, and not least the wretched traitor whom he had led to commit so many crimes against faith and family.

This may be the best place to refer to the extraordinary pedigree of the Fitzherbert family, now in the Public Record Office, which was drawn up by Topcliffe about this time. It is wrongly calendared under 1594 but its true date is 1591, since Sir Thomas is referred to as "now in the Tower." † It is endorsed in Topcliffe's peculiar style—"The petygree of yᵉ Fitzherbertz from the Judges Father untill them that nowe Lyve and be dyvers beyond sea, trators and most of yᵉ resedew yᵗ bee in England daingeroos Persons."

Sir Thomas is noted as the third son of the Judge, the two eldest dying young without issue. "Now in Tower" is written below his

ment that this was the date of the old knight's death, *e.g.* in an Exemplification of Letters Patent, 14 Car I. 1639, preserved at Swynnerton.

Some confusion has been caused as to both the place and date of Sir Thomas' death by a document preserved at Swynnerton (Norbury, No. 39), an Exemplification of Letters Patent of King James I. (26 June, 2 Jac. I. 1604) appointing Sir John Bentley, Knight, Francis Fitzherbert, of Tissington, and others to inquire as to the manors and lands of Nicholas Fitzherbert, who stood attainted of treason committed 1 January, 31 Elizabeth 1589. It recites the Inquisition taken at Derby, June 11, 1604, before Sir John Bentley and Lawrence Wright. The jury declared that John Fitzherbert died November 8, 1590, at Norbury, and that Sir Thomas died November 30, 1591, also at Norbury. Neither of these statements is correct, any more than their further declaration that Thomas (the traitor) and Nicholas himself were then living at Norbury. Altogether this document is a mystery.

* *Acts*, vol. xxii. p. 519.

† *S. P. Dom. Eliz.* ccxxxv. No. 88. Foley gave a facsimile in his second volume of *Records of the English Province S.J.* p. 198, and Cox has done the same, *Journal*, vol. vii.

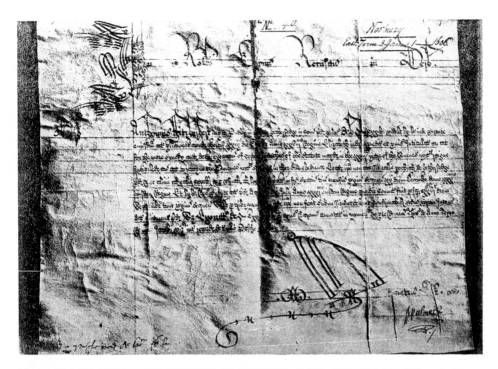

## ANTHONY FITZHERBERT'S QUIETUS FOR RECUSANCY, 1606
*From the original deed at Swynnerton.   Photo by the author*

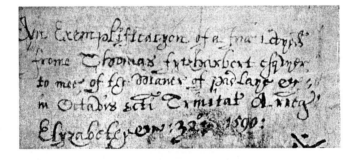

## TOPCLIFFE'S ENDORSEMENT OF THE
## FINE OF THE MANOR OF PADLEY
*Photo by the author*

*To face page* 58

name. John has the note, " Next brother to S$^r$. Tho. to whome and to whose sone S$^r$. Tho. assured ye lande 5 tymes." Then comes, " Rich. fytzharbert ye 5 brother, a feugetive outlawed and now in prison for rec$^g$ pste." Then, " Wm. fytzharbert ye 6 sone dead and left sev$^n$ child$^n$ and is called Fitzherbert of Swynerton."

This brother has hardly been mentioned in our record, since he was fortunate enough to die in the year of Elizabeth's accession. But he is important in the pedigree as the ancestor of the present family. The marriages of the three daughters are then noted.

Of the sons of John Fitzherbert, Thomas has the note, " A good subject and is her Maj$^{ts}$ servant & thought to be disinherited by S$^r$ Tho. his said Uncle verye wrongfullye."

Nicholas is " a canonist at Rome. Now in service with Card. Allen. a trator " ; Francis is noted " A frier, a trator " ; Geordge, " a fhezewt [Jesuit !] iff he like, a trator " ; Anthony " in ye Gaole at Darby for receiving of Sem Preasts." " A tratoroos fellowe now enlarge out of Darbye Gaole," is added below.

Richard's two sons, William " a youthe brought upp with Abram Sutt$^n$ a seam$^{ry}$ Priest," and Anthony " a youthe bro$^t$ upp w$^h$ ye sam Sutt$^o$ ye seam$^y$ Priest " are labelled " daingeroos." William Fitzherbert of Swynnerton's three children are Thomas, " fled for treason & now with Stanley in Spaigne—a trator " ; Anthony, " a skoller of ye Seaminary now in England—danidgeroos," and Anne, " a doughter married by S$^r$. Tho. to Walt. Hevenningham in Stafford—verye badd and danidgeroos."*

Any family might be proud of such a pedigree as this !

Though Thomas got possession of Norbury by fraud, Padley, for which he had sinned so foully, never became his. It fell for a time into Topcliffe's hands, but only for a time. He was turned out of it by Lord Shrewsbury, as we shall see. Thomas and his accomplice did not profit greatly by their villainy after all. Thomas' cruelty and oppression to his tenants soon brought him into trouble.

The Council received complaints, July 28, 1592, that he had forcibly evicted a poor tenant of Hamstall Ridware, by name William Sutton, with his wife and seven children, out of their dwelling, pulling down the house, so that they had nowhere to shelter their heads. The Council thought this " to be a hard and extreme course " and directed the neighbouring magistrates to inquire into the facts. Again we find him in September, " presuming on a protection from her Majesty whereby he supposeth himself to be exempt from suit of law," forcibly carrying off,

* After this the reader will probably be grateful to us for having modernised the spelling elsewhere.

with the aid of threescore persons, certain lead and lead ore to a great value, belonging to one Richard Hurt of Nottingham, and wrongfully detaining it for his own profit. On November 19 it was ordered that he should be arrested at Norbury, and in December the matters were referred to arbitration.* The wretched Thomas, in fact, ended as we should have expected. He became almost as evil as his master, Topcliffe, than whom hell had no more accomplished servant.†

The two scoundrels soon quarrelled over the spoil. In November, 1594 (as we have seen), Topcliffe sued his accomplice in the Court of Chancery in a bond for £3000. "For whereas Fitzherbert entered into bonds to give £3000 unto Topcliffe, *if he would persecute his father and uncle to death, together with Mr. Bassett.* Fitzherbert pleaded that the conditions were not fulfilled, *because they died naturally*, and Bassett was in prosperity. Bassett gave witness what treacherous devices he had made to entrap him, and Coke, the Queen's Attorney, gave testimony openly that he very well had proved how effectually Topcliffe had sought to inform him against them contrary to all equity and conscience." ‡

" This was rather too disgraceful a business to be discussed in open court, and 'the matter was put over for secret hearing,' when it would seem that Topcliffe, standing somewhat stiffly to his claim, lost his temper, and let fall some expressions which were supposed to reflect on the Lord Keeper and some members of the Privy Council, whereupon he was committed to the Marshalsea for contempt, and there kept for some months. While he was incarcerated, he addressed two letters to the Queen, which have been preserved, and two more detestable compositions it would be difficult to find. In one of them, dated 'Good or evil Friday, 1595,' he says, '. . . I have helpt more traitors [to Tyburn] than all the noblemen and gentlemen of the court, your counsellors excepted. And now by this disgrace I am in fair way and made apt to adventure my life every night to murderers, for since I was committed, wine in Westminster hath been given for joy of that news. In all prisons rejoicings, *and it is like that the fresh dead bones of Father Southwell at Tyburn and Father Walpole at York, executed both since Shrovetide will dance for joy !* '" § So far Dr. Jessopp.

* *Acts of Privy Council*, vol. xxiii. pp. 72, 165, 314, 338.
† The late Thompson Cooper, in the *D.N.B.*, says Topcliffe had authority to torment priests in his own house, and that he boasted he had a machine there of his own invention, compared with which the common racks in use were mere child's play.
‡ Stonyhurst MSS. Angl. A.N. 83.
§ He had actually seduced (if not worse) Anne Bellamy, the daughter of Father Southwell's host, whom he got into his power, having carried her off to prison on one of his raids. He then used her for playing upon her own father, and betraying the secrets of the house, so that he was enabled through her means to apprehend the holy martyr

# THE TRAGEDY OF THE FITZHERBERTS

From these letters (which we have taken the trouble to copy at the Museum, and print in full in the appendix) it would appear that Topcliffe's chief offence was his indiscreet allusion to the £10,000 paid to Puckering, the Lord Keeper, (and apparently to other members of the Council) for the life of Mr. John Fitzherbert. It is little wonder that Topcliffe should have thought this piece of villainy hardly better than his own. But it was also very important to stop his mouth. So Puckering lost no time in committing the miscreant to prison.

We also print in the Appendix the absurd and outrageous charges which Thomas Fitzherbert concocted against Mr. William Bassett. They are indeed very instructive. It is well to note that Thomas was now "Her Majesty's sworn servant," i.e. one of that miserable band of pursuivants who were the plague of all good Catholics, and a disgrace to the Government that employed them.

Though his adversary had fallen into disgrace, it is a comfort to know that Thomas had not escaped scot-free. We find him, at this very time, a prisoner in the Fleet, and, as usual, making mischief.

In the same volume of MSS. which contains the articles against Bassett, are the records of an enquiry* into the conduct of a "James Rither, Esquire, now prisoner in the Fleet," who was a cousin of Topcliffe's, and had been boasting of his relative's influence with the Queen, and encouraging his fellow prisoners to appeal to her Majesty over the heads of Judges and Privy Council, with the promise of Topcliffe's support. This was, of course, to be given for a consideration, and a certain Catholic lady in the prison, Mrs. Jane Shelley, had been induced by the precious pair to pay over to them more than £100 in gold, in the hope of gaining her liberty. When she grew restive, they resorted to threats. Mr. Patrick Sacheverell (one of the Derbyshire Catholics of that name) testified that he, "standing one day under the vine in the Fleet Garden, about a month past, saw them bring Mrs. Shelley into Mr. Rither's chamber, where Mr. Topcliffe did threaten her with many evil words, saying he could procure her utter undoing, and Mr. Rither replied that her life lay in Mr. Topcliffe's hands, and that the said Topcliffe was the man that could do her good ; and Mr. Topcliffe charged her that she had deceived him, saying that she had divers goods, as jewels and other things in her chamber in New Holborn, which he could not find."

Thomas Fitzherbert testified that Rither had abused the Lord Keeper,

there and bring the whole family to ruin. He married the unhappy girl to one of his own low tools. The italics in the text are Dr. Jessopp's. Harleian MSS. 6998, No. 50, fol. 185. *One Generation of a Norfolk House*, pp. 70–72.

\* Harleian, 6998, fol. 190.

and said that he had tasted already too much of his bitterness, that the new Orders of the Fleet were illegal, ungodly and intolerable, and that he would have his cousin Topcliffe move the Queen's Majesty of them, and put the new Warden out of his office. Also that he had got money, at least £100, out of Mrs. Shelley, under pretence to procure her liberty, and had persuaded her that the Lord Keeper and Mr. Beale were her enemies. Rither, of course, denied everything, and said he had been made quite ill by these cruel accusations. He now found to his cost that it was no longer an advantageous thing to be the cousin of Richard Topcliffe.

We do not know how long Fitzherbert remained in the Fleet, but it was probably not long. Topcliffe and he were both valuable servants to the Government, and now that they had had a warning no doubt they would be more prudent in future. "Topcliffe was out of prison again and at his old tricks in October, the restless ferocity of the man never allowing his persecuting mania to cease for an hour. . . . What became of him at last it is not worth while to inquire, though it is the fate of such monsters of iniquity that their names can hardly go down to oblivion. Even enormous crime insures a measure, if not of fame, yet of infamy." *

As to Thomas Fitzherbert, he went on selling all the property he could, and heavily mortgaging the rest. Topcliffe kept him out of Padley, getting a grant of the manor from Queen Elizabeth, and even tried to get hold of Norbury, though in this he was unsuccessful.

There are numerous deeds at Swynnerton showing how Thomas played ducks and drakes with his fortune. Fortunately he had a brother worthier than he, or Norbury itself would have been lost for ever to the Fitzherberts. Anthony, as we shall see, did all in his power to save the property for the family.

By 1598 Thomas was a fugitive from justice. On April 14 the Council directed a warrant for his arrest. He took refuge in the Cold-harbour in Thames Street, which, it was claimed, was a privileged place where criminals were safe from arrest.

He was charged not only with "force and violence offered unto one Malden," but with owing "great sums to divers poor women and other her Majesty's subjects." The Council, on April 26, ordered the Attorney-General and Francis Bacon to inquire into the pretended privileges of the Coldharbour, and inform them what charter or authority there might be to warrant the liberty of that place.†

On February 26, 1598–9, he was still at large, in spite of the writ of the King's Bench.

* Jessopp, p. 72. † *Acts of the Privy Council,* vol. xxviii. pp. 410, 424.

# THE TRAGEDY OF THE FITZHERBERTS

" Now forasmuch as the said Thomas Fitzherbert being of very evil name and fame . . . lurketh and lodgeth secretly in divers places in and near to the city of London, thinking that by the occasion of some privileged places to continue still in his said evil demeanour, whereby her Majesty's process cannot be served and executed . . . these are therefore to will and require you [all her Majesty's public officers] in her Majesty's name, immediately upon sight hereof . . . to enter into the said pretended places of privilege and other liberties, and to attach the body of the said Thomas Fitzherbert and to commit him to prison." *

This is the last mention that I find of the wretched man, save for the account given in his brother's petition, which follows. To understand it, it must be explained that the next brother, Nicholas, was heir after Thomas, but, as he had been attainted for treason, his estates were forfeit to the Crown. An inquisition as to his property was taken at Derby, June 11, 1604.

The petition from poor Anthony to Lord Salisbury, Lord High Treasurer of England, is in the Public Record Office.† It discloses new villainies on the part of his eldest brother :

" Whereas Thomas Fitzherbert was seized of the manor of Norbury in the county of Derby for term of his life, remainder to Nicholas Fitzherbert and the heirs male of his body (which Nicholas living beyond the seas was in the life-time of Queen Elizabeth attainted of treason), remainder to your petitioner and the heirs of his body, Thomas did in the 39th year of her Majesty's reign [Nov. 1596-7] acknowledge a recognisance of one thousand pounds to Mr. Robert Harcourt ‡ for the performance of covenant, and after sold the said manor of Norbury, being a small part of his lands, together with all other his lands to the value of £2000 by year to divers persons.

" This petitioner, for that the said manor of Norbury had continued 500 years in his name and blood, bestowed his whole fortunes to purchase the estate that Thomas had sold, and also paid for his Majesty's title which was escheated unto him by the attainder of the said Nicholas, £1200.

" Robert Harcourt neither being indebted to his Majesty nor upon any other consideration, by the instigation of the said Thomas Fitzherbert, about Christmas last assigned this recognisance to his Majesty, and procured only the land in the possession of this petitioner to be extended upon this recognisance at the value of £10 per annum. And now

---

* *Acts of the Privy Council*, vol. xxix. p. 614.
† *S. P. Dom. James I.* xlv. 63.    ‡ Husband of his sister Elizabeth.

laboureth by some of his Majesty's servants to obtain lease thereof from his Majesty to hold for the rate of £10 until £1000 be satisfied.

"Now my humble petition to your Lordship is, that forasmuch as this practice is intended to dispossess your petitioner of his whole estate of living, to his utter overthrow and undoing of his wife and children, That out of your honourable mind that never favoured practise, you will stay the granting of any such lease : And that your petitioner may be admitted to show to the Court what in law and equity he can for the discharging of his lands of the said debt. And so will daily pray to God for your Lordship's long life in all honour and happiness."

Endorsed—
22 Maii, 1609. "Let this petitioner come to me on Tuesday next at 7 o'clock in the morning."

Jo. ALTHAM.

Taking these statements in conjunction with facts disclosed by the deeds at Swynnerton, we find that in 1597 Thomas Fitzherbert borrowed from his brother-in-law, Robert Harcourt, of Stanton Harcourt in Oxfordshire, the sum of £1000, for which he gave an annuity of £70, issuing out of his lands in Derbyshire and Staffordshire. He afterwards sold the lands. Anthony having bought Norbury, Robert Harcourt assigned his debt to the King about Christmas 1608, and then sought to enforce it against Anthony. Harcourt, who seems to have been a person after Thomas Fitzherbert's pattern, was afterwards outlawed "in divers personal actions at the suits of several persons." In 1619 arrears of £1226 13s. 4d. were due upon the annuity, which the King had granted to friends of his own.

Again, in 1595, Thomas borrowed £100 of a butcher named Areton for which possession of Norbury was granted till repaid. Anthony repaid it in 1610. Other portions of the property he bought for £280 from Sir John Ferrers, of Tamworth Castle.

Thomas Fitzherbert seems to have died between May 18, 1613, and May 23, 1615. At the former date he gave a general release of all claim to the manors of Norbury, &c., to Martha Fitzherbert, widow of Anthony, and at the latter date a deed at Swynnerton speaks of him as deceased. He is described as "of London," so he probably ended his miserable days in the great city.

He had sold his faith and his honour, the lives of his father, kinsmen, and benefactors, his happiness in this life, and perhaps in the next, for the miserable baits of the world and the glory of being called "a good servant of her Majesty" by Richard Topcliffe. And what had he gained in this devil's bargain but misery, infamy, and eternal disgrace ?

64

# THE TRAGEDY OF THE FITZHERBERTS

His accomplice, Topcliffe, also found his great friends turn from him at the last. He who had been flattered by Burleigh, and caressed by the great Queen, died in obscurity and universal contempt. Only for a time did he enjoy the fruits of his villainy at Padley.

We give some extracts from a letter of his to Gilbert, Lord Shrewsbury, written in the last year of his evil career.*

"Now give me leave (I beseech your Lordship) to be somewhat tedious in a cause that doth concern mine undoing, because I did receive no answer from your Lordship to my last letter sent you by Mr. Fenton, one who honoureth you, and seemeth to love me, for I was then loath, and still am so, that any person but a well wisher to us both should know that your Lordship . . . should now go about to offer to heave me (with your strength) out of Padley, a delightful solitary place, in which I took threefold the more pleasure for the nighness of it unto three of your chief usual houses, so there I thought that I should (in my old days) take comfort in your Lordship's presence. . . . I trust that no practising enemy of mine shall interest your Lordship to offer to me that requital for my long loving you, either for their revenges against me or for their own gainings ; for such fugitive changes which brokers do not wish Padley to your Lordship for duty or love, but for other devices. And if I had not known in my heart that there is a God, who will call mighty and mean unto an account, how they heap up land unto land, houses to houses, and also towns to towns, and often towns to one house, I could have had further foothold in Hathersage, Norbury, Ridwaye, and in all those stately manors and parks than any purchaser as yet hath. And with bitterness of soul some purchaser will buy his bargain dearly. For Padley, I did know it was no part of Fitzherbert's ancient inheritance, but given to Sir Thomas, and to him by Dame Anne Fitzherbert, and Thomas Fitzherbert did assure it to me and my heirs, I dearly paying for it and for the residue adjoining to it, partly with my purse, with adventures, with charges, and with above seven years toil and travail with him.

"I therefore hope that your Lordship whom God hath blessed with so many thousand pounds of stately lands since I did first know you, and since your Lordship did first love me as entirely as you did any gentleman in England . . . will continue your good opinion of me and suffer me to enjoy with your favour Padley and the residue assured to me : To whom I can prove good Queen Elizabeth intreated your Lordship's favour and assistance under grant of her

* Printed by Cox, *Journal*, vol. vii. p. 249, from the Talbot Papers at the College of Arms, M. 184.

I

Councillors' hands in the defence of my right unto Padley when you were first Earl."

The hypocrite then goes on to make the most abominable charges against the unfortunate tenants at Padley, whom he accuses of all sorts of hateful crimes and vices. This letter is dated "from my solitary Sumerley yᵉ 20 of February 1603," and signed,

"Your Lordships auncyent honorrer

"As yᵉ Lorde Godd dothe know

"Rɪᴄ. Tᴏᴘᴄʟʏꜰꜰᴇ." *

This appeal was not successful; perhaps Lord Shrewsbury was already in treaty with Anthony Fitzherbert. We know he came into possession of Padley not very long afterwards. No doubt he had to pay a good price for his inheritance. Topcliffe died before December 3, 1604, when a grant of administration was made in the Prerogative Court of Canterbury to his daughter Margaret.

The family deeds at Swynnerton show that Padley remained in the possession of the Fitzherberts till 1657.

## FAITHFUL UNTO DEATH

Wᴇ have finished with the sickening record of treachery and crime. It only remains to gather together a few brief notices of those who remained faithful unto death.

We have seen that Nicholas Fitzherbert had been attainted of treason, 1st January, 1589.† This was on account of his zeal for the Catholic cause, and especially for his fervent co-operation with Cardinal Allen in his great work for the English colleges. Nicholas was born in 1550, and was educated at Exeter College, Oxford. He stayed about four years at the University, being senior undergraduate of the College in 1572. He was not able to take his degree on account of his religion, and so, like many another at that time, he made his way abroad

* The deed at Swynnerton already referred to (Norbury, No. 39) recites the Inquisition taken at Derby, June 11, 1604, as to the manors and lands of which Nicholas Fitzherbert was seized January 1, 1589, or since, which by reason of his attainder should accrue to the King. It is characteristic of the time that already in February 29, 1603-4, James I. had made a grant to Henry Butler, Francis Cartwright, George Gorse and their heirs of such remainder in the manors of Padley, etc. "as may accrue to the King by the attainder of Nicholas Fitzherbert." (S. P. Dom. James I. vol. vi. No. 84.)

† Dictionary National Biography, by Thompson Cooper, F.S.A. Fitzherbert's description of the University of Oxford in his time is exceedingly interesting. It has been reprinted in recent years. Oxoniensis in Anglia Academiæ Descriptio, Romæ. 1602, 8vo. Reprinted, Oxford Historical Society, vol. vii. Elizabethan Oxford.

66

in order that he might freely profess his faith. He went to Allen's College at Douay, and after matriculating at that University, proceeded to Bologna, where he studied Civil Law. He afterwards settled in Rome, receiving from Pope Gregory XIII., as the note below shows, an allowance of ten golden scudi a month.

When Dr. Allen was raised to the purple in 1587 Nicholas became his Secretary, and continued to reside with him till the Cardinal's death in 1594. He was extremely attached to his great master, and has left us a beautiful little sketch of his life.*

His humility was so great that he never could be induced to take sacred orders, though his friends considered him worthy of a mitre. Dom Augustine Bradshaw, Prior of the English Benedictines at Douay, indeed recommended him as the most worthy person to be raised to the episcopate, when in 1607 proposals were made to send a bishop to England. He did not sympathise with the Spanish proclivities of so many of the exiles, and had some difficulties in consequence with the redoubtable Father Robert Persons, S.J. But, on the other hand, he was a special friend of the Benedictines, and one of their most devoted supporters.

At Allen's death a report was made to Philip II. as to the members of the Cardinal's household whom he had specially recommended to the King of Spain's generosity. The following is a translation of the note as to Nicholas Fitzherbert.

"Nicolo Fierberti, copyist and servant from the beginning of the Cardinalate. A gentleman of very noble birth and fortune, whose relatives have suffered much for the Catholic faith. He is a cleric (*i.e.* tonsured), capable of receiving a pension as such, though he does not wear the clerical dress. He knows how to serve well, and has been seven years in the service of the Lord Cardinal, by whom he was greatly beloved in Rome, where he had lived many years before, and had ten gold scudi a month, to enable him to study, from Pope Gregory XIII., of blessed memory. His father died in imprisonment of 26 years for the faith, and his uncle also left this life in prison for the same cause, after having been incarcerated for 32 years continuously."

Mr. Fitzherbert continued to reside in Rome after his great patron's death. He was drowned while travelling near Florence, November 6, 1612, and was buried by his beloved Benedictines in the beautiful Church of the Badia, at Florence. He left all he had to the Procurator of the English Cassinese monks. Thus while three of the elder generation had died in prison for the faith, Nicholas was the first to die in exile, stripped of all he possessed, for the same holy cause.

* *N. Fizerberti de Alani Cardinalis vita libellus*, Romæ, 1608. Reprinted in *Letters and Memorials of Cardinal Allen*, London, 1882 (No. I. pp. 3–20).

Nor did the remaining members of the family escape persecution. We have already seen how Anthony Fitzherbert, John's second son, had been arrested at the time of the first raid at Padley on Candlemas Day, 1587–8, and carried off to Derby gaol. Dr. Cox prints a letter from the Talbot MSS. in which he promises to conform.* It is dated May 21, 1591, when he had been three years and more in prison. As Dr. Cox says, "We must not judge him too harshly : Derby gaol seems to have been enough to unnerve any one." His father had died a few months before of gaol fever, no doubt contracted there, and he himself had been very ill of the same wasting disease. He implores to be released in a pitiful way, since he has been no "meddler in matters of state, but only misled in points of religion, wherein I have been houseled up from my infancy (never tasting any other pap)." Now he was ready to conform himself and come to the Church. "Pardon me my Honour : good Lord (I humbly beseech you), my unfortunate boldness for the straitness of this place, and most odious for many causes, which the loathsome and unsavoury smells, and the cumbersome companions which be hither remitted for all vices, wherewith I am pestered, do so daily increase the many infirmities of my weak body . . . that unless I find your Honour to stand my good Lord, I shall rather wish a short and speedy death than so weary and consuming a life."

This letter seems to have brought about his release, but he was again apprehended shortly afterwards, and for a time imprisoned in London. Evidently he returned to the Faith immediately after his release, and he proved faithful for the rest of his life.

He had been convicted of recusancy July 4, 1589, and at Swynnerton s still preserved a Receipt and Quietus for £120, of which £60 was due for absence from Church for three months from December 20, 1587, and the other £60 for refusing to submit after his conviction till S ptember 22, 1589. These fines were not paid till the Easter Term, 3 James I., 1606, the date of the Receipt. He is described in this document as "nuper de Padley," and the church he refused to attend is the parish church of Hathersage.

We give, facing p. 58, a facsimile of this very interesting document.

Anthony died in 1613, his will (of which the original Probate copy exists at Swynnerton) being dated December 24, 1612, and proved in London March 23, 1613. He gave the whole of his estate to his wife Martha (daughter of Thomas Austen, of Oxley, County Stafford), and appointed her sole executrix. He left one son and five daughters. The son, Sir John Fitzherbert, was a gallant cavalier, and colonel in King Charles I.'s army. There is a fine portrait of him at Swynnerton.

* *Journal*, vol. vii. p. 254. (Talbot MSS. H. 289.)

THOMAS FITZHERBERT, S.J.
*From his portrait at Swynnerton*
*Photo by the author*          *To face page* 68

He died childless, and was succeeded, in 1649, by his cousin, William Fitzherbert, great-grandson and heir of William Fitzherbert, Sir Thomas' brother, who had married the heiress of the Swynnertons.

From this date Swynnerton was the principal residence of the family, and (apparently in 1682) Norbury was reconstructed on a smaller scale, and used as a farm residence. A doorway in the Great Hall still bears this date.

The husbands of three of the five sisters of Anthony Fitzherbert (Draycott, Barlow and Eyre) all suffered fines and imprisonment for recusancy. Maud Barlow was imprisoned in the plague-stricken gaol at Derby for more than three years, while her sister, Jane Eyre, and a third sister were placed in private custody. Their gaolers were William and Richard Sale, rectors of Aston and Weston-on-Trent, both staunch Protestants. However they could make nothing of these brave ladies. A letter of the Privy Council, August 17th, 1589, speaks of the " obstinacy and superstitious and erroneous opinion " of these last two ladies, and directs that as there was no hope of their conformity they might be placed with their kinsfolk, the charges of their gaolers being disbursed by selling some of the goods of Mr. John Fitzherbert, their father.*

There is one more member of the Fitzherbert family whom we cannot altogether pass over, although it is impossible to devote to him the space which his merits deserve.

This is Thomas Fitzherbert of Swynnerton, son and heir of William Fitzherbert, and therefore first cousin of Nicholas and Anthony. He had a very eventful career, and his life, if adequately treated, would require almost a volume. The State Papers are full of his name, and extensive biographies of him are found in the works of Jesuit writers, such as Father Henry More and Brother Foley.

Thomas Fitzherbert was, in fact, a very remarkable man. He was born in 1552 at Swynnerton, and studied at Oxford, probably at Exeter College, with his cousin Nicholas. As early as 1572 he was imprisoned for recusancy. In 1580 he became one of the most active of that little band of heroic young men who, under the leadership of George Gilbert, devoted themselves to assisting Blessed Edmund Campion and Father Robert Persons, S.J., in their wonderful missionary work.

The story of those adventurous days has often been told. In another part of this book we shall see how Fitzherbert helped Campion in one of his most important undertakings. In 1580 he married Dorothy, the only daughter and heiress of Edward East of Bledlowe, County Bucks, by whom he had one son, Edward. Two years later he was forced to retire to France, and the rest of his life was spent in exile. After his

* *Acts, Privy Council,* vol. xviii. p. 45.

wife's death in 1588 he went to Spain where he received a pension from Philip II. He was accused, without any reason, of plotting the Queen's assassination. Ordained priest at Rome, March 24, 1601–2, he for twelve years acted as agent to the English secular clergy; in 1613 he joined the Society of Jesus, and from 1618 to 1639 was Rector of the English College at Rome. He died in the College, August 7, 1640.

Anthony Wood's opinion of him is as follows : " He was a person of excellent parts, had a great command of his tongue and pen, was a noted politician, a singular lover of his countrymen, especially those who were Catholics, and of so graceful behaviour and generous spirit that great endeavours were used to have him created a Cardinal some years after Allen's death, and it might have been easily effected, had he not stood in his own way."

He was a prolific writer of controversial books. His refutation of Macchiavelli entitled *A Treatise concerning Policy and Religion*, dedicated to his son Edward (Douay, 1606–10), was greatly esteemed both by Catholics and Protestants. But far more than all this, he was a man of great and fervent sanctity. Father Henry More speaks of the tears that would frequently well from his eyes as he explained a verse of Holy Scripture, or quoted some familiar English hymn.

Some passages from his own account of his inner life written at the command of his General, when at the age of sixty-two he entered the Society, may be fitly quoted here.

" I ever, by the Grace of God, venerated the Blessed Virgin with special devotion ; and so, when about twenty years of age, I made a vow daily to recite her Office, I also added other obligations, not only to fast on her vigils, but also to abstain from eggs, fish, milk of any kind ; also to recite daily one chaplet and on Saturdays two, also on her feasts to confess and communicate and to recite the whole Rosary, even during the Octave, finally to fast on all Fridays when I was at home. . . .

" . . . But as I have also to answer regarding particular favours, I acknowledge that the divine bounty has bestowed divers upon me, though I am a most worthless and grievous sinner, meriting nothing less than hell itself. And first and foremost, that, although being born in the reign of the heretical King Edward VI., in the year 1552, when there was no public profession of the Catholic religion of England, both my parents were by the singular providence and mercy of God, Catholic, and that I was baptized with all the ceremonies of Holy Church, and was educated a Catholic. And I remember when I was a boy of five or six years of age, I possessed the light and gift of faith, being accustomed to stand and contemplate the heavens and to meditate upon God, especially upon His eternity, and that it had existed without a beginning; and I strove much to comprehend how this could possibly be; and although I could not understand it, nevertheless I believed it with much amazement.

"God, moreover, planted within me other seeds of virtue, in my infancy itself, although from want of discretion, and the many evils of my nature, they did not bring forth due fruit. For when I had attained nine or ten years of age, I was seized with a great desire of almsgiving, which as I could not satisfy otherwise, I would secretly abstract food from the stock of the house, and hiding it, would afterwards distribute it among the poor. I fasted also sometimes indiscreetly, not having any spiritual father to guide me; for instance, not being above twelve years old, I would fast the last three days of Lent upon bread alone and a little fruit. And when I came to understand many things about the Fathers of the Society and their Institute, I was strongly affected towards them, and towards all who were attached to them. And in that early age I conceived a great desire of martyrdom, and often prayed God to bestow that favour upon me. With increasing years the light of faith also increased, and by the gift of the good God a zeal towards the Catholic faith, and a hatred of heresy; nor would I willingly converse with Protestants, or attend their sermons. Upon which point I cannot omit a benefit accorded me by God, for when sixteen years old I was a student in the University of Oxford, a temptation came over me, out of curiosity, to hear a heretical sermon. Nevertheless, I would not do so without the advice and consent of my confessor, an aged and not a very learned priest, who on account of the persecution lay concealed in Oxford. I asked his opinion, which was that I could be present without sin, provided I did not go to learn, but merely to hear. Indeed, in those times but very few Catholics abstained from attending Protestant sermons, although they would not be present at the prayers. Therefore having heard the opinion of my confessor, I sallied forth on a certain day to hear a special famous preacher, who had already ascended the pulpit before I arrived; but no sooner had I put my foot in the church, than I was seized with so violent a horror that I could not possibly remain there; I therefore rushed out, the only word I heard being the name of Jesus Christ. And from that time I openly professed myself before all to be a Catholic, and took every opportunity of defending the Catholic religion against the ministers and other heretics, and of confirming the Catholics in their faith. On this account I was forced to be hid for two years, and being at last seized, I bore an imprisonment to my great consolation. On the arrival of Fathers Campion and Persons in

England [1580], I associated with them, and rendered them what assistance I could, until the heat of the persecution became too strong for me. I determined to emigrate and live in exile as long as heresy was dominant.

"I acknowledge also the high favour and goodness of God which never suffered me, as far as I can recollect, to remain for twenty-four hours in any sin, although when a youth, I very frequently offended Him grievously, ungrateful and unworthy of such mercy!

"The Divine Majesty likewise, even from my childhood, excited within me vehement feelings and spiritual affections, with great emotions in my soul. For when my mother suggested to me, being then a boy of ten years of age, to prepare to receive the most Holy Communion, as I was going into the fields, and reflecting upon the greatness of the mystery, and begging of God to make me worthy of so great a benefit, such a feeling of consolation suddenly seized my soul, that I burst into a flood of tears, which affection lasted until I had, as I hope with great profit, confessed and communicated; and from that time even until the present, many similar visitations have occurred to me in England, France, and Spain, especially after my making the vow of chastity. And (to omit other cases) when in Spain, for several days the representation of our Lord Christ crucified remained so indelibly imprinted upon my memory, that, except when actually asleep, it was always present to me; which favour I lost by my own fault, since, ungrateful as I was, I did not esteem it as it deserved, nor did I endeavour to preserve it.

"At another time, whilst I read the Life of St. Benedict, written by St. Gregory, I was melted into tears, and experienced during the greater part of the night great consolation and sweetness of soul, lasting until overcome by sleep. But after my admission to the Society I enjoyed these kinds of visitation much more copiously; and I appeared to myself to be sometimes totally inflamed with divine love; and one night being unable to sleep, whilst praying in bed, it seemed to me as though a stream, or rather I should say, a certain torrent rushed into my heart, filling me with inexpressible sweetness, giving me an assurance of the presence of God in my soul, whereupon I began to praise God with great jubilee and copious tears, frequently repeating, *Bene venerit Dominus meus, bene venerit Dominus meus*—'Welcome my Lord, welcome my Lord,' and returning thanks for so sweet a visitation.

"Also, another time, when on the night of the Nativity of our Lord, I was singing Mass in the English College, and was administering the most Holy Eucharist to the scholars, I was overtaken by so great a consolation and flood of tears, as to be unable to proceed in giving

72

THE CHRIST OF SWYNNERTON
*Photo by the author*

*To face page* 72

Communion, or to finish the singing part of the Mass, although I made many and great efforts to do so. This happening in public caused me so great a confusion and distress, that I begged of God to be pleased to remove from me this vehemence of devotion; nevertheless, it was quite impossible for me to sing, and it was with difficulty that I read the remaining portion of the Mass in secret, my utterance being choked by tears and sighs. This holy consolation and joy lasted for two or three days. From which may be gathered how great was the kindness and mercy of God towards me, a wretched and ungrateful sinner.

"Lastly, God was pleased to confer the greatest favour upon me, in placing me under the protection of His most holy Mother during the whole course of my life, and especially on her feasts, which I experienced in many and great necessities, both spiritual and temporal, and especially in observance of the vow of chastity which I had pledged in her honour. Also in a case of grievous calumny and false witness borne against me in Belgium, in which my life was in peril; and likewise in many dangers both by sea and land in which I experienced the manifest help of the most holy Mother of God, so that I might justly repeat what my blessed Father Ignatius was accustomed to say of himself with the most profound humility—that it was impossible to find these two things combined at once in any other individual, viz., to have received from God such great and excellent favours, and nevertheless to have been so ungrateful towards His Divine Majesty."

With this self-revelation of a beautiful soul, this chronicle may fitly end. For here, at least, we get into close touch with the spirit that inspired these Fitzherberts to face suffering and death so gladly for their Master's sake. "Ung je serviray" was their device, and they never forgot it. To One their hearts were given, to One their loyal service was pledged, to One they were faithful even unto death.*

It is thus not without significance that the principal relic of our Catholic past, which has been preserved by the family, is the great statue of Our Blessed Lord, pointing to the wound in His Sacred Heart, which is now to be seen in the Fitzherbert Chapel of the old parish church at Swynnerton. We give an illustration which, though it does not do it justice, gives some idea of the singular dignity and beauty of the original. Tradition says that it was formerly the central figure on the west front of Lichfield Cathedral, and was saved from desecration by the piety of the

* For Father Thomas Fitzherbert see H. More, *Historia provinciæ Anglicanæ S.J.* (St. Omers, 1660), p. 233, &c.; Foley, *Records S.J.* vol. ii. p. 188 (Life), also vol. vii. (Collectanea), p. 258; Gillow, *Bibliographical Dictionary*; *Dictionary of National Biography*; de Backer, *Bibliothèque des Ecrivains S.J.* and the Calendars of State Papers *passim*.

K

Fitzherberts, at the Reformation. It was buried in their chapel for safety, and dug up again in more peaceful times. A drawing of the statue in the Family Book shows it intact, with the right hand raised in blessing. It probably is meant to portray Our Lord in judgment, and if so, the central scheme of statuary on the west front of Lichfield will have been, like that at Wells Cathedral, a representation of the Doom. However this may be, it is touching to find that the Fitzherberts preserved this noble figure of the Lord whom they so faithfully served, and to whom alone they looked for the reward of their fidelity.

THE RUINED TOWER, WARBLINGTON CASTLE

THE PRIORY CHURCH, CHRISTCHURCH, HANTS
*Photo by J. Miller*

*To face page* 75

# A RUINED CASTLE BY THE SEA

IT was the writer's lot, in the year 1905, after enduring the ordeal of a severe surgical operation, to spend the days of convalescence amid the sea-breezes of Hayling Island. This little island, now known to fame chiefly by its golf-links, is closely attached to the coast of Hampshire, where that county borders on Sussex. It is four miles long, and contains some ten square miles. It is connected with the mainland by a swing bridge, erected in 1824, and by a railway bridge, and boasts of two interesting old churches, and the ruins of a Priory, which was a dependency of the famous Norman Abbey of Jumièges.

At first it was sufficient happiness just to lie upon the sands and listen to the countless sky-larks which filled the air almost continuously with their thrilling notes of joyous melody. And when the sun's rays shone down too hotly on the beach, one could always seek refuge in the garden under the cool, dark shade of the ilex trees, which spread their sombre branches almost to the edge of the shore.

But as bodily strength returned, the archæological instincts of the pilgrim revived also, and in the cool of the day many an interesting expedition was made to the relics of Christian antiquity, which abound in the neighbourhood. And thus after due homage had been paid to St. Richard of Chichester and his Cathedral shrine, and the pilgrim had stood in the Saxon Church of Bosham, where Harold knelt before the coming of the Conqueror, and gazed upon the stone that covered the grave of the little daughter of Canute, there came a day when he went to seek one of those Forgotten Shrines which are dearest to his heart, and to muse among the ruins of the once stately castle, where a royal martyr lived, a castle that was for some two centuries an outpost of the persecuted faith.

Crossing the bridge on to the mainland one bright June day, a walk along the water-side, under great trees of chestnut and beech, brought us in half an hour to Warblington. Unfortunately the tide was low at the time, and the prospect seawards was marred by long stretches of mud-flats, whose odour was even less pleasant than their aspect. But when the tide is in, the view must be fair enough, with Thorney Island in the foreground, and out far beyond the long, low promontory of Selsea Bill, which recalls so vividly the memory of St. Wilfrid, the great apostle of Sussex. Before us, on the very edge of the creek, the spire of Bosham gleamed, while further inland the taller spire of Chichester rose stately in the blue distance; for Warblington lies on the border-line between Hampshire and Sussex.

# FORGOTTEN SHRINES

We turn inland across a field or two, shadowed by gigantic elms, and soon find ourselves at the little church, which stood here when the great Norman compiled Domesday Book, and which in the days of his Plantagenet descendants was re-dedicated in memory of "the holy blissful martyr," St. Thomas of Canterbury. A most charming little church it is, indeed, a whole epitome of English history. Its central tower has three stages, the lowest Saxon, the next Norman, and the third Early English of the thirteenth century. In this last period the church was rebuilt, and within we still find the south arcade with delicate clustered shafts of Purbeck marble, which was built in the days of the third Henry. In the reign of his warlike son, Edward Longshanks, other additions were made, and of the fourteenth century are also the two recumbent effigies of noble ladies that lie in the nave.

On the north side of the chancel is what is probably an anchorage, where once an anchoret lived enclosed: a little low building, which has a low window or squint opening on to the High Altar, so that the solitary could ever see from his cell the Blessed Sacrament hanging in its veiled pyx above the altar, and at the sacring of the Mass could, in the beautiful old words of our forefathers, "see and adore his Maker." How vividly these little out-of-the-way country churches bring back to us the days of long ago! And yet how difficult it is fully to realise a time when English men and women were found all over the country ready to devote themselves to a life of such absolute self-abnegation, such a death in life, as that of the anchoret walled up in his narrow cell. Well might the Bishop read the funeral service, as he blessed the aspirant to so extraordinary a life, and enclosed him in the tiny chamber which he was never more to leave.

But the peculiar glory of this church is not within. It consists in the extraordinarily fine north porch with timber front of fourteenth-century date. The massive oaken timbers could hardly be matched nowadays; such trees are rarely found in England in our degenerate time. The porch was an important part of the church in mediæval days. Here the first portions of the Sacraments of Baptism and Matrimony were celebrated, and here women knelt to be churched.

The churchyard is shadowed by grand old yew trees, one of which has a circumference of 26 feet, and must be of extraordinary age. Another feature of this pretty churchyard was new to us. At either gate we found a small low building, the use of which was very hard to understand. We were told that they were built for watchers at the time when hired miscreants, called "Resurrectionists," used to come at night and violate the new-made graves in order to carry off the corpses and sell them to the surgeons for purposes of dissection. It seemed strange

THE GATEWAY, WARBLINGTON CASTLE
*Photo by E. S. McEuen*

*To face page 76*

THE PORCH, WARBLINGTON CHURCH
*Photo by E. S. McEuen*

that this hideous trade should have been so prevalent in this secluded spot, that it was necessary to have nightly watchers to secure the sanctity of God's acre, but its vicinity to the sea may be the explanation, for it would be easy thus to carry off bodies to sell at Portsmouth.

As we stood in the porch of this little sanctuary of St. Thomas the Martyr, we looked across the churchyard northward to where a lofty ruined tower raised its battlemented crest amid the trees.

This indeed, rather than the church, was the sanctuary we had come to seek, for this, and one great gateway close by, is, alas ! all that remains of the once famous Castle of Warblington. And Warblington Castle must be ever dear to the Catholic pilgrim for the sake of the great lady who made it her home, and was torn from its peaceful shelter to witness for Christ in prison and on the scaffold. For Warblington was the favourite home of Blessed Margaret Pole, then the last surviving member of the royal house of Plantagenet, the direct descendant of Edward III. and niece of Edward IV.

This is what makes the beautiful porch and the little church so profoundly interesting, for though the castle had its own chapel, doubtless on Sundays and feast days Blessed Margaret would be careful to assist at the Parish Mass, and here at Easter-time she would come to kneel beside the poor and humble at the Table of the Lord, and be fortified with the Bread of the Strong.

A modern house, built by a worthy alderman of Portsmouth, occupies part of the site of the martyr's castle, and still contains traces of the older building, and we were kindly given permission to inspect and photograph the ruins. The illustrations will give a better idea of them than any word-painting of mine could do. It is still possible, though somewhat risky, to mount to the summit of the ruined tower, the base of which is used as a stable, and which is the haunt of innumerable pigeons. It now stands a solitary beacon to proclaim the glories of the past. This tower is one of the four which formerly stood at the angles of the castle. The building, which dates from the end of the fifteenth century, was in good order until 1633, but was dismantled in the time of the Commonwealth.

Part of the moat still remains, but the great gateway is shorn of drawbridge and portcullis. An ancient local history thus describes the old castle :

"The walls are stone and of great thickness, but those of the tower and gateway are faced only with stone, the inside being of brick. A deep moat and corresponding fosse surround the ancient site on three sides, but on the fourth the earth has been levelled. Ivy clings to the mantles and shattered turret, and the arches of the porch are festooned with it. The foliage of the elm and of the ash is to be seen through the ruined casements, and though desolation has completed her work, yet the hand of nature has been busy to compensate for the wanton destruction apparent at every step.

"The building originally formed a quadrangle, surrounded on every side by a moat 30 feet wide and 10 feet deep, fronting the west, with an entrance under an arched gateway flanked by turrets, a porter's lodge to the south, and an armoury to the north.

"The southern side of the quadrangle comprised the chapel, 42 feet by 32 feet, and the great hall, 58 feet by 32 feet, communicating at one end with a small cellar, and at the other with the buttery, kitchen and brewery. The state apartments occupied the northern side, with a fair gallery and sleeping-rooms above. The interior was of brick, faced with stone, brought from the Isle of Wight, or from Caen in Normandy. A very particular description of the building, when perfect, is to be found in a survey of the Manor of Warblington taken in the eighth year of Charles I. (1632), by William Luffe, general surveyor to the right worshipful Richard Cotton, Esq., the lord of the manor, and by his command."

From this we learn that the court was 200 feet in length and in breadth, and that the four towers were covered with lead. "There is a fair green court before the gate, containing two acres of land, and near to the said place, a grove of trees containing two acres of land, two orchards, and two little meadow-plots containing eight acres, and a fair fish-pond near the said place," and so on.

The Blessed Margaret Pole was, it will be remembered, the daughter of George, Duke of Clarence, who was murdered by his brother, Edward IV., having been, according to popular report, drowned in a butt of his favourite wine. The son of "murdered Clarence," her only brother, Edward, Earl of Warwick, the true heir to the throne, was legally done to death on this account by the jealous Henry VII. Queen Catharine of Aragon used to believe that the sorrows which afflicted her in later years were a judgment of God, for, as she said, her marriage had been "made in blood," the blood of this innocent, whose only crime was his right to the throne. She believed that her father, King Ferdinand, had refused to give her in marriage to the Prince of Wales as long as a male heir of the house of York was living. Queen Catharine lavished her affection on the victim's sister, for looking upon herself as the innocent cause of the Earl of Warwick's death, she was anxious to make her every reparation in her power. She made her godmother and "Lady Governess" to her infant daughter, Princess Mary. In 1513 the Lady Margaret was permitted to succeed to her brother's vast estates, and was granted the title of Countess of Salisbury. Her property chiefly lay in Hampshire, Wiltshire, and Essex, and she seems to have preferred the first of these

78

A View of the Front of this Palace of Beaulieu commonly called NEW HALL in Essex, built by K. Henry VIII.

counties. It was at Christ Church Priory that she prepared the magnificent chantry in which she wished to be buried, and at Warblington, at the opposite extremity of the county, she made the home of her old age, when the fickle cruelty of Henry VIII. had driven her, like her royal mistress, from the Court, and his wicked persecution of her family had accumulated sorrow upon sorrow on her grey head.

She was the bravest and most constant of women, as her most bitter enemies freely admitted, truly a *mulier fortis*. When the time came that every one in England was obliged to take a side, Margaret of Salisbury clung to the hapless Catharine's cause, and took the place of the poor mother as guardian of her daughter, Princess Mary. But even this was not long permitted. In February, 1534, the royal commissioners descended upon the Princess's peaceful retreat, at New Hall in Essex, and tore her from the arms of her venerable relative. This was a blow more bitter than the mere deprivation of rank or titles, for thus the Princess lost for the second time a mother's care. It was as great a sorrow to the Countess. The Spanish Ambassador wrote to the Emperor that the Lady Governess, " a lady of virtue and honour, if there be one in England, has offered to follow and serve her at her own expense. But it was out of the question that this would be accepted, for in that case they would have had no power over the Princess."

The whirligig of time brings strange revenges. New Hall, which witnessed this sad and final parting, is now a convent, the English home of the Canonesses of the Holy Sepulchre. The ancient presence-chamber is now the conventual chapel, and the altar occupies the place where once was the royal daïs. On the wall opposite the entrance may be seen a splendid achievement of the arms of King Henry VIII., carved in stone and richly coloured, which is said originally to have adorned the great gateway tower. Under the arms runs the inscription :

> " *Henricus rex octavus, rex inclitus armis*
> *Magnanimus struxit hoc opus egregium.*"

And outside, above the entrance to the chapel, is another coat-of-arms— that of Mary's triumphant rival, Queen Elizabeth, with a fulsome Italian description calling her the most shining star in heaven and on earth, the most beauteous, the most learned, and the most virtuous of Virgins and of Queens! But with a most happy instinct, the good nuns have placed just above this a large statue of our Blessed Lady, so that the words now seem to refer rather to the Queen of Heaven than to the apostate daughter of Henry VIII. Thanks to the kindness of the good Canonesses of the Holy Sepulchre, who now preserve with loving care the once royal mansion, I am able to give some views of the convent-

BLESSED MARGARET OF
SALISBURY

*To face page* 80

THE ACHIEVEMENT OF ARMS OF HENRY VIII
*From New Hall*

palace, where once Princess Mary and her faithful guardian spent days of comparative peace and happiness, before the tragedy of their separation.

New Hall was either rebuilt, or at least extensively repaired, by Thomas, Earl of Ormond, to whom the Manor had been granted by King Henry VII. He was the great-grandfather of Queen Anne Boleyn, whose headless ghost is said to haunt the avenue. But long before that unhappy woman came to her end, after dragging to a violent death some of England's noblest sons, the most illustrious of her victims must often have wandered through these lime-tree alleys, when, as a young light-hearted lover, he came to court a bride at New Hall.

For here lived one Mr. John Colt, an Essex gentleman, with his three daughters, and among his most frequent visitors was young Thomas More, of Lincoln's Inn. Here, in 1505, the future Chancellor of England wooed and won his host's eldest daughter Joan, and thus the stately old Tudor mansion has its memories of more than one of Christ's Blessed martyrs.*

We give reproductions of two old prints by G. Virtue, published in 1786, showing the house as it was in Tudor days.

Henry VIII. purchased it in 1517, and was so charmed with it that he gave it the name of Beaulieu, which, however, it did not long retain. He greatly enlarged and improved the house, and here he spent the feast of St. George in 1524. The noble gate-house which he built, and the buildings on either side, as well as the Chapel and Great Hall, have long since disappeared. In fact, what remains is, as at Audley End, but the south side of the great quadrangle.

In the Chapel (on the left side of the engraving) was a large east-window, containing the beautiful painted glass now so much admired in St. Margaret's, Westminster. It is said to have been intended as a present to Henry VII. for his Chapel at Westminster from the magistrates of Dort in Holland, but it was set up at Waltham Abbey, and at the dissolution was removed to New Hall.

It was here that, after the dispersal of her household, the unhappy Princess Mary still continued to live, save for a time when at the height of Anne Boleyn's power she was actually sent to Hunsdon to act as attendant on the favourite's infant daughter, Elizabeth. After Anne's execution, she regained possession of New Hall, and lived there quietly until 1553, the year of her accession to the throne. She had much to suffer during the reign of her young brother, Edward VI., because of her refusal to give up having Mass celebrated publicly in her chapel. Here, too, we know she had the Blessed Sacrament reserved all through the worst days of Protestant ascendency.

* Morant, *Essex* i. 490.

L

81

# FORGOTTEN SHRINES

The illustrations show the entrance to the present chapel, and Elizabeth's arms with the inscription :

" *En terra più savia Regina. En Cielo la più lucente Stella.*
*Vergine Magnanima, Dotta, Divina, Leggiadra, Honesta e Bella.*"

And in the general view of the façade, we see the same doorway, with the statue of Our Lady above the coat of arms. The trophy of armour round the escutcheon of Henry VIII. is of later and much inferior workmanship to the shield itself. A curious stone dragon, now in the park, formerly stood on the gates erected by Henry VIII. It represents the red dragon of the Princes of Wales.

But we must leave New Hall with its once magnificent avenues of lime trees, and follow our royal martyr to her retirement at Warblington. Blow after blow fell upon her, for she had earned the resentment of the most cruel and relentless of tyrants. Her fidelity to the Queen and the Princess was not her only offence ; she was also the mother of Reginald Cardinal Pole, who in his book, *De unitate ecclesiae*, had dared to denounce the King's iniquities in vigorous terms, and had added to his crimes by persisting in remaining safely abroad, and by politely but firmly refusing to return and put himself into the power of the infuriated monarch. Attempts were made to procure his assassination in Italy, but when these also failed, vengeance fell heavy on the innocent heads of the Cardinal's family. Cromwell openly avowed this : " These that have little offended (saving that he is of their kin), should feel what it is to have such a traitor for their kinsman." Lord Montague, the Cardinal's brother, was arrested and executed for having sought absolution from the Holy See for having taken the oath of supremacy. The King told the French Ambassador that he intended to exterminate the whole family. Sir Edmund Nevill, Lady Montague's brother, the Marquis of Exeter, grandson of Edward IV. and Sir Nicholas Carew, were all barbarously executed. The King did not even spare little children. Edward Courtenay, the little son of Lord Exeter, and Henry Pole, the child of Lord Montague, were thrown into the Tower by this " Western Turk." The pathetic inscriptions carved by these children on the walls of their dungeon may still be seen.

We can imagine the grief inflicted on the Lady of Warblington by the murder of her son and her other relatives. But this was not enough to satisfy Henry's vengeance. It might have seemed impossible to touch the Countess herself. She was venerable for her age, she was a royal princess, she was revered for her virtues ; in earlier days the King himself had honoured her and had been wont to say " that the kingdom did not contain a nobler woman." But her destruction was now decreed,

82

a The Chappel Window

The inside Prospect of the House the Chappel & the Hall of Beaulieu.

London Sold by Sanford LONDON

Publish'd as the Act directs 11 April 1786.

or to put it better, she was now to earn the crown and palm of martyrdom. The King commissioned Fitzwilliam, Earl of Southampton, and Goodrich, Bishop of Ely, to arrest her at Warblington. They arrived there on November 12, 1538, ten days after the apprehension of her sons. We can imagine the confusion into which the castle was thrown by this sudden and ominous arrival.

But the King's agents could neither frighten nor entrap the brave lady of the castle into any admission of guilt : though as they reported to Cromwell next day they had " travailed with her all day, both before and after noon, till almost night." "Surely," they protested, " we suppose that there hath not been seen or heard of a woman so earnest, so manlike in continuance, and so precise as well in gesture as in words, that wonder is to behold."

But they continue, " Now that we have seized her goods, and given her notice that the King's pleasure is she shall go, she seemeth thereat to be somewhat appalled. And therefore we deem that it may be so, she will then utter somewhat when she is removed. This we intend shall be to-morrow, so that we have caused inventories to be made of her said goods, and of such things as may be easily carried, as plate, &c., and our purpose is to take them with us."

They accordingly carried off the venerable lady to Cowdray Park, near Midhurst, where again they pestered her with their cross-examination, but still to no purpose. No trace or shadow of treason could be found in her ; she was evidently perfectly innocent of any crime. " We assure your lordship," the agents wrote to Cromwell, " that we have dealt with such a one as men have not dealt before with. We may call her rather a strong and constant man than a woman." However, the searchers left at Warblington had sent " certain bulls granted by a Bishop of Rome," found in one of the rooms, and this was sufficient in those days to condemn the most saintly.

Meanwhile the martyr was left some months at Cowdray, where she was subjected to the grossest indignities by her unmannerly gaoler. During her imprisonment there her rooms and trunks were searched more than once, and in one of her coffers was found an embroidered vestment, which was to play a prominent part in the final tragedy. This was a tunicle of white silk on which were embroidered the Five Wounds of Christ, and other instruments of His Passion.

This the King pretended to believe connected the Countess with the Pilgrimage of Grace, in which the Catholics of the North country had risen "for God, Our Lady, and the Catholic Faith," under the banner of the Five Wounds. It was also stated in Parliament that bulls from the Pope were found in her house, that she kept up correspondence with her

84

REGINALD CARDINAL POLE
ARCHBISHOP OF CANTERBURY

*To face page* 84

son, the Cardinal, and that she forbade her tenants to have the New Testament in English or any other of the books that had been published by the King's authority.

On such evidence as this a bill of attainder was passed through the House of Lords in two days, the accused having no opportunity of defence, and no witnesses being examined! The Commons were equally ready to gratify the King's thirst for blood, and the attainder was finally passed on June 28, 1539, and on this day the Countess was removed from Cowdray to the gloomy dungeons of the Tower. Here she lingered for nearly two years, "tormented by the severity of the weather and the insufficiency of her clothing." At last, quite suddenly as it seems, her martyrdom was decided on. Early in the morning of May 27, 1541, she was led out to die. She could hardly believe the news at first, and protested that no crime had ever been imputed to her; but soon, resigning herself to the divine will, she walked with a firm step to the place of execution, on East Smithfield Green, within the precincts of the Tower. Here she devoutly commended her soul to God, and begged the spectators to pray for the King and the royal family. She desired to be commended to them all, but especially to her beloved god-child, Princess Mary, to whom she sent her last blessing.

She was then commanded to make haste and lay her head upon the block, which she did; for the story of her refusal seems to be incorrect.

The regular executioner being busy in the North, "a wretched and blundering youth had been chosen to take his place, who literally hacked her head and shoulders to pieces in the most pitiful manner." Her last words were: "Blessed are they who suffer persecution for justice' sake."

Thus was consummated a piece of iniquity which it would be difficult to match in the annals of this country, even in those of this blood-stained period. And thus ended the kingly race of Plantagenet, winning in its death-throes a glory more brilliant than that of earth. For this noble victim of unnatural and savage tyranny entwined the golden boughs of the *planta genista* with the palm branches of martyrdom.

"Hitherto," said her son the Cardinal, when the cruel news was brought to him, "Hitherto I have thought myself indebted to the divine goodness for having received my birth from one of the most noble and virtuous women in England; but from henceforward my obligation will be much greater, for I understand that I am now the son of a martyr. May God's will be done, and may He in all events be thanked and praised."

In meditating on these facts amid the ruins at Warblington, our thoughts flew swiftly across Hampshire to the western limit of the country,

85

where it borders on Dorsetshire. There, wedged in between the estuaries of the Avon and the Stour, hard by the sea, rises the little town of Twyneham, encircling its Norman castle and its stately Priory Church. So important indeed was the Priory, that its name eventually gained the mastery over the old name of the borough, and now to all the world Twyneham is known as Christ Church. This is no place to describe the glories of that magnificent church, with its splendid Norman nave and fifteenth-century quire, its mediæval reredos and quire-screen, its Lady chapel, which still retains its ancient altar, and its quaintly carved quire-stalls, where once the Austin Canons sang God's praises night and day. But here, amid a group of glorious chantries, stands out one pre-eminent in beauty, the chantry-chapel erected by the Blessed Margaret Plantagenet as her chosen place of sepulture. Even now, cruelly and savagely defaced as it has been, it is still, both within and without, a structure of ideal beauty, designed at the time when the old Gothic traditions were still strong, and yet the breath of Renascence was in the air, and the skill of Italian sculptors had begun to adorn, with detail of infinite and exquisite variety, the framework of English Perpendicular. This wonderful monument was intended to be the burial-place, not only of the martyred Countess, but of her son, the Cardinal. Needless to say that neither of them has found a resting-place within it. The splendid fan tracery of the vaulting within the chapel bears the royal arms of Plantagenet, and these were shockingly and of set purpose defaced by the " visitors " who came to suppress the Priory, on November 28, 1539. The notorious and infamous Dr. London was one of these, and he was shortly afterwards put to open penance for adultery and died in prison. He, too, no doubt, found pleasure in defacing the shield, sculptured with the five wounds, which may still be seen over the place where the chantry-altar once stood, another touching memorial of the martyr's love for this sacred emblem. She may indeed be called the " Martyr of the Five Wounds."

Her martyred body lies in the gloomy chapel of St. Peter ad Vincula, within the precincts of the Tower, amid a company of fellow-victims, some like herself illustrious for their virtues, and others notorious for their crimes. There, side by side with the unhappy Anne Boleyn, and Henry's other murdered wife, Catharine Howard, lies this noblest victim of his rage ; and near her, in all probability, still lie her fellow-martyrs, John Cardinal Fisher, and Sir Thomas More. They all received the honours of beatification from Pope Leo XIII. in 1886, and we hope that the day will come when we may reckon them among the canonized saints.

But Warblington has other memories yet for the Catholic pilgrim.

THE CHANTRY OF BLESSED MARGARET
OF SALISBURY, CHRISTCHURCH, HANTS
*Photo by J. Miller*                     *To face page* 86

# A RUINED CASTLE BY THE SEA

The influence of the royal martyr seems to have lingered long there, and her spirit to have inspired its later owners. The Cottons of Warblington were foremost among the faithful Catholics of the penal days. The castle and estates which had been confiscated by the Crown had passed to the head of this family, during the Protestant reign of Edward VI. But Mr. George Cotton of Warblington deserves a high place in the roll of these heroic men, who suffered themselves to be despoiled of their goods rather than compromise their faith. These Recusants were ground down, as we have seen, by a most cruel and oppressive system of fines. The Parliament of 1581 imposed a penalty of £20 a month on all persons absenting themselves from church, and such as could not pay the same within three months were to be imprisoned until they should conform. The Queen, by a subsequent act, had the power of seizing two-thirds of the Recusant's land and all his goods for default of payment. Hallam says, " These grievous penalties for recusancy established a persecution which fell not at all short in principle of that for which the Inquisition had become so odious. Nor were the statutes merely designed for terror's sake—to keep a check over the disaffected, as some would pretend. They were executed in the most sweeping and indiscriminate manner."

Abbot Gasquet, in a valuable paper on the *Hampshire Recusants* has shown, from a careful examination of the Exchequer Receipt Books, and of the Recusant Rolls preserved at the Public Record Office, that Hallam's severe censure is more than justified. In the last twenty years of Elizabeth, the amount received by the Exchequer in fines from Catholic Recusants amounted to the enormous sum of £120,305 19s. 7½d. ; and we must multiply this sum by at least ten to get the equivalent in modern money.

The special Recusant Rolls do not begin till 1590, and are divided out into counties. In that of Hampshire, for this year, the first name of those fined at the rate of £20 a month, and thirteen months in the year, "for not going to church, chapel or other place of common prayer," was the name of George Cotton of Warblington, who pays £260 on this score. He actually paid the same enormous sum annually for at least twenty years. Abbot Gasquet says : " Imagine what such payments mean ; actually, in hard cash, this gentleman—a man of considerable property about Havant—in these twenty years paid in fines some £5200 in money of those days, or something over £60,000 of our money. I did not myself for some time believe that this could have been the case, and supposed that although he was nominally fined that amount, the money was not actually paid. I have, however, satisfied myself that the cash was in fact handed into the royal treasury. In what are called the

*Pells Receipt Books* . . . each six months is recorded a receipt of a moiety of the £260 which Mr. George Cotton is stated on the Recusant Roll to have paid. He begins in 1586 by a small payment of £15 6s. 8d. In 1587, on May 20, he pays £140, and the other moiety of the £260, namely £120, on November 24 ; on this day he also pays £199 6s. 8d., said to be "in part payment of the sum of £1199 6s. 8d." arrears of fines for not going to his parish church. By degrees he is forced to pay off these arrears. Thus on November 28, 1588, besides his usual six monthly moiety of the £260, he pays into the Queen's purse £433 6s. 8d., and a like sum at two subsequent dates."

In 1586 the Catholics had been given hopes that they might perhaps purchase toleration by the payment of a yearly sum to the Queen. A commission was appointed, on April 13, to examine the Hampshire Recusants as to their ability to pay. Few were able to offer anything. Many of the Catholic gentry were in prison for their faith. But Mr. George Cotton promised to pay to the utmost of his power, which, however, is "but weak of itself, and hath been of late not a little diminished as well by ordinary charges of children and servants necessarily depending on me, as by manifold losses sustained, partly by long imprisonment, partly by the evicting of a great part of my living." He adds that he has lately arranged marriages for three daughters, and has seven children more depending on him. Still he concludes, "besides the great sums which I have paid for the statute of Recusancy, I offer £30 a year ; " and this he afterwards changed to £40.

But this slight hope of toleration soon passed away, and as we have seen, for the next twenty years, Mr. Cotton was paying the crushing fines, seeing his estates and goods gradually melting away, and himself little by little reduced to penury. We find that at the end of Elizabeth's reign there were only sixteen Catholics left in the kingdom who were able still to pay the fine of £20 a lunar month. The rest had forfeited two-thirds of their estates. These lands were leased out by commissioners appointed by the Crown for the purpose, and the lessee paid a certain rent into the Exchequer.

Mr. Cotton of Warblington was one of the sixteen still not utterly impoverished. But beside the loss of property, he had to endure many another trial. His house at Warblington was a castle indeed, but it was no castle to him. At any moment, by day or night, it might be broken into by the pursuivants searching for priests or "Church stuff." The house was known to be a place of refuge for many a hunted priest, but if ever one should be found there, it would bring total ruin, yes, even a felon's death, upon his generous host. Yet shelter and a welcome was never refused at Warblington to any of the persecuted missionaries ; nay,

THE ARMS OF BLESSED MARGARET OF SALISBURY, FROM
THE ROOF OF HER CHANTRY AT CHRISTCHURCH,
DEFACED BY HENRY VIII. *The centre boss has a carving of the
Coronation of Our Lady, also much mutilated. Photo by J. Miller*

SHIELD OF THE FIVE WOUNDS, FROM THE
CHANTRY OF BLESSED MARGARET OF SALIS-
BURY. *Photo by J. Miller*

*To face page* 88

they were received there as angels of God. The house was so near the sea that it became a convenient shelter for the young priests who came over from Douay or Rheims, at the peril of their lives, and landed at dead of night at some quiet nook of the Hampshire coast. The great gateway that had seen the Blessed Margaret of Salisbury borne out on her way to imprisonment, now witnessed many a furtive arrival at midnight, and the gates that were cautiously opened to let in the priests of God, too often rang to the blows of the pursuivants hot in pursuit. In the State Papers we find more than one report from spies, mentioning prominent priests or Jesuits who found shelter at Warblington. One, dated 1609, informs the Lord Treasurer that "in the house of Mr. Cotton, of Hampshire, there is harboured a Jesuit who names himself Thomas Singleton. He teaches the grandchildren of the said Cotton." Among other priests who made their abode at Warblington, we find Father Thomas Lister, S.J., a companion of the martyred Father Oldcorne, who had known imprisonment and exile, and the famous Father Baldwin, whose exciting adventures in the company of a band of church students I have described at length elsewhere.* The Government having released him from Bridewell, under the impression that he really was the Neapolitan merchant he pretended to be, this distinguished Jesuit took refuge with Mr. Cotton at Warblington, where he rendered great assistance to the Catholic cause.

Warblington was in fact for many years a constant hospice, opened not only to priests but to the persecuted Catholics of every grade and condition. It went by the name of the Common Refuge. Mr. Cotton, who was an intimate friend of his saintly neighbour, Thomas Pounde, of Belmont (that noble confessor who was so dear to Father Edmund Campion), vied with him in doing his utmost to propagate the faith, and was in fact one of the most zealous to enlighten those blinded by the errors of heresy, and to confirm any Catholic who might be wavering. He suffered long years of imprisonment in Winchester gaol and in other places, and finally had the honour to die a confessor in chains. A letter written in 1614 records his end. The old man was despoiled of all his goods and consigned to a dungeon to the end of his days, which was hastened by hardships, filth, misery and a chronic malady. "The ministers, as if he were unworthy of Christian burial, would not allow his corpse to be buried in their churchyard, hence his remains are deposited in an open field."

May we not say truly that our castle by the sea was the home of two most glorious martyrs of Christ; for we cannot doubt that such prolonged constancy crowned by so blessed a death merited for George Cotton of Warblington the martyr's crown and palm?

* In the Brave Days of Old, "A Jesuit in Disguise." Burns & Oates. 1906.

M

His family were worthy of him. One of his sons, John, was a student at Oxford, when Father Campion's fame attracted him to Lyford that he might hear the famous Jesuit preach. He was in consequence apprehended with the martyr, and suffered a year's confinement in the dungeons of the Tower. He was again cast into the Tower in the time of King James I., and remained there for five years, a close prisoner. Many other sufferings he bore for Christ, with a cheerful and joyous heart, and crowned a life of self-sacrifice with a saintly death in the year 1638. Other members of the family are found inscribed on the rolls of the Jesuits, the Benedictines and the Poor Clares ; for the holy example of their martyr moved them to a generous emulation in renouncing home and all earthly delights for the love of Christ.

Nor were they less loyal to their earthly sovereign than to their heavenly king.

Richard Cotton, our martyr's heir, was one of the most devoted adherents of Charles I. On him, as on all loyal Catholics, the vengeance of the victorious Parliament fell with double force, as the object both of civil and religious hatred. The exact date of the demolition of the splendid castle at Warblington is not known, but tradition assigns it to Cromwell's soldiers, and there is every reason to believe it, in this instance, to be correct. A detachment of troops was probably sent by Sir William Waller to dismantle it, either when proceeding to besiege Portsmouth, or after having recovered Chichester from the hands of the king's partisans, both of which events took place in 1642.

After the building was reduced to a heap of ruins, its materials were dispersed over the country, and may be traced in various old houses in Emsworth, Havant and the neighbourhood. Even Portsmouth is said to have shared in the spoliation, and a street in that great town still bears the name of Warblington street, because it is believed to have been built out of the ruins of the old home of the Blessed Margaret and her faithful successors.

The last of the Cottons of Warblington died unmarried about 1736. Thus they have passed away and left but little visible memorial behind them (we could find but one of their monuments in the church), yet the fragrance of their memory still seems to linger round the ruins of their ancient home, and it is good that their example should not be forgotten.

# STONOR PARK AND ITS MARTYRS

CERTAINLY for a place of pilgrimage it would be difficult to imagine a spot more beautiful and romantic than Stonor Park, the seat of Lord Camoys, head of the great Catholic family of Stonor.

It is situated some five miles north of the famous riverside town, Henley-on-Thames, and lies in Oxfordshire, indeed, but so close to the Buckinghamshire border that the boundary-line on the south and east runs along the outskirts of the woods that crown the heights above the house.

It is attractive for more reasons than one; for its own picturesque beauty, for the long and honourable descent of the family that has owned it since the Norman conquest, and for the fact that it has ever remained Catholic, boasts of a chapel in which the Protestant service has never once been said, and has been the home of one illustrious martyr, and, in time of bitter persecution, the refuge of another yet more famous.

It was, therefore, with feelings of unusual joy that the pilgrim found himself one bright autumn day making his way to Stonor. Would he not have the privilege of offering the Holy Sacrifice within walls seven centuries old, beneath a roof that had never echoed to any other sounds but the solemn chants and sacred words of the Latin liturgy? Was he not to see a place which had been so dear a home to the Blessed Adrian Fortescue, Knight of St. John and martyr for the faith, and as sure a refuge to the Blessed Edmund Campion, the glory of Oxford and of the Society of Jesus?

So, with glad heart, he leaves behind him the fair wide river, gleaming bright in the sunshine, and drives quickly down the stately avenue, well called "The Fair Mile," that stretches straight as a dart, northward from the town. The five-mile drive seems long until the little village is reached at last, and the carriage pauses at the park gates. And then the beauties of the park unfold themselves. The drive curves round to the left and the great house lies before us.

Very fair and stately it looks, stretching out before us on the hillside, built in the form of an E, with the Church adjoining the eastern wing. And yet there was a dash of disappointment in the view. The house, though undoubtedly ancient, has been sadly modernised in the dark days of the eighteenth or early nineteenth century. The picturesque gables have gone, gone are the mullioned windows, gone the old front of timber, brick, and flint which Leland saw. Ugly modern sash windows, more suitable for a factory than for such a mansion, deface the façade, and there is little left to tell of antiquity but the general outline of the building, and the porch with its carving and statuary. And here, indeed, as we drive nearer, and pass from the deer-park into the enclosure of lawn and garden which surrounds the front of the house, we see something that almost compensates for all the rest. For in the gable over the porch is still seen the stone image of Our Blessed Lady keeping watch over the house. She stands upon the crescent-moon, and her hands are folded in prayer. She has stood there through the bright days and the dark, and, as the present head of the family said—"we hope we are under her special protection." As we gazed on this glad symbol of our faith, we thought of Blessed Edmund Campion, drawn on his hurdle towards Tyburn, and striving with his fettered hands to make obeisance to the image of Our Lady of Newgate, which still stood above the arch under which he passed. How his brave heart must have been cheered and gladdened by the sight of Our Lady of Stonor, how often must he have bared his head to greet her during those secret breathless months, while the printing-press, hidden under the gables, was labouring out the burning words which were to put the adversary to silence and to shame! *

And there again to the right of us is the little Church of the Most Holy Trinity, which has stood there since the days of the third Edward. Happy little church, more happy than any of the great cathedrals which make England so famous! Here then, where Mary has lingered almost alone in all this desolate land, here where Jesus in His Blessed Sacrament has deigned to dwell through seven centuries of sunshine and of storm, who can distress himself about mere antiquarian details, or fret over the loss of externals when the essential has been preserved?

Still, it must be acknowledged that it is with a pang that the eager pilgrim first enters the little Church of the Most Holy Trinity of Stonor. For think what it might have been! Of course reflection should have warned him not to expect too much. In the perilous days of Elizabeth and James and Cromwell, how could it be possible that a papist chapel should preserve the splendours of its past intact? Who could expect to find the sacred pyx still hanging under its canopy before the fourteenth-century altar; the statues set up in 1349 still smiling from their niches in 1909; the screen with the Holy Rood and Mary and John still spanning the sanctuary as of yore; the storied glass unbroken; the frescoes undefaced?

Alas! the whole sad truth must be told—there is absolutely nothing left! The very tracery is gone from the windows, the tesselated pavement has been torn up, not a fragment of ancient glass, not a trace of

* A tiny sketch of this statue will be found within the initial letter of the Preface to this work.

Stonor Park.

mediæval fresco, not a piscina, not an altar, not a statue, not a wreck or a fragment remains from the ages of faith. The new broom of a drastic restoration has swept away every trace of antiquity left by the heretical foe ; and the lovers of the past have to mourn a loss irreparable.

And it is still more sad when we realise that most of this was done, with the best intentions, by the faithful, not by the foe. But these regrets are vain ; Stonor has its consolations that nothing can ever destroy.

It should be explained, before we describe the house, that the east wing, apparently the oldest portion of the house, has been partly cut off, and turned into a residence for the chaplain. There is, however, communication on the upper storey between the main part of the house and a tribune in the church, which is reserved for the family and their friends.

The porch is the most attractive part of the modernised house. On either side of the sixteenth-century doorway are two curious figures, with an enigmatical inscription below them, which has completely baffled the antiquaries. The inscription runs,

| *On the left,* | *On the right,* |
|---|---|
| OMNIBUS JUDICIO | MEMET SINE |
| AEQUE TAMEN | COGNOSCO FRAUDE |

which seems to mean : " In all things justly, yet with judgment, I know myself to be without fraud." But what this refers to, or what the two pairs of figures mean, is a complete enigma. The house faces south and is built against the side of a hill, so that what is the first floor in the front of the house is the ground floor at the back, and opens on to the garden. The interior has been modernised at the same melancholy time as the front and the chapel, and the great hall has been cut up into rooms and disfigured by a staircase.

The most interesting features of the house to the pilgrim are naturally the secret passages and hiding-places which the zeal of the Stonor family for the ancient religion made necessary. From the butler's pantry a secret underground passage used to run into the hill and emerge in a clump of trees in the park. It was in this tangled dell, amid shrubs and bracken, that the secret printing press of Blessed Edmund Campion was set up. At least so we were told by Lord Camoys. Another tradition has it that the press was concealed amid the labyrinth of attics and passages underneath the roof. At any rate, the passage referred to was used by the martyr and his assistants to convey the books and materials in and out of the house. The passage has now fallen in, and has become impassable, and the entrance from the pantry, long concealed by a cupboard, is now bricked up.

There is also a secret passage in the roof of the house and a hidden

94

THE PORCH, STONOR PARK
*Photo by the author*

*To face page* 94

place where holy Mass was offered during the days of persecution. This is entered from a room over the porch, the room which is guarded by the image of our Lady that stands outside it. In this room stands a wardrobe, which, being pushed aside, discloses a concealed door, opening into a small room beyond. In this room a triangular piece of the partition lifts up, and thus a hole is made through which a man of average size can just creep.

From this hiding-place, which is small and dark, a rough ladder leads up into the roof of the central gable of the house, and another leads down from thence into a large attic under the roof of the main building.

The religious history of Stonor begins (so far as public documents are concerned) with a licence of mortmain granted by King Edward III. to Sir John de Stonore in 1349. This document grants the royal leave to "give and assign a certain suitable place within his manor of Stonor for the sojourn and dwelling-place of six chaplains, regular or secular, to celebrate divine service for ever, in a certain chapel, founded within the said manor, in honour of the most Holy Trinity, for the good estate of Us and of the said John himself, during our lives, and for Our souls after that we have departed out of this life, and for the souls of Our progenitors and successors and the ancestors and heirs of the said John de Stonore, and of all the faithful departed."

When the time came for the family to prove their attachment to the old religion they were not found wanting. The first sufferer for the faith who was connected with Stonor, was not indeed a member of the family by birth but by alliance. Sir Adrian Fortescue, Knight of St. John, now numbered among the Blessed Martyrs of England, was married to Anne, daughter of Sir William Stonor by the latter's wife Anne, daughter of John Neville, Marquis Montagu, and co-heir of her brother, George Neville, Duke of Bedford.

Sir Adrian Fortescue was born in 1486. He came of an illustrious house, which owed its origin, it is said, to the Battle of Hastings, where Richard le Fort having saved the Conqueror's life by the shelter of his "Strong Shield," was henceforth known as Fort-Escue. In reference to this tradition his descendants took for their motto, *Forte scutum salus ducum*, "a strong shield the safety of leaders." Our martyr's father, Sir John, held important posts at Court, and fought on the side of Richmond on Bosworth field. He married Alice Boleyn, and thus Sir Adrian was cousin to that unhappy woman whose rise was to bring about the fall of the old religion in England, and the shedding of rivers of innocent blood besides that of her kinsman.

Sir Adrian is first mentioned in 1499, when he was already married.

He was doubly connected with the Stonors, for in 1495 his wife's brother, John Stonor, married his sister, Mary Fortescue. On the death of her brother John, Lady Fortescue inherited Stonor, but her right to it was disputed by her uncle, Sir Thomas, and, after his death by her cousin, Sir Walter. Stonor Park was, however, retained by Sir Adrian Fortescue till Michaelmas, 1534.

Lady Fortescue died in 1518, and in April 1534, the conclusion of his long lawsuit with the Stonors is recorded by the martyr in his book of accounts. His own plea was that, "by the courtesy of England," he was entitled to his wife's property for his life and her children after him. He waited on the King at Greenwich, but he was already suspected as "evil in religion," and before the summer was out, not only had he lost Stonor and all its broad lands, but was himself committed a prisoner to the Marshalsea Prison. He was released some time in 1535, and returned home, but no longer to the "fair park" of Stonor, for Stonor was his no more. Nor had he a long respite of freedom. Arrested once more in February 1539, he was attainted for having "most traitorously refused his duty of allegiance" to the King's Highness, or, in other words, of having refused to recognise his title of Supreme Head of the Church of England. For this "crime" (of which he was certainly guilty) he was condemned without trial, and beheaded on Tower Hill on July 9, 1539.

He has left an imperishable name behind him, and in 1895 he was numbered among the Blessed Martyrs who have made England glorious. And Stonor, his home for more than twenty happy years, is irradiated with the glory of his aureola.

In the church at Husband's Bosworth is preserved Blessed Adrian's book of Hours, on the fly-leaf of which he has written and signed with his own hand a series of maxims or rules of the spiritual life, of which we may quote a few:

"Above all things love God with thy heart."

"Desire His honour more than the health of thine own soul."

"Take heed with all diligence to purge and cleanse thy mind with oft confession, and raise thy desire or lust from earthly things."

"Resort to God every hour."

"Be pityful unto poor folk and help them to thy power, for there you shall greatly please God."

"In prosperity be meek of heart and in adversity patient."

"And pray continually to God that you may do all that is His pleasure."

"If by chance you fall into sin, despair not; and if you keep these precepts, the Holy Ghost will strengthen thee in all other things necessary, and this doing you shall be with Christ in Heaven, to Whom be given laud, praise and honour everlasting."

"ADRYAN FORTISCUE."

BLESSED ADRIAN FORTESCUE,
KNIGHT OF ST. JOHN
*From his picture at Malta*                    *To face page 96*

# STONOR PARK AND ITS MARTYRS

We must now pass over more than forty years, to find ourselves in the midst of the reign of Elizabeth, in the very thick of the persecution. Stonor was now to be glorified as the abode of a martyr even more illustrious than the Knight of St. John. The Blessed Edmund Campion was in the midst of his romantic mission, risking his life many times a day and all day long for the sake of the souls for whom he burned and hungered.

At this time Stonor was in the hands of a lady, Dame Cecily, widow of Sir Francis Stonor,* who was the nephew and heir of the Sir Walter who had dispossessed Sir Adrian Fortescue. Though the martyr had had to give up his beloved home, it seemed that his spirit still lingered there, and that there was something in the very air of Stonor which gave, not only men, but women, courage to risk goods and lands and life in the cause of Christ.

It was Dame Cecily's privilege to grant a shelter to the hunted priests of God, and not only that, but to give to the great Jesuit martyr the opportunity he needed for launching against triumphant heresy a thunderbolt which shook it to its very foundations. For his little book, the *Rationes Decem* or *Ten Reasons* for the faith which was in him, addressed to the great University of Oxford, which was printed with infinite trouble and infinite risk in the shelter of Stonor Park, did perhaps more for the cause he had at heart than any book which has ever been issued in England. It was steeped in the life-blood of martyrs, for not only its writer, but one at least of its printers owed to it his crown and palm.

It is not too much to say that the effect it had, first at Oxford and then throughout the country, can only be compared with that caused by Newman's *Essay on Development*. And Stonor is immortalised, if only that it gave birth to the ripest fruit of Campion's genius, a work of which grave men judged that it was " a truly golden book written with the finger of God." Father J. H. Pollen, S.J., in a valuable article in the *Month* (January, 1905), has given at length the history of the secret press at Stonor. We cannot do better here than epitomise his story.

Campion was asked in November, 1580, to " write something in Latin to the Universities," and especially to Oxford men, of whom he had been the idol. And he proposed very characteristically to choose as his theme " Heresy in Despair." When his friends laughed at choosing a title so wildly inappropriate at a time when heresy was flourishing as it had never done before, he answered, that the very cruelty of the persecution evidently proceeded from despair, for if the heretics had any confidence at all in the truth of their cause, they would never proceed in such a way.

Campion was just about to start on an arduous missionary journey

* He had died in August, 1550.

through the Midlands to Derbyshire and Lancashire. How was he to get time for writing, still less for study, amid labours so manifold and perils so tremendous! His days were spent on horseback, his nights in preaching and administering the Sacraments. Death dogged him at every step, and the need of being ever on the alert must have been a continual distraction. Books he could not carry with him—his task seemed an impossible one. Yet he persisted in it, and overcame the difficulties triumphantly. Within a very few weeks, in February and March (1581), he had written the noble book which was to set England on fire.

Circumstances, fresh attacks and fresh needs, led him to alter and improve his original plan. He resolved " to render to the Universities the 'Ten Reasons,' relying upon which he had offered disputation to his adversaries in the cause of Faith." In the introduction, however, he deals with his original theme, " Heresy in Despair." The present writer can never forget the delight with which he first came across a copy of this famous book. It was in the old monastic library of the great Abbey of Monte Cassino that he found it, and having found it, eagerly devoured it. The glow of Campion's eloquence, the romantic history of the book, the fame of its author, but recently raised to the altars of the Church, its dedication to the Oxford men of a bygone day, were enough to inspire interest in a modern Oxford convert ; and, as he read, interest quickened into enthusiasm. Surely never man wrote like this !

The wit and eloquence of the book are so amazing, amazing too the extraordinary dexterity with which he wields his rapier, piercing his adversary first in one point then in another, with inexorable skill, with bewildering dash and rapidity, with inimitable art. Eloquence clothed in the most majestic Latin, for Campion was a master of style ; humour and sarcasm mingled with passionate pleading ; fierce indignation against the falsehoods and blasphemies of heresy, melting into cries of anguished love which recall the plaints of One Who wept over Jerusalem—all these and how much more—are here.

The " Ten Reasons " include Holy Scripture, the notes of the Church, the Œcumenical Councils, the Fathers, History, the paradoxes, sophisms, and crimes of the Reformers ; and they are all put forth with vigour, logic, and conviction. But what perhaps most amazes the reader is the extraordinary learning displayed. The martyr has the controversy at his fingers' ends, the quotations from the Fathers he has by heart, the infamies of Luther and his followers are quoted by one who knows of what he speaks. How was it possible to write such a book under such circumstances ? We can only reverently repeat : " the finger of God " —*Digitus Dei hic.* This burning stream of controversy is poured out from the furnace of a heart white-hot with the love of God, even now after these centuries. The book is alive, it is afire ; it enkindles and inflames. It is twelve years and more since I read it, but it lives with me still, and still I feel the glow.

Well might Father Persons be amazed when he received it, some time before Easter, and saw the multitude of quotations with which it bristled. His prudence would not, however, allow him to publish it to the world without having the citations verified, well knowing how every slip would be seized upon by the adversary. Some young laymen, who had devoted themselves to helping the apostolic work of the Fathers, and had given up their wealth, their time, and their all to this noble cause, were glad to undertake this task. The most diligent of these was Thomas Fitzherbert of Swynnerton. He was then just married, but after his wife's death he became a Jesuit,* and a most distinguished member of the order. " At Persons' request," writes Father Bombino, " he visited the London libraries, for being a good man and a noted scholar, he could do so in safety. In fine, *having found that all was quite accurate*, he brought the good news to Persons, and urged on the publication of the work.

Campion was now sent for, to see his book through the press. And now new difficulties came in crowds. Mr. Stephen Brinkley was the name of the devoted Catholic gentleman who had given himself to the printer's trade for the love of God, and he had already, at the most deadly risk, printed off three little books for Father Persons. But the old house near London was no longer safe, and it was necessary to find a surer hiding-place. And now another member of the gallant little band of laymen came forward with help. This was John, second son of Lady Stonor, and as devoted a Catholic as his mother. He suggested that Stonor would be a safe place, and convenient, being hidden in woods, near the river, and within reach of Oxford and London. Both he and his mother well knew the risk they were running by this generous action —the risk of a cruel death for themselves and absolute ruin for their family. But no such fears could shake the resolution of these brave hearts. Lady Stonor's quality may be gauged from her answer to her judges when she was "convented" before them. Having been reproved for her constancy in the Catholic religion, she replied : " I was born in such a time when Holy Mass was in great reverence and brought up in the same faith. For King Edward's time, this reverence was neglected and reproved by such as governed. In Queen Mary's it was restored with much applause, and now in this time it pleaseth the State to question them, as now they do me, who continue in this Catholic profession. The State would have these several changes, which I have seen with my

* See page 69.

99

eyes, good and laudable—whether it can be so, I refer it to your Lord-ships' consideration."

This brave widow, then, was not likely to shrink from the danger of harbouring priests and assisting in their great work. She gladly gave up her house to the Jesuit Fathers and their assistants, among whom John Stonor was proud to be reckoned. And so to Stonor " were taken all the things necessary, that is, type, press, paper, etc., though not without many risks. Mr. Stephen Brinkley, a gentleman of high attain-ments both in literature and in virtue, superintended the printing. Father Campion went at once to the house in the wood, where the book was printed and eventually published." So far Father Persons.

There was grave risk of discovery from the number of extra men about the house, of whose fidelity it was not always possible to be abso-lutely sure. Traitors, indeed, there were among them, and one of them during this time caused the loss of all Persons' papers and other effects in London, and the apprehension of the Blessed Martyr Alexander Briant. But the work at Stonor went on safely. It was begun late in April and finished about the end of June, 1581. The time taken to print so small a book (it consisted of only about 10,000 words) seems surprising at first sight, but Father Pollen has shown very ingeniously, from intrinsic evidence, that the stock of type was very small. " The printers had to set up a few pages at a time, to correct them at once, and to print off, before they could go any further. Then they distributed the type and began again. When all was finished they rapidly stabbed and bound their sheets." There were only seven workmen at most, of whom five, including Stephen Brinkley, were subsequently arrested. Another was the Venerable William Hartley, afterwards a glorious martyr for the faith.

For many years it was supposed that no copy of the edition printed by the martyrs was still in existence. Now, however, two copies are known, of which one was given to Stonyhurst College by the late Marquis of Bute. Father Pollen shows that the printing-frame was so small that it would have been covered by half a folio sheet, 9 by 13 inches. Each little sheet had to be printed off by itself. They had no Greek font, and though the book was printed in the new " Roman " type, they had to use the query-sign which belonged to the old English black-letter font. Their stock of diphthongs was also but a small one, and, as the text shows, soon gave out. Otherwise the little volume is distinctly well got up. There is nothing, indeed, at first sight to indicate the peculiar circumstances under which it was printed.

Meanwhile Campion was not content to spend all the precious time at Stonor. Father Persons tells us that " he preached unweariedly, some-times in London, sometimes making excursions. There was one place

IHS

EDMVNDVS CAMP
O·PRÆ·SOC
LOND
PRO·CAT·FIDE·MA
CONSVMAVIT

THE BLESSED EDMUND CAMPION, S.J.

*To face page* 100

whither we often went, about five miles from London, called Harrow Hill. In going thither we had to pass through Tyburn. But Campion would always pass bare-headed, both because of the sign of the Cross, and in honour of some martyrs who had suffered there, and also because he used to say that he would have his combat there." The hour of that combat was, indeed, soon to sound.

The book was finished in time to be distributed at Oxford at Commemoration. On Tuesday, June 27, the congregation who assembled in St. Mary's Church to hear the responses of the students, found the benches strewed with the little books, hot from the press at Stonor. Four hundred copies had been brought post-haste to Oxford by the Venerable William Hartley, who had disposed of them partly in this way and partly in gifts to various persons. The audience seized upon them with avidity, and the disputations of the students passed unnoticed, so absorbed were all in reading Campion's burning words. " Some were furious, some amused, some frightened, some perplexed; but all," says Simpson, "agreed that the essay was a model of eloquence, elegance, and good taste."

Three weeks later Campion was captured at Lyford, and led in triumph to London. It was probably the crowd of Oxford students,

Ego dabo vobis os & sapientiam

TITLE-PAGE OF BLESSED EDMUND CAMPION'S
*Ten Reasons*, PRINTED AT STONOR PARK

who had journeyed to Lyford to hear him preach, that did most to bring about his apprehension. For he had done his work, and the heart of Oxford was moved to its very depths. He had now but to seal the work with his blood.

When William Hartley, in his turn, won his reward at Tyburn, in 1588, his mother, we are told, made a great feast to which she called her

101

neighbours and friends as to a marriage, bidding them rejoice with her, for she was the mother of a martyr of God. Thus St. Felicitas and the Blessed Mother of the seven Machabees had worthy followers in Elizabethan England.

Campion was arrested July 17, 1581, and by the 2nd of August the Council was in possession of information which enabled them to seize the little colony at Stonor. They wrote to Sir Henry Neville, at Billing-beare, and ordered him " to repair unto the Lady Stonor's House and to search for certain Latin books dispersed already in Oxford at the last commencement, which . . . have been there printed in a wood. And also for such English books as of late have been published for the maintenance of Popery, printed also there, as is thought, by one Persons, a Jesuit, and others. And further for the press and other instruments of printing, thought also to be there remaining."

And so, two days before the Feast of our Lady's Assumption, the Madonna who looks down on Stonor might have seen a sad sight. A night raid by armed men upon that peaceful park, torches gleaming in the darkness, fierce battering down of doors and wainscot, triumphant arrest of the little band of faithful men. But they, like Campion himself, had done their work, and no more could it be undone. The press was seized, the books and papers, and a large quantity of " massing-stuff," chalices, vestments, altar-stones, all sanctified by a martyr's use. The Council ordered that the " massing-stuff " should be defaced, and the proceeds given to the poor, and the press, books, and papers were despatched to London.

John Stonor was lodged in the Tower, and it is strange that his life was spared. One of the most romantic episodes of that strange time is connected with his name. Cecily, daughter of Sir Owen Hopton, Lieutenant of the Tower, saw her father's prisoner and fell in love with him. Whether or not he returned her affection, he succeeded in converting her to the faith for which he was suffering. Henceforth, while her father's rule lasted, she was ever ready to give her secret assistance to the Catholic prisoners. In 1584 she was denounced to the Government as conveying " letters and messages between the prisoners in the Tower and the Marshalsea," and her conversion and active ministry to the prisoners of Christ, became the principal cause of her father's subsequent disgrace. John Stonor afterwards gained his freedom and went abroad, where he served in the army of the Prince of Parma.

There would be much to add about the ufferings of the Stonors for the religion to which they clung so faithfully, but our space does not permit.

In later times the family have given distinguished prelates to the Church. One of the best-known of the Vicars Apostolic who ruled the

Church in the eighteenth century was John Talbot Stonor, Bishop of Thespia, who died in 1756. And there are few to whom the name of Stonor does not recall a venerable prelate, the titular Archbishop of Trebizond, still happily living at Rome, and so well known for his kindness to all English pilgrims to the Holy City.

Such then are the thoughts which Stonor Park suggests. And yet how little, in these days of freedom, can we even imagine what the grinding tyranny of that century and a half of persecution meant to the faithful few. To be branded as traitors for fidelity to conscience, must have been keenest pain to descendants of the heroes of Crecy and Agincourt. "Unless they will forget God," writes one, "and profess the errors which are here established, they will not only lose lands, liberty, and perhaps life, but, through these laws now passed through Parliament, they may leave tainted names to their children."

"It is small wonder," says Falkner, in his *County History*, "that the Romanist creed was gradually battered out of Oxfordshire under such assaults as these. And yet there were some who dared to profess it in face of all, and the 'Recusants' were duly registered by the Protestant rectors in each town and village. There is a list of eighty-eight such returns made by the parsons in Oxfordshire, preserved in the library at Stonyhurst. . . .

" Many of the Recusants were in humble life, and quite unable to pay the fine, and in the case of those who could pay it, it is to be hoped that it was sometimes not exacted. But, although the Catholic gentleman was left very largely to himself, except in time of popular excitement, he was a pariah for more than two centuries, cut off from his fellow squires and looked on with a mixture of dislike and fear, exiled from the bench of magistrates, from all office and from public life in general, debarred from sending his sons to public school or university."

But Catholic families, like the Stonors of Stonor, had taken for their motto the words of David : " *Elegi abjectus esse in domo Dei mei, magis quam habitare in tabernaculis peccatorum.*" Outcasts and abjects they may have been in the eyes of their fellow countrymen, but how dear and how noble to God and His angels !

# MARKENFIELD HALL AND THE RISING OF THE NORTH

> " IT was the time when England's Queen
> Twelve years had reigned, a sovereign dread ;
> Nor yet the restless crown had been
> Disturbed upon her virgin head ;
> But now the inly-working North
> Was ripe to send its thousands forth,
> A potent vassalage, to fight
> In Percy's and in Neville's right,
> Two Earls fast leagued in discontent,
> Who gave their wishes open vent ;
> And boldly urged a general plea,
> The rites of ancient piety
> To be triumphantly restored,
> By the stern justice of the sword."
>
> WORDSWORTH, *The White Doe of Rylstone.*

SURELY one of the most romantic houses left in England ! This is the thought that first strikes the mind of the pilgrim who is fortunate enough to discover Markenfield Hall. And if as he gazes upon this grey pile of buildings—already " an ancient house " in the days of Elizabeth—he is able to recall the stirring story of its past, he is thrilled yet more with the sense of its romance. This splendid old pile, built in purest fourteenth-century Gothic of the time of the Third Edward, enlarged by its lords in the two following centuries, but happily untouched since then, stands as a monument of heroic deeds and knightly prowess. From its stately gateway mail-clad warriors passed forth to fight at Agincourt and Flodden, and in less happy days it was here that faithful hearts planned the desperate attempt to rise in arms for " God, Our Lady and the Catholic Faith," against the persecuting violence of heretical power. The great court-yard, now so peaceful and deserted, was once filled with armed men, each with a crucifix hanging on his breast, and a red cross upon his arm, grouped beneath the banner of the Five Wounds of Christ. It was from Markenfield that they rode forth, those loyal " rebels " of the faithful North, over the three miles of park and road to Ripon, there in the City of St. Wilfrid to proclaim the restoration of the ancient Faith and to cause Holy Mass to be sung again within the stately Minster. Surely the bones of St. Wilfrid, that doughty champion of Rome, must have thrilled with the joy of that day, when amid the glad tears of the faithful, Thomas Markenfield of Markenfield set up once more the High Altar in the desecrated sanctuary, and the Great Sacrifice which they had lost for ten sad years was pleaded once again in Ripon Minster.

104

MARKENFIELD HALL.    *Photo by C. M. Parker*

*To face page* 104

# MARKENFIELD HALL

Alas, how short-lived was the joy of that day! But before we tell the story of the ill-fated Rising of the North, let us examine more closely the home of the Markenfields.

It is not so easy to find nowadays, for it is hidden away among fields far from the main road. The motorists who rush along the road from Harrogate to Ripon little think what a world of beauty and of interest lies concealed among the hills to their left, approached by a mere cart-track, through fields of waving corn. And perhaps this is for the best, for automobiles are not quite in harmony with the old-world charm of Markenfield.

The Hall was begun about the year 1310, when John de Merkingfield, who had been Chancellor of the Exchequer under Edward II., obtained licence from the King to crenellate Markenfield, that is, to build a fortified and battlemented castle.

The approach is not what it once was, for the stately park filled with magnificent timber which so delighted the Elizabethan Commissioners has given place to arable land and farm buildings. Markenfield, like so many stately homes of the past, has fallen from its high position, and is now a farm, though certainly a farmhouse that is unique of its kind.

The moat is crossed by a solid stone bridge which has replaced the drawbridge of ancient days, and we pass under a simple but dignified perpendicular gate-house into the great court. This, as my photographs show, is a stately enclosure. Opposite the entrance, and on our right, lies the original fourteenth-century building, raising its lofty battlements and turret over the roofs of the humbler portions of the pile.

This original part of the building is in the form of the letter L; the great Hall with its splendid Gothic windows is immediately opposite the entrance gateway, and in the portion to the right is the ancient Chapel and priests' chamber. The Chapel is duly orientated, and has a very beautiful east window which we shall see from the opposite side. It is the south side of the hall which we now have before us.

The entrance to the Hall was originally, according to Parker, by a doorway in one corner, from an external staircase, of which the foundations and the weather-moulding of the roof over it remain. Unfortunately a very ugly interior staircase has lately been erected which greatly spoils the fine old Hall, though it no doubt adds to the comfort and convenience of its present occupiers.

The southern front of the building is continued to the west by a lower range, built in the fifteenth century. This front is adorned by a row of shields carved with coats of arms. It contains the present kitchen, a magnificent old-world room, of which we give a drawing; its huge fire-place is big enough to roast an ox, and with its great beams

o

of oak, it gives a vivid idea of the hospitality of ancient days. The original kitchen seems to have been under the Chapel. The whole of the ground floor of the fourteenth-century house is massively vaulted in stone, and this applies not only to the main building, which contains the Chapel and Hall, but also to the retainers' lodgings which form the right side of the court, and also date from the fourteenth century. I give a good photograph of one of the richly moulded doorways of this range; the beautiful little window of the upper story will be noticed. Opposite the "lodgings" on the left side of the court are ranged the stables and outbuildings. Thus we have at Markenfield a very perfect picture of a mediæval Manor House of the nobler sort.

Before entering the house we should stroll round the moat and gaze at the different aspects of this glorious building.* Every view of it is a picture that will linger long in the memory. The eastern side shows us the back of the lodgings, and beyond them the exquisite tracery of the Chapel window. Beyond this are seen the windows of the Solar or family parlour which adjoined the Hall. One most charming little lancet can just be seen peeping above a fine yew-tree. At the time we took these photographs the moat was dry, as part of the wall had fallen into it, and was under repair. This detracts from the picturesqueness of the view, but enables us to see the depth of the moat. We should notice the battlements pierced cross-wise for arrows. Coming round to the north we have before us the windows and buttresses of this side of the Hall, and note that one of the windows has been blocked by a huge chimney of later date.

The interior of Markenfield, as is the case with so many old houses, is less interesting, because more modernised than the exterior. The Hall has lost its ancient open roof, although the stone corbels that supported it still remain. The modern floor is cut up by the staircase already mentioned and by hideous glazed holes which serve as skylights to the passages below.

It is some consolation to find the doorway to the Chapel intact, and to find that it still retains its ancient bar of wood, which slips into a hole in the jamb of the doorway. The Chapel itself, which is entered from the Hall, is still impressive, though now so desolate and changed. It is at least a consolation to find that it is not used for any domestic purpose. A piscina and aumbry still remain, and on the sill of the east window is a curious block of stone. This seems to have formed part of the reredos, and perhaps was a pedestal for the crucifix. It is grooved down the front, and the groove continues down the wall below. Altogether it forms a curious archæological puzzle. On the south side of the Chapel is a

* See facing pages 112 and 114.

THE KITCHEN
Markenfield Hall
JPke 1912.

doorway leading to the priests' chamber, and close by is the staircase turret. This is octagonal in plan, and is crowned with a conical roof of stone. It leads to the flat roof, from which a fine view may be had. To the north-west of the house is a conical hill called How Hill, which overlooks the famous Cistercian Abbey of Our Lady of Fountains, on the summit of which the monks had a sanatorium of which some remains still, we believe, exist. Fountains Abbey, the most wonderful and romantic ruin in all England, is only about two miles distant from Markenfield.

The old Hall belongs to Lord Grantley, who bears as a secondary title the name of Markenfield. He has hung on its walls many of his family pictures, and among them one of surpassing interest, the portrait of his ancestor, old Richard Norton of Norton Conyers, the Patriarch of the Rising of the North.

He and Thomas Markenfield were indeed the true originators and leaders of this second Pilgrimage of Grace. It was their zeal which almost forced into action the heads of the great northern houses of Percy and Neville, and although once they had been joined by the Earls of Northumberland and Westmoreland, their own part in the Rising necessarily became a secondary one, yet it was constantly asserted by both friend and foe that "Old Norton" and Markenfield were the mainsprings of the cause.

It is to the memory of old Richard Norton and his heroic sons that Wordsworth has devoted some of the fairest fruits of his genius in his *White Doe of Rylstone*, though it would be a mistake to take the poet's song for history. And Lord Grantley, who is the descendant of the Nortons, as well as the owner of Markenfield, has done well to hang the portrait of old Richard Norton on these historic walls. We think ourselves fortunate at having secured so excellent a photograph of this portrait of the hero, who with his white hair streaming in the wind, carried the standard of the Crucified before the insurgent host.

Richard Norton of Norton Conyers was at this time an old man of seventy-one. But years had not dampened his ardour, nor dimmed his zeal for the old religion. He had a very large family, eleven stalwart sons and eight fair daughters, by his first wife, Susan, fifth daughter of Richard, Lord Latimer. He was governor of Norham Castle and a member of the Council of the North under Mary the Catholic, and at the time of which we are writing he held the very important position of High Sheriff of York. The reasons which finally decided him to join in the Rising, in spite of the official position which he held under the Crown, were his attachment to the Catholic faith and his warm regard and friendship for Blessed Thomas Percy, Earl of Northumberland.

DOOR IN THE LODGINGS, MARKENFIELD HALL

*Photo by the author*                    *To face page* 108

# MARKENFIELD HALL

Camden describes Norton as " an old gentleman with a reverend grey head, bearing a Cross with a streamer."

> " The Norton's ancient had the Cross
> And the Five Wounds Our Lord did bear."

In his portrait,* which is well painted, the countenance is florid, the hair grey, but the slight beard is of a sandy colour. The eyes are small and grey, the colour is pleasing, and the general expression is grave but not stern—vigilant, wary and contemplative. He looks like one better fitted to shine at council-board than " to rise in such a fray." The arms of Norton—*azure a maunch ermine debruised with a bend gules*—are painted on the picture. It is said that there are also portraits of two of the sons at Wonersh near Guildford.

> " Thee, Norton, wi' thine eight good sons,
> They doomed to die, alas! for ruth!
> Thy reverend locks thee could not save,
> Nor them their fair and blooming youth——"

runs the old ballad of the *Rising of the North*. It is quite true that they were all condemned to death, but they did not all perish, as the ballad followed by Wordsworth in his *White Doe of Rylstone* would have it.

The sons were Francis, the eldest, who escaped with his father; John, who became a glorious martyr at the age of seventy-six, for having harboured the seminary priest, Venerable Thomas Palasor (they suffered at Durham, August 9, 1600); Edmund, who does not appear to have taken part in the Rising, and who is lineal ancestor of the present Lord Grantley, owner of Markenfield Hall; William, who was confined in the Tower some time, and was probably pardoned, on composition; George, also condemned to die, but perhaps pardoned for a consideration; Thomas, who had no part in the Rising; Christopher, who was executed at Tyburn with his uncle Thomas, May 27, 1570; Marmaduke, the eighth son, who was still a prisoner in the Tower on July 14, 1572, but was probably pardoned on composition. He died at Stranton in the County of Durham, November 2, 1594. The ninth son was Sampson, who died in exile abroad, probably in 1574, and there were two younger yet, Richard and Henry, who seem to have had no share in the Rising. Beside these eleven sons, " old Norton " had eight daughters, who all married scions of good old families in Yorkshire or Durham.

But to return: Thomas Markenfield of Markenfield Hall, in 1569, had already been for some years an exile for his faith. To him, as secret envoy from the Holy See, came Dr. Nicholas Morton, an old friend and connection of his family, who had in happier times been Prebendary

* See facing page 116.

of York. He brought news that the Pope was about to take action against the Queen, and persuaded Markenfield to return with him to England to assist in preparing men's minds for the coming struggle.

Markenfield naturally first sought out his old friend and neighbour, Richard Norton of Norton Conyers. Norton is only some five miles distant from Markenfield on the other side of Ripon. It is still a very fine place with a grand old park.

According to Francis Norton, the main instigator of the Rising was Dr. Morton. "He used such persuasions to the Earl of North-umberland, and to my father, whom he had served in times past, and to many others where he had travelled to and fro for the same purpose." He told them that the Queen was about to be excommunicated, and that they would run both their own souls and their country into the greatest danger, if they did not seek at once to restore the ancient faith. For they would share in the excommunication if they held to the Queen, and if they did not reform things from within the realm, other Christian princes would invade the Kingdom to depose the excommunicated Sovereign. This was indeed no imaginary danger, and we can well understand how it would affect men who were at once passionately devoted to the old religion, now proscribed and persecuted, and at the same time ardent lovers of their country. From this point of view the Rising of the North has a patriotic as well as a religious aspect, and scrupulous consciences like Northumberland's might well doubt if it were lawful to uphold a monarch certainly illegitimate, and denounced by the Head of the Church as a heretic and an enemy of the pure faith.

Francis Norton goes on to tell how Blessed Thomas Percy sent for his father and broke his mind to him, "declaring the great grief he had, for that they all lived out of the laws of the Catholic Church ; for the restitution of which he would willingly spend his life." By his father's command Norton had then an interview with the Earl in a field, in which he was won over to the cause.

The two motives which induced the Earl of Northumberland to take action were, as we know from his own "confession," the restoration of religion and the naming of an heir to the throne. The true heir was undoubtedly Mary Queen of Scots, and the fear that she would be set aside or got out of the way, to the utter destruction of Catholic hopes, forced the great nobles to take action. "It was thought," says B. Thomas Percy, "that all the realm would be in a hurly burly about the same ; which occasion moved me most especially not only to send to the Duke [of Norfolk], but also to assemble my friends, and to advise with them, and to know their inclinations." But this assembling brought such suspicion upon the Earl and his brother of Westmoreland, that they were peremptorily summoned to York to give an account of their doings to the Council of the North, a summons which forced them into premature action. The Earl confided his dangerous position to old Richard Norton (as we learn from the "confession" of his young son, Christopher), "which grieved him exceedingly, for it was his duty as a Queen's officer to disclose what the Earl had told him ; but the Earl reminded him that he had been a servant in his grandfather's house, and that he confided in him as a man of honour, and his countryman."

Francis Norton, Leonard Dacre, and Markenfield were eager to release the Queen of Scots and conferred with B. Thomas Percy as to how it might best be effected. The two former went secretly to Lord Shrewsbury's to see if there were any chance of getting her conveyed safely out of his hands, but returned after two days' absence reporting that they could not bring it to pass. Their intention in releasing her, says the Earl, was "that we hoped thereby to have some reformation in religion, or at the least some sufferance for men to use their conscience as they were disposed, and also the liberty of freedom of her whom we accounted the second person [in the Kingdom] and the right heir apparent."

Norton and Markenfield were more earnest in persuading Northumberland to join the rising ; urging that they had already gone so far that they could not draw back without disgrace, and that they would have to fly the country. "This would be a marvellous blot and discredit, thus to depart and to leave off this godly enterprise, that is so expected and looked for at our hands throughout the body of the whole realm."

Markenfield had the confidence of Dr. Morton, and told the Earl of Northumberland that the Doctor thought it was lawful for him to take up arms against Queen Elizabeth, as having been lawfully excommunicated by the Head of the Church. And he said, according to Markenfield that, since the Queen refused to receive the Pope's ambassador, she was for that cause lawfully excommunicate, and so it was lawful to take arms against her. "This much did Markenfield report of the said Dr. Morton. . . . 'The most of us,' adds Francis Norton, 'thought it was rather his own imagination, to advance the matter than otherwise ; yet, notwithstanding, the other two divines consulted thought it not sufficient, unless the excommunication had been orderly published within the realm.' "

Whatever may be thought of these arguments, it was, according to Northumberland himself, old Norton and Markenfield who finally prevailed with the Earls to take active measures, and their counsel was seconded by that of the two Countesses. Their motives may be judged by the declaration of another member of their party, Mr. Smythe of Eshe, near Durham. He is reported to have told a friend who met him riding, muffled, to Brancepeth, that the setting up of religion was their purpose. "How can that be, when you shall be rebels to our Queen, and so act against your consciences?" he was asked. "No," he said, "that is not so, for the Pope has summoned this land once, and if he summon it again, it is lawful to rise against the Queen, and to do it if she will not; for the Pope is Head of the Church."

These conferences were held during the early days of November, 1569, at Brancepeth Castle near Durham, the seat of the Earl of Westmoreland, where the leaders of the movement had assembled.

Brancepeth Castle, a magnificent feudal pile, much added to and modernised at the beginning of the nineteenth century, stands on the side of a steep and wooded dell, through which runs a rivulet. The situation is very romantic. The country west and north of Brancepeth is poor and bare, and soon stretches into bleak and comfortless hills, which are now seamed with collieries and covered with hideous mining villages. But the home view to the river is rich and cultivated, and the castle is surrounded with a noble park hemmed in by luxuriant woods. Between the dell and the castle walls lie lawns and gardens, shrouded by the rich foliage of the trees which spring from the bed of the rivulet. The fine old church lies within a stone's throw of the castle gates, and is one of the most interesting in the country.

To Brancepeth then the eyes of all the North Country were turned, and the assembly there speedily became an object of suspicion to the government officials. Thanks to the publication of the State papers, we are now able to read the reports sent up to the government day by day from the perturbed officials in the North. Foremost among them were the Earl of Sussex, Lord President of the Council of the North, and Sir George Bowes, who was stationed in the county, or as it was then called, the Bishopric of Durham. Durham had indeed a peculiar position in the country. It was the Patrimony of St. Cuthbert, a palatinate governed by its Bishop Palatine, who enjoyed full secular as well as spiritual jurisdiction. The change of religion had not affected this mediæval arrangement, and the bitterly Protestant Pilkington, who now usurped the chair of St. Cuthbert, was also civil ruler of the Bishopric, of course in due subordination to the Sovereign.

On November 7 we find Bowes reporting to Sussex that "the retainers of the Earl of Westmoreland with the most part of all his tenants of his Lordship of Raby, being furnished with armour and weapons, in their warlike apparel repaired to Brancepeth yesterday, and this night past, and that his other tenants had been ordered to set out at an hour's warning." He adds that Norton was there with the Earl of

MARKENFIELD HALL FROM THE EAST
*Photo by the author*

To face page 112

Northumberland. On the 10th he reports that Francis Norton and divers of his brethren, with twenty-nine horse, all armed, had gone there, and that in another company had ridden Thomas Markenfield with the Sheriff of Yorkshire and thirty horsemen, all armed in corslets under jerkins.

The riders who left Markenfield Hall, to obey the summons of the head of the Nevilles, no doubt wore their armour concealed under their ordinary attire, in order not to attract attention. Sir George Bowes reported that the Earl of Northumberland was armed in a privy coat, under a Spanish jerkin (which was open so that the coat of armour could be seen), and a steel cap covered with green velvet. He says "marvellous great fear ariseth here in these parts; for they pass in troops, armed and unarmed, so fast up and down the country that no man dare well stir anywhere, and it is every hour looked that they will do some evil enterprise, and make open stir . . . and yet for anything that in certainty I can perceive, *they gather rather for their own safety than to annoy*, for they are not as I well know, above three hundred. . . ." "All their faction" could not exceed more than this number, he thought, that had any arms or weapons, but "they presently sweep up all manner of weapons and armours that can be gotten for money; for this day they bought all the bows and arrows in Barnard Castle, and, as I hear, at Durham."

He adds in a postscript: "But now presently it is advertised to me that their enterprise shall be set forth before Sunday, and that should be to make open call of men for alteration of religion, and to spoil such as will not follow their directions, and prove if this will move the multitude to follow them, and if it will not, they have a ship ready to pass away. But this is a report, delivered upon great uncertainty."

The alarm was now given. Sussex wrote in haste on the 13th that he heard that they "were to have an open Mass this day in Durham. I pray you understand the truth."

The news was true. The scruples of Blessed Thomas Percy had been finally overcome, or rather he was almost forced into action. And now the die was cast. On November 14, the great gates of Brancepeth were flung open and the venerable form of Richard Norton was seen advancing with the standard of the host, a gleaming crucifix. His white hair streamed in the wind, and his face was fired with high enthusiasm for what he deemed a holy and a sacred cause. Behind rode the Earls, with their banners, Markenfield and the other leaders, each with a large golden crucifix around his neck. The horsemen that followed them all bore the cross, as for a new crusade.

Rapidly they rode over the four miles which divide Brancepeth from the City of St. Cuthbert.

P

What they there did let Bowes report :

"Yesterday at 4 o'clock in the afternoon, the Earls accompanied by Richard Norton, Francis, his son, with divers others of his said sons, Christopher Neville, Cuthbert Neville, uncles of the Earl of Westmoreland, and Thomas Markenfield, with others, to the number of three score horsemen, armed in corslets and coats of plate, with spears, arquebuses and dagges [pistols], entered the minster at Durham and there took all the books but one, and them and the communion-table defaced, rent and broke in pieces."

This letter of Bowes' was written in such haste and confusion of mind that it is actually addressed to "my singular good Lord *the Earl of Westmoreland*, Lord President of the Queen's Majesties counsell established in the North parts," instead of to the Earl of Sussex ! "It is also (says Sir Cuthbert Sharpe) exceedingly difficult to read."

It is not difficult to imagine the enthusiasm with which the restoration of the ancient worship was welcomed at Durham on November 14, 1569. Though the Earls and their company only stayed a few hours there, returning to Brancepeth that evening, and setting out next day with their army southwards, they had lighted a fire at Durham which could not be easily extinguished. They found a watch of twenty-four of the townsmen quite sufficient to guard the city, for, as Sussex had afterwards to admit to the Queen, "there was no resistance made, nor any mislike of their doings." The Protestant clergy, with their worthy Bishop, fled from the city, and those who had remained faithful took their places. The majority of at least the inferior clergy attached to the Cathedral were eager to help in the good work. Faculties from Rome had been entrusted to certain leading priests (including the chaplain of the Earl of Westmoreland) to absolve from schism and heresy both clergy and people, and we have stirring accounts of the joy with which the people flocked to hear High Mass sung once again in the great Church of St. Cuthbert and of their eagerness to receive upon their knees the public absolution from censures which was solemnly pronounced on Sunday, December 4. The Protestant service-books from the churches were publicly " burnt at the bridge end," the ruined altars rebuilt, the holy water stoups set up again, and from many a hidden store, hands trembling with joy brought forth the sacred vestments and ornaments of the Church which had been carefully concealed in the hope of a better day. Thousands flocked to the great Minster to hear once more the old familiar chants of Mass and Vespers, and say their beads again in public to the honour of God's Mother, and, best of all, to be shriven from their sins and receive once more the Bread of Angels in the Sacrament of Love. Later on, when the Rising had been

MARKENFIELD HALL FROM THE NORTH

*Photo by the author*

*To face page* 114

quenched in blood, these poor people had to suffer for having (in the words of authority) "by the instigation of the devil, come to Mass, Matins, Evensong, procession and like idolatrous service, thereat kneeling, bowing, knocking, and such like reverent gesture, used praying on beads, confession or shriving to a priest, took holy water and holy bread," and, above all, for having "among other like wicked people, knelt down and received absolution under Pope Pius' name in Latin, false-terming this godly estate of England to be in schism or heresy."

If in that sad day not all were faithful, not all courageous, who shall dare to blame them too severely? Many at least were true, for years afterwards the Protestant Bishop angrily complained of the Church of Durham that "its stink is grievous to the nose of God and men, and which to purge far passeth Hercules' labours." The same scenes of joyful reconciliation to the Church of Christ were seen wherever the army of the Earls appeared. At Staindrop, at Darlington, at Richmond, and Northallerton, Holy Mass was sung again amid indescribable scenes of joy and devotion. It was about the 20th of that fateful November that they came to Ripon. Here in the market-place they raised the banner of Christ's Five Wounds, and in St. Wilfrid's Minster celebrated the Holy Sacrifice. The stately halls of Norton and Markenfield were in gala that day. All Yorkshire thrilled with joy. "There are not ten gentlemen in all this country," wrote Sir Ralph Sadler to Cecil, "that favour the Queen's proceedings in religion. The common people are ignorant, superstitious, and altogether blinded with the old Popish doctrine, and therefore so favour the cause which the rebels make the colour of their rebellion."

The Proclamation of the Earls ran as follows :

" Thomas, Earl of Northumberland, and Charles, Earl of Westmoreland, the Queen's most true and lawful subjects, and to all her highness's people sendeth greeting :

" Whereas divers new set up nobles about the Queen's Majesty, have and do daily, not only gone about to overthrow and put down the ancient nobility of this realm, but also have misused the Queen's Majesty's own person, and also have by the space of twelve years now past, set up and maintained a new found religion and heresy contrary to God's word. For the amending and redressing whereof, divers foreign powers do purpose shortly to invade these realms, which will be to our utter destruction, if we do not ourselves speedily forefend the same. Wherefore we are now constrained at this time to go about to amend and redress it ourselves, which if we should not do and foreigners enter upon us we should all be made slaves and bondsmen to them. These are, therefore, to will and require you, and every of you, being above the age of sixteen years and not sixty, as your duty towards God doth bind you, for the setting forth of His true and Catholic religion ; and as you tender the common weal of your country, to come and resort unto us with all speed, with all such armour and furniture as you, or any of you, have. This fail you not herein, as you will answer the contrary at your perils. God save the Queen."

Leicester and Cecil "and others of the most painful and dutiful servants to the Queen's Majesty" were specially aimed at. Sussex issued a counter proclamation on November 19, by virtue of the Queen's warrant, denouncing the Earls, Norton, Markenfield, and the rest as rebels against her Majesty and disturbers of her realm. He promised, at the Queen's own suggestion, to pardon those "of the mean sort" who would desert their leaders and return home by November 23, but expressly exempted from this pardon the Earls themselves, Christopher Neville, Egremond Ratcliffe, Richard Norton, Thomas Markenfield, John Swinburn, Robert Tempest, Francis Norton, and Thomas Gennye (Jennings).

On November 20, the Council at York write to the Queen that the levies come in slackly. "The people like so well of their cause of religion, as they do flock to them in all places where they come ; and many gentlemen show themselves ready to serve your Majesty, whose sons and heirs, or other sons, be on the other side." And Sir George Bowes writes to Sussex from Barnard Castle on November 23 : " Daily the people flee from these parts to the Earls, and I know not what should be done to stay them, for I have notified their unloyal and rebellious dealings, and with fair speech and bestowing of money, used those that came to me in the most gentle manner I could. But it availeth nothing, for they still steal after them. . . . Many be not gone, that yet concealeth them in woods and other places, and will not come before me, for any precept or commandment, and the Earls have caused two or three lewd fellows of theirs to proclaim me a traitor and heretic."

The whole number engaged in the insurrection was computed at twenty thousand. "For all the inhabitants of the Bishopric and Richmondshire, a few only excepted, were all rebels," writes the Lord President of the North to Cecil in 1573. But Lord Huntingdon ascertained that there were never more than five thousand five hundred on the field together, of whom one thousand seven hundred were light horsemen, and three thousand three hundred foot soldiers. But of these latter there were not more than five hundred properly armed, and those only with bows and arrows, jacks and bills.

As a matter of fact the movement was doomed to failure from the first. Hurried into action, the leaders had no time for proper prepara-

RICHARD NORTON, OF NORTON CONYERS,
STANDARD-BEARER OF THE NORTHERN
RISING.  *Photo by the author*         *To face page* 116

tions, nor did the hoped-for succour from abroad come to their assistance. Their host was badly disciplined and ill-equipped, and it may be doubted if the leaders themselves had many of the necessary qualities for success. They were no match for the crafty and resolute Sussex, who was biding his time in York till reinforcements could arrive from the south, and steadily making his preparations for attack. If, however, the Earls had marched on to York, and arrived there while Sussex was still unprepared, they would have had a good chance of victory. Sussex's letters to Cecil betray his great anxiety. But, after reaching Wetherby on November 23, the failure of supplies and money, and unfortunate differences of opinion among the leaders, put a stop to further progress. They turned again northwards, and henceforth their cause was lost.

Much time was wasted in besieging Barnard Castle, where Sir George Bowes had entrenched himself. Here a remarkable proof of the popularity of the Rising was given by the conduct of the garrison, no fewer than 226 of whom during one day and night leapt from the castle walls to join the Earls. Thirty-five of these, we are told, " brake their necks, arms or legs in the leaping." Ten days later Sir George Bowes had to capitulate, and was allowed to retire to York. But Sussex was now in the field, and proceeding most vigorously to the attack. Little by little the insurgent host melted away. The last council of war was held at Durham on December 16, only a month and a day from the beginning of the Rising, and the conclusion was *Sauve qui peut*.

The leaders rode towards Hexham, quickly pursued by Sussex and his army, and from Northumberland they crossed the border into Scotland. Here, among the hereditary foes of England, they were comparatively safe.

The whole North was now at the mercy of Sussex, whom the Queen had specially charged to execute on the offenders the full severity of martial law. The only consideration that could temper her fury was a pecuniary one, for Elizabeth loved money even better than blood.

On December 25, Lord Sussex writes to Cecil from Hexham : " Touching present commodity, I find that all the forfeitures by this late rebellion [which] should grow to the Queen's Majesty in the Bishopric, will indeed by the laws of the realm, fall out in the end to the Bishop ; which will be too great for any subject to receive. And, therefore, before I proceed against the offenders that have estates of inheritance or great wealth, I think it very necessary that the Queen's Majesty should either compound with the Bishop for his royalties, and keep them still in her hands, or translate him to some other Bishopric ; whereby, *sede vacante*, all might grow to her Majesty."

The Queen's frugal mind had been greatly vexed by the expense of the expedition, and Cecil sent on her letters to Sussex showing how "earnest she was to have you take care to diminish her charges, wherewith she seemeth to be much grieved."

She had had to send ten thousand pounds in gold to York, which indeed vexed her sorely.

Sussex wrote to Cecil on December 28 : "I mean to pass to Durham where I intend to remain some days, to take order for such of the common people as shall be executed by the martial law ; among whom I mean to execute specially constables and other officers, that have seduced the people (under colour of the Queen's Majesty's service) to rebel ; and such others as have been most busy to further those matters, so as there shall be no towne that hath sent men to the rebels, or otherwise aided them, but some of the worst disposed shall be executed for example : the number whereof is yet uncertain, for that I know not the number of the towns, but I guess it will not be under six or seven hundred, at the least, that shall be executed of the common sort, besides the prisoners taken in the field ; wherein I trust to use such direction, as no sort shall escape from example ; and that the example shall be (as it is necessary that it should be) very great, wherein I could not orderly deal, before I had first directed the former and principal matters.  I mean also, if I be permitted, to execute my office without abridgement, to fine all others of all kind of sorts that be offenders and shall not be executed, and thereby to raise a commodity to the Queen's Majesty.  And herewith, I trust, that her Majesty will not mislike, that with the goods of some persons, where I think fit, I reward some that have served, as all others in my place, and like cases have done.

"I had, before the receipt of the Queen's letters, resolved, with Mr. Sadler, not to execute the martial law against any person that had inheritance or great wealth ; for that I knew the law in that case."  By this Sussex means that by the law the property of those executed would go to their families, while if their lives were spared, they could be stripped of all that they possessed.

Among the prisoners in Durham Castle (January 1, 1570) under Sir George Bowes, Knight, Provost-Marshal, we find "John Markenfield, brother to Thomas Markenfield, Christopher Norton and Marmaduke Norton, younger sons of Richard Norton," and the representatives of many of the noblest Catholic names of the North.

The gentlemen paid 6s. 8d. a week for their "meat and drink," and the "meaner sort" 3s. 4d.  On January 25, the two Nortons and John Markenfield, with others, were sent to York Castle.  Some were saved from the Queen's vengeance by an appeal to her cupidity.  Thus Lord Sussex writes that he had ventured to pardon John Sayer, a very young

118

man, on consideration of his father paying a fine of five hundred pounds —if the Queen's Majesty be so pleased : *which if he be executed she should have nothing.*

Meanwhile Lord Warwick and the Lord Admiral had arrived on the scene, after the rebellion was over, and proceeded, as Sussex bitterly complained, to ravage the whole country, making their headquarters at Durham. "They have driven all the cattle of the country, and ransomed the people in such miserable sort, and made such open and common spoil, as the like, I think, was never heard of. . . . Their men ride daily about the country, seizing and spoiling and ransacking at their pleasure." Worse than this, "the pardon proclaimed by the Queen's Majesty's commandment is (to her dishonour and my shame) no surety to such as received it." He earnestly begs the Queen to "maintain him in his first authority, allow of his well doings, and defend him from defacings without desert. . . . If I weighed not the quiet of my Queen more than any other matter, I would have stopped them from crowing upon my dunghill, or carrying of one halfpenny out of my rule."

The ruthless directions for wholesale executions are terrible to read. At Durham, at Darlington, Richmond, Northallerton, Thirsk, Ripon, and in all the towns and villages around, the gibbet was erected in the market-place or in the centre of the village street, and soon was loaded with its ghastly burden. It was expressly directed that no village should escape. In three days in January over three hundred perished in the Bishopric. Even the fiercely Protestant Bishop Pilkington was touched at the state of his unhappy diocese, and wrote, "The cuntre is in grete mysere. . . . The number off offendors is so grete, that few innocent are left to trie the giltie." The red rain fell thick on every village green, and the carrion-crows feasted as they had never done before.

Meanwhile two anxieties only filled the heart of the virgin-queen, first that exemplary punishment should be meted out to "the meaner sort," and next that "her charges should be diminished to the utmost compatible with safety." It would be difficult to tell whether ferocity or avarice held the stronger sway over that virgin heart.

To do him justice, the Earl of Sussex did his work very systematically. He first obtained the approximate number of those who had joined the rising from each village, and then settled the number that were to be executed there. Thus, for instance, under Richmondshire in Yorkshire, we find :

| Joined in Gilling West, | 141 | To be executed, | 30 |
|---|---|---|---|
| „ „ Hang East, | 241 | „ „ | 42 |
| „ „ Hang West, | 293 | „ „ | 47 |
| „ „ Hallikeld, | 341 | „ „ | 57 |
| „ „ Gilling East, | 225 | „ „ | 37 |

The comforting intelligence was duly sent to her Majesty, together with the Lieutenant's assurances that all that was possible was being done to spare the royal pocket. But the Queen was annoyed that the executions took so long, and Sussex had to hurry on his Provost-Marshal : " I pray you make all the haste you can, to avoid offence, *for a little matter will stir offence where charge groweth by it.*"

Poor Sussex was indeed worried to death by her Majesty's letters. Writing again on January 19, he tells Bowes that he has received letters from court whereby he perceives " the Queen's Majesty doth much marvel that she doth not hear that the execution is yet ended, and that she is disburdened of her charges, that was considered for that respect :— and therefore I heartily pray you to use expedition, for I fear that this lingering will breed displeasure to us both. I would have you make the examples great in Ripon and Tadcaster, and therefore if you find not sufficient numbers within the town that be in the doings of the late rebellion, take of other townes and bring them to the execution to those places ; for it is necessary that the execution be great in appearance in those two places. . . . The like thereof shall be convenient to be done at Thirsk."

The cruelty with which the rebellion was punished was no doubt sound policy. As Sir George Bowes, the Provost-Marshal writes : In this circuit and journey through the Bishopric, Richmondshire, Allertonshire, Cleveland, Ripon, and Wetherby, " there is of them executed, six hundred and odd ; so that now the authors of this rebellion is cursed of every side ; and sure the people are in marvellous fear, so that I trust that there shall never such things happen in these parts again." And indeed they never did.

To sum it up in Lingard's words, there was not " between Newcastle and Wetherby, a district of sixty miles in length and forty in breadth, a town or village in which some of the inhabitants did not expire on the gibbet."

But to the great chagrin of the Queen the leaders had escaped her. It was now her darling wish to get them once more into her power. Norton and Markenfield and the two Earls were all safe in Scotland. But the Regent, the crafty Moray, was the Queen's friend, and his influence was invoked to compel the half independent clans on the border to give up the fugitives.

The Queen found a spy in a certain Robert Constable, the representative of a noble Catholic family and a relative of the Earl of Westmoreland, who volunteered to follow the fugitives to Scotland ; where he might, " percase, work some feat to betrap some of them." He was himself ashamed of his mission, which he declared to be " a

BLESSED THOMAS PERCY, EARL OF NORTHUMBERLAND

*From a Bartolozzi print in possession of Mgr. Owens. The signature is from the answers to his examination before his judges, now in the Public Record Office*

*To face page* 120

traitorous kind of service that I am waded in, to trap them that trust me, as Judas did Christ." But he persevered in it. He found at Cavers Mr. Richard Norton, who inquired about his sons William, Christopher, and Marmaduke, and rejoiced to hear that they were still living. Constable advised him and his son Francis to come to England ; but happily they did not trust themselves to his protection. Mr. Markenfield, he learned, was at Brauxholm with several other of the leaders.

With the exception of the Blessed Thomas Percy, who, to the eternal disgrace of the Regent, was sold to the Queen for a sum of £2000, the leaders of the Rising succeeded in escaping abroad.

Old Richard Norton told Constable that he had had to fly for his life so suddenly, that he had taken away with him "neither horse, apparel nor money, but was glad to ride of a horse of his son's." Francis and Sampson, who had escaped with him, "brought neither apparel nor money, but were as bare as Job."

From Scotland, old Norton and his sons managed to get over to Flanders, where they obtained a pension from the King of Spain. The period of the old man's death is uncertain, but as Sir Cuthbert Sharpe remarks, "worn down with age and trouble, it is not probable that he was long burdensome on the bounty of the King of Spain." Francis did his best to buy his pardon by a full confession, but his humiliating disclosure won him no mercy from the implacable Queen.

On January 16 Elizabeth directed that William and Christopher Norton, and Thomas Norton, their uncle, should be sent up to court, under separate escort, so that they should have no conference by the way together nor with others. This was accordingly done.

On April 6 they were arraigned at Westminster, and pleaded guilty to the charges brought against them.

Christopher was but a boy, and we do not know why he was signalled out for execution, while William and Marmaduke were spared, but the probability is that he had no property with which to buy his life.

There is an official account extant of the execution of young Christopher Norton and his uncle Thomas, who suffered on May 27, 1570. They were drawn on a hurdle from the Tower to Tyburn. Being pressed by the preacher to acknowledge his offences against God and his prince, Thomas Norton answered that for offence made and committed toward the Queen's Majesty, he had the law for it, and therefore must suffer death, and to that end he was come thither ; and so he only asked pardon for his offences against God. He was then requested to say the Lord's prayer in the vulgar tongue. "Sir," quoth he, and answered very obstinately, that he would pray in Latin, and therefore prayed him that he would not molest his conscience. Another minister bade him, if he must needs say it in Latin, to say it then secretly to himself, and so he did. His Latin prayers being ended, the preacher exhorted him very earnestly to say the Lord's prayer and belief in English. This he at last agreed to, and so said the Lord's prayer in English, to which he added the Ave Maria. And then he desired not only the audience, but, also the saints in heaven to pray for him, both then and at all times. He hung a certain space, and then was taken down and quartered in presence of his nephew, who presently must drink of the same cup.

Christopher, poor lad, was not so brave as his uncle. He acknowledged that he had worthily deserved his death, and therefore besought God and all men to forgive him. As the horrible butchery proceeded, he cried out in his agony, "'Oh, Lord, Lord, have mercy upon me!' and so he yielded up the ghost."

Let us pray that he found that mercy with God, which he had sought in vain from man. Sanders speaks of him and his uncle as suffering " a noble martyrdom"; and it is certain that they died in the cause of the Catholic religion.

The Lord of Markenfield, after spending some time under the protection of Lord Hume at Hume Castle, fled, like his kinsman and friend, to Flanders, to linger out the rest of his days, a ruined and a broken man. His wife, Isabel, daughter of Sir William Ingleby of Ripley Castle, and sister of the martyr, Venerable Francis Ingleby, was allowed a small pension for life, out of her husband's confiscated estates. We find from time to time mention made of Thomas Markenfield in the reports of Government spies. Thus in October, 1571," Markenfeld is said to be gone to Spain or Rome, and there is one Dr. Morton, that was said was coming from the Pope with letters and money to the English now at Louvain." A letter addressed to Markenfield at Madrid, dated from Tournay, May 19, 1593, from a cousin, states that he has received his letter from Portugal, "written upon the back of a target," and that he was glad to hear from him, as he had been reported dead. The writer adds, "Your wife is poor, but prayeth hard for you. I fear she is in great lack of worldly comforts."

We hear, from the reports of spies, picturesque details as to the life of the exiles at Louvain. "Those who were at Louvain for religion before the rebels came used not to come in their company." A spy saw "Sir Francis Englefield refuse to meet or speak with the Earl of Westmoreland in the street, whereat the Earl was much offended; but every Thursday all the English in Louvain went to church to hear Mass and pray for England. Many persons were continually coming from England

### THE ARMS OF BLESSED THOMAS PERCY

*From his Book of Prayers, written and illuminated with his own hand. Now in the possession of the Duke of Northumberland*

*To face page 122*

into Flanders." Coming towards England, one Henry Simpson, whose report we quote, "met a wagon with fourteen men, women and children from Oxfordshire, their servants walking on foot with sky-coloured cloaks laid on with green lace." Mr. Markenfield had a cook called Francis, who spoke French, and who remained in Paris in order to get the news from England (October 21, 1571).

Thomas Markenfield is finally mentioned in a book called the *Estate of English Fugitives* as one of " those that are only for want of things necessary, and of pure poverty consumed and dead." His younger brother, John, a boy of nineteen, was unjustly attainted at York, and narrowly escaped execution. The Commissioners report that "he is very young, under twenty, and was attainted only to bring his title to his brother's lands (if he have any) to the Queen; and it was not meant he should die, for that he hath no land, and is within the compass of the commission for compounding."

Of another reprieved prisoner, Henry Johnson, the Commission reports : " He is very simple, was abused [*i.e.* perverted] by his wife, who is Norton's daughter, and he hath made a state [*i.e.* settlement] of his lands to her at the time of his marriage; so as by his life the Queen shall have his lands, and by his death his wife shall presently have them according to the state." The same was reported of other prisoners, *e.g.* "*so the Queen shall win by his life ana lose by his death.*" In reply the Queen, after remarking that she had "always been more inclinable to mercy than to severity," doubted whether since such a great number of the poorer sort of people had been executed, it would not seem "an inordinate compassion to have no greater example upon the richer than upon the four only" already executed. " We are pleased that Henry Johnson for his simplicity, and John Markenfield for his youth . . . shall be forborne from execution. As for the other four . . . we are in nothing moved to spare them, for any respect of the profit that might come to us by their life"; however, she left it to the judgment of the Commission.

It only remains to learn the fate of Markenfield Hall. The Commissioners who were surveying the confiscated property of the insurgent leaders write as follows to Cecil (April 21, 1570) :

"We are now at Ripon, surveying Richard Norton and Thomas Markenfield's lands. Norton has a brick house, which looks fair, but is all out of order within. It is well placed, with apt grounds for garden and orchards, wherein he had pleasure; within half a mile of his house, he has a park of $1\frac{1}{2}$ miles, well stored with timber. It has been stored with deer and conies, which are now almost spoiled. Of his demesnes, part is good ground lying about the river Ure, but the grounds on the river are not so good as those by the rivers in the south. His demesnes are about 650 acres."

"As Norton's house lies two miles from Ripon, N.E., Mr. Markenfield's is one [*sic*] mile S.W. An ancient house, built all of stone, to the outward show fair and stately ; the hall and the lodging side embattled, more in length than breadth, and three sides environed with an evil moat ; but the house is served with a conduit very plentifully. Against the entry of the court is built the hall and kitchen, on the right hand of the court the lodgings, and the left the stables, brewhouses, and offices. The hall and lodgings are all vaults and were at first built all about one high room. Besides the vaults the walls are of a great height, without order, whereof part is divided at the mid-transom of the window, so that the rooms are all out of order. The house is placed in a park of the like quality with Mr. Norton's, but better ground, and well planted with large timber. There is a demesne adjoining of 800 acres, with no quantity of water meadow, but much hay is made in seasonable years."

Before we finish our story let us go for a moment into Ripon Minster and look at the magnificent tomb of Sir Thomas de Markenfield and Dionisia, his wife, which forms one of the glories of the ancient church. It lies in what was once the Chapel of St. Andrew, in the north transept of the cathedral. Sir Thomas is clad in armour of the time of Edward III., and when he was alive the famous hall was in all the freshness of its beauty, if indeed he did not see it building. Round his neck is a collar composed of park palings with a hart lodged within it, which according to Planché is the special badge of the town of Derby. The hands of the warrior are folded in prayer, his sword in its richly ornamented scabbard lies by his side, and his feet rest upon a lion *guardant*. Upon the tomb and upon the hilt of the sword are sculptured the Markenfield arms—*argent, on a bend sable three bezants*. The sides and west end of the tomb are panelled and bear shields, among which we may still detect the famous saltire of the Nevilles.

This knightly effigy is surely a fitting representation of the lord of such a house as Markenfield.

Another Sir Thomas lies by the north wall of the transept, beside Eleanor, his wife. Both effigies are greatly disfigured and mutilated. They are of the time of Henry VII., and this Sir Thomas was probably the great-grandfather of the last lord of Markenfield Hall. Of Sir Ninian, who fought and bled at Flodden Field, no monument remains. It is said that the family became extinct in the male line at the beginning of the nineteenth century, in the person of Metcalf Markenfield, who died at Slingsby, January 2, 1808, aged ninety-three. But this is not certain. On one of our visits to Markenfield Hall, we

124

TOMB OF SIR THOMAS MARKENFIELD
AND DIONISIA HIS WIFE, RIPON MINSTER
*Photo by the author*

TOMB OF SIR THOMAS MARKENFIELD
AND ELEANOR HIS WIFE, RIPON MINSTER
*Photo by the author*

*To face page* 124

were told that the name still exists, if not in England, at least in America, and that in recent years one who claimed to be a descendant of the ancient family whose name he bears had come across the Atlantic to visit the home of his ancestors.

What could be more striking to the imagination than the contrast between this feudal house, hidden away in its fallen majesty, forgotten as it were by time itself, and the stirring life of the great republic of the West, in which perhaps the last scion of its ancient lords lives and moves!

The glory of Markenfield has departed, and its name is long forgotten. The vast demesnes of its last lord were granted to Sir Henry Gates of Seamer in Yorkshire, as a reward for his efforts in putting down the Rising.

And with the passing away of the Percies and the Nevilles, the Nortons and the Markenfields, it must have seemed indeed to the men of the North country that the old order had departed for ever. In a sense this was true. The last remnant of the great feudal nobility had been ruthlessly destroyed. The times were changed indeed, and England was no longer the Merry England of old. Could it be that the ancient religion now proscribed and persecuted, was also to pass away? It may have seemed so to some of little faith. And yet we know that the old religion which flourished when Markenfield was in its prime was not and could not be extinguished with the ruin of its noble house; rather in its imperishable strength it has thrown out new roots across the very ocean, and men come from a land unknown and undreamed of to the builders of Markenfield, to muse over the fallen splendours of the place, with the same zeal burning in their souls which drove Thomas Markenfield forth from his home to strike a blow for God, our Lady, and the Catholic Faith!

*Transit gloria mundi, fides Catholica manet* ("The glory of the world passeth away, but the Catholic faith remains") is a motto inscribed upon the walls of another ancient Manor House, and it might be well written over the gateway of Markenfield Hall. The cause seemed lost indeed for a while, but God's cause can never fail, and the blood of the faithful North has born its seed in due season.

In conclusion we may quote some verses of "Claxton's Lament," a contemporary poem which describes the fate of Robert Claxton, of Old-Park County, Durham, who was engaged in the Rising. It might have been written equally well of the Markenfields:

> "Listen, English merchants brave,
>   To Robert Claxton, woeful man!
> Who once had lands and livings fair,
>   Most like an English gentleman.

# FORGOTTEN SHRINES

" But the flower is shed and the spring is fled,
   And he wanders alone at the close of the day ;
And the sleety hail in the moonshine pale,
   Glistens at eve on his locks of grey.

" To Wetherby the Earls are gone ;
   A message came, so fair and free—
' Now swear thee, on the holy rood,
   I charge thee, Claxton, ride with me.'

   \*      \*      \*      \*      \*

" ' We only stand to guard our own,
   Our lives are set in jeopardy—
And if thou wilt not ride with us
   Yet shall thy lands forfaulted be.

" ' Now, foul befall the venomed tongues
   That slandered two such noble peers ;
And brought such woe and misery
   On silver hairs and failing years.

" ' To Wetherby I needs must ride—
   No better chance since I may see :
My eldest son is full of pride ;
   My second goes for love of me.

" ' Now bide at home, my eldest son ;—
   Thou art the heir of all my land.'
' If I stay at home for land or fee
   May I be branded in forehead and hand.

" ' The Percies are rising in the north ;
   The Nevilles are gathering in the west ;
And Claxton's heir may bide at home
   And hide him in the cushat's nest ?'

" ' Now rest at home, my youngest son,
   Thy limbs are lithe, thy age is green,'
' Nay, father, we'll to Wetherby,
   And never more at home be seen.

" ' We'll keep our bond to our noble Lord,—
   We'll tine our faith to the Southern Queen ;
And when all is lost, we'll cross the seas,
   And bid farewell to bower and green.

" ' Our towers may stand till down they fall,—
   That's all the help they'll get from me ;
False Southrons will be lords of all,
   But we'll ne'er hear it o'er the sea.'

# MARKENFIELD HALL

" Now the Percies' crescent is set in blood ;
   And the northern bull his flight has ta'en ;
And the sheaf of arrows are keen and bright
   And Barnard's walls are hard to gain.

" *The sun shone bright, and the birds sung sweet*
   *The day we left the North Countrie ;*
*But cold is the wind, and sharp is the sleet,*
   *That beat on the exile over the sea.*"

# RIPLEY CASTLE AND ITS MARTYRED SON

IN the valley of the Nidd, that most picturesque of Yorkshire rivers which flows between its lofty cliffs of limestone by St. Robert of Knaresborough's Hermitage, and that gloomy castle where the murderers of St. Thomas of Canterbury "dreed their weird" for twelve long months after the sacrilegious crime, there rises a wooded hill, upon which stands a tiny village, clustering round its fourteenth-century church and the castle of its lords.

Ripley is situated about four miles from Knaresborough and a little less from the well-known Spa of Harrogate, in the midst of a country full of Catholic memories. As you mount the hill from Nidd bridge you come first to the village, and a charming village it is. The mediæval Ripley has indeed disappeared, for the old town was pulled down and a new one built on a different site by Sir Wm. Ingilby in 1827. The old pre-Reformation market-cross, consisting of a plain shaft resting on five well-worn tiers, still occupies an open space in the midst of the present village ; and beside it stand the now long-disused parish-stocks. An ancient priests' house with a chantry chapel, which once occupied this spot, has also disappeared, together with the mediæval town.

Though the archæologist has reason to regret the result of this act of benevolent despotism, it must be confessed that the model village it created is a very pretty one. Nor do I imagine that the people of Ripley have any complaints to make. For Ripley belongs to its Lords, the Inglebys, as it has done for the past five hundred years, and the old feudal relations that have existed all these centuries are very strong and close.

The beautiful little church is full of Ingleby monuments, the " estoile argent" of the family is seen everywhere, and the village seems to exist but for the splendid castle in which the Inglebys have dwelt since the days of Edward III.

Let us first enter the church, as is but right. It stands just opposite the castle gate-house, a typical English parish church, of the Decorated or Edwardine period of Gothic architecture, embowered in a God's acre full of magnificent trees. It is dedicated to All Saints. On the north side of this churchyard is a very curious ancient cross, of unknown antiquity. It is mutilated indeed, like most of these ancient Catholic memorials in Protestant England, but what is left of it is unusually interesting. The circular base is 2 feet high and $15\frac{1}{2}$ feet in circumference, and in it there are indented eight deep hollows, apparently meant for those who might wish to kneel in prayer around the symbol of salvation. It is called a Penitents' or Weeping Cross,* and is, of its kind, unique in

* See facing p. 146.

128

TOMB OF SIR THOMAS INGLEBY

*Photo by the author*

*To face page* 128

England.  It probably dates from the fifteenth century, but this is not
certain.  It is thought that the upper stone (33 inches in diameter and
28½ inches high) supported a rood of wood.

Other curious relics of great antiquity, such as stone-coffins and
sculptured tomb-slabs, lie by the walls of the church, memorials, it would
seem, of an earlier building which once stood lower down upon the river
bank.

Within we find a quaint old rood screen of black oak, which, however
(at the restoration of 1862), has been removed from its proper place, cut
short, and re-erected in the south chapel.  So few screens remain in this
part of Yorkshire, that this has all the interest of a precious relic.  But
the interior of the church gains most of its charm from the Ingleby chapel
and monuments.  The members of this family, though staunchly Catholics
throughout the fiercest days of the persecution, were laid to rest within
the walls of the desecrated sanctuary which in life they never entered.
The reason of this, of course, was that in the penal days Catholics could
not be buried anywhere else, for Popish chapels and cemeteries were alike
proscribed by law.

And thus the silver star of the family gleams out from the monuments
not merely of the Inglebys of Catholic days, such as that of Sir Thomas
and Edeline, his wife, of the time of King Edward III., but from many a
slab to the memory of men who lived and suffered, in the darkest days,
" for God, our Lady, and the Catholic Faith." *

It is, indeed, sad for the pilgrim to find that the ancient faith is no
longer the heritage of those who now bear this ancient name.  For that
name can never be anything but dear to those who love the memories of
the past, and who also reflect that the family has been made for ever
illustrious by giving one of its sons to the white-robed army of martyrs
who witnessed to that faith with their blood.  And it is with the

---

* This Sir Thomas was the first Ingleby of Ripley, having married the heiress, Lady
Edeline de Ripley, about 1330.  He was a judge of the King's Bench from 1361–77,
when presumably he died.  His tomb " is one of the most perfectly fashioned types of the
camail period of the time of Edward III. extant.  The Lady Edeline appears on the right
of her husband to indicate her prerogative as heiress.  This altar-tomb of wrought limestone is said to have been brought from the older church about A.D. 1400."—(SPEIGHT,
*Nidderdale.*)  Mr. John Foster, who is descended from the Inglebys, and is a great authority
on their history, informs me that in his opinion Speight is mistaken here, and that the
Lady Edeline belonged to the Thwenge family.  The arms on the tomb impaled with
those of Ingleby (and also on an illuminated pedigree in possession of Sir Henry Ingilby)
are of Thwenge, viz., *or, a fess between three popinjays vert*.  He thinks Sir Thomas Ingleby
got Ripley in some way from the Crown, for Knaresboro' and all the neighbourhood then
belonged to the Crown.  Originally Ripley was probably a sort of fortified Peel Tower,
and Padside Hall was the family residence.  In time of war the family migrated to the
shelter of Ripley.

R

invocation of the Venerable Francis Ingleby in our hearts and on our lips that we stand to gaze at the fair picture presented by his ancient home.

Looking from the north, we see on our left the castle, belted round by its park, mirrored in the waters of the stream, which here widens out into a lake. A little to the right stands the gate-house, a fine specimen of its class, still untouched by the vandal hand of the restorer, just as it was when the future martyr passed in and out of it.

The gate-house opens on to a private road which divides it from the churchyard, and which, skirting the old wall of the park, runs down the hill towards the water. Beyond the gate-house we see the church-tower rising from its bower of trees, and still further to the right, a large old-fashioned house, the vicarage. The whole picture is a charming one, such as, indeed, can hardly be seen elsewhere than in England. It is the old mediæval picture, the village, the castle, and the church, where our Catholic forefathers worshipped God, side by side, peasant and knight together; and it embodies to the understanding eye a long story of chivalrous deeds and simple pastoral life, carrying us back to the good old days when England was merry because she was Catholic.

But to the pilgrim, Ripley Castle has a far higher, deeper interest; to him it is a shrine. And hither one afternoon on a bright August day, the writer made his way to glean what he could of the life of the martyr of Ripley from the stones of his ancient home. He was hospitably and kindly received by those who now bear the ancient name, and the first thing that he was shown was the martyr's portrait, hanging over the fireplace in the Castle library. This portrait was discovered not many years ago in some lumber-room of the Castle, whither no doubt it had been relegated when the Inglebys lost the faith for which their ancestors had died. But now it has been brought to light again, and hung in its place of honour. It is a small painting on panel, and has never before been reproduced. We owe it to the kindness of Sir Henry Ingilby, the present Baronet, that we are able to show it to our readers, for it has been photographed expressly for this purpose. Curiously enough, the picture, as it is now hung, has a pendant, and that is the portrait of the Queen who sent Francis Ingleby to his death !

We found that little was known of the martyr's life at Ripley Castle, and it was even supposed that he had committed the crime for which he nominally suffered—that of high treason. This account, therefore, of his life and martyrdom was compiled in the first place for the martyr's family, that they might honour him as he deserves. But here we venture to lay it before a wider circle, that God may be glorified yet more in His saints.

130

RIPLEY CASTLE

Yorks:    White Aug 1910.

But before we close this introduction, we may add a few details as to the Castle and the family history.

The illustration gives a good idea of the former. The fine old gate-house dates from the middle of the fifteenth century. Over the archway are sculptured the arms of Ingleby impaled with those of Strangeways. This fixes the date, for John Ingleby, who married Margaret, a daughter of that knightly house, was born in 1434 and died in 1457.

The present Castle is of later date, and has been sadly modernised. When Pennant visited it in 1773 it was still unchanged. He describes it as partly a tower embattled, but "a more ancient house still remains of wood and plaster, and solid wooden stairs. The entrance to this house is through a porch, the descent into it by three steps ; the hall is large and lofty, has its bow windows, its elevated upper table, and its table for vassals, and is floored with brick." Not long after this all these ancient features disappeared. The massive tower at the angle of the building, which is shown so prominently in the drawing is the least altered part. It dates from 1555. It was, in fact, built by Sir William Ingleby, our martyr's father, at this time, as we learn from an inscription carved on the frieze of the panelling of the "Knight's Chamber," which is the principal feature of the interior of the tower, and is approached by a staircase in the turret. This inscription runs : "In the year of our Ld. M.D.L.V. was this house buylded by Sir Wyllyam Inglbi, Knight, Phelip and Marie reigning that time." *

This upper chamber is a fine room, as the drawing shows, and the only one in the Castle which has maintained its ancient appearance. Here are preserved some very precious manuscripts, many of which were saved by the Ingleby of the day from the wreck of Fountains Abbey. This famous Cistercian House of "Our Lady of the Fountains" is situated only some five miles away, as the crow flies. Thus the Inglebys had good opportunities of saving these grand old illuminated books, opportunities which they, fervent Catholics as they were, were not slow to use. The writer spent a very happy hour among these treasures, which were kindly laid out for his inspection by his host. There is also a fine collection of ancient armour and various weapons, and a valuable collection of gold and silver coins and medals.

The park and gardens of the Castle are exceedingly pretty and well

---

* In another place the following quaint carving occurs :
"Better ys povertie with mirthe and gladness
Than ys riches with soro and sadness.
I.H.C.—I.H.C. be our spede . Amen . Mon Droit. made by me
Sir Willyam Ingilby Kt. in the second yeare of our Sovereign
Lord Kynge Edward, 1548. I.H.C., Keep, keep the Founder."

THE KNIGHTS CHAMBER
Ripley Castle.

laid out. During the summer months the gardens are kindly thrown open to the public, and visitors to Harrogate are not slow to avail themselves of the privilege. The Castle, however, is not shown.

The family was one of the most faithful of Yorkshire, and was allied with many of the chief knightly families of that Catholic shire. Thus the Inglebys of Ripley were closely related to their near neighbours, the Mallorys of Studley Royal, the Nortons of Norton Conyers, the Markenfields of Markenfield, the Brimhams of Knaresborough, the Yorkes of Goulthwayt, the Plumptons of Plumpton, the Vavasours or Newton Hall, all famous for their devotion to the ancient faith in the midst of persecution. If they have now lost that faith, it is some compensation that their neighbours, the Radcliffes of Rudding, have happily regained it, while the late Catholic Marquis of Ripon, the Lord of Studley Royal, was a direct descendant of the Mallory who defended the faith in the days of the sixth Edward. The hamlet of Bishop Thornton, close to Ripley, is still a stronghold of the old religion, which has never died out there. The Trappes of Nidd Hall, and the Slingsbys of Scriven, close to Knaresborough, were also staunchly Catholic; so that here, if anywhere in England, the pilgrim finds the very air laden with historic memories of his faith.*

Our martyr's great-grandfather, John Ingleby, of Ripley, died in 1502. His wife was Elinor, daughter of Sir Marmaduke Constable of Everingham, another grand old family of Yorkshire Catholics. Their son, William Ingleby, married Cecily, daughter and heiress of Sir George Talboys of Kyme, and their son, our martyr's father, Sir William Ingleby, married Anne, daughter of Sir William Mallory of Studley Royal. Sir William Ingleby died in 1578 or 1579 (he was buried at Ripley) leaving a large family of five sons and eight daughters. His will is dated from "Padsidehead" in the Forest, a homestead apparently as commodious as the Castle itself. His interment in Ripley Church must have been a memorable event in the Dale. He left £23 6s. 8d. (equal to about £200 of our money) for the "charges of the funerall dinner." His portrait is still preserved in the Castle. He is clothed in the armour of the period, with neck-ruff and mail collar, and épaulières with ornamental edge which nearly meet across the cuirass.

To show that our martyr came of good Catholic stock on either side

---

* A recent historian of Nidderdale (Mr. H. Speight, to whose industry I owe many details of topographical interest) writes: "In the reign of Elizabeth there was probably hardly a family in this neighbourhood that was not Roman Catholic at heart. In 1604 there were at least one hundred persons declared Recusants in the three neighbouring parishes of Farnham with Scotton, Nidd, and Ripley. No part of Yorkshire was more rampant with Romanism."

we may quote a story, told in the *Chronicle of St. Monica's, Louvain*, of his maternal grandfather :

"This Sir William Mallory was so zealous and constant a Catholic that when heresy first came into England, and Catholic service commanded to be put down on such a day, he came to the church, and stood there at the door with his sword drawn to defend, that none should come in to abolish religion, saying that he would defend it with his life, and continued for some days keeping out the officers as long as he possibly could do it." This must have been in the time of Edward VI. when the ancient services were abolished, and the First Book of Common Prayer substituted for them, in the year 1549. The church the good knight so stoutly defended was no doubt the old chapel at Aldfield near Studley Royal. This chapel has been replaced by a splendid modern church, built by Lady Ripon, which forms a prominent feature of the landscape, at the end of a long avenue in the park of Studley Royal.

The spirit of Sir William Mallory lived long in his descendants. In the same *Chronicle* a very similar story is told of Sir William Babthorpe, the great-grandson of his daughter Ann, Lady Ingleby.

"He came at length into great trouble for his zeal in defence of religion, by reason that having two priests found in his house, he would have agreed with the pursuivants for money to let them go, but when he saw that by no fair means they would do it, he determined by force to rescue them out of their hands. Therefore, being a tall, strong man, he made no more ado, but drew out his sword, and made the priests to depart away, keeping the pursuivants the while in such fear with his naked sword that none of them durst resist him. But afterwards they complained to the Justice, and it was esteemed a great contempt so to resist these vile officers, wherefore he was fined to pay such a sum of money as brought him to great poverty, besides imprisonment almost a whole year."

But to return to Sir William Ingleby and his children.

The eldest son, also Sir William, died without surviving issue, although he married twice, his two wives being both heiresses, the first, Anne Thwaites of Marston, who died in 1570 ; the second, Catherine Smythe or Smethley of Brantingham. He was buried at Ripley, January 25, 1617–18, and his second wife survived him only ten months. The second son, David, married Anne, daughter of Charles Neville, Earl of Westmoreland, the leader (with Blessed Thomas Percy, Earl of Northumberland) of the second Pilgrimage of Grace, the famous Northern Rising of 1569. We have already told the story of their fate in the account of Markenfield Hall. David Ingleby had three daughters, Mary, Frances, and Ursula. The third son was John, who

135

died in infancy; the fourth, Francis, our martyr, who, as it is quaintly put in *Betham's Baronetage*, "died young." The fifth was Sampson, who married Jane, the daughter of Mr. Lambert of Killinghall, and whose son William (born in 1594 at Spofforth Castle) was heir to his uncle, Sir William. Sampson Ingleby became steward of the Yorkshire estates of Henry, ninth Earl of Northumberland in succession to Thomas Percy, the Gunpowder Plot conspirator. He lived in this capacity, for some years, at Spofforth Castle, the ancient home of the Percies, whose splendid ruins may still be visited, close to the railway line between Harrogate and Wetherby. He is said to have been a very trusty man, and his portrait still hangs on the wall of Ripley Castle. He died July 18, 1604, and his widow was presented as a Recusant by the minister and churchwardens of Spofforth parish in the same year. Sampson Ingleby left besides his son, five daughters, Anne, Catherine, Mary, Jane and Elizabeth; the last named became a Franciscan nun at the English monastery at Brussels, the community which is now flourishing at Taunton. All these daughters of Sampson Ingleby were good Catholics, but I fear that their brother Sir William (who was created a baronet in 1642 and died in 1657–8) must have given up his faith and conformed to the new religion.

But to return to the martyr's own family.

His next brother was John, the fifth son of Sir William, who married Catherine, daughter of Sir William Babthorpe of Babthorpe and Osgodby, and relict of George Vavasour of Spaldington, Esquire. The Vavasours and Babthorpes are among the most famous of Yorkshire families, and were always staunch Recusants.

Jane, our martyr's eldest sister, married George Wyntour, second son of Robert Wyntour of Coldwell and Huddington, County Worcester. This is noteworthy, for it throws a light on a tragic episode of English history.

Jane Ingleby, by this marriage became the mother of two sons, Robert and Thomas Wyntour, well known for their share in the Gunpowder Plot. A Protestant writer,* who has lately written the sad history of these Wyntours of Huddington, most truly remarks: "Great was their crime, monstrous in its conception, and mad in its development. But equally criminal was the Government, which denied to its subjects liberty of conscience and freedom of religious worship"; and he reminds us that the story of the sufferings and martyrdom of Francis Ingleby, their uncle, was doubtless learned by the Wyntour brothers at their mother's knee, making a deep and lasting impression upon their young minds. Jane

* Mr. John Humphreys, F.L.S., *The Wyntours of Huddington and the Gunpowder Plot.* (Transactions of the Birmingham Archæological Society, 1905.)

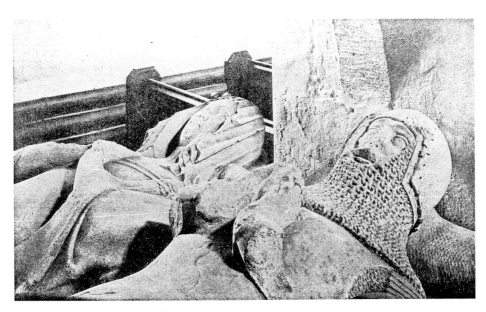

SIR THOMAS AND DAME EDELINE INGLEBY
*From their tomb in Ripley Church.   Photo by the author*

THE TOMB OF SIR THOMAS AND DAME EDELINE
FROM THE SOUTH.   *Photo by the author*

*To face page* 136

Ingleby, happily, did not live to see the tragic fate of her sons, and that of John Grant, the husband of her daughter Dorothy, who was also one of the conspirators.

The next sisters of the martyr were Dorothy, Susanna and Isabel, the last named married Thomas Markenfield of Markenfield Hall, son and heir of Thomas Markenfield, one of the principal supporters of Charles, Earl of Westmoreland, in the Crusade of 1569. The grand old Gothic Hall of the Markenfields was built, as we have said, about 1310 and added to in the fifteenth and sixteenth centuries. Francis Ingleby must often have visited it ; he prayed doubtless in its exquisite Gothic Chapel ; though he was but a boy of twelve when, after the failure of the Rising, the Markenfields had to fly for their lives, and their ancestral estates were forfeited to the crown.

Francis had four other sisters, Elizabeth, wife of Peter Yorke of Goulthwaite, eldest son of Sir John Yorke ; Katharine, wife of William Arthington of Arthington (who was presented for recusancy by the parish of Dacre Pasture in 1604), Frances, and Grace, wife of William Byrnand of Knaresborough, who became mother of one noble daughter, Grace, Lady Babthorpe, of whom we shall hear more.

The Yorkes, the Byrnands and the Arthingtons were among the noblest families of the West Riding of Yorkshire. They were all staunch to the old faith.

It only remains to give the ancient arms of the Ingleby family, before we proceed to recount what is known of the life of its most illustrious scion. They are thus given by Glover (*Yorkshire Visitations*, 1612). Arms : Quarterly, 1. *Sable, an estoile argent*, Ingleby of Ripley. 2. Gules, *a lion rampant argent, within a border engrailed or*, Mowbray de Colton. 3. *Argent, a fesse crenellé between three falcons' heads erased sable, beaked or*, Chaumont de Colton, and 4. *Argent, a chevron between three lions' heads erased gules*, Rocliff de Rocliff.

Crest : *A boar's head, couped erect argent, armed or*. Motto, *Mon droit.**

For those who are uninitiated in the fascinating mysteries of heraldry, a word of explanation may be useful.

The Ingleby arms are those first named ; they show a six-pointed silver star upon a black field. By marriage with heiresses they have become entitled to quarter these arms with those of the other three families mentioned, *i.e.* to divide their shield into four divisions, their own arms taking the place of honour in the top left hand (dexter) corner. So that the whole shield shows in the first quarter the silver star of the

---

* Legend says that the crest was granted to the family by one of the Edwards, whose life was saved by an Ingleby from the tusks of a wild boar.

Inglebys ; in the second, the silver lion of the Mowbrays, rampant on a red field, within a border engrailed of gold ; in the third, the three black falcons' heads, with golden beaks, of the Chaumonts, separated by a horizontal battlemented bar, which makes a black line across the silver shield, and lastly the three red lions' heads of the Rocliffs, separated by a red chevron (which is a figure in the shape of the letter V inverted), so that one of the lions' heads is in the lower part of the field below the chevron, and the other two in the corners above it.

The crest, which surmounted the knightly helmet of the Lord of Ripley, was a silver boar's head, upright, with golden tusks.

We have said that it appears that Sir William, the first baronet, son of Sampson Ingleby, was the first of his family to conform. We are not sure of this, but from this date the Inglebys made no more Catholic alliances. Their kinsmen, the Inglebys of Lawkland Hall, retained the faith until the beginning of the nineteenth century. The legitimate succession of the Inglebys of Ripley failed in 1772 at the death of the fourth baronet. Curiously enough there have been two new creations of the baronetcy, in 1781, and again in 1866. The family now spell their name Ingilby, as, indeed, they often did from the beginning.

So much by way of introduction to the life of the martyr of Ripley Castle.

The venerable Servant of God, Francis Ingleby, was the fourth son of Sir William Ingleby, of Ripley, County York, Knight, treasurer of Berwick, and Dame Anne, his wife, daughter of Sir William Mallory of Studley, Knight. He was born in 1557, the last year of Queen Mary the Catholic, only two years after his father had rebuilt his ancient home. Thus his birth almost synchronised with the change of religion, which was to bring such grievous suffering to his family, and gain for him the martyr's crown.

He at first studied law in London. Father William Warford, S.J., writes : "I saw him in 1582, when he had made a good start in his profession, and heard him commenting with great discretion, but very fluently, on the frauds practised by the Earl of Leicester in perverting the laws of the country."

But he resolved that he could serve God better as a priest, and he therefore left his profession, and went over seas to the English seminary established at Rheims, where he studied theology and prepared himself for the perilous duties of a missionary priest in England. He arrived at the English College, August 18, 1582.

He received the subdiaconate at Laon, May 15, the diaconate at Rheims, from the hands of the Cardinal de Guise, September 24, and on December 24, 1583, he was ordained priest in the grand old cathedral
138

The Shambles, YORK.

Joseph Pike
Aug 1910.

that surmounts the hill at Laon.   He said his first Mass on Christmas Day.   On April 5, 1584, he left Rheims on his return to England. His short missionary career was spent in the North, principally if not entirely in his own county.   Though the persecution of Catholics was then at its height, yet in the worst of times his labours are said to have borne great fruit.

Among his chief friends and supporters was the saintly Margaret Clitherowe, who, at the risk of her life, sheltered him in her own house in the Shambles at York, and provided him with all that was necessary for fulfilling his sacred office.

In 1585 the cruel and sanguinary law was passed by which it was made high treason for any Englishman, made priest by the authority of Rome since the first year of Elizabeth, to return into the kingdom or remain there ; and felony for any person to harbour or relieve any such priest.   By these statutes it was only necessary to prove that a man was a Catholic priest, in order to condemn him to the most cruel and shameful death ; and many were the victims who were sacrificed under these unjust laws.   When these laws came into force, a priest (perhaps Mr. Ingleby himself) who had frequently said Holy Mass in Mrs. Clitherowe's house, came to warn her of the risk she was running in relieving priests.   But she, being filled with the desire for martyrdom, was greatly rejoiced at the news, and said, " By God's grace all priests shall be more welcome to me than ever they were, and I will do what I can to set forward God's Catholic service."

On March 10, 1586, in the beginning of Lent, the sheriffs of York came to search her house.   They whipped a little boy until he showed them the priest's chamber, and the hiding-place where she concealed the church vestments, Catholic books and other treasures.   These they carried off, but they could not find Mr. Ingleby.

Margaret Clitherowe was committed to prison, and on the feast of the Annunciation, March 25, 1586 (which was also Good Friday), she suffered a most cruel and barbarous martyrdom, being pressed to death in the Tollbooth on Ousebridge, at York, for having harboured Mr. Francis Ingleby and another priest, Mr. John Mush.

They stripped her and laid her on the ground, tying her hands (outstretched in the form of a cross) to two stakes.   They then put upon her a door, and on that heaped stones to the weight of five or six hundredweight.   She was a quarter of an hour in dying, and in the very pangs of death she cried : " Jesu, Jesu, help me.   Blessed Jesu, I suffer this for Thy sake," and so in terrible agony she yielded up her blessed soul to God.   One of her hands is kept as a relic at St. Mary's Convent, York, to this day.

"Jam hiems, transiit, imber-
abiit, et recessit: surge, amica
mea, et veni." — Off. Parv.
B. Mariæ ad Vesperas.

VENERABLE MARGARET CLITHEROWE

*To face page* 140

BISHOPTHORPE
YORK THos Pike 1910.

Francis Ingleby, for whom this heroic woman had gladly given her life, did not, however, escape long, if indeed he had not already been taken before her martyrdom on March 25. The manner of his apprehension is related by two contemporary writers.

"On a certain day he left York on foot in the dress of a poor man, without a cloak, and was courteously accompanied beyond the gates by a certain Catholic of that city, named Mr. Lassie (Lacy). The gentleman, though intending to return at once, stayed for a few moments' conversation with the priest on an open spot, called Bishopsfields, which, unknown to the priest, was overlooked by the window of the Archbishop's palace of Bishopthorpe. It happened that two chaplains of the Archbishop, idly talking there, espied them and noticed that the Catholic, as he was taking leave, frequently uncovered to Ingleby, and showed him while saying good-bye, greater marks of respect than were fitting towards a common person meanly dressed."

The other account says that Mr. Lacy knelt down on parting and craved the holy priest's blessing. In any case the two clergymen were struck by the marks of respect paid to the unknown, and suspected that he was a priest. They ran, therefore, and made inquiries, and finding that he was indeed a priest, they apprehended him and had him brought before the Council of the North, then sitting at the Old Palace, York, under the presidency of the Earl of Huntingdon, for the suppression of the Catholic religion.

The Council said to the martyr that "they marvelled that he, being a gentleman of so great calling, would abase himself to be a priest. He answered that he made more account of his priesthood than of all other titles whatsoever."

He was therefore committed a prisoner to the Castle, where he had a pair of fetters laid upon his legs at the prison door. The Catholic prisoners, who were confined there in large numbers for their religion, craved his blessing. With a smiling countenance he said: "I fear me I shall be overproud of my new boots," meaning his fetters. At the time of his imprisonment a minister, as usual, came to him to dispute about religion.

"After Whitsuntide next following (1586) at the gaol delivery, Sir Thomas Fairfax, vice-president, Henry Cheeke, Esquire, Ralph Huddlestone, Esquire, and the rest of the Council, arraigned Mr. Ingleby, and condemned him as a traitor because he was a priest of Rheims. With him they used much guileful dealing that they might entangle him with an oath to disclose in what Catholic men's houses he had been harboured, but they could not deceive him. When he was about to speak anything, they stopped him with railings and blasphemies,

The Guildhall. York.                    Joseph Pike. 1910.

overthwarting him in every word, and interrupting him by one frivolous question after another, so that before he had answered two words to one matter, they came upon him with another, inasmuch that many noted how they could not suffer him to make a perfect end of any one sentence, and this they did to make him contemptible in the eyes of the people." When he refused to take the oath of supremacy, which acknowledged the Queen to be the supreme governor of the Church, he said : "I will give unto the Queen subjection in so far forth that she has protection." And when he was condemned to death he spoke these words : "*Credo videre bona Domini in terra viventium*" ("I believe that I shall see the good things of the Lord in the land of the living.")

Mr. Henry Cheeke, a member of the Council, openly derided and scoffed at the martyr because, when standing at the bar, he made the sign of the cross. It was noted at the time that within a few hours this man fell downstairs and broke his neck. Huddlestone had also a sudden and terrible death, falling down dead while waiting, in the ante-chamber of the Archbishop, for leave to put some poor Catholics to the torture.

When the martyr was led from the place of judgment (no doubt the ancient Guildhall) back again into the Castle, the Catholic prisoners, looking forth of their windows, craved his blessing. Privily he gave it them, saying : "O sweet judgment!" After his condemnation he showed such tokens of inward joy that the keeper (named Mr. Meverell) said that he took no small pleasure to observe his sweet and joyous conversation, and though he was a very earnest Puritan, he could not abstain from tears. He suffered on June 3, 1586, at the Tyburn at Knavesmire, which was situated about a mile and a half beyond Micklegate Bar, on the London road, near the present race-course. The place is still well known to the York Catholics, and an annual pilgrimage is made to it on Whitsun Tuesday in honour of the martyrs. Hither Margaret Clitherowe had been used to come in pilgrimage at midnight, walking barefoot from her house in the Shambles, and praying to the priests who had suffered there that she, too, might gain the martyrs' crown.*

The sentence ran that he was to be drawn to the place of execution, where he was to be hanged, and then the halter was to be cut immediately, and while still fully alive, the sufferer was to be disembowelled and dismembered, and his heart torn out before his eyes. The body was then to be quartered, after being parboiled in a cauldron, and set up on the various gates of the city. All this was carried out in the case of the holy martyr, Francis Ingleby.

* An old print of York preserved in the Merchant Adventurers' Hall in that city, shows the Tyburn with its gallows. It was a triple tree like that of London.

THE VENERABLE FRANCIS INGLEBY
*From the original portrait at Ripley Castle*     *To face page* 144

But the persecutors could not touch his blessed soul, which was received into the joy of its Lord, and obtained the unfading crown of those who persevere to the end, and who give the supreme pledge of love by surrendering even life itself for conscience' sake.

"Great was the loss to York," writes his friend, Father Warford, "for he was most highly esteemed by all Catholics on account of his great zeal for souls, and especially for his remarkable prudence. He bore himself most constantly and bravely, and left all Catholics sore afflicted at his loss. They have preserved the memory of many of his sayings and doings, which are indeed worthy of note, though I cannot now recall them in detail.

"He was a short man, but well made, and seemed thirty-five years of age or thereabouts. He was of light complexion, wore a chestnut beard and had a slight cast in his eyes. In mind he was quick and piercing, ready and facile in speech, of aspect grave and austere, and earnest and assiduous in action."

It may be noted that his eldest brother William's wife, then Mrs. Ingleby, was a most devout and fervent Catholic, who suffered much for her religion. On March 25, 1592, she was with Lady Babthorpe, Lady Constable, Mrs. Metham, Mrs. Lawson, and Mrs. Hungate, committed by the Lord President to Sheriff Hutton Castle, where they were locked up, each separately, and not allowed a maid to wait on them, or to see their husbands or friends. They also had to pay large sums for their board. Here they were kept for nearly two years, the President sending every now and then ministers to dispute with them. They could have gained their release at any time, if they had been willing to go to the Protestant service. The keeper told them that he was bound in four hundred pounds that they should not speak with each other. But Lady Babthorpe told him he was very simple to bind himself in such manner, "for," said she, "a man hath enough to do to keep one woman, and would you undertake to keep and rule six women ?"

As a matter of fact, they contrived sometimes to meet, and even get a priest into the prison to give them the Holy Sacraments.

This was chiefly owing to the courage and resource of young Lady Babthorpe, our martyr's niece. She had "a hundred tricks and devices to cozen the keepers," and actually contrived to remove a whole window, so that the priest might enter. "For, taking a chisel and a hammer, and getting some to play at shuttlecock, that they might not hear her at such times as she cut the freestone of the window on the inside, where bars of the grate went in, so long time till she could take in the whole window, and let in the priest, and when he was gone, put up the grate again, and nothing was seen on the outside."

T                                                                    145

When the Lord President, "a most rank heretic," examined her as to when she had gone to the Protestant services, she answered him: "Never." He then demanded how many Masses she had heard. She said: "So many that she could not reckon them." At this he began to stamp!

Her companions were of the like courage, more courageous indeed than their husbands, some of whom had yielded to the times so far as to go to church, though it seems probable that they all died good Catholics.

These brave ladies were connected with one another by blood or marriage. Lady Constable was Margaret, daughter of Sir William Dormer, sister of the first Lord Dormer, and of the saintly Jane Dormer, Duchess of Feria, who had been Queen Mary's favourite lady-in-waiting. She was thus a grand-niece of the Carthusian martyr, Blessed Sebastian Newdigate. She was the wife of Sir Henry Constable of Holderness in Yorkshire, and her only son was created Viscount Dunbar in 1620. She is described by Strype as "an obstinate Recusant not to be reformed by any persuasion nor yet by coercion."

Her saintly daughter, Dorothy, married Roger Lawson, of Heaton, the son of her fellow prisoner, Mrs. Lawson. This Mrs. Lawson was the wife of Ralph Lawson (afterwards Sir Ralph), of Brough, near Catterick, in Yorkshire, a family still Catholic. She had nine children, one of whom was born while she lay a prisoner in Sheriff Hutton Castle. This nearly cost her her life.

Mrs. Ingleby was probably Catherine Smythe or Smethley of Brantingham, the second wife of William Ingleby. Grace, Lady Babthorpe, was her niece by marriage, being the daughter of Grace Ingleby, our martyr's sister. Lady Babthorpe had been left an orphan at an early age and had been brought up at Ripley Castle by her grandmother, Lady Ingleby. Thus she must have been on intimate terms with her saintly uncle, whose spirit she had certainly imbibed. Her wonderful life story is told in the fascinating *Chronicle of St. Monica's, Louvain*, where she died a professed nun in 1635, aged about 64.

Mrs. Hungate was Margaret Sotheby, wife of William Hungate of Saxton, Esquire; both she and her husband were presented for recusancy in 1604. The Methams of Metham were also among the staunchest of Yorkshire Catholics, and Father Thomas Metham, S.J., died in prison for the faith.

Sheriff Hutton Castle, where they were confined, is still a most imposing ruin. It lies about two miles north of Flaxton Station, on the line between Malton and Scarborough. It was a royal castle, and had served as a prison for even more illustrious captives, the Princess Elizabeth of York, afterwards Queen of Henry VII., and Edward

146

THE WEEPING CROSS, RIPLEY

OLD OUSE BRIDGE, YORK
*With the Chapel of St. William converted into a prison*     *To face page* 146

Plantagenet, Earl of Warwick, the only brother of Blessed Margaret Pole, the martyred Countess of Salisbury. It was built about 1410 by Ralph Neville, First Earl of Westmoreland, on so great a scale that Leland says, "he saw no house in the North so like a princely lodging."

It had, however, fallen into much decay at the time of which we are writing, and was by no means a princely lodging for these Catholic ladies. But here they were kept, and if the Lord President had had his way, here they would have remained for the rest of their lives.

At last, however, after two years, their husbands got them released, through bribing some of the ladies at court to intercede with the Queen for them.

We have gleaned one or two more allusions to Venerable Francis Ingleby. At his martyrdom, one Humphrey Mountain, who would have taken some of his blood as a relic, was arrested and carried off to prison at the castle.

"When Sir Francis Ingleby, priest, was to come over Ousebridge on a hurdle to execution, Robert Bickerdyke, going over the way to the Tollbooth (which stood on the bridge), a minister's wife in the street, on his way, said to her sister, who was with her: 'Let us go into the Tollbooth and we shall see the traitorly thief come over on the hurdle.' 'No, no thief,' quoth he: 'as true as thou art.' He said no more words than these, but they were the cause of his death, for he was denounced as a Catholic and he suffered martyrdom in his turn." Robert Bickerdyke was born at Low Hall, near Scotton, in the parish of Farnham, near Knaresborough, so that he was a neighbour of the Inglebys, and must have known our martyr well. He may very probably have been reconciled to the Church by Francis Ingleby. He could have saved his life by consenting to go to church, but preferred to die; and so he bravely suffered at the York Tyburn, October 8, 1586, only four months after the priest whose fair fame he had defended at the cost of his life.

There are still Catholic Bickerdykes in the West Riding, who claim relationship with this brave, chivalrous young martyr.

One most precious relic of Venerable Francis Ingleby still remains to us, the martyr's right hand, now preserved among the many relics of the English martyrs at the Franciscan convent, Taunton. It was brought to that community by his three nieces, Elizabeth, the daughter of Sampson Ingleby, and Marie and Grace, daughters of John Ingleby and Katherine Babthorpe. These three nieces of our martyr made their profession in the community, then settled at Brussels, on September 17, in the year 1624. The confessor at the convent was at that time the glorious martyr, Venerable Francis Bell, O.F.M., and he has himself written the record of their profession in the community archives, which are still preserved. The Rev. Father Andrew à Soto, Commissary-General of the Order this side of the Alps, presided at the ceremony. Elizabeth Ingleby, who took the name of Sister Elizabeth Joseph, had been born at Spofforth. She was in her twenty-third year at her profession. She died September 9, 1662, and the Annals quaintly say, " She was a parson of a most exemplar and labourious life, and prudent and discreet." She was buried at Bruges, whither the community migrated the year of her death. Her two cousins had predeceased her, and had died during the sojourn of the community at Nieuport.

Grace, called in religion Sister Francis Clare, died December 6, 1639, in the forty-second year of her age. She had been Mistress of Novices for ten years, when " by an edifying, confident, and most pious death, she left us to enjoy her more desired Spouse and Saviour, Christ Jesus . . . whose blessed departure comforted her sorrowful friend and so unworthy confessor, who, as he assisted her passage and buried her ashes, so is he confident of her intercession."

Marie, called in religion Sister Marie a Sta. Cruce, died May 25, 1658. These two sisters were born, Marie at Harewell and Grace " at the same place, within a mile, at Dacres Hall in Yorkshire."

Their peaceful lives and deaths in holy religion form a striking contrast to the cruel martyrdom of their saintly uncle, whose hand they cherished as their greatest treasure, and gave to their community as the most precious portion of their dowry.

# AN OXFORD MARTYR*

THE visitor to Oxford cannot fail to be impressed by a stately monument erected in a commanding position in the old city, hard by the beautiful Church of St. Mary Magdalen. It looks down the magnificent avenue known as "St. Giles'," while opposite to it, at the other end of that avenue, stands the old-world church of that name. The monument, though evidently modern, is designed after the pattern of those Eleanor Crosses which the first Edward raised to the memory of his beloved consort. So fair is it that it awakes the admiration of the stranger, and he stops to ask what it may be. He is told that it is called the "Martyrs' Memorial."

He then observes that the figures which ornament this beautiful Gothic Cross are not those of Catholic saints, but of Protestant divines, clad in the garb of Geneva. And he gathers, if he has patience to decipher a long inscription, that this Memorial was erected in 1841 as a tribute of homage to three famous Anglican Bishops who here suffered the penalties inflicted in their day on obstinate and relapsed heretics—in a word, this is the monument of Cranmer, Ridley, and Latimer, who were executed hard by in the reign of Queen Mary.

This gives rise to various and varied reflections. The Catholic regrets, as much as the Protestant, the barbarities of the past, or, rather, his regrets are far more poignant, for he realises how much harm they have done to the sacred cause he cherishes. Perhaps he feels with the great Pugin that this is "the most painfully beautiful" monument in Oxford, and perhaps he envies the blissful ignorance of the Catholic Bishop from China, who admired it so much that he wished he could carry it off with him and erect it outside his Cathedral! On the other hand, Oxford Anglicans themselves regard it with mingled feelings. There was one old dignitary of High Church views who used to salute it as he passed, explaining to his scandalised companion that he was "thanking God that he belonged to the University which burned those blackguards!" Others, without going to these lengths, heartily regret the erection of the Monument, and console themselves with the reflection that the "martyrs" were all of them Cambridge men! "Cambridge nurtured them, and Oxford burned them," they say, not without a spice of malice.

But to the Catholic pilgrim Oxford has memories of martyrs far more glorious and more real. Almost every one of her stately Colleges has given recruits to that white-robed army which has glorified God by their

* The writer wishes to express his acknowledgments to Miss Louise Imogen Guiney, who has most generously given him all her notes on the martyr and his home. Many passages from these appear here without quotation-marks.

blood poured out like water for the ancient Faith and the primacy of
the Apostolic See, in the dark days of national apostasy. Oxford, indeed,
is only of late waking up to this fact. She hardly knows the names
of many of these martyrs of hers, yet there are signs that she is at last
beginning to appreciate her treasures. Two years ago in the " Oxford
Magazine," the principal organ of the University, appeared an epigram,
which, though but a trifle, may yet serve to show the direction of the
wind. It ran as follows :

> " To be mother of martyrs, proud Cambridge is fain,
> Cranmer, Latimer, Ridley, whom Oxford hath slain :
> But of martyrs less doubtful, which boasts the chief store ?
> True, Cambridge has Fisher, but Oxford has MORE "—

and to the epigram was appended the note that of the Catholic martyrs
beatified by Leo XIII., not only the Blessed Thomas More, but the
vast majority were Oxford men.

It is in honour of one of these true martyrs of Oxford that we are
about to make our pilgrimage.

A quaint old street, full of delightful old houses, leads from the
heart of Oxford, where stand the Bodleian Library, the Sheldonian
Theatre, and the great group of University buildings around them,
down by the outskirts of New College and the ancient wall of the city
towards the ancient Manor of Holywell. Here we are out of the city
proper, in a charming quarter of playing-fields and parks, where young
Oxford takes its pleasure. These green fields form a noble setting for the
picture of the towers and spires and old grey Colleges, which make the
unique beauty of the place.

And here is an ancient Church dedicated to the Holy Cross of Christ,
and beside it a precious fragment of an Elizabethan Manor House—
the Manor House of Holywell.

Our photographs reveal the old grey group of buildings at a glance.
The little chapel with its flèche is, of course, modern, though it contains
the Holy Well which, since Saxon days, has given its name to the place.
Modern, too, and deplorable in its ugliness is the red brick addition of
which the photograph reveals as little as may be. But the building
which lies between these modern intrusions is genuine Elizabethan, and
is something more, for it is the home, if not the birthplace, of a
martyr of Christ.

This old Manor House is the shrine where the sanctuary lamp was
kept burning, in those dark days when Oxford had lost the light. Here,
in some hidden sanctuary, the Holy Mass was celebrated in secret for
two weary centuries of persecution, when the names of Oxford's colleges

150

THE MANOR HOUSE AND CHURCH OF ST. CROSS

HOLYWELL MANOR HOUSE

*To face page* 150

# AN OXFORD MARTYR

—Corpus Christi, and All Souls, and Our Lady of Oriel—had ceased to have any meaning for the sons of Oxford.

Here, at least, the Holy Cross was still venerated, nay more, was fervently embraced, long after it had been forgotten in the Church hard by. And here there grew to manhood a son of Oxford who carried that Cross to his Calvary in Oxford town.

It is the story of the Venerable George Napier of Holywell Manor House that we have to tell.

The Manor was there in Saxon days, we know, and, after the Norman Conquest, came, as did so many other rich properties in this neighbourhood, to Robert d'Oilly, the builder of the Castle. King Henry III. gave it to Merton College, then newly founded. A bundle of rolls, entitled "Holywell," is preserved in Merton College treasury, containing many curious particulars of the Manor. The College, on its own immense lands, had anciently the privilege of its own pound, pillory and gallows, and even a court where wills were proved.

We think of the Manor House standing alone, as it does in Loggan's chart, a grey bulk between the Church and the stream, with fields all about it, and the walls of Oxford, still unbroken, lying north, with glimpses of her towers over or through them. In Elizabeth's time, the south side of Holywell Street began to spring up. There was a group of low roofs facing the churchyard, taken away not many years ago ; and the old sloping cottages opposite the Manor gate may well have slept at the angle of the road, while the sworded Napier men were yet coming and going in the saddle, escorting some quiet stranger who was a "massing-priest" in disguise.

The more antique portion of the present structure is all that remains of the house rebuilt in the latter half of the sixteenth century ; the thick walls, the drip stones, the dark interior panellings, and the little high windows for defence, all date from the Napier days. There is a tiny supposed priest-hole upstairs. If it were not for the modern additions, the whole building would still be in a great measure romantic. It is certainly still interesting, and challenges instant attention, in its quasi-isolation.

The Manor takes its name from the Holy Well, which was dedicated to St. Winifred and St. Margaret. Though long venerated, it was covered up, and practically lost for centuries. Hearne, the antiquary, apparently thinks that the Well and its pilgrims lived on secretly, under the favour of the Napiers. He says : "The ordinary devotions performed by the sick people and other vigilants [at the Well] might be made in the House where distinct rooms were appointed to that end, and all the other suitable accommodation prepared for reception of all

151

comers."* When the Manor passed out of the hands of Catholics, this, of course, all ceased.

The Holy Well came to light again only in our own day, after the old Catholic Manor House had passed into the possession of a Community of Anglican Sisters who there carry on a work of rescue for poor girls. Their little Chapel was built, inadvertently, directly over the Well. In the north wall of this building there is now fixed a tablet, which reads : "Beneath this stone the Holy Well was discovered, 1896, in enlarging this Chapel. The ancient tabular Anglo-Saxon stone was found in its original position outside the existing north wall of the Well chamber. The upper rim of the stone was about 3 ft. 3 ins. from the floor level of the Chapel ; its lower rim was set up on the three stones it still rests on, in the well-chamber below. These three unworked stones were found placed an equal distance apart in the sandy bed of the spring, and upon them the old tabular stone rested."

The small, clean crypt, or well-chamber, is entered by means of a sliding door and steps, from the nave. While the Well was yet "in the garden," but in ruins, it was turned for a while into a bathing-place. It is probable that a chapel, or shrine, stood directly over the Well in mediæval times.

Holier than the Well which gives its name to the place, are the memories of the martyr whose home it was. Let us gather up what history tells of him.

In the reign of Henry VIII., the Manor was leased by Merton College to one William Clare, a well-to-do grazier, who was one of the bailiffs of the City.†

Upon this good man's death, Joan, his widow, married, apparently about 1530, a Fellow of All Souls, one Edward Napier, M.A., who was still a young man.‡ This Edward Napier (or Napper) was from Swyre, in Dorset, and was descended from the Napiers of Merchistoun and Rosky in Scotland, who were scions of the ducal house of Lennox ; while his grandmother was Anne, heiress of John Russell of Swyre, of the family of the Earls (now Dukes) of Bedford.

Edward Napier settled down at Holywell, though not in the present house. His wife died in 1545, leaving him one daughter, Joan, who married Thomas Greenwood, an Oxford barrister. Their family remained faithful Catholics till its extinction in the nineteenth century, and their eldest son, John, of Brize Norton, married a great-granddaughter of

* Hearne's *Collections*, vol. iii. (1710–12). Oxford Hist. Socy, 1889. P. 403.
† *Oxford Post-Reformation Catholic Missions*, by Mrs. Stapleton (University Press, 1906), p. 211. We are greatly indebted to this valuable work.
‡ He was elected Fellow in 1527 and proceeded M.A. in 1530. Boase, *Register*, vol. i.

Blessed Thomas More. Thomas Greenwood himself died in 1577, and was buried in Holywell Church.

Edward Napier, left a widower, married, in 1547,* Anne, daughter of Sir John Peto, of Chesterton in Warwickshire. She was a niece of the famous Cardinal Peto, the Franciscan of Greenwich, who had so boldly withstood Henry VIII. to the face, when he projected his miserable divorce.

By his second wife, Mr. Napier had two sons, William and George. Both were to prove worthy of their father and of their heroic uncle, and the younger was destined to gild the family name with imperishable glory. From the accounts of George Napier's martyrdom, we learn that he was already an old man, and one document (in the Vatican archives) gives his age as about sixty. He was probably born as early as 1548, so that he would be ten years old at his father's death.

For that sad year which saw the death of the Catholic Queen, and that of the last true Archbishop of Canterbury, saw also Holywell Manor House left desolate. Edward Napier was, indeed, happy in the time of his death, for he was spared the sight of the evils to come. He had been a great benefactor to the University, and had given liberally towards the repair of the schools, especially of the Divinity school, which "had been either pulled down or quite ruinated in the time of Edward VI." †

The solemn Requiem Mass at Edward Napier's funeral will have been one of the last that were ever sung in the fine old parish church of St. Peter-in-the-East, where he was laid to rest "in our Lady's Chapel under the upper window by the side of his first wife." ‡ Henceforth Holy Mass in England was to be said in secret at the risk of liberty or life.

In his will, our martyr's father left all his lands in South Petherton, Somerset, to his own College of All Souls, upon condition "that they keep his obit yearly, and give to three of the poorest Fellows of the said College, to be chosen by the Warden, 26s. 8d. apiece yearly, so that they were actually priests, or else within three years after they had first partaken of the said Exhibition." §

Alas! in that most beautiful Chapel of Chichele's foundation, dedicated to the blessed English dead of Agincourt and "to all Christen soules" it is much to be feared that no "obit" is kept for Edward Napier.

---

* The licence is dated January 25, 1546–47. Chester's *London Marriage Licenses,* ed Foster. London, 1887.

† Wood, *History and Antiquities of the University,* vol. ii. part ii. p. 764.

‡ Wood, *City of Oxford,* iii. p. 254.

§ Wood, *History and Antiquities of the University* (1786), vol. iii. p. 264.

U

The widow, Anne Napier, thus left with two little boys (and, as it would appear, some little girls also) re-married with Philip Huckle, of Merton College, a worthy man who leased a large estate from his College. It was he who built the Manor House, which was yet unfinished at the time of his death in 1576.* His wife died some four years earlier.

It was a long time before Elizabeth succeeded in de-Catholicising Oxford, and during the early years of her reign the old religion was still powerful in the University.

George, the future martyr, was educated at an Oxford grammar-school and then at Corpus Christi College, and we have an interesting account of the part which he took in defending that most Catholic foundation against the assaults of the Government.

Anthony Wood may be allowed to tell the story in his own words.†

Thomas Greenway, President of Corpus, having resigned in 1568, the Queen recommended to the choice of the Fellows "one William Cole, sometime Fellow of that College, afterwards an exile in Queen Mary's reign, suffering then very great hardships at Zurich. But the Fellows, who were most inclined to the Roman Catholic persuasion, made choice of a Robert Harrison, M.A., not long since removed from the College by the Visitor for his . . . Religion, not at all taking notice of the said Cole, being very unwilling to have him, his wife and children, and his Zurichian discipline introduced among them.

"The Queen hereupon annulled the election, and sent word to the Fellows that they should elect Cole, for what they had already done, was, as she alleged, against the Statutes. They submissively give answer to the contrary, and add that what they had done was according to their consciences and oaths. The Queen, not content with that answer, sends Dr. Horne, Bishop of Winchester, Visitor of the College, to admit him, but when he and his retinue came, they found the College gate shut against them. At length, after he had made his way in, he repaired to the Chapel, where, after the Senior Fellows were gathered together, told them his business, not unknown (as he said) to them, and then asked each person by seniority, whether they would admit Mr. Cole; but they all denying, as not in a possibility of receding from what they had done, he pronounced them *non Socii*, and then, with the consent of the next Fellows, admitted him.

"About the same time (viz. July 21) a Commission was sent down from the Queen, directed to the Chancellor of the University, the said Bishop of Winchester, Sir William Cecil, Principal Secretary, Thomas Cooper, Lawrence Humphrey, Doctors of Divinity, and George Acworth,

---

* Stapleton, *op. cit.* pp. 211–12.　　†　Wood, *op. cit.* vol. ii. part i. p. 165.

154

CORPUS CHRISTI COLLEGE, OXFORD
*Exterior view from Merton Street*

CORPUS CHRISTI COLLEGE, OXFORD
*From an old print*

*To face page* 154

# AN OXFORD MARTYR

Doctor of the Laws, to visit the said College, and to correct and amend whatsoever they found amiss, and to expel the principal delinquents. The sum of all was that after a strict enquiry and examination of several persons, they expelled some as Roman Catholics, curbed those that were suspected to incline that way, and gave encouragement to the Protestants. Three of those so ejected were Edmund Rainolds, Miles Windsore, and George Napier. The first . . . receded to Gloucester Hall * (a place to which lovers of the Catholic religion retired for their quiet) where he living in great retiredness, arrived to the age of ninety-two, and died a wealthy man . . .

"As for the third, George Napier, he went afterwards beyond the seas, where spending some time in one of the English Colleges, that was about these times erected, came again into England, and lived as a Seminary Priest among his relations, sometimes in Holywell near Oxford, and sometimes in the country near adjoining among those of his profession." †

We may here break off Anthony Wood's narrative. In 1568 George Napier was still a young man, probably about twenty years old. This was not exceptionally young for an Oxford Fellow in those days. Some have indeed conjectured that the Fellow of Corpus cannot have been the martyr, but there is no record of another George Napier in the family history. Wood too, besides his "constitutional accuracy," was an intimate friend of the Napier family, and cannot have been mistaken on so important a question.

As to the President, whom Elizabeth and that bitter Protestant, Bishop Horne, intruded with such violence on a Catholic College, he was no credit to their choice. "As for Mr. Cole," continues Wood, "(who was the first married President that Corpus Christi College ever had) he, being settled in his place, acted so foully by defrauding the College and bringing it into debt, that divers complaints were put up against him to the Bishop of Winchester, Visitor of that College." Horne was obliged to take his friend to task. "Well, well, Mr. President, seeing it is so, you and the College must part without any more ado ; and therefore see that you provide for yourself." Cole was thunderstruck. "What, my good Lord, must I then eat mice at Zurich again ?" he faltered. This allusion to their common exile so touched Horne that he allowed the defaulter to remain, and in

* The ancient Benedictine Hall, now Worcester College.

† It is worth while to point out here that this proceeding of Queen Elizabeth is hushed up and almost unknown : whereas because James II. did the very same arbitrary thing at Magdalen College a century later, a most tremendous "to-do" has been made about it by historians.

155

the end he got no worse punishment than translation to the Deanery of Lincoln !

George Napier, who preferred to be expelled rather than submit to see Bishop Fox's glorious foundation in honour of the Adorable Sacrament desecrated by the government of a married apostate, had no such worldly honours to look for. His was henceforth to tread the Royal Highway of the Holy Cross.

After his expulsion, unfortunately, the records of his movements during the years that follow are very scanty, and there are gaps which it seems impossible to fill up ; but it would seem probable that for some years he lived quietly in England, no doubt chiefly at Holywell.

His stepfather died in 1576, and was succeeded at Holywell by William Napier, our martyr's elder brother. William was a very staunch Catholic, who was willing and glad to risk the terrible dangers of harbouring priests in the new Manor House, which he was left to finish. No doubt he took care to provide several hiding-places in the building. He had provided others elsewhere, as we shall soon see.

Mr. Napier was possessed of considerable property, and no doubt had to pay the cruel recusancy fines. He was himself a Brasenose man, and took his M.A. in 1568, the year of his brother's expulsion from Corpus. George Napier was not, indeed, the only future martyr to be expelled from that College. In 1560 the Venerable James Fenn had been deprived of his fellowship for Popery, and had retired for a time to Gloucester Hall.

William Napier made a good marriage, in the worldly sense of the word, when he espoused Isabel, daughter of Edmund Powell, of Sandford-on-Thames. This family was an important one, but unfortunately it became entangled with the fatal possession of monastic lands, and, though always Catholic, it did not escape the usual fate of such owners. Sandford Manor itself was anciently a Preceptory of the Knights Templars, and the Powells also owned the Mynchery at Littlemore, and the site of the White Friars' Convent at Oxford. Little wonder, then, if they soon became extinct.

Isabel Napier bore her husband seven children, and at her death, in 1584, she must have still been well under forty. Her husband never shrank from sacrifices for the faith he loved so well. Wood tells us that he had a farm at Cowley, near Oxford, and that he let part of the land to a good Catholic mason, named Badger, "who built a house thereon, about the latter end of Queen Elizabeth's reign, for a hiding-hole for a priest, or any other lay-Catholic in times of persecution." We may easily imagine that George, as well as the other priests whom Mr. Napier harboured, used this house.

156

# AN OXFORD MARTYR

Our martyr's life from the time that he was expelled from Corpus in 1568, to his ordination, in 1593, is, as we have said, exceedingly obscure. Only some scattered notices remain to us, which we have pieced together as best we may. The entries in the *Douay Diary* suggest that his career was a very chequered one, but we have no clue as to the reasons, whether of health or other difficulty, which deferred his ordination so long.

In 1574, a "Mr. Napper" was staying at a Mr. Tyrrell's at Rawle, in Essex, and a "false brother," one Davy Johnes, a Protestant minister masquerading as a Catholic, betrayed him to the authorities, but did not succeed in getting him arrested.* From the context it would appear that this Mr. Napper was a priest, but this is not at all certain. George Napier may have been just as obnoxious to the Government for his religious zeal before his ordination as after it. His fidelity at Corpus would have made him a marked man. In 1579, on August 24, a Mr. Napper came to the College at Rheims ; this will no doubt have been our martyr.† He did not, however, stay long in the College, for the next thing we hear of him is that he was in prison in England.

He came to Rheims just in time to see Dr. Allen, who, only three days later, left for Rome with his brother Gabriel and a little party of friends. It is probable that George may have come over principally to see his old Oxford friends at the College, and possibly, also, to consult them about his vocation.

In December, 1580, news came to Rheims that Blessed Ralph Sherwin and other priests had been arrested and thrown into prison, and that besides the priests there had also been arrested four laymen—John Paschall (Sherwin's friend and protegé), Mr. Vavasour, Mr. Dibdale, and Mr. George Napper. Paschall was, we know, in the Marshalsea, but George Napier seems to have been imprisoned in the Counter or Compter, Wood Street, Cheapside. At least we find him there in 1588 or 1589. There is no certainty that his imprisonment lasted all these years ; he may possibly have been released and arrested again in this interval, but it seems more probable that he lay in prison for some nine years. The cause of his imprisonment was simply recusancy, that is to say, the Catholic religion. This we know from the persecutor's own admission.

In the *Lansdowne MSS.* in the British Museum, is a paper ‡ dated September 30, 1588, and endorsed "Certificate of Seminary Priests and Recusants in the prisons in and about London." The prisoners are classified according to their degree of "guilt." The first class are those

* Morris, *Troubles*, series ii. p. 303.   † *Douay Diaries*, p. 155.
‡ Printed C.R.S. vol. ii. (1906), pp. 282–84.

157

" by their own confessions guilty of treason or felony," *i.e.* persons who had confessed that they were Seminary priests, or that they had been reconciled to the Church since 1585, when by statute it had been made treason to be ordained priest abroad and return to England, and felony to be reconciled. Then come other classes, and finally, No. 7 : " These persons are only Recusants." Among this last class is our martyr's name, " George Napper."

Unable to pay the heavy fines for not attending the Protestant service, he had been thrown into prison. We find the reason for his being classed among the least " guilty " of the confessors, in a paper which has fortunately been preserved in the Public Record Office. It is calendared as the " Submission of George Napper," and assigned to the first half of 1589. It is probably, however, somewhat earlier in date. It has never been printed before, so we give it in full.

"I, George Napper, unfeignedly profess and with my whole heart, that I am thoroughly and altogether persuaded, and do truly think in my conscience that the Lady Elizabeth, the Queen's Majesty that now is, is our lawful, true, natural and rightful Queen, and that she hath, and of right ought to have, all superiority, jurisdiction, pre-eminence and authority on all persons within England and Ireland and all other her dominions which any other prince hath, or at any other time hath had, over his own dominions in Christendom : and that no foreign prince, prelate, estate or potentate, may or ought any way to pre-vindicate the said superiority, jurisdiction, pre-eminence or authority within her Majesty's dominions, countries and seignories : and I unfeignedly protest likewise that I have, and ought to have, such care of her Majesty's most royal person, that I will with all my endeavours seek to overthrow and persecute even to the very death all such as shall any way impugn her Highness' life or go about or intend any such traitorous practice, yea, or lift up their finger against her, either to take any drop of blood from her, or to diminish any iota of her foresaid titles within her Majesty's countries, of what estate, condition or degree so ever they be ; which I am, and always will be, ready to aver and justify against all men with my blood.

" In witness whereof I have hereto set my hand.

" By me, GEORGE NAPPER,
" Prisoner in the Compter in Wood Street."

This evidently sincere and heartfelt profession of loyalty to his temporal Sovereign ought, one would imagine, to have saved the writer from the cruel imputation of treason. Yet, as we shall see, it is under that imputation that he died. His statement, as a prisoner, does but

158

embody the sentiments of the vast majority of English Catholics, who were conspicuously loyal throughout the long reign of a Sovereign who, heaping ever new burdens upon their devoted heads, seemed determined to test their heroic fidelity to her person by trials more cruel than death.

That George Napier's loyalty to his Sovereign was without prejudice to that higher loyalty which he owed to the Church and to Christ's Vicar, his whole life and his heroic death sufficiently prove.

We do not know how much longer he remained a prisoner, but he was certainly at Douay in 1594. In the summer of the previous year, the English College had been moved back from Rheims to its original home and George Napier matriculated at the University of Douay on April 1, 1594.* Two years later he was ordained priest.†

About 1591 a well-known priest, who became later on in life a Jesuit, came to stay at Holywell Manor House. This was William Warneford (or Warford) a Yorkshireman of Trinity College. He had been ordained in 1584, and we owe to him some interesting reminiscences of the martyrs he had known at Oxford and elsewhere. Cardinal Allen himself suggested "that Dr. Walford will be well provided for in Oxford with Mr. Napper, a renowned and virtuous Catholic." ‡

Oxford had lately been the scene of martyrdoms,§ therefore it instantly became a most desirable place to those whom a King of England once called "God Almighty's fools." With Father Warford came from abroad one "Napper of Oxford," and eight others. One of the ubiquitous spies reports in July, 1591, "These ten came in one company, arrived about a month since, were brought by a merchant man of London who had £60 for reward. Landed in an out-creek near Plymouth." ‖ We cannot be certain, but it is most probable that it was George Napier, now released from prison and at Rheims, who took this opportunity of visiting his home, and that he came with his friend to Holywell, though it is, of course, just possible that Mr. Napier of Holywell had himself gone abroad in order to bring back the priest in safety to Oxford.

If it were George, he must have soon returned to the College to continue his preparations for the priesthood.

Even after his ordination he did not enter upon his mission work for

---

* *Douay Diaries*, p. 282. The scribe, in the official list of matriculations, calls him, by a slip of the pen, *Gregorius*, instead of Georgius.

† *Ibid.* p. 16.

‡ Cal. Dom. Eliz. 1591–94, p. 28.

§ Ven. George Nicols, Richard Yaxley, priests, Thomas Belson, gentleman, and Humphrey Pritchard, a servant at the Catherine Wheel Inn, were martyred at Oxford Castle, July 5, 1589.　　　　‖ Cal. Dom. Eliz. 1591–94, p. 79.

some years, but went to live at Antwerp, where, according to Challoner, he spent the next seven years, till the end of the reign of Elizabeth. Only after the old Queen's death do we get the entry in the College Diary of George Napier's being sent to labour in the vineyard. It was almost the eleventh hour.

"Anno 1603, [in Angliam missus] Georgius Napperus." *

Seven years of fruitful work still, however, lay before him, though he was already past middle life. The clear, late evening had gloriously set in. "The rain is over and gone."

We have little or no details as to the seven years of his missionary life. Dr. Worthington compresses them into one sentence—one, indeed, which could be predicated of all our martyr-priests—*Strenuam navavit lucrandis animabus operam*, or, as Challoner translates it, " he was remarkably laborious in winning souls to God." Wood tells us that he " lived as a Seminary Priest among his relations, sometimes in Holywell near Oxford, and sometimes in the country near adjoining, among those of his profession."

It must have been a happy home-coming to the dear old Manor House, then indeed new in all its fresh beauty, to the faithful brother who loved him so tenderly and respected his sacred office so intensely that he was glad to risk his life and fortune by sheltering the proscribed priest beneath his roof. The family at Holywell had grown since George Napier's imprisonment and exile. William's eldest son, Edmund, was born in 1579, so he may have already known his uncle. William, the third, was born three years later, on the feast of St. Gregory, 1582, when George was probably already in prison.

There were also three other sons, Maurice, Christopher, and Thomas, and a daughter named Mary.† They lost their mother in 1584, perhaps at the birth of the youngest child ; she was interred in the Chancel of Holywell Church, on July 7, 1584. Her husband remained faithful to her memory during the seven and thirty years that he survived her. Probably one of his sisters (whose names we do not know) lived with him at Holywell.

It was thus to a widower's house that George Napier was welcomed in the first year of the new reign, that reign which opened with such bright hopes for Catholics, for was it not the son of Mary Stuart who now filled the throne ? They had yet to learn that one who could betray

* Cal. Dom. Eliz. 1591–94, p. 33.

† William married into the Devonshire family of Gandy ; Thomas married Mary Collins, of Cowley ; Christopher died, a bachelor, in London. Only from a note of Hearne's do we learn of the existence of Maurice, whom he calls the second son. Bodl. Hearne's MSS., 60, f. 142.

his own mother to a cruel and shameful death was not likely to shrink from breaking his promises to others, if he could gain anything by doing so.

However, in the wonderful revival of Catholic activity that heralded the new *régime*, George Napier took his full share. He divided his time between Holywell and Temple Cowley, making excursions into the neighbourhood wherever there were Catholic souls to tend, or hope of bringing some stray sheep into the fold.

No doubt he had the happiness of giving the nuptial blessing to his nephew Edmund, when, in 1609, he married Joyce, daughter of John Wakeman, Esq., of Beckford, County Gloucester. The bride had good Catholic blood in her veins (her mother was a Giffard of Chillington), and she was to have the honour of suffering imprisonment for her faith.

Their first child, William, was born in June and died in August, 1610, the year of George Napier's martyrdom. But this union was blessed with ten other children, one of whom bore his martyred uncle's name, and this younger George Napier, though the fourth son, eventually succeeded to the Holywell estates. Two more, William, the third, and Charles, the eighth, son, became Franciscans, and of these William (or Father Marianus as he was called), had the honour of being condemned to death for his priesthood, like his holy uncle. This was during the Oates Plot, in 1679, but unlike his uncle, the Franciscan was reprieved, though detained in prison till 1684, when he was exiled.

But we must return to our martyr. Though we know so little about his apostolic labours, we have at least the most minute details of his glorious end.

An account has come down to us, written by an intimate friend and fellow-prisoner, which is one of the most touching and exquisite memorials of the days of persecution. It is strange that this should never yet have been printed in full, though Bishop Challoner *more suo* abridged and paraphrased it in his *Memoirs of Missionary Priests.** One manuscript is preserved in the Bodleian Library at Oxford,† and we have collated it with another copy which belongs to the Archives of the See of Westminster,‡ and with the copy used by Bishop Challoner himself, which is at Oscott College. Challoner's copy is taken (as he informs us) from a MS. in the Knaresborough collection. The Bodleian MS. is contained in a large quarto volume, which formerly belonged to Hearne, the Oxford antiquary. It is entitled, "Account of yᵉ Apprehension and Execution of Mr. George Napper, Priest," and is written in a contemporary hand.

---

* The latter part he has transcribed accurately enough.
† *Rawlinson MSS.* D. 399, ff. 213-16*b*.
‡ *Arch. West.* ix. n. 90.

# FORGOTTEN SHRINES

We have modernised the spelling, but have made no other alterations in the narrative.

"My Reverend Friend, according unto your request, as near as my memory will give me leave, I have set down all accidents that have fallen out from his first apprehension until his farewell in this world.

"Imprimis, I have heard him say many times upon occasions of speeches, that he did pray to God that it would please His Majesty that if ever he should fall into the hands of his enemies, that he might not be taken in his friend's house; and it seemed that God heard his prayers, for being seen by a young wretched companion, or, as I think, rather, by a couple, to go into an honest woman's house on July 18 (being on a Wednesday) towards evening one of the knaves said to his other companion that there was a priest gone to such a house, wishing that the Vicar might have understanding of it.* Whereupon one of them went to the Vicar's house and demanded of his daughter where her father was, who answered him, he was not within, fearing he did come to do her father some harm. The cause of the fear was that there had passed many words between the fellow and her father a little time before. And another reason moved her, too, by reason of a dream the Vicar's daughter had dreamed the night before which was, as she confessed, that her father was killed, therefore she cried to her mother that she should in no case tell where her father was.

"The fellow, all this while standing at the door and hearing the maid's fear, called to her mother that she should not doubt any such matter, for his coming was to let him understand that there was a priest in such a house, requesting his aid and counsel in apprehending of him. The Vicar's wife, hearing such news, leapt from her stool with great joy and called her husband to the fellow, who presently united themselves in friendship, and concluded how to take him, which was that they would forbear him that night, and watch his coming out, and then to apprehend him; and so they did, for the next day being the 19th of July and Thursday, the blessed man departing and going down a close, one of the knaves met him, stayed him, and said unto him that he must have him before a justice to be examined whether he was a priest or no.

"And so the good man went quietly back again with the fellow, who brought him to the constable and charged him to keep him safe, and to have him before Sir Francis Evers,† and so he did. And going on the

---

* This happened at Kirtlington, a village about four miles north-east of Woodstock, and nine miles north of Oxford.

† Sir Francis Eure, or Evers, of Heyford Warren. Heyford lies on the Cherwell, seven miles north-east of Woodstock. The old Elizabethan Manor House still stands here.

way he called to mind a Pyx which he had about his neck with a couple of consecrated Hosts which he took great care of, lest They should happen into the hands of his enemies, and thinking within himself what he might do to preserve Them, he prayed to God to save Them, until such time that he might receive Them with reverence. He made an excuse to withdraw himself to a bush seeming to untruss a point, and so thinking to convey Them into the bush to save Them, but they had so vigilant an eye over him that he could not hide Them. And still praying in his mind and seeming to move his neckcloth (by reason it rained a little) by God's appointed goodness he did untie the knot, and the Pyx fell down between his shirt and his skin, down to his knee and there stayed. And likewise having a little bag of relics about his neck he loosed that, so that it slid down to the other knee, and there stayed.

"And when they brought him before Sir Francis Evers, he caused the Constable who dwelt in the town to search him from top to toe, pulling off his shoes, and as the blessed man did think, the Constable did many times touch both the Pyx and the bag, but God of His marvellous mercy saved them both from being found. And in the dead time of the night, as he told me, he did rise and with as much reverence as time and place would give him leave, he received the consecrated Hosts, and saved Them from being polluted.

"Sir Francis used him very kindly and so did my Lady, and provided him a mess of broth for his supper and likewise in the morning a mess of milk with cinnamon and sugar ; and when the Constable had thoroughly searched him and found many things about him, as his service book and a book of notes, a little oils, his needle case, thimble, and thread, he told him he was but a poor priest, and, in his conscience, he was no statesman. The knight willed the High Constable to take him to look well to him ; he answered that he would make him sure, for he would put him into the stocks, but the Justice said he should not do so by no means, and prayed him to let him have a good bed, and anything that he would call for. So the next day they brought him to Oxenford, being 20th of July.

"The Assizes drawing on and being come, he was brought to the Bar and was called by the name of George Napper to answer his indictments, which was that he was a traitor ; then Justice Croke asked him if he were guilty ; he said, 'No.' 'How will you be tried ?' He said, 'By God and the country.' He asked him if he were a priest. He said if any man could prove him so, let him have the laws. 'Will you,' said the Justice Croke, 'deny that you are no priest ?' He answered, 'If any man can prove me a priest, let him say so.' Then the Judge said to the Jury, 'My Masters, you hear he will not deny that he is a priest, therefore you may well think what he is ; but if he will say he is no priest, I will believe him. But these things that were found about him doth manifestly show that he is one, and therefore you have wisdom sufficient.' But concerning the arraingment and the particulars such as I have set down, I think my Reverend friend may know and learn the certainty of them, better than I can report, by some of the Sheriff's men who were both at the beginning and the ending, for myself was not there, nor I never heard him make repetition of it, and so I will say no more of that."

We may here break off the narrative for a few observations. At this wretched travesty of a trial, the like of which was only too familiar to the indignant, broken hearts of contemporary English Catholics, William Napier was present. After hearing his brother's sentence, he "made the greatest interest," as the phrase went, to get him a reprieve, and he never rested until he had obtained it. Probably our martyr would have been reprieved and banished, had it not been for the interference of the Vice-Chancellor of the University. This was that Dr. John King of Christ Church, who afterwards became Bishop of London. As bishop, he took a prominent part in the trial and condemnation of the venerable martyr, John Almond, in 1612. It is said that he not only mourned for this crime as long as he lived, but that he was actually granted the grace, so seldom given to persecutors, to become himself a Catholic, and to die in the communion of that Church which he had so cruelly persecuted.* Like Saul of Tarsus he had the blood of more than one martyr on his hands, and we may hope that the Catholic tradition of his conversion is an authentic one. Dr. King's portrait still hangs in the splendid Hall of Christ Church.

It was hoped, almost up to the last, that our martyr's life would be spared. There is a letter of November 2, 1610, signed by the Rev. George Lambton, now in the Archives of the old Clergy Brotherhood in London, which refers to him as follows: "Our miseries are daily multiplied. Divers priests have been banished of late and now more are apprehended. . . . We hope for all this that God will give us patience to bear these afflictions, and strength to pass through such terrible wars. Your old friend, Mr. George Napper, lieth in Oxford Gaol, condemned but reprieved, and might have escaped for taking the Oath. It is thought he shall be banished." † A week later, and our martyr passed through the last fiery trial to his crown.

To continue the narrative: "There was a poor fellow that was con-

* Challoner, _Memoirs_, &c. (Derby, 1843), vol. ii. See _The Bishop of London's Legacy_, a book put out at the time of Dr. King's death in 1621. The rumour as to his conversion is not widely credited.

† Foley, _Records English Province S.J._, series x. part i. p. 391.

demned for felony (his name was Falkner) and the poor man took great
care to die as a good Christian, and whether it were God Almighty's
extraordinary goodness, as I am persuaded it was, to put him in mind to
come to the blessed man for his ghostly comfort and help, or whether
some good-minded man willed him to go to him for help, I know not.
But to him he went and requested his charitable help to save his soul,
and he most lovingly received him and brought him into the state of
grace, and so the poor creature made it known that he died as a good
Christian man ought to die, which confession of his made divers malicious ministers fret against the blessed man ; and some of them, as it was
reported, rode presently to Abingdon to the judges and told them what
the poor man had confessed at the gallows, and entreated them that the
good man might be executed out of the way, or else he would do great
harm.   And this being given to understand to the blessed man, he constantly thanked Almighty God that he had done so good a deed, and
said if the judges would come unto him, he would do as much for them,
for he came into the country to exercise his functions, and to save men's
souls ; and this much he told me himself.

"But shortly after Justice Croke sent his warrant or his letter that he
should be executed, but the High Sheriff thought his letter not sufficient,
being reprieved, and so stayed the execution, and when that Justice Croke
returned home, all his service being ended, he sent another warrant or
letter to the High Sheriff again that he should be executed ; and yet the
Sheriff would not do it.   Between these two (as I remember) the High
Sheriff and Mr. Chancellor sent for that blessed man to come to Christ
Church.   There he was examined about the poor man, his recon-
cilation and by whom it proceeded ; the blessed man answered that
being condemned and both put together, as the order of the Castle is,
the poor man of his own voluntary forwardness beseeched him to give
his counsel how he might die a good Christian, for he said that he had
lived a very bad and lewd life a long time, not knowing the true way
how he should carry himself, and therefore he craved his help at that
instant.   The blessed man received him most willingly into the bosom
of his Mother the Catholic Church ; and he desired the Vice-Chancellor
not to charge any other man with it.   For there was a prisoner in the
house whose name I know not, that was brought in to be an instrument in the business.   The Vice-Chancellor asked him if he would
take the oath of allegiance ; he answered he would so far as it
concerned [temporal] affairs and yielded unto his Majesty as much
power and authority as ever any king had heretofore, or of right
ought to have ; but that would not prevail unless he would take it as
it [is] appointed in the book.   And if he would take it, so they would

promise his life should be saved. But he answered that he could not nor would not.

"Then they persuaded him to read Mr. Blackwell's book concerning the oath, and then to consider of it, and with much persuasion he took the book and promised he would ; and so he told me himself he did read it, but would not take the oath for all that. And as I think he told me, he sent the Vice-Chancellor a draft of [it] that he would take if it would please him to accept of it ; but they would accept of no other form but that which was set down by the Act of Parliament, for they sent him word they could not. And then his friends caused a petition to be delivered to his Majesty for his life by the hands of a sister of his, Mrs. Gunwell, who delivered it, and also a pheasant hen, which petition the King received (and the pheasant also) and willed the poor gentlewoman should have an angel, but she had never a penny ; and he promised he would consider of the petition, but it was to no purpose, as the event followed.

"After all this Judge Croke coming up to London to the term, went to make an end and to send him to eternal glory, and to that end sent down his warrant with the copy of his indictment and all other things belonging to the order of law, that he should die by the 9th day of November. This warrant being come down, a dear friend of his sent him word of it, that he should prepare himself to die, for there was no other hope. The blessed man received this [message ?] most lovingly, not being appalled at it ; and so desired his friend to pray for him that he might be constant and valiant to the end ; for he thanked God he he found no fear in himself. This warrant being known, it caused one of his nephews to post up to London, who procured Colonel Cecil to go to Justice Croke for a reprieve ; and with much ado he procured it for one day longer ; which was the 10th of November ; and in the meantime he should confer with some learned men, and that they should certify his good behaviour.

"The Vice-Chancellor and divers others at that time being at London about the election of [the] Chancellor, and Doctor Hamon being at home, was willed to do him what pleasure he could ; and before the tenth day the Vice-Chancellor did come home, and another of his nephews went unto him, and delivered the commendations, which was commendable ; but he made light of it, and said if he would take the oath of allegiance he would do what he could to save him ; otherwise he would not do anything. And when these that were at London had intelligence how all things passed, they laboured further for a pardon. But as matters were handled, it came too late : for those which bent themselves to be his most enemies, proved to be his best friends. For myself is, and was, of that opinion that it was Almighty God's pleasure that he should now come to receive his wages, or rather, a crown of glory for working in His vineyard.

"His friends this time marvelled they could not hear from London whether he should die or live ; and Thursday being coming we thought to have received some news by letters, what the blessed man should certainly trust to. And that Thursday, at night, he caused a breast of mutton to be roasted, and willed a couple of poorer Catholic men to be at supper with him, and so they did. And the same Thursday, there was a good man * had sent a very great present to him and myself, to be merry together, giving us to understand that by God's grace he would sup with us that night, which news caused Mr. Napper to rejoice much, for he took great care to speak with one. And truly this is to be noted, that every time that it was given out that he should die, it pleased God that a good man unlooked for came unto him ; and [as it is reported] one of them which was with him but four days before he suffered, is now gone to heaven unto him. † Little did he eat that supper, only a piece of pigeon-pie, and after, a few stewed prunes which one of his sisters had brought him.

"Very merry he was that evening ; and being at supper, I said unto him, 'Mr. Napper, if it be God's holy will that you shall suffer, I do wish with all my heart that it might be to-morrow, being Friday' ; and [I] said that ' our Saviour did eat the Paschal Lamb with His disciples on Thursday at night, and suffered the Friday following, and therefore I do wish, if you must die, that it might be to-morrow.' He answered me very sweetly, saying, 'Welcome be God's grace, and I pray God that I may be constant' : praying us all to pray for him.

"And thus much I must let you understand that every time he heard the news that he should suffer he gave to some poor body which was Catholic some of his clothes, and I would say unto him : ' Methinks you should make reservation of them again, if you do not die !' His answer was that he had more upon his back than he had brought into the world, and 'if I live, I will put myself to God's Providence' ; and truly, if he had lived, he had left himself little more than he brought into the world, for he had given all away. After supper he and the other good man drew themselves to a secret place, to confer upon some essential matter ; ‡ and when they had made an end, they took their leave the one of the other, and so did all the company, every man to his chamber.

* *i.e.* a priest.
† Either the Venerable John Roberts, O.S.B., or the Venerable Thomas Somers, who were martyred at Tyburn, December 10, 1610.
‡ *i.e.* to make his confession.

"The next day being Friday, 9th of November, about nine of the clock in the morning, the Under-Sheriff sent to the keeper's wife to tell Mr. Napper that he should prepare himself to die, for that was the day, between one and two in the afternoon, that he should be executed. The poor woman took it very grievously, and fell a-crying coming to me, who hearing her, marvelled what the matter should be, and asked her what the matter was : who answered me, crying : 'Oh, the blessed man must die this day, and I cannot find [it] in my heart to tell him of it !' I answered her : 'Welcome God's grace, for now I am sure it is God's blessed will to have it so ; and therefore I will go tell him myself and let him understand of it.' So I went to his chamber, knocking at the door. He opened it ; I saluted him, and asked him how he did ; he answered me : 'Well, I thank Jesus.' I asked him how he had slept that night, and he said 'Very well, I thank God.' Then I said unto him that the bell had tolled and rung out also. He asked me what I meant by those speeches ? I said to him that now he must put on his armour of proof, for he must fight that day a great battle. He took me in his arms and embraced me, and said it was the best news that ever was brought unto him, and I was most welcome for declaring it unto him, saying further that he found himself thoroughly scoured from all the rust which had troubled him long before, [and thereat] * he rejoiced very much, and asked me if he might not serve God † that day ? I said the day was far spent, but if it pleased him I would make all things ready, and he prayed me that I would.

"So he was ready ; and surely methought he did consecrate that day as reverently in all his actions, and with as much sweet behaviour as ever I did see him in all my life, for I did especially note him ; and he showed not fear in any respect. When he had made an end and all things laid aside, he fell to his devotions, and by the end of our service many scholars were coming to the Castle yard and into the Court ; and after he had prayed above an hour, I came to him and asked if I should send for some comfortable thing for him to drink. He answered, no, he would neither eat nor drink, hoping in his Saviour that he should have a sumptuous banquet, and shortly.

"After a little stay, I considered that the time drew somewhat near ; I came to him again, and put [him] in mind of shifting him with a fair shirt. He said he would willingly. Then I made him a fire, and warmed his shirt. And coming to him again to put it on, he made a step down among the poor prisoners, and did distribute certain money amongst them. Coming up again, he brought a piece of silver of half a crown, with a little money besides ; he laid it in my chamber window.

* Conjectural : Corner of page missing.          † *i.e.* say Mass.

I asked him what he would do with that piece of silver having the picture of St. George ? And he told me he would give it to the executioner for his pains, and the rest he would give to some poor people ; and so he did.

"When he had put on his clean shirt he fell to his prayers again. He had prayed but a small time when came two scholars, Masters of Art, and I think one of them was a minister. They began to offer some speeches to him concerning the oath of allegiance. He prayed them to give him leave to prepare himself, for he had not long to stay, and it stood him upon to call to mind all his reckonings which he was to make to his Lord and Master, and therefore, with most mild and sweet words, entreated them not to trouble him ; and they, like honest-minded men, stayed their speeches, seeming they were sorry for him. Then the Pro-Proctor coming to the Castle to speak with him (for both the Proctors were gone to London), and the Vice-Chancellor, he sent the keeper to bring Mr. Napper to him, who stayed in the keeper's chamber, with divers other scholars. The blessed man being coming to him, he began to use some speeches to persuade him to take the oath ; but the good man prayed him to give him leave to spend that little time which was lent him in prayer ; so knelt down at a table and prayed a little.

"But by that time the Under-Sheriff willed him to make haste, for all things were ready to the execution. Then he rose up and went into a little chamber by, put off his doublet and woollen breeches and his boot-hose, and put him on a white waistcoat and pair of white linen breeches, a pair of white stockings, a pair of shoes, and borrowed the keeper's gown (to save his own from the hangman), and being apparelled to the end that the law had appointed, he came again to the keeper's chamber. And I, meeting my keeper, he asked me if I had taken leave of him ? I answered him I would willingly see him again, [and]* so I went with him up into his chamber, and as I was coming the * [bless]ed man was about to kneel down, and seeing me he stayed, and I pressed down through the scholars and came unto him and knelt down. He blessed me ; rising up, he embraced me and kissed me.

"The Proctor asked what I was. I heard one answer him that I was a gentleman, and a prisoner for my conscience. And then the blessed man began to kneel down, and the Proctor said : 'Mr. Napper, shall I pray with you ?' And he answered him thus : 'Good Mr. Proctor, you and I are not of one religion, therefore may not pray together.' The Proctor said : 'Shall I pray for you ?' The blessed man said : 'I would to God you were in state of grace to pray for me.' Then he knelt down, and I knelt by him the space of saying a Pater noster.

* Corner of page gone.

Presently the Under-Sheriff called very earnestly to come away, and so, [he] prostrating himself to the ground, kissed it, and made the sign of the Cross, and went forward to go to the dungeon door, where the hurdle stayed for him, and coming by the Proctor, he said : 'Mr. Napper, if you will yet take the oath of allegiance, I make no doubt of your life.' He said : 'Good Mr. Proctor, do not wrong me when I am [*sic*] gone, for I know many speeches will go of me ; and now I say again unto you that I have prayed most heartily for the King, the Prince, and all his children, as any subject he hath in the world, and will yield him as much power and authority as ever any Prince had, or ought to have.'

"Then the hangman came and asked him forgiveness. The blessed man embraced him and said : 'I most lovingly forgive thee, and for a pledge I have willed one of the Sheriff's men to give thee a piece of silver.' The hangman said he had it and thanked him for it ; and so, being called for again, went down to the stairfoot ; the door being opened, I followed him. And he, seeing the hurdle there, laid himself down upon it, and with a most lively courage blessed himself, and had not so much as thread to bind himself with ; I think never any but was bound but himself. When they offered to draw forward, one of the [pieces ?] of the trace broke, so they stayed until it was made fast again ; and the people were so unreasonable in pressing themselves to see him, that they pressed me downwards upon the hurdle ; then I called to the Proctor to command the people to give back, and I took both his hands in mine, and I prayed God to comfort him. He looked upon me and prayed God to bless me, and with much [ado] I got from the throng of the people ; and more than this I cannot set down of my own knowledge.

"And this that now is to write, is the report of Mr. Charles, his own hearing at the place where he suffered his martyrdom. [What follows is in the same hand.]

"The 9th of November being Friday, 1610, it pleased God to appoint the time in the which Mr. George Napper, priest, was to be tried in the furnace. Being brought out of prison, laid upon a hurdle, with his hands conjoined a[nd his] * eyes fixed towards heaven, without moving any way, he was drawn to the place of execution where, being took off and set on his feet, beholding the place where he was to suffer, he signed himself with the sign of the Cross, and advisedly began to speak as followeth : 'Gentlemen, you must expect no great speech at my hands, for indeed I intend none : only I acknowledge myself to be a most miserable sinner.' And therewithal, joining his hands together with an intent to pray, was interrupted by a minister who said unto

* Corner of page gone.

him, 'Mr. Napper, confess your treason.' Wherewith bending himself towards him, he said : 'Treason, Sir ? I thank God I never knew what treason meant.' To the which the minister answered, 'Be advised what you say. Do you not remember what the Judge told you, that it was treason to be a priest ?' 'For that I die, Sir ; and that Judge that condemned me, as well as I, shall appear before the Just Judge of Heaven to whom I appeal.'

"Then again turning to the people he said : 'I confess I am a Catholic priest, and withal protest that none but Catholics could be saved.'

"After these words, he desired he might have leave to pray. Whereunto the minister replied, 'Pray for the King now.' With that he lifted up his hands and said : 'I pray God bless his Majesty and make him a blessed saint in Heaven.' Then he desired the company that he might pray to himself. The minister interrupted him the third time and said : 'Go to : pray, and we will pray with you.' To which he answered and said : 'Sir, I will have none of your prayers ; neither it is my will that you should pray with me. But I desire all good Catholics to join with me in prayer.'

"And [he] addressed himself to pray and said : 'In te Domine speravi, non confundar,' etc., then lifted up his hands and heart and said the psalm 'De Profundis'; after that, 'Beati quorum remissæ sunt'; lastly the psalm 'Miserere.' These being ended he plucked down his nightcap over his eyes and the most part of his face, and often repeated these words : 'In manus tuas, Domine, commendo spiritum meum'; and yielding himself to one side of the ladder, having his hands still enjoined, he being turned off, he struck himself three times on the breast, and yielded his blessed soul to Him that gave it to him, showing yet a perfect memory was joined with a constant resolution.*

"Thus, beseeching God to defend you from your enemies, I must humbly desire you to remember me in your prayers.

"From my cell, this 19th day of December, 1610.

"His charity was great, for if any poor prisoner wanted other meat to fill him or clothes to cover him, he would rather be cold himself than

---

* We do not know, unhappily, the exact spot chosen for the martyrdom. At that time, very much more remained of the great Norman Castle than outlasted the Civil Wars ; and from the gaol to the gallows was a considerable journey. On Wood's authority, we may accept the place of execution as that immediately connected with the Castle, perhaps in the great enclosure itself, perhaps in Broken Hayes across the road, along the line of what is now George Street and its northern boundaries. Otherwise it might well seem as if, by a refinement of cruelty exceedingly common in Elizabethan and Jacobean days, the martyrdom was consummated on the green at Holywell, in sight of the Napier home.

they should ; if any would pray him to give his word to the keeper for them he would do it, if he paid it himself, as sometimes he did, and he would write for the poorest prisoner in the house.    There was one wretch went away with twenty shillings and ninepence of his, promising him he would send it to him honestly, but he never heard of him. Another he lent his cloak to wear a days to keep him warm, and hath willed that as long as he stay in the gaol he must wear it, which I fear me will be so long that he will wear that out and such another.    And thus beseeching you once more of your prayers, I in all duty commend me." *

And thus the tragedy was consummated, and George Napier of Corpus entered into the joy of his Lord.

There is but little to add to the beautiful story that we have quoted, save some fragments from other writers which we insert, " that nothing be lost."    A paper, preserved at Stonyhurst by the Jesuit Father Coffin † gives a few details.    At his first apprehension he was thrown into the Bocardo prison, where for some days the " venerable old man " was scarcely kept alive on a little bread and water.    Here, in spite of great weakness, he had to hold daily disputations with eager graduates and undergraduates, who flocked to the prison, hoping to refute and convince him.    But he addressed to them such fervent exhortations that they were silenced, and not a few converted.

The Bocardo prison was over the North Gate of the City, next the Church of St. Michael.    It was famous as the place where Cranmer, Ridley and Latimer had been confined.    For this reason, the old door of the prison is now kept as a relic in the Church of St. Mary Magdalen, hard by.    Father Coffin also gives a long speech in which the martyr comforted his weeping sister, and so animated her with his own supernatural joy, that, like another Scholastica, she would fain have spent the whole night before the martyrdom in hearing him discourse upon the joys of heaven.    He tells us, too, that when the martyr addressed the people at the gibbet, many Protestants, as well as the Catholics, were seen to weep, which much annoyed those in charge of the execution.    The crowd interfered to prevent them cutting the rope before the martyr had breathed his last, and some of the lower people, thrusting themselves through the guards, rendered the dying man what they thought to be an act of charity.    Thus they hung on his feet and dragged them down and struck him on the breast, and so on, moved by a zeal not altogether according to knowledge, with the intention of making his death more swift and easy.    It is at least a comfort to know

* Here there follows yet another postscript, which we postpone till its proper place in our story.    † *Anglia*, iii. n. 103, f. 207.

that the cruel butchery that followed was not carried out upon a living breathing man.

Father Coffin adds that he was about to close his letter, when "Our Father Rector" came into the room, and told him some more wonderful things about the holy martyr. These the Archpriest had himself written to tell the Holy Father, and the rector had heard of them from Cardinal Blanchetti.

He then goes on to narrate, on this excellent authority, that after the martyr's quarters were exposed on the city gates, a bright star appeared for some days above one of them, and when this same limb fell by some chance to the ground, at once a spring of most pure water burst out on this very spot, which ran as a sparkling rivulet through the streets of the city, and caused wonder to all who saw it. This sentiment was greatly increased by a miracle that followed. A blind man, hearing of this spring, full of faith and trust in the martyr's intercession, caused his guide to lead him in haste to the spot, where he washed his eyes, and at once recovered his sight.

At this the heretics were filled with fury, and proceeded to choke the spring with mud, but the waters broke out again. A second time they stopped it up, but once more it burst through the obstruction. The third time they were determined not to be beaten, and so rammed it down with clay and rubble that they succeeded in closing it.

It is also in a postscript that the anonymous writer, whose account of the martyr's last days we have transcribed, treats of these wonders. We have purposely postponed these closing paragraphs of his narrative until now.

"Since his death he appeared to one who saluted him by his own name, 'Mr. George Napper'; who answered him, 'Not now George Napper, but *Rex in magna gloria*.' *

"Again, in Lent last, there brake out water under that forequarter of his which was set up on a pole at the South Gate in Oxford, which is hard by Christ Church; by the virtue of which water some thought themselves to have help (I [keep back] † their names, lest they should have trouble from it), so that many went to take of it, and it [was] now so famous that it [was] called Mr. Napper Well, and it seemed that the fingers of his hand pointed to the said water.

"Whereupon the Vice-Chancellor, Dr. King, returning from London, caused that quarter to be secretly taken down and cast into the Thames, and the well spring to be rammed up." ‡

* "A King in great glory."
† The words within square brackets are not clear, but this is evidently the sense.
‡ From the copy in the Westminster Archives.

# FORGOTTEN SHRINES

" . . . Mr. Hunt used to mention one Mr. Knapier (of the family of Knapier of Holywell) that was hanged and quartered in Queen Elizabeth's time, and one of his quarters being put up upon some place in the city of Oxford, under it there sprang up a fountain, which so vexed several of the principal men of the city that they took it down and threw it into the Thames.

[¶] "A miller of Sandford one morning seeing it, acquainted Mr. Powell's great-grandmother with it, who had it taken up and buried in the chapel (now a barn) on the south side of Sandford old Mansion House." *

The writer of the narrative does not tell us (perhaps he thought it would not be safe) what happened to the rest of the sacred body. But, happily, Anthony Wood has supplied this omission. Here is his touching story :

"The next day [after George Napier's martyrdom] his head and quarters were set upon the four gates of the City, and upon that great one belonging to Christ Church, next to St. Aldate's Church, to the great terror of the Catholics that were in and near Oxford.†

"He was much pitied for that his grey hairs should come to such an end, and lamented by many that such rigour should be shown on an innocent and harmless person. No great danger in him (God wot), and therefore not to be feared, but being a Seminary [priest], and the laws against them now strictly observed, an example to the rest must be shewed. Some, if not all, of his quarters, were afterwards conveyed away by stealth, and buried at Sandford, near Oxford, in the old chapel there, joining to the Manor House, sometime belonging to the Knights Templars." ‡

The present writer will not easily forget with what delight he came across this passage, some years ago, in good old Anthony Wood. Till then, he had no idea that the sacred relics of this great son and martyr of Oxford had been preserved for the veneration of posterity.

Nor was he satisfied till he had made pilgrimage to Sandford, and visited the sacred spot where the mangled limbs were laid.

The City gates have all disappeared, § and even Tom Gate has been

---

* From Hearne's *Collections*, Oxford Hist. Soc. vol. viii. p. 45 (A.D. 1723–24).

† It was the head that was placed on Tom Gate (not on Christ Church steeple, as Challoner says). The South Gate stood across St. Aldate's, between Christ Church and the old Almshouses, now the house of the chaplain to the Catholic undergraduates, Monsignor Kennard.

‡ *History and Antiquities of the University* (Oxford, 1796), vol. ii. p. 166.

§ They were the North, or Bocardo Gate, the South Gate by Christ Church, the East Gate near Magdalen College, and the West Gate (or Water Gate) by St. Ebbe's Church. There are illustrations of them in Skelton's *Antiquities of Oxford*.

altered almost out of recognition by Wren's stately additions, for it had remained till then in the unfinished state in which Wolsey left it. But, happily, Sandford Chapel remains, though degraded to the uses of a barn.

How long the sacred relics remained exposed in rain and sun, for the birds of the air to devour, we do not know. It seems, however,

The Commandery from the river.
Sandford

from the old writer's mention of "last Lent," that they must have been left there for some months at least.

Perhaps, when the martyr's arm, on the South Gate, was taken down and thrown into the river, the Napiers felt that an effort must be made to preserve the rest of those sacred limbs from further desecration.

It was William Napier, we may be sure, who, with heart-broken but subdued sorrow, carried his sainted brother to his rest on the quiet acres of the Powells ; perhaps by water, so that a walk from Christ Church to Sandford Lock by the tow-path may become for us a veritable pilgrimage in his wake.

Our picture shows the present house across the river. The old chapel is seen on the right, looking what it is now, a barn. The house has been entirely rebuilt in our own time by Magdalen College, to which the estate now belongs. The large walled garden is seen on the left. Though the house is modern, much of the old materials have been used, and the house is well built in the Elizabethan style. Within, the great oak beams that support the ceilings date from the time of the Powells, and every vestige of antiquity that could be preserved has been incorporated with the modern building.

The place is thus described in *A Guide to the Architectural Antiquities in the Neighbourhood of Oxford.* *

" The farmhouse, in a field on the north-west side of the Church, has usually been looked upon as the remains of the old preceptory of the Knights Templars in this place, but the only ancient parts of it are some slight traces of early English work in what was formerly the chapel. These consist of a portion of the east window, and a roll-moulded string-course. The doorway is much later, of Perpendicular character. The chapel was dedicated to St. Mary the Virgin. . . .

" In the garden is a gateway bearing the date 1614, on each side of which there are fragments of architectural ornaments built into the wall, and among them a reversed shield of late date, having carved on it a cross pattée, the badge of the Knights Templars, and also of their successors, the Knights Hospitallers of St. John of Jerusalem."

The preceptory was moved to Sandford from Temple Cowley about the year 1274.

In 1542, soon after the Dissolution, this house of the Knights Hospitallers was granted to Edward Powell, whose descendant, Winifred, Lady Curzon, alienated it in the year 1760.

On June 29, 1661, the antiquary, Anthony Wood, made a visit to Sandford, then the seat of Mr. John Powell, which he thus noted :

" Mr. Francis Napier of Holywell and myself walked over to Sandford, two miles distant from Oxon, where we saw the ruins of an old priory and a chapel there adjoining. . . . This house at the Dissolution came to the Powells, who enjoy it to this day." The antiquary then proceeds to note coats of arms of the family and their alliances, which he found in a window of the hall.

Francis Napier, who accompanied Anthony Wood, was the great-nephew of our martyr, being the sixth son of Edmund, William Napier's son and heir. He was a great friend of Wood's, who often mentions walking with him. He was born in 1623, and died a bachelor in the house of his grandfather Wakeman, at Beckford in Gloucestershire. No doubt it was he who told his friend the antiquary the touching story of his martyred uncle, and of the translation of his relics to Sandford, and we can see from Wood's account how much the story moved him.†

* Parker, 1846.

† Mr. Gillow is mistaken in saying that Francis became a Franciscan (*Cath. Record Socy.*, vol. i. p. 135). It was Charles, the youngest brother, born in 1631, who died at

176

It is probably only the eastern part of the barn which really forms a part of the old chapel. The early English window is now walled up, and the upper part of it, as well as of the wall, has disappeared, and is replaced by boarding. The old fifteenth-century doorway on the south side fortunately still remains intact, with its door, and we give an illustration of this precious relic. (See facing p. 206.)

When we visited the place, and begged to inspect the interior of the barn, we were kindly welcomed by the present occupiers. Standing by the old doorway, through which the mutilated body of the martyr had been carried nearly three centuries before, we found ourselves in a huge barn filled with waggons, farm implements, and the like. The eastern end, however, with its walled-up window, was happily free. We asked the man who showed it us, and who seemed to be a native of the place, if he had ever heard of any one being buried here. "Why yes, sir," he said, "there's a man lies here who was hanged, drawn, and quartered." "Do you know why he was executed?" "Well, sir, they say it was because he was a priest." "And is it known exactly where he lies?" "Yes, sir, just below where you stand, in front of where the altar was, on a line with the doorway by which you came in. There have been Roman Catholics here to visit the place, and there were many who wanted to dig to find the body, but my father's old master, sir, he always used to say, 'Leave him there in peace; he has been there all these hundred years, let him rest in peace.'" *

It was consoling to find that the tradition of the martyr's resting-place was not lost. Edmund Powell, his brother-in-law, still lived at Sandford when the sacred remains were brought there, and we like to think that the beautiful gateway in the garden may have been raised as a sort of triumphal archway in commemoration of the martyr's coming home.

The sacred burden was doubtless carried up from the river-side, through this sweet enclosed garden, to the ancient Chapel of Our Lady, and as the faithful sons of the house went out to meet it and escort it in procession with flaming torches to its last resting-place, they may well have thought that there should be some memorial of the passage of the King—*Rex in magna gloria*, who had thus come to honour their home

Holt, County Leicester, in 1678. He took the name of Francis in religion, hence the confusion. *Cf.* Wood, *Life and Times*, vol i. (in a pedigree).

* Since this was written, it has come to the knowledge of the writer that search has been made by Catholics in this very spot, but without any result. Though two perfect skeletons were found, the quarters of our martyr could not be discovered. It therefore seems probable that when the Powell family left Sandford they translated these precious relics elsewhere. Perhaps they were taken abroad. In any case it would seem certain that they are no longer at Sandford.

z

with his presence. And so, a few years later, the gateway was built and the date inscribed above it as a perpetual memorial to his passing, to whom no more direct memorial could safely be reared.

No doubt, at that delayed funeral, one of the " good men " who had been so assiduous in visiting the martyr in his dungeon, was there to offer the Holy Sacrifice over his sacred remains. And many another secret Mass must have been offered there, through that long dark night of our Church's sorrow, in honour of the martyr and the Martyr's King. And among the priests who offered there must often have been found the Franciscan brothers, William and Charles Napier, of Holywell.

The little Norman Church, close to the old preceptory, though almost rebuilt, contains one precious relic of the ages of faith, which was found buried in the churchyard in 1723. This is an exquisite carving in alabaster, representing the Assumption of Our Blessed Lady. The figure of the Mother of God, crowned and vested in royal raiment, is surrounded with a *vesica* of rays, and supported by six angels. Below her feet are two smaller angels, kneeling, and supporting between them a reliquary, now broken and empty. This beautiful memorial of the piety of our forefathers was, on its discovery, placed with praiseworthy liberality within the Church and attached to the south wall of the chancel, where it may yet be seen. No doubt it owes its preservation to the influence of the Powell family.

But we must leave Sandford and return to Holywell. If we do not cross the river, we may return by Littlemore, which will be for ever associated with the memory of the greatest of all Oxford Catholics, John Henry Newman. The Mynchery, that old monastery which he so greatly loved to contemplate from his hermitage, or to visit on his daily walk, also belonged to the Powells. And it is a consolation to mount the hill from Sandford to Littlemore, and to reflect that " the winter of our discontent " is past, and that we have lived to see the blossoming of the second spring. For the seed which fell into the earth and died has surely brought forth great fruit.

It would be interesting to follow the fortunes of the dear old house at Holywell and of the Napier family in detail, but we can only do so briefly. William Napier survived his martyred brother some eleven years, dying in 1621. His heir, Edmund, then forty-three years old, reigned in his stead. He left behind him a folio commonplace book in which he noted the family births and deaths, and inserted copies of the various leases held by the Napiers from an early date. The book was the gift of his brother Christopher. It is now in the possession of Mr. Joseph Gillow, who edited the Family Register from it for the

178

THE GATEWAY IN THE GARDEN,
SANDFORD

*To face page 178*

THE DOOR OF THE OLD CHAPEL,
SANDFORD

Catholic Record Society in 1905.* This has naturally been of the greatest service to the present writer.

It is touching to read the prayers which good Mr. Edmund Napier writes after the record of the birth of each of his children : " God make him his servant," " *Sit sibi corde servire Deo, det illi deus de rore cœli et benedicat ei,*" and so on, he writes, evidently with a full heart. In 1643 he had to suffer a cruel blow ; within three days (July 12th and 14th) both the wife of his bosom and his eldest surviving son Edward were taken from him. An epidemic was raging at Oxford, and no doubt these two precious lives were among the victims. King Charles I. was holding the University city and keeping his court there in this first year of the Civil Wars, when what was called " the camp fever " broke out and swept away a whole company of his most devoted adherents, the poet Cartwright among them. Edmund Napier seems to have thought that he could not long survive his loved ones, and within a week of the double funeral in Holywell Church, he made his own will. The death of his heir (who was in his thirtieth year) no doubt also made this necessary.

The will,† which begins in the usual pious fashion, " In the name of God, Amen," is dated July 22, 1643. The testator leaves " my lease of the farm of Holliwell" and all his Oxfordshire estates, except one at Wolvercote, to his son George and his heirs, with annuities to his younger sons William, Edmund, and Charles. William and Charles, as we have seen, were Franciscans. Edmund tried his vocation among the Jesuits, and after failing there, sought to become a secular priest, and entered at the English College in Rome in 1652 ; but in 1656 he had to be dispensed from the missionary oath for the same reasons of ill-health which had driven him from the noviciate, and he returned to Oxford, where he married, and lived as " a Popish schoolmaster in the parish of St. Mary Magdalen." ‡ He lived in a house which is now part of Nos. 63 and 64 St. Giles's, § and dying in 1685 was buried with his ancestors in Holywell Church. Mr. Napier, however, survived his wife for nearly twelve years. He lived to see two-thirds of his property sequestrated, under the Commonwealth, for recusancy, and died February 26, 1654, aged seventy-five. He was buried in the chancel of Holywell Church, and his son George succeeded him. He had married, during his father's lifetime, Margaret, heiress to Mr. Arden of Kirtlington, who brought him a considerable fortune, but gave him no son, so that,

---

* *Miscellanea*, vol. i. pp. 133–37.
† It is in the *British Museum*, Add. MSS. 34,679, f. 746.
‡ Wood, *Life and Times*, vol. i. p. 193, and vol. iii. p. 124.
§ Stapleton, *op. cit.* p. 214–15.

when he died in 1671, the Napiers of Holywell were represented by three girls—Margaret, Mary and Frances, of whom the eldest was twenty-two. She married Mr. Henry Nevill of Nevill Holt, in Leicestershire, and took with her the family estates.

The last male survivor of the Napiers of Holywell was George's brother William, known as Father Marianus Russell, the Friar Minor. In him the family ended gloriously, for, as we have seen, he was a notable confessor of the Faith. Born in 1619, he left for Douay on June 14, 1630. Russell, the *alias* he assumed, according to the universal custom of the students of that famous College, was the name of his great-great-grandmother. Nine years later he entered the English Franciscan Convent of St. Bonaventure's at Douay, and took the name of Marianus. Professed in 1640, he was approved for preaching and hearing confessions in 1650. He was Confessor to the English Poor Clares at Aire, from 1651–1656, when he was sent on the English Mission. He was titular Guardian of Coventry, 1674–1677 (his younger brother, Charles, being titular Guardian of Oxford); Rector of Mount Grace in Yorkshire in 1675 and 1676, and Chaplain to the Spanish Embassy in London in 1678. It was the year of national madness, the year of Titus Oates's colossal lie. In the memorable *True and Exact Narration of the Horrible Plot and Conspiracy of the Popish Party*, now preserved in the Public Record Office, Article lxxii. purports to be a Papal Bull, shown to Oates by Father Blundell, containing a prospective list of dignitaries in England, that England in which his Sacred Majesty and the Protestant Religion shall have been done away with by Popish plotters. In this document " Napper, a Franciscan Friar," is set down over against the Bishopric of Norwich !

Therefore the innocent Franciscan was, on January 17, 1679, indicted for treason at the Old Bailey. Once more, during that unquiet century, a man of his lineage had the chance to confess before an English court the Catholic Faith of Christ. But the joy of martyrdom, once given to a Napier, was now denied.

The trial was, of course, a farce. Those evil inventors, Oates and Prance, were the only persons who could be found to witness against him, except Sir William Walter, who had arrested him, and deposed to finding vestments in his chamber. Father Napier asked time to prepare some defence. Lord Chief Justice Scroggs replied : " The only use you can make of time is to repent," and promptly condemned him to death. He was returned to gaol ; and the moment public excitement was a trifle allayed, King Charles II. proceeded to grant the kinsman of his loyal Giffards a reprieve. If we are sure of anything about this complex King, we are sure of his personal sympathy for Catholics. If he let them, innocent as they were, suffer and die through these cruel years of national madness, it at least became extremely plain, on occasions, that he hated their tormentors, who mastered him. William Marianus Napier was one of two Franciscans, and one of thirty priests, thus condemned and reprieved, of whom sixteen, then and after, died in prison from ill-usage.

For his own part he did not die, though he was not liberated for six years; and then, in 1684, he went into exile. In exile, at St. Bonaventure's Convent, in Douay, on St. Francis's day, October 4, 1693, he slept in Christ, seventy-four years old.

And in this son of sweet St. Francis, like his holy father a martyr in will, died the last of the Napiers of Holywell. They were marked with the cross of the family shield, even to the last. Nor did they forget that on that shield were emblazoned also the red roses of martyrdom.*

But little remains to be told of the fate of the old Manor House, which, after the death of George Napier, came, as we have seen, to the Nevills of Holt. They did not live there, but it was still inhabited by Catholics. In 1686, Wood notes that " an ancient man and one of the King [James II.'s] chaplains came to Oxford, and next day visited Obadiah Walker [the Catholic Master of University College]. He said Mass at Soladin Harding's, by Holywell Church, where all Papists there retired to do their devotions by him." †

Soladin Harding died in 1684, and was succeeded by Thomas Kimber, who acted as steward to the Manor under the Nevills. At the Revolution, in December 1688, Wood notes that all the Popish houses in Oxford had their windows broken by the mob, among them being Kimber's in Holywell.

Mr. Kimber died in 1716, aged eighty-nine, and his son, Thomas, in 1725. Old Mr. William Joyner, a convert Fellow of Magdalen, lodged with the Kimbers at Holywell; he was a great friend both of Anthony Wood and of Hearne.‡ He was a man of considerable learning, who suffered much for his religion; he died in 1706, aged eighty-four, and is buried under a freestone slab in Holywell churchyard.‡ He was somewhat eccentric, and after his death it was discovered that he had kept all his money hidden in the books of his library.

Holywell, like Sandford, thus remained in Catholic hands till well on in the eighteenth century. Alas! that they do so no longer.

Hearne has left us a minute and sympathetic account of the old house, as it was in his day. Not a trace of any of the antique painted glass which he noticed and recorded, is now to be seen. No

---

* The arms of Napier of Holywell are, *argent, a cross saltire between four roses gules*.
† *Life and Times*, vol. iii. p. 45.     ‡ Stapleton, *op. cit.* p. 221.

wonder, for in the nineteenth century the place was used, first, as the parish workhouse, and then as a public-house known as the Cock-pit, from the place where cocks were fought hard by ! Now, at least, it is in reverent hands, though we could wish it had been left unspoilt by modern additions.

One piece of glass, noted by Hearne, seems to have a striking significance. It was in "a small arched room over the passage to the bowling-green," which he takes to have been an oratory. The inscription ran :

*" Requiescens accubuit ut leo*
*quis suscitavit eum . . . gentes ergo ? "*

He thinks it dated from the time of Henry VIII. This has an evident reference to Numbers xxiv. 9, though it differs from the Vulgate text. The "Authorised Version" is more like it : "He couched, he lay down as a lion, as a great lion ; who shall stir him up ? "

Now the lion, in mediæval symbolism, is the emblem of Christ Our Lord, and it is possible that this window, of which Hearne saw but a fragment, originally contained a representation of the Entombment of our Saviour. Whatever it was, the faithful generations who looked upon the legend below it, must have applied it in their hearts to the oppressed and sacred faith, seemingly driven to bay and wounded to death in the city once fragrant above other English cities with religion and loyalty. It gives one a strange thrill of comfort, after all the years, to think that the lion has slept with open eye ; that Catholicism never really died on this soil ; that the English priests of the Society of Jesus who came to our University town in the seventeenth century caught up alive the Eucharistic light which at Holywell Manor had burned on, feebly but steadily, ever since England broke with her merry past and with the Holy See.

THE QUADRANGLE, HOGHTON TOWER
*Photo by James Watts*

# IN A MARTYR'S FOOTSTEPS

## SOME LANCASHIRE TRADITIONS OF VENERABLE EDMUND ARROWSMITH, S.J.

LANCASHIRE, it has been said, is now "a melancholy land, devastated with its own inner wealth. The roads are worn with toil and traffic. The clouds are dull and lowering, shutting out the brightness of the sky." That is true for a great part of Lancashire, but north of the Ribble the country is still fair enough, and not yet made ugly by mill-chimneys and coal-pits. The district which is the object of the present pilgrimage lies, indeed, a few miles south of the Ribble, but it is still fairly unspoilt; the hills that close in Brindle and Hoghton are well wooded, and the fields that encircle the lonely farms and ancient Halls that stud the district are still green and fertile. Brindle, in fact, though it lies in the midst of a triangle, of which Preston, Blackburn and Chorley form the angles, and is thus hemmed in by smoky towns, is even now an oasis in this grimy land.

The Catholic church, plain but commodious, is hidden away in a maze of leafy lanes which seems to have been designed to perplex the wayfarer, and to conceal the House of God. Rhododendrons and flowering shrubs border the path, and the priest's large walled garden is a pleasant resting-place. Brindle, like so many other missions hereabouts, is, and has been for over two hundred years, under the charge of Benedictines, and in these favoured spots religion flourishes as in the golden days of England's faith.

On a lofty hill, with a perfectly straight drive leading to it for more than a mile in length, stands the splendid old castellated mansion, known as Hoghton Tower. Once itself a stronghold of the faith, it seems to dominate all the country round. At the foot of the hill winds the little river Darwen, that once ran red "with blood of Scots imbued." "Not many centuries ago," says Mr. Fletcher Moss, in his fascinating *Pilgrimages to Old Homes*, "all this land was wood or forest, noted for its wild cattle and deer; and the wild white bull is still the cognizance of the family. We toil upwards to a large, massive castle, whose battlemented gatehouse is flanked by towers. . . . Crossing the first courtyard, we come to a steep flight of rounded steps with an inner court or enclosure beyond them, then more steps, and another gatehouse." Within, a splendid quadrangle of Tudor buildings, the Great Hall like that of an Oxford College, with the "screens" and oriel, where James I. in his cups knighted the loin of beef and made it first a sirloin.

183

# FORGOTTEN SHRINES

The " Howse which Hoghton of Hoghton, Esquier, enterprysed to buylde and ffynysh in 1562," thus still looks down from its proud height upon the country-side. Thomas Hoghton the Elizabethan builder was a man of faith, nay, a confessor of the faith under the Virgin Queen : a friend of William, afterwards Cardinal, Allen, he had the honour of entertaining that great man under his roof. It was a dangerous honour, for no man was more obnoxious to the new rulers of England than the intrepid Cardinal.

We do not know whether Allen ever lodged under the stately roof of Hoghton Tower, for it was being built between 1563 and 1565, just at the time that Allen paid his last visit to Lancashire. Mr. Gillow, however (and there is no better authority), thinks that he was present at the house-warming of the great mansion. But if Allen lodged at the old manor-house at Hoghton Bottom, which had sheltered the family

" E'er since the Hoghtons from this hill took name,
Who with the stiff, unbridled Saxons came,"

he must have watched with interest the rising of those majestic towers, which still look down on busy Lancashire.

But a greater guest even than he certainly rode up the long steep drive to claim a shelter in the stately Tower of Hoghton. This was Allen's beloved son, the blessed martyr, Edmund Campion, who came here on his missionary tour through Lancashire in the winter of 1580–1581. But at that time the builder of Hoghton Tower had already died in exile, not having long enjoyed the splendours of his house ; for, five years after he had completed it, the persecution drove him from his native land. Mr. Gillow in his invaluable *Dictionary* tells us that "feeling he could not remain in the country and keep his conscience, Hoghton took the advice of his friend, Vivian Haydock (whose son William married Hoghton's sister Bryde),* and in 1569, or the beginning of the following year, he hired a vessel and sailed from his mansion of The Lea, on the Ribble, to the coast of France, and thence proceeded to Antwerp. For this he was declared an outlaw, and possession was taken of his estate." He remained in exile till his death, in June 1580, and was buried in the Church of St. Gervais, at Liége, where a handsome monument was erected to his memory bearing his arms and the following inscription :

" Hic e regione sepultus est vir illustris D. Thomas Houghton Anglus qui post decem·annos exilium spontaneum variasque patrimonii et rerum omnium direptiones propter Catholicæ fidei confessionem a sectariis illatas

* Thus Mr. Hoghton was connected by marriage with the glorious martyr, Venerable George Haydock (1558–84) who in his boyhood must often have visited Hoghton Tower.

184

THE GREAT HALL, HOGHTON TOWER
*Photo by James Watts*

*To face page* 184

obiit 4 Non. Jun. 1580, ætat 63," which, roughly translated, may run as follows :—

"Over against this spot lies buried the illustrious man Mr. Thomas Houghton, Englishman, who after ten years of voluntary exile, despoiled by the sectaries of his patrimony and all his goods for his confession of the Catholic faith, died June 2, 1580, aged 63."

An instrument relative to his estate, drawn up by Dr. Allen at Rheims (June 26, 1580), relates that Mr. Hoghton, "our deceased friend of godly memory," disposed of all the money he had in hand a year before his death, and among other things bequeathed £100 to buy a pair of organs, one fair table, and as many books of music as should cost £7 (which money be placed in the hands of John Sacheverell, Esquire, and Hugo Charnock, Gentleman, his friends and fellow-exiles), for the Parish Church of Preston, of which the Hoghtons were patrons, "when time should serve." But his executors, seeing little hope of being able to fulfil their friend's bequest, agreed with his faithful servants, Anthony Stamper and Edmund Stubbes, to give the money to Allen for the use of his Seminary, he undertaking to pay it back to Preston Church when times should change.

He had already been a great benefactor to the College, and so, finally, on July 5, 1590, his body was carried from Liége to Douay, and translated to its last resting-place under the predella of the high altar on the Epistle side, when the first High Mass was sung in the new church of the English College there, July 13, 1603.

He was the author of a most pathetic ballad, entitled :

### "THE BLESSED CONSCIENCE.

" At Hoghton hygh, which is a bower
   Of sports and lordly pleasure,
I wept, and lefte that loftie tower
   Wich was my chiefest treasure.
To save my soul and lose ye reste
   Yt was my trew pretence :
Lyke fryghted bird, I lefte my neste
   To kepe my conscyènce.

" At Hoghton, where I used to reste
   Of men I hadd great store,
Ful twentie gentlemen att least,
   Of yeomen gode three score.
And of them all, I brought but twoe
   Wyth mee, when I cam thence.
I left them all, ye world knows how,
   To kepe my conscyènce.

# FORGOTTEN SHRINES

" Fayr England ! nowe ten tymes adieu,
  And frendes that theryn dwel ;
Fayrwel my broder Richard trewe,
  Whom I dyd love soe wel.
Fayrwel, fayrwel ! gode people all,
  And learn experience ;
Love not too much ye golden ball,
  But kepe your conscyènce."

The son of this brave confessor, also named Thomas, went with his father into exile, and studied at Douay for the priesthood. Bereft of all his patrimony, his devotion to the faith cost him also his life. On arriving in Lancashire to labour on the mission, he was at once seized and thrown into Salford Gaol, where we find him in 1582, and still in 1584, and where in all probability he died. He is noted in 1582 as one of those Catholic prisoners who " do still continue in their obstinate opinions, neither do we see any likelihood of conformity in any of them."

Mr. Hoghton's brother Richard, who entertained Father Campion at Hoghton Tower, was arrested in the summer of 1581, immediately after the martyr's own apprehension. It appears that a number of Catholic books and papers had been left by Father Campion at Hoghton Tower, and these he was on his way to fetch, when he was arrested at Lyford Grange. Richard Hoghton survived his imprisonment, but was pursued with relentless persecution to the end of his life.

The Hoghtons only lost the faith through the cruel system, then so widely practised, of seizing the head of the family when a minor and bringing him up in the new religion. Thus, in the next generation, the young Lord of Hoghton was given in ward to Sir Gilbert Gerard, Master of the Rolls, who married him to his daughter whilst still under age, and brought him up as a Protestant. The same thing happened to Thomas Hoghton's great-great-grandson (descended from his only daughter Jane), Sir Roger Bradshaigh of Haigh Hall. The rest of the Hoghton family retained the faith, and but for these unjust proceedings, the Sir Richard Hoghton who entertained our Scottish Solomon on August 17, 1617, would have been, like his forefathers, a faithful Catholic.*

When the Lords of Hoghton lost the faith, it might have been feared that Brindle and the neighbourhood would not keep it long. But the Catholics of Lancashire are of sturdier stuff than that, and though the protection of the great house was gone, the farmers and labourers on the Hoghton estate have remained firm, for the most part, to this very day.

* I owe most of these details to Mr. Gillow's *Haydock Papers*. He prints the ballad in full.

186

THE VENERABLE EDMUND ARROWSMITH, S.J.
*From the original oil-painting at Stonyhurst College*

*To face page* 186

# IN A MARTYR'S FOOTSTEPS

We must now seek for the traditions of the penal days, not in the castle on the hill, but in the farm-houses and villages that cluster in the valley below.

Nowhere, perhaps, in England does the Catholic pilgrim find a more consoling spectacle than in this tract of country that lies between Preston and Blackburn. Nowhere, perhaps, does he find himself brought more into touch with the Merry England of the good old days, before the Tudor schism devastated the land.

Here stands many an old chapel, dating almost from penal days, surrounded, as of yore, by a sturdy flock, English to the core, and all the more true to the faith for the sufferings they have endured for its dear sake. Here, too, stands many an old farm-house, in which Holy Mass was said by some devoted priest during the dark days when no public worship was possible. Here, too, there yet linger priceless traditions of the good shepherds who did not fear to lay down their lives for their sheep ; and still may be gathered from the lips of aged men, the thrilling stories of those days that now seem so far off—stories handed down from grandsire to grandchild, traditions all the more precious, because they are, as it were, family heirlooms, never given to the public, but guarded with jealous care by their possessors. But the old houses are gradually falling into decay, the old generation quickly passing away. It is well "to gather up the fragments that nothing be lost."

Thus it was that a pilgrim spent some days in this neighbourhood, trying to gather up the memories of one of the glorious martyrs who once ministered there, and here is the result of his labour of love.

We have no intention of writing a life of Venerable Edmund Arrowsmith, S.J. It has been fully done already by Brother Foley in his *Records*, and again, most charmingly, in a little Catholic Truth Society pamphlet, by the veteran historian, Father Francis Goldie, S.J. But we may briefly sketch the martyr's career in order to introduce him to our readers. He was a Lancashire man, born between Wigan and Warrington, at Haydock, in Winwick parish, to Robert Arrowsmith, yeoman, and Margery Gerard his wife. The Gerards were, and still are, a family ennobled both by ancient lineage and faithful adherence to the old religion.

Our martyr was born in 1585, and was christened Bryan, or Barnaby. He took the name of Edmund in Confirmation, no doubt because it was the name of his uncle, who was a distinguished professor at Douay College. Bryan was a very pious child : we learn that he used to recite the Little Hours of Our Lady's Office on his way to school with his brothers, and her Vespers and Compline on the way home. This school seems to have been the Grammar School at Senely Green (built in 1587), which now serves as a Catholic Infant School attached to the Mission of Birchley. It was not till he was twenty that Bryan got across to Douay, and there received the Sacrament of Confirmation and the name by which he was henceforth known. He was a delicate lad, and twice during his studies had a serious breakdown, but he recovered his health and persevered in his vocation to the priesthood, to which he was at last raised at Arras, December 9, 1612. And thus at the age of twenty-seven he came back to England to labour in God's vineyard. We are told that he was small and rather uncouth in appearance, but of a bright and pleasant disposition and very attractive in conversation. He was also full of fun. After ten years' arduous labour in Lancashire, he was arrested and lodged in Lancaster Castle. He was, however, released, and made use of his liberty to join the Society of Jesus, which he had for years longed to do. This was in 1624. Each year he retired to some out-of-the-way spot in Lancashire to make a retreat of ten or twelve days with other of his fellow religious.

And so we come to the summer of 1628, when the quarrel between King Charles I. and the Parliament was running high; this year found Father Arrowsmith labouring in the neighbourhood of Brindle. Frequently he said Mass on the old Missionary Altar, described in another place, belonging to the Burgess family, and now preserved at Bolton-le-Sands. They were settled at that time at Denham Hall, Brindle.

Another house in which he used to say Mass, and in which it is said he celebrated what was probably his last Mass, is still standing in Gregson Lane in Brindle. One end of it now faces the entrance to Gregson Lane Mill. "It is believed to have been erected about 1580, and is a fine example of the comfortable yeoman's dwelling of that period, an interesting feature of the building being a small room in which the ironwork around the fire-place is hammered into a representation of the wheat and vine, emblematic of the bread and wine used in the Mass. It is said that at the beginning of the eighteenth century this house was the residence of the Gregsons of Gregson Lane, one of whom placed his initials, 'G.G.,' with a cross and the date, 1700, on the lintel of the porch, thus giving later generations the erroneous impression that the building was erected in 1700. Near this house was dug up in 1899 a very ancient font, possibly of the ninth century, and in the garden of a cottage close by stands a beautiful old wayside cross. Local tradition asserts that at this same old house the Venerable Edmund Arrowsmith, the Jesuit martyr, said his last Mass. There are other interesting traditions of his presence in the neighbourhood. The writer possesses a tiny statue, enclosed in an ivory niche, which Father Arrowsmith is said to have dropped as he

188

THE HOUSE OF THE LAST MASS, GREGSON LANE
*Photo by W. T. Bateson*

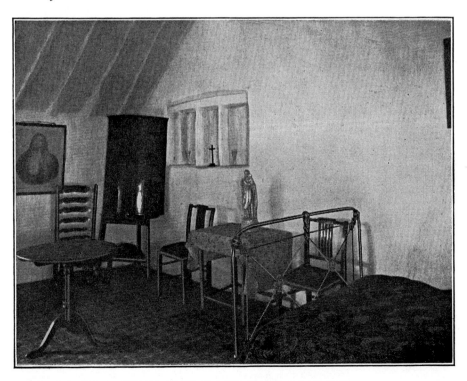

THE ROOM WHERE THE LAST MASS WAS SAID
*Photo by W. T. Bateson*

*To face page* 188

escaped from the Old Blue Anchor Inn at the Straits in Hoghton Lane."*
An illustration of this relic is here given. So far a local antiquary—but
we must now return to the house in Gregson Lane. There still exists a
dark attic under the thatch, corresponding to the secret oratory of Father
Postgate at Egton. There is no light in this attic, and it is only reached
by a ladder and a trap-door. It is situated in the gable end of the house,
to the right as you enter the porch, and was probably a priest's hiding-
place. A mullioned window
in this end of the house
lights the room that leads
to this attic. Alas! the
thatched roof has recently
been replaced by hideous
corrugated iron, a truly
lamentable vulgarisation of
this fine old dwelling. Our
martyr's last Mass is said
to have been celebrated in
a bedroom at the east end
of the house, of which we
give an illustration. A
cross is faintly seen in the
gable-end of this room near
the top.

One very remarkable
fact must be mentioned
about this house. It is
vouched for by several
members of the Walmesley
family who have lived there,
including the present occu-

IVORY SHRINE — SAID TO HAVE BELONGED
TO THE VENERABLE EDMVND ARROWSMITH.
SCALE OF ⊢—————————⊣ INCHES

pants. It is said that a cross of light appears at intervals on the wall of
the room in which the last Mass was said, and remains visible for some
little time. My informants, including a Catholic doctor of the neighbourhood, tell me that there is no possible natural explanation of this
phenomenon. The present occupier, Mr. Walmesley, has seen it several
times. It appears high up on the wall. The previous occupant, whose
name is Worden, has also frequently seen it.

In the year 1841, while some earlier occupants, also named
Walmesley, lived in the house, a great storm of wind blew down part

* Kindly communicated by Mr. George Hull, from his *Historical Sketch of St. Joseph's,
Brindle.*

of a wall in the attic, and behind it was discovered a hiding-place in which was found a box containing a chalice and two vestments, and two altar-stones, one broken. The chalice appears to have been given to a Mr. Thomas Parkinson, who was then studying for the priesthood, but I have been unable to trace it further. One of the chasubles and the altar-stones were given by Mrs. Walmesley to Father Ildephonsus Brown, O.S.B., of Ampleforth Abbey, who was pastor of the Brindle Mission from 1874 to 1884. He, considering that these treasures were relics of a Jesuit martyr, very generously gave the chasuble to the museum of Stonyhurst College. This beautiful vestment is powdered with Gothic flowers of the conventional type, and further adorned with a charming little figure of St. John the Baptist. It is made of inferior silk, and is much worn, especially in front, where the mending is of the rudest character. The groundwork is now brown. It was once red, with a blue cross on the back. The pillar in front has floral designs like the back. The neck-piece is Y-shaped, and can be drawn together by a hook and eye. The front is very much narrower than the back. The lining is of coarse linen. The stole and maniple are lost. We should take the date to be late fifteenth century.

A former occupant of the house writes to me: "I think that there is still something hidden in the house, as in one room, where there is a very thick wall, there is plainly marked in black a cross with three lines below, and no matter how often the wall is whitewashed, the cross always reappears." This is in the pantry, which is approached through the kitchen, at the west end of the house. This pantry is only about 7½ ft. by 6 ft., and could not hold more than six people. The cross is on the north side, about 2 ft. from the west wall. Undoubtedly Holy Mass was sometimes said in this small room. An altar-stone, broken in half and enclosed in a coarse canvas bag, so as to be folded and put into the pocket, was found here. But it is not known what has become of it, though it may possibly be found at Ampleforth Abbey.

The Walmesley family still cherish as a very precious relic a part of the other less perfect vestment which Father Arrowsmith is said to have worn in their house. My informant writes: "It must have been purple, but it is very much faded. It was put on the bed when I was confined of my first child, with a promise, if all went well (of which there were grave doubts), the child should be either a priest or a nun. The girl who was then born has always had a desire from her birth to be a nun."

The dark blue lining of this chasuble was given to Father Ildephonsus

Brown, who still possesses it. The silk vestment was divided among friends of the Walmesleys, they naturally keeping the largest portion. The altar-stone and half the broken one are in possession of Father Brown, who is now stationed at Parbold near Southport. It is of course not *certain* that these relics really were used by our martyr, but it is at least extremely probable.

Across the railway at the modern Hoghton Station runs Hoghton Lane, leading directly to Preston through Walton-le-Dale. A few hundred

THE OLD BLUE ANCHOR INN, HOGHTON. *from which the
Ven. Edmund Arrowsmith, s.J. escaped.
The + shew position of hiding place.*

yards in the direction of Gregson Lane and Walton is a part of the road called the Straits. Here, on the left-hand side of the road, formerly stood a picturesque old half-timbered house with a thatched roof. This was the old Blue Anchor Inn, and I am able to give a drawing of it, from an old photograph, for unhappily it has been pulled down in recent years. This old house was used by Father Arrowsmith as a place of refuge, and contained a hiding-place, the position of which is marked in the sketch. It was entered from a bedroom at the south end of the building. One of my kind informants, Mr. William Bolton, tells me that he has frequently visited this hiding-place. It was from this house that the martyr fled on his last fatal journey, dropping as he did so, for he was heavily laden, the little ivory statuette already mentioned.

We have now to consider the history of the martyr's arrest, as given by his own lips at his trial, supplemented by the topographical details which the devout Catholics of the neighbourhood have carefully handed down. My principal informant as to these traditions is Mr. Peter Worden, now of Bolton-le-Sands, near Carnforth, whose forefathers have lived in the same locality from time immemorial. He lived as a boy with his parents for ten years (1843–1853) in the nearest house to the spot where Father Arrowsmith was arrested.*

He says : " I believe there was little change in the place up to that time. The Moss Ditch (which, as we shall hear, played so fatal a part in the tragedy) was then open. It was drained about thirty years ago. I left that district in 1864, and have only visited it once or twice a year since."

" There is little doubt that the last few years of Father Arrowsmith were spent in the neighbourhood of Brindle. He rode about on horseback a good deal, and a man often rode with him, and brought the horse back which Father Arrowsmith had ridden, after he had dismounted near the place where he was about to celebrate Holy Mass. No doubt he had a large area. I have heard that he said Mass at Lower Hall, Church Bottoms ; Fleetwood Hall, in Samlesbury ; Jack Green, Brindle ; Wickenhouse Farm, Withnell ; Wheelton ; Denham Hall, near Clayton Green ; Woodcock Hall, Cuerden ; and Livesey Hall, near Blackburn."

The occasion of our martyr's apprehension was his zeal for the sanctity of marriage. Two first-cousins, of whom the man was a Catholic, named Holden, had been married by the Protestant minister. They seemed to have lived with the man's father in the old Blue Anchor Inn already described. Father Arrowsmith was engaged in procuring a dispensation to make the marriage valid when the young woman also became a Catholic. When the dispensation came from Rome, the Father would not make use of it unless the parties had separated for the space of fourteen days. This incensed them so much that they determined to betray him. They knew that he used to stay in their father's house, and, knowing the time when he was to return there, they had the wickedness to send word to Captain Rawsthorn, a Justice of the Peace (the Rawsthorn family still reside at Penwortham, near Preston), to come and apprehend the priest. The Justice was unwilling to injure old Mr. Holden, who was a neighbour of his, and sent to warn him, bidding him send the Father away before he came to search the house. Our martyr hastily left the house, and set out on horseback, as we shall hear, with his books and belongings, intending to seek shelter, as it is supposed, in an out-of-the-way farmhouse at Withnell. The pursuers

---

* I have also to thank Mr. George Hull and Mr. William Bolton for much valuable information about places and traditions which they have known from childhood.

192

were sent off on the Blackburn Road, but Father Arrowsmith had taken the opposite direction. However, in doubling back on his track, he came across some of his pursuers, and was apprehended by the servant of the Justice, and his son, a boy of only twelve years old, who were returning

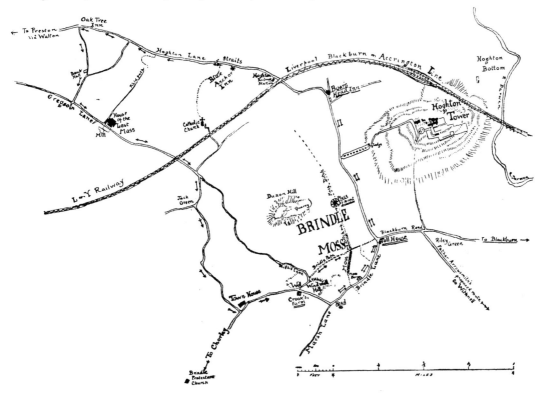

from the search. They witnessed against him at his trial that he had tried to withdraw them from the Protestant religion.

We will now give the martyr's own account of his arrest, from the records of his trial.

"The servant of God upon this humbly begged leave to speak, which being granted, he spoke to this effect: 'My lord, as I was upon the road, that very man, as I take it, rushed out upon me with a drawn sword. He was meanly dressed, and upon horseback. I made what haste I could from him, but being weak and sickly, was forced by him at last to the Moss, where I alighted, and fled with all the speed I was able—which yet could not be very great, seeing I was loaded with heavy clothes, books, and other things. At length he came up to me at the Moss Ditch, and struck at me, though I had nothing to defend myself with but a little walking-

2 B                                                                      193

stick, and a sword, which I did not draw; with the blow he cut the stick close to my hand, and did me some little hurt. I then asked him if his design was to take my purse and my life. He answered that perhaps it was: and then I fled again from him, but was soon overtaken. Then came up this youth (the Justice's son), who has given evidence against me, with others to assist him. They used me with much indignity, and took me to an alehouse, and searched me to the skin, offering insults which modesty forbids me to relate, and which I resisted as far as I was able. That done, they fell to drinking, and spent nine shillings of my money in an hour; they told me that the Justice of the Peace, by whose warrant I was apprehended, was there in person, but that I would not believe. Upon this occasion, my Lords, I began to find fault with the man's wicked and rude behaviour who seemed to be the ringleader; and I besought him for Jesu's sake to give up his disordered life, drinking, dissolute talk, and whatever might offend Almighty God. Upon my word and my life, this, or to this effect, is all I said to him. Let him look on me and gainsay it, if he can. As for that youth, I deny not to have told him, that I hoped when he came to riper years, he would look better into himself, and become a true Catholic, for that, and that alone, would be the means to save his soul; to which he made no answer at all. And I hope, my Lords, that neither they, nor any other can prove ill against me."

So far the martyr. If now the reader will examine the map which we append, he will be able to trace the very route taken by the holy man in his flight, and if good fortune ever take him to Brindle, he will be thus in a position to make a pilgrimage in the martyr's steps.

"It is thought," writes Mr. Worden, "that he intended to go to Wickenhouse Farm, Withnell, an isolated place where he sometimes said Mass. A man accompanied him on horseback. They set off in a contrary direction to Withnell, going on the road towards Preston, but turned to the left past the Oak Tree Inn, and went up Gregson Lane. They passed over Jack Green, by the Town House (a gentleman's house now known as 'The Nook'), and then turned to the left towards Marsh Lane Head. They turned again to the left at the Well, where there is a farm-house, then occupied by a family named Crook, past Windmill Hill, on to Brindle Moss. Meanwhile the pursuer had got on the scent, and inquired at the farm at the Well which way the two horsemen had gone. Crook, the farmer, directed him, as he had observed the fugitives pass his house. The pursuer overtook them at the Moss (which abuts on Duxon Hill), and ran on our martyr with his drawn sword. Finding that his horse refused to jump the Moss Ditch, the Father dismounted and ran along by its side, hoping to reach the place higher up where the ditch is much

194

narrower. The ditch still exists, but is now roughly bridged over with thick stones or flags. He ran on for some little time till he came to this narrower part, but here, as he tells us, the pursuer overtook him. Meanwhile, the man who should have been his protector deserted him. The martyr was apprehended, with the help of the rest of the party who soon came up, and was carried by them first to the toll-house at Marsh Lane End, and thence to the Boar's Head Inn in Hoghton Lane, not far from the present railway station. Here he was subjected to the infamies of which he complained at his trial. He was then carried off to the dungeons of Lancaster Castle.

"If his horse had jumped the Moss Ditch he would soon have been on the Blackburn Road. By turning to the right at Riley Green, he would have got to Billy Street on the Chorley Road. Then to the right, they would soon have reached the occupation road leading to Wickenhouse Farm. Father Arrowsmith could then have dismounted and walked by this secluded road to the farm unobserved. The man would have gone on with both horses to Wheelton, then by Copthurst, Waterhouse Green, and through Brindle, home. That is supposed to have been the plan."

The late Mr. William Brindle, of Brimmicroft, Hoghton (whose mother was a Livesey), when an old man, told Mr. Worden that Wickenhouse Farm had been inhabited by the Liveseys since the Reformation. The room was still shown in which Father Arrowsmith and other priests had said Mass. Unhappily the old farm is now in ruins. It began to fall into decay about the year 1899, and was then demolished in order to provide stones to repair another old farm-house, near at hand, to which the Livesey family removed. This is now called New Wickenhouse Farm, though its old name was Taylor's Farm.

Mr. Worden continues : " My uncle, William Walmsley, told me that Crook, the farmer, went after the pursuer of Father Arrowsmith, and was given his cloak as a reward for the information he had given. He had a fine boy about eleven years of age, and he got a tailor to come to the house to make the child a suit out of the martyr's cloak. When he put it on, the family was much pleased with his appearance, and to celebrate the event he was put on the back of a horse, to take a triumphal ride. But though the child had previously ridden this horse, which was a quiet one, it at once, on feeling his weight, set off at a gallop and threw him. His head struck a stone on the roadside, and the poor boy was killed on the spot. The stone was visible for a long distance when I was a boy, but the road has been raised at that part and the stone covered. The family were so frightened that they returned to the Catholic faith. They were up to that time noted for their good looks, but the children of their descendants were for long afterwards in some way deformed or dwarfs. My uncle said that God had punished them severely, though they afterwards kept the faith and were very striving. One of the last I remember was James, alias 'Turk,' a dwarf. They lived at a place called Bullocks, on the river Darwen side, above Samlesbury Mill. He was drowned in the river Darwen in February, 1862.*

"I have often heard it said that Father Arrowsmith was once disputing about religion with the Vicar of Brindle, near the church wall, and he said : 'If my religion is right, my foot will leave its impression on this stone,' and he sent his foot back against the wall, and left the impress of his boot." So far Mr. Worden.

This last story is very interesting, as parallel legends may be found about many of the saints, notably about SS. Peter and Paul at Santa Francesca Romana, in Rome, and St. Benedict at Monte Cassino. The impress of Our Lord's Feet are shown at the "Domine quo Vadis," on the Appian Way, and on the Mount of Olives, in the Church of the Ascension. We are informed that the stone has been built over or reversed so that the impression can no longer be seen. This was done because of the reverence shown to it by Catholics.

The rare printed Life of the Martyr,† written probably by Father Cornelius Morphy, S.J., and published in London in 1737, adds : " There is a letter extant of this blessed man, the first he wrote after he was imprisoned, which hath these words : 'All particulars did so co-operate to my apprehension and bringing hither, that I can easily discover more than an ordinary providence of Almighty God therein.' " The author then mentions, among others, these : " When the blessed man was flying from his persecutors at the time of his apprehension, he was extraordinarily well mounted ; and yet whatsoever desire he had and diligence he used, it was not possible to put his horse to any speed. . . . A kinsman of his own, whom he had in nature of a servant, well known to be a stout man, forsook him and fled away, when the least resistance might have preserved him."

Another tradition of the martyr in Brindle is, that an old " malt-

* I have received a very touching letter from Mr. William Crook, one of this family. He ends as follows : "Dear Father, our family may have suffered for their folly in the past, but let us hope there is a brighter day before us. I would ask you to remember us at the altar, as we will remember you in our prayers." The writer is a nephew of the poor man who was drowned in the Darwen. No doubt the martyr's prayers have won for the family the grace of the true faith.

† *A True and Exact Relation of the Death of Two Catholics Who Suffered for Their Religion at the Summer Assizes, held at Lancaster,* 1682.—A copy is in the Library of Oscott College.

P. Edmundus Arosmithœus Angl. Soc. IESV pro Fide Ca
tholica suspensus et dissectus Lancastriæ in Anglia 7 Sept.A.1628.

## THE MARTYRDOM OF FATHER
## ARROWSMITH
*From an old print*

*To face page 196*

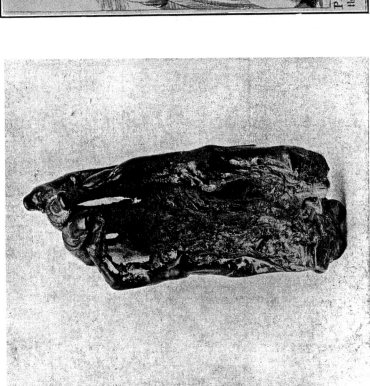

## "THE HOLY HAND"
*Venerated at Ashton-in-Makerfield*

house" in the neighbourhood was used as a hiding-place by Father Arrowsmith and two or three other priests. This old malt-house is in good preservation. It is situated in a field off Brier's Brow, Wheelton (near Chorley), close to the present Catholic Church of South Hill. It is some considerable distance from the high road going from Preston to Chorley, and on the left side. The malt-house now forms several cottages, but it was formerly used as a farm-house. A new farm-house has been built just behind. An old holy-water stoup is still to be seen in the house, and the hiding-place of the martyr still exists. Another place where Father Arrowsmith is said to have celebrated Holy Mass in this neighbourhood is a house at Lockett Lane, close to Wheelton, the residence of a branch of the Andertons of Euxton.

Yet another forgotten shrine is Slate Delph Farm, Wheelton. Only last year the original steps to the humble loft where the martyr said Mass were removed, as I am informed by Dr. Thomas P. Leighton of Brinscall. The plain glass chalice used by the martyr at Slate Delph Farm is still preserved in Catholic hands. This is an exceedingly interesting relic, for glass chalices must be very rare. At Slate Delph Farm (as at other places) " washed linen " was put out on a certain hedge to inform the people that Mass was to be said there that day.

We need not follow the holy martyr to his glorious death at Lancaster. The incidents of his trial and cruel martyrdom have been admirably recounted by Father Goldie. We may, however, give the fine old print of the martyrdom from Tanner's *Societas Jesu usque ad sanguinis et vitæ profusionem militans* (Pragae, 1675). It took place on August 28, 1628. The martyr was forty-three years old. The gallows was erected about a quarter of a mile from the Castle. Near it were a cauldron, boiling high over a vast fire, the butcher's knife and other apparatus of torture. " Nothing grieves me so much as this England which I pray God soon to convert," he cried from the ladder ; and with an earnestness which moved his auditors to tears, he bade them bear witness that he died a steadfast Roman Catholic, and exhorted them to become members of the one true Church. His last words were *Bone Jesu*—" Good Jesus ! " as he was thrown from the ladder and the butchery began. From that cruel agony his soul fled to heaven. His name is still greatly honoured at Lancaster, and when the present writer made his pilgrimage to the Castle, the custodians took care to point out to him, without even being asked, the place where the trial took place, and the exact spot on John of Gaunt's Tower where the sacred quarters were exposed on high, according to the orders of the brutal judge.

197

Finally, let us mention one or two other relics and memorials of the martyr which have been handed down to us.

At Ampleforth Abbey is now preserved an old sideboard, which is said to have been frequently used by Father Arrowsmith as an altar. It was in the possession of the Dennet family at Appleton, in Lancashire, who lived within three hundred yards of a house occupied for some years by the venerable martyr. A member of this family was the Mother Prioress of the nuns of St. Sepulchre, now at New Hall in Essex, and the present Abbot Smith, of Ampleforth, remembers an old relative who died about 1859, at the age of 91 or 92, who knew this prioress, and handed down the tradition from her. The marks left by the two Mass candles on the *mensa* of this improvised altar are still clearly visible. The vestments were kept in a cupboard at the side. The altar passed into the possession of Miss Ellen Nightingale, a niece of the Dennets, who afterwards married John Smith, of Sutton, County Lancaster, and was the mother of the Right Rev. Abbot Smith, and of Mrs. Dawson, of Preston. The latter presented the altar to Ampleforth Abbey in 1905, and it is now in St. Peter's Chapel there. I owe these particulars to the kindness of the Abbot.

At Stanbrook Abbey is preserved a little cross, which has been handed down in the Talbot family of Padgate near Warrington, as having belonged to the martyr. These Talbots claimed to be relatives of Father Arrowsmith, and they cherished this tiny cross as a very precious relic. One of them, Margaret Talbot, became a lay-sister at Stanbrook, under the name of Sister Elizabeth. She received the cross from her mother, who gave it to her because she thought it would be safer than with her son. I have been unable to learn more particulars of the history of this little cross. On the obverse side Our Lord is represented, and on the reverse Our Lady. The inscription on the latter runs : " Vir. Imm. vitam præst. pusam " (*sic.*)—*i.e.* "Virgo Immaculata vitam præsta puram" (Virgin Immaculate, grant to us a pure life.)

We need not be surprised that relics of our martyr came into the hands of his friends. Brother Foley prints a very interesting letter from a certain Henry Holme, who seems to have been a warder in Lancaster Castle, to a priest named Thomas Metcalfe, attesting the authenticity of certain relics he had given him.* In it he says : " The certainty of those things which I did deliver you at your being at Lancaster, I will affirm to be true, for the hair and the pieces of the ribs I did take myself at the going up of the plumbers to see the leads, when they were to mend them ; and the handkerchief was dipped in his blood at the time

* Foley *Records*, vol. ii. p. 59, from the Westminster Archives.

of his quarters coming back from the execution to the Castle, by me likewise with my own hands. You know the handkerchief was your own which you gave me at your departure, and for the piece of the quarter, both I and some others had taken part of it for our friends, which Mr. Southworth can witness ; and that which I gave you, John Rigmaden, our keeper, gave me leave to take. . . ." This letter is actually endorsed by John Rigmaden, the keeper of Lancaster Castle, so it is evident that then as now, the martyr had sympathetic friends in his very prison.

Indeed the people of Lancaster always sympathised with him. At his martyrdom their behaviour, says his ancient biographer, was very remarkable. " In proof of their detestation of this judicial murder, no man could be prevailed upon to undertake the execution, except a butcher, who though ashamed to become the hangman himself, engaged for five pounds that his servant should despatch the martyr. This the servant, out of a feeling of humanity and respect for that good man, refused, and when informed of his master's shameful contract, he fled from his service, and was never seen by him again. Within the gaol itself the same spirit was displayed. Felons and malefactors, though offered their own lives, would lend no hand to injustice ; till a deserter, under sentence of death for leaving his regiment, offered for the sum of forty shillings, the prisoner's clothes, and his own liberty, to be the vile instrument of the murder. But this made him so detested by the good people of Lancaster, that none would lend him an axe wherewith to slay the servant of God."

We learn from a contemporary report that the martyr's clothes and the knife that cut him up came into the possession of a devout Catholic, Sir Cuthbert Clifton. Thus we are not surprised that the martyr's near relatives, the Gerard family, were able to secure for themselves no less a relic than his right hand. No record, apparently, remains as to how they secured it, but it was in their possession at Garswood, Ashton-in-Makerfield, for many generations. It is at present preserved with great reverence in the church of St. Oswald, at Ashton, wrapped in linen and enclosed in a silver casket.

In the " Life " of the martyr, published in 1737, is a very circumstantial account of a miracle of healing, worked through the means of this holy hand, on Thomas Hawarden, a child of twelve, at Appleton-within-Widnes, in Lancashire. It is certified by no fewer than nineteen witnesses, several of whom have signed as Protestants. Since that time the miracles worked through this holy relic are innumerable, and continue down to our own day, nor was this the first cure recorded. Some twenty to sixty pilgrims still visit the " Holy Hand " every week, and after Mass every day it is applied to those who are suffering. More than this, linen which has touched this relic is frequently sent to the sick who are not able to make the pilgrimage, and in many cases cures are recorded. The present writer remembers meeting at Bournemouth in 1893 Father O'Reilly, the then priest of Ashton, who told him that a few days before he had taken to a poor woman, who was expecting an operation for cancer or tumour in the infirmary at Bournemouth, a piece of linen, which she had applied to her breast. That very morning the surgeon had come to perform the operation, and had found to his astonishment that the tumour had entirely disappeared, and that no operation was needed. Many other most wonderful cures are recorded at length by Brother Foley and Father Goldie.

We may quote one which they do not give, but which appeared in the *Messenger of the Sacred Heart*, for December 1900. " At Seaforth, a little boy was in danger of losing his sight through the recurrence during two years of malignant ulcers. Specialists were consulted, but no good effected. One eye was almost lost, and the other was going rapidly. Many Masses were offered and novenas made. At last the little fellow was taken, in a state of intense suffering, to be touched by Venerable Father Arrowsmith's hand. He returned home happy and free from pain ; the eyes gradually healed, and are now bright and clear, only a slight mark remaining to remind one of the time of trial, and of worse suffering averted. With grateful hearts his family now fulfil their promise of publication."

Another recent miracle has the merit not only of making a very pretty story, but of being recounted by a medical man. Dr. Leighton of Brinscall writes (March 31, 1910) as follows : "One of my collectors, John James Denhurst, who, when four years old, could not walk or talk, was taken by his mother and touched by the Holy Hand. He immediately exclaimed, "Mother Mary."

A lady, Miss Almond, of Badminton Road, Balham, tells me that when living at Liverpool she herself witnessed two miracles through the application of linen that had touched Father Arrowsmith's hand. The second one, which happened about 1870, was the cure of a little girl who through severe illness had entirely lost the use of her legs. She was instantaneously cured, to her doctor's amazement, by the touch of the linen.

Another correspondent from St. Katherine's Convent, Queen Square, tells of a friend of hers who was instantly cured of complete lameness by the same means. A novena was made to the holy martyr, and afterwards the linen was applied to her knee. The pain caused was so great that she screamed aloud, but the next instant she was perfectly and completely cured. She had been so helpless till then that she had to be carried up and down stairs.

As our glorious martyr was being hanged, an eye-witness of credit declared that he saw, at the moment the holy man expired, a very brilliant light extending in a stream from the Castle to the gallows, like resplendent glass. Never in his life before had he seen anything of the kind. " But the path of the just, as a shining light, goeth forward and increaseth even to perfect day." (Prov. iv. 18).

# THE SKULL OF WARDLEY HALL

## THE "SKULL HOUSE"

SOME of the pleasantest recollections of the writer are woven round a visit paid in company with the present Bishop of Salford to the historic Hall of Wardley. It is true that the day was a deplorable one, Manchester and its environs being wrapped in a heavy pall of dense fog, which made it impossible even to see across the moat of Wardley Hall, yet the interest of the visit was so great, the hospitable welcome we received so kind and cordial, the sense of having at last been able to fulfil a long-cherished wish so delightful, that this day of pilgrimage is marked henceforth with a white stone in the tablets of memory. For it was no mere historic mansion that the good Bishop took us to visit ; the interest of Wardley is more than antiquarian : it is not only a beautiful old house, it is a martyr's shrine.

Beautiful it undoubtedly is, and fascinating to the antiquary beyond many old houses, but its unique glory is signified in its name of the "Skull House," for it guards in its very innermost heart the head of one of Christ's chiefest martyrs in England. For as all Lancashire now knows, the skull that is enshrined on the staircase wall of Wardley is that of the Venerable Servant of God, Edward Ambrose Barlow, monk of the Holy Order of St. Benedict, who shed his blood for his faith at Lancaster, September 10, 1641.

This has indeed not always been so clear as it happily now is, for as we shall see, various popular legends grew up around the relic, and gave rise to much confusion. But the skill and learning of Mr. Joseph Gillow have unravelled the tangle for us, and we may now be morally certain that the Skull House of Wardley enshrines the head of the martyr-monk of Manchester.

Before we proceed to recount the life of this holy and venerable priest, it may be well to give some account of the old house which is so closely associated with his memory. Wardley Hall has found a most competent historian in the person of its present tenant, Colonel Henry Vaughan Hart-Davis (late R.E.), Chief Agent to the Earl of Ellesmere, to whom the house belongs. The splendid volume which appeared in 1908 bears witness not merely to his antiquarian research but to his artistic skill, for the illustrations which give so much charm to the book are all reproduced from the talented author's own drawings. In his careful and tender hands the venerable mansion has been repaired and restored to much of its pristine beauty and magnificence, after a long period of

WARDLEY HALL FROM THE NORTH-WEST

*Photo by James Watts*

To face page 202

neglect and degradation.   He is intensely proud of it, as well he may be, and no little of our pleasure in visiting the old place was derived from his own enthusiasm for its manifold beauties.   It is always a joy to see an ancient house in good hands, and Wardley is indeed happy, for it could not have fallen into better keeping.

It is from Colonel Hart-Davis that we have gleaned what we know of the history of Wardley.*

The Hall is situated in the township of Worsley, about six miles from Manchester, on the famous Bridgewater estate.   It is certainly by no means an ideal situation for such a quaint and venerable building. Hemmed in by coal-pits, whose seams stretch around and even beneath its walls, this ancient seat of early manorial lords, with its wide moat and protecting woods, now forms an oasis in the midst of a grimy and unattractive neighbourhood.   Perhaps indeed we value its beauty the more on account of the contrast it presents to its surroundings.   It is said to have been built by one Thurstan Tyldesley, in the reign of Edward VI., though there is distinct evidence of the existence of an earlier house since about the year 1300.

A manorial residence in those days needed means of defence, and Wardley Hall was amply supplied with them.   The services of two small streams have been controlled to form the unusually large moat, and the direction of these streams has influenced the plan of the building, which consists of an irregular quadrangle, the eastern and western sides of which converge towards the south.   The inner court is about fifty feet by thirty-five feet in extent.   The main entrance is under a handsome gate-house on the north side, but the drawbridge has disappeared, for the moat on this side has been filled up in quite modern times.   On the east of this gateway was the ancient Chapel, now, alas! completely modernised and degraded into a store-house.   The quadrangle is extremely beautiful.   Half-timbered, with quaint gables, projecting eaves, carved oak beams, and mullioned windows, the old fabric has a picturesque charm which is only enhanced by its irregularity of plan.   Unhappily the old half-timbering of the northern or gate-house side has disappeared, but the contrast that this brick wing makes with the rest is not un-pleasing.   The chimneys of moulded brick are very picturesque.   The front door is not placed directly opposite the entrance gate, as it should be, but almost in the south-east corner.   This is no doubt due to the irregularity of the plan.   It opens, as in all old houses of this type, on the "Screens," *i.e.* a passage which goes through the house, and has on the right the Great Hall, and on the left the buttery and kitchen, an

* We have to thank him, and his publishers, Messrs. Sherratt and Hughes of Manchester, for leave to reproduce two of the illustrations from his book.

arrangement familiar enough to all who know the colleges at Oxford or Cambridge. The domestic offices on the left have, in this case, disappeared, since the eastern wing has been completely remodelled, and the ancient banqueting hall no longer serves its original purpose.

The Great Hall has been mutilated by a party-wall which cuts off a portion used as a boudoir. What is more grievous is that the height has also been reduced by the later addition of a floor across it at about half its height. Colonel Hart-Davis thinks that this was done as early as 1551. Thus the beautiful open-timbered roof, exposed once more at the restoration, can only be seen by going upstairs, where the upper story of the hall makes a very fine apartment. The original proportions of the hall were forty feet in length by twenty-one feet in width.

The fireplace in the Great Hall is of stone, standing in a deep overarched recess. This has a particular interest, for, as Colonel Hart-Davis reminded us, it was here that Francis Downes, the Catholic lord of Wardley, converted to the old faith the Puritan, Sir Cecil Trafford of Trafford, and thus secured to the Church a family which has ever since been conspicuous for its fidelity and devotion. But of this more anon. On the northern side of the Hall, west of the great window that looks on the courtyard, and just opposite the fireplace, is the glazed niche in the wall which contains the martyr's skull. It is high up, for it is on a level with the first landing of the great staircase, which is just behind this wall. The niche is in fact a square hole cut right through the wall and opening on the one side to the hall and on the other side to the staircase. Oaken doors close over the glazed openings, so that the relic can be entirely screened from prying eyes. It is best examined from the staircase, as there it is on a level with the eye.

It certainly gives a thrill to the stranger whose gaze lights for the first time on this relic of mortality thus enshrined in the principal apartment of this noble mansion. Some, no doubt, are shocked and disturbed by being brought into such close contact with a human skull, and may wonder at the strange taste which has thus exposed a death's-head in a living-room. But to those who know its history, the skull of Wardley is encircled with a sacred aureole, and even those who do not share the faith for which the martyr died, honour with deep and simple reverence the memorial of one who was loyal to his conscience even unto death.

Thus, far from being troubled at its presence, the family which now occupies the old Hall looks upon the martyr's skull, we are assured, as a protection and an honour to their home, and this reverence is fully shared by the noble owners of Wardley.

The staircase by which it rests is a very magnificent one, dating no doubt from the time when the Great Hall was divided into two stories,

WARDLEY HALL FROM THE SOUTH

WARDLEY HALL FROM THE SOUTH-EAST
*Photos by James Watts*

*To face page* 204

*i.e.* about 1550. It is, of course, all of oak, with splendid carved newels and balusters, and of a most stately amplitude. Ten steps lead to the landing, from which it is possible to examine minutely the martyr's skull.

Opposite the staircase opens the door of the panelled chamber, now used as a dining-room, which occupies the south-west corner of the quadrangle, and represents the ancient solar, or family withdrawing-room, abutting on the Great Hall. A more beautiful dining-room it has never been our fortune to visit. The oak-panelling round the walls rises to a richly carved cornice, upon which rest the huge moulded oak beams of the ceiling. Round the east side of the room runs an oak bench, worked into the panelling of the walls. This panelling is of the usual square Jacobean type.

But let us go outside into the garden. The moat is of unusual width, and part of it has been filled up and forms a delightful sunken garden. The streams which feed the moat flow down into a deep ravine, the sides of which are beautifully planted with rhododendrons and other flowering shrubs, and beyond is a wood, bedded with bracken growing waist-high, where, within green recesses, it is easy to forget the coal-mines and the railways and the other symbols of "our national commercial pre-eminence," which surround one on every side.

Colonel Hart-Davis has painted two charming views, taken across the moat, from the south-east and from the north-west respectively. Viewed from these two aspects, the old Hall, mirrored in the calm waters of the moat, looks extremely picturesque, with just that air of romance and mystery which beseem a house having so weird a reputation. It is well known that the wildest tales have been circulated about the Hall, known for nearly two hundred years as the "Skull House," and about the treasure it contains. It is said that if it is moved from its niche strange sounds are heard at night, and that the inhabitants have no peace until it is restored to its place. The head, indeed, it is said, defied an attempt to bury it, and, in a terrific storm of thunder and lightning, betook itself to the recess in the staircase wall. Thrown into the moat, it avenged itself by bringing on storms and disturbances of every sort, until the water was drawn off and it was recovered and replaced in the Hall. A recent writer says: "If anything was done to it, or it was not treated with proper respect, such commotions arose about the house that no one dared live in it. Windows were blown in, cattle pined in the stall, and the things were bewitched. . . . There is plenty of testimony to the ill-luck that has happened when the skull has been disturbed; and this has not come from the superstitious only, but from shrewd observant men of business, whose word is as good as their bond." *

* Fletcher Moss, *Pilgrimages to Old Homes*, vol. ii. pp. 267–268.

However this may be, Colonel Hart-Davis gives only the true story, which has, probably enough, given rise to all the others.

## THE STORY OF THE SKULL

It was in the famous '45, when the Jacobite army under "Bonnie Prince Charlie" was encamped in a field near Wardley Hall, still known as the "Rebel Field," that the skull was first brought to light in the old house.   Up to this date its history is conjectural.   The Hall then was held by one Matthew Moreton on a life lease from the Lady Penelope Cholmondeley.   It was this lady who sold Wardley in 1760 to Francis, Duke of Bridgewater, the ancestor of its present owners.   She was the granddaughter of Richard, Earl of Rivers, who had married Penelope, the heiress of the Downes of Wardley.

Moreton was a farmer, and as the Jacobites marched along Wardley Lane on their return to the North, a detachment visited the Hall to demand carts and horses for transport purposes.   They threatened to fire the buildings unless their demands were complied with, so that, in spite of moat and raised drawbridge, the farmer had to yield.   His son Matthew was sent with the carts and horses.   But the Duke of Cumberland coming up with the Jacobites, young Moreton, to save his life, abandoned his property, and made his way home.   The loss so impoverished the family that they determined to take up hand-loom weaving to retrieve their fortunes.

" Moreton commenced to pull down a somewhat ruinous part of the building in order to make room for the looms, and as the work of demolition was proceeding, a box or chest fell out of the ruins.   Thinking it to be a treasure-chest, he ordered the bystanders to stand back, and himself broke off the lid with a pick-axe.   The box was found to contain a skull furnished with a goodly set of teeth, and having on it a good deal of auburn hair.

"A maid-servant of the Moretons, knowing nothing about the skull, being set to clean the room in which it was kept, mistook it for the head of an animal and threw it into the moat.   The same night there was a furious storm, and Matthew Moreton, the younger, being a superstitious man, and having ascertained that the skull had been thrown into the moat, ascribed the storm to the indignity to which it had been subjected.   He, therefore, at once caused the water to be run off, recovered the skull, and restored it to its place." So far Colonel Hart-Davis.

The impression of the Moretons was that the skull belonged to a

206

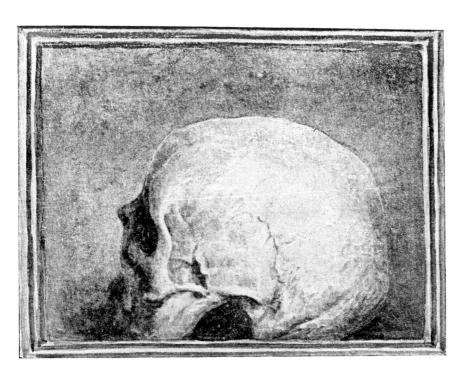

THE SKULL OF WARDLEY HALL

THE OLD CHAPEL OF THE COMMANDERY,
SANDFORD, WHERE THE MARTYR'S BODY
WAS LAID (*see p.* **177**)                *To face page* 206

# THE SKULL OF WARDLEY HALL

Catholic who had been executed for his faith during the times of persecution, and we shall see that this conjecture was substantially correct.

Wardley Hall was sold by Thurstan Tyldesley in 1563 to the Sheringtons of London, and from them it passed, about 1601, to one Roger Downes. He came of an ancient Cheshire family, the Downes of Worth, who bore arms, on a field *sable* a stag lodged (or couchant) *argent*, that is, a white stag lying on a black shield. Roger was reader to Gray's Inn, and Vice-Chamberlain of Chester, and he represented the borough of Wigan in the Parliaments of 1601 and 1620. What is more important to us is that he was a kinsman of Sir Alexander Barlow, of Barlow Hall, near Manchester, the brother of our martyr. In his will, dated April 4, 1631, Sir Alexander nominates him overseer, together with Sir George Gresley, and speaks of him as his "loving cosen." Though Sir Alexander was a most devout Catholic, in fact, a confessor of the faith, it does not appear that his kinsman and executor was himself a Catholic, although the latter's wife, Anne Calvert of Cockerham, was certainly one. But just before he died, it is probable that Roger Downes of Wardley had the happiness of being reconciled to the Church of his fathers by the venerable Benedictine monk, Dom Richard Huddleston. Roger died in July 1638, and we find that Francis, his eldest son and heir, was reconciled at this very time. No doubt the Catholic wife had long implored this grace for both husband and son.

The good priest, whose ministry thus gave to the Church one of the most faithful of its sons, belonged to a branch of the old Catholic family of Huddleston of Sawston, settled at Farington Hall, near Leyland, County Lancaster. He was born there in 1583, and ordained priest at Douay in 1607. After labouring for some time on the English Mission, he retired to the Continent, and was professed a Benedictine at the famous Abbey of Monte Cassino. There he spent some years in study and devotion by the tomb of the holy Patriarch St. Benedict, and then returned, like the Benedictine monks of old, to preach the Gospel of Christ in England. This was in 1619, and he appears to have taken up his abode at Farington Hall, the residence of his brother Joseph. "Here, like another St. Austin endued with an evangelical spirit, he exercised his talents in preaching, teaching, disputing, and reducing his stray'd countrymen to the sheepfold of Christ. And it pleased ye Divine goodness to bless his endeavours and second his words with extraordinary success. In all, as well public debates as private conferences, he still came off a conqueror, in so much yt many chiefe families . . . in Lancashire, with numberless others of all states and conditions, owe next to God their respective reconciliations to this worthy Benedictine."

207

Amongst the families, which the old chronicler we have quoted enumerates, is that of the Downes of Wardley Hall.

In the good old Father's treatise, *A Short and Plain Way to the Faith and Church*, edited by his still more famous nephew, Dom John Dionysius Huddleston, O.S.B., we are told that the work "was long since composed for the medicinal instruction of a private friend," whom there is good reason to assume was Francis Downes. It was by help of this celebrated work that the latter was able to overcome the arguments of Sir Cecil Trafford, and win him to the faith. But the most illustrious conversion due to the good Benedictine's *Short and Plain Way* was that of King Charles II. It was while hidden in the apartments of Dom John Huddleston at Moseley House, after the battle of Worcester, that Charles perused the treatise, which was then still in manuscript. He acknowledged himself convinced; and though, unhappily, he had not courage to proclaim his convictions to the world, yet, when he lay upon his deathbed, he was reconciled to the Church by that same Benedictine who had helped to screen him, and probably to save his life, at Moseley.

It was Francis Downes who welcomed to Wardley his friend and kinsman, Edward Barlow, in religion, Dom Ambrose, O.S.B. As we shall see, Father Ambrose came from Douay in 1617 to labour on the mission in his native country. He ministered chiefly in the private and secret chapels in the Halls of Wardley and Morleys. At the latter Hall he was taken on Easter Sunday, 1641. After his martyrdom at Lancaster Castle, on September 10 of that same year, the martyr's sacred head was impaled on a spike, probably upon the tower of the old Collegiate Church of Manchester, now known as the Cathedral. From this place it must have been rescued by Francis Downes, just as that of Blessed Thomas More was ransomed by Margaret Roper from the gate of old London Bridge. And having secured the relic of his old chaplain, we can imagine how Mr. Downes would cherish it. He himself was then nearing his end, for his will is dated February 1643, and in it he declares himself to be "much impaired and weakened in body by a long consuming sickness." Nevertheless, he lived till 1648, when he was succeeded by his brother John, also an excellent Catholic, who, however, only survived him by a few weeks. Colonel Hart-Davis suggests that some epidemic was probably raging at the time, since John and his wife both died very soon after Francis, leaving a son, Roger, and a daughter, Penelope, the former being only a few months old. Poor little Roger and his sister, bereft of their natural guardians, were, according to the cruel laws of the time, brought up as Protestants. Nor did Roger do much credit to the new religion. He became one of the wildest blades at the Court of Charles II., and was finally killed by a watchman in a drunken brawl at Epsom Wells,

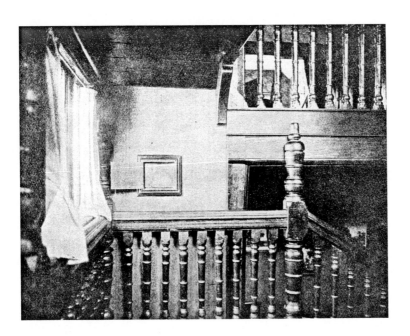

THE SKULL ON THE STAIRCASE

THE STAIRCASE, WARDLEY HALL
*Photos by James Watts*

*To face page* 208

aged only twenty-eight. Thus the male line came to a sad and tragic end.

We should not have thought it necessary even to mention poor Roger Downes, were it not that a comparatively modern popular tradition identified the skull of Wardley as belonging to this young rake, rather than to the martyr-priest. At least, one eighteenth-century tradition did so ; another, and older tradition, seems always to have asserted that it was the head of a "Father Ambrose." Fortunately the doubt was set at rest by the opening of Roger Downes's coffin in the family vault at Wigan, when it was found that the skeleton was perfect, head and all, except that the upper portion of the skull had been sawn off, just above the eyes, no doubt by the surgeon, who wished to ascertain the cause of death. This operation possibly gave rise to the tradition which connected the mysterious skull with this unfortunate young man.

Thus, in the words of Mr. Joseph Gillow, the antiquary to whose researches we owe the identification of the skull, "the Hall passed into alien hands, and though the skull of the martyr was religiously respected, the local Catholic tradition concerning it had almost died out and given place to the worthless stories which the gullibility of Lancashire antiquaries has perpetuated in the literature of the county."

## BARLOW HALL

The Saxon name of Barlow is thought by Whitaker to mark the locality as a favoured haunt of the wild boar, at a time when beasts of chase overspread the country.

Nothing could well have been more desolate than the site of Barlow Hall in those early days when the Saxon family of that name first made its abode there, on the wild northern moors where Lancashire and Cheshire meet. Fixing their home on a slope above the marshy levels of the Mersey, protected by the great belt of boggy and rush-grown land which ran through the district, the Barlows, no doubt, found that the situation had its advantages, and there, indeed, they took root, and for no less than seven hundred years grew and flourished.

On the south of the Hall, the Mersey wound its sluggish course, while to the north there was a stretch of marshy ground, still known as Barlow Leys, while Barlow Wood is said to be the only remains now standing in the neighbourhood of the great Forest of Arden which stretched up well into these northern districts.

The present Hall is interesting from its high antiquity rather than from any distinctive architectural merits. The original building probably dates from the time of Edward I., but it is very doubtful if any part of the ancient house survived the rebuilding in the days of Elizabeth. In late years it has been sadly modernised and pulled about, partly owing to a disastrous fire during the late Sir William Cunliffe Brookes's tenancy, and the original outline of the house is almost lost in the mass of alterations and additions which have transformed and disfigured it.

So far as can be made out, it consisted of the usual quadrangle erected in the quaint half-timbered style so characteristic of the neighbourhood, with the addition of a large wing built out at right angles to the Hall. "The framework consists of great oaken timbers, resting upon a foundation of solid masonry connected by beams, and strengthened by bracing ribs firmly bolted into the main timbers, filled with a composition of plaster of lime and mud, mixed with straw, and laid upon laths. Very little of the timber-work now remains exposed to view, the greater portion having been covered with plaster, and being also covered with ivy, as are many aged trees which stand around."

The fire which occurred on March 19, 1879, has necessitated much rebuilding, and it is difficult now to trace the original plan. Even the banqueting hall is mutilated by party-walls, and its splendid oriel now stands in a passage cut off from the room it was designed to light. The fire destroyed the beautiful panelling of this hall, only a fragment being preserved. There are some magnificent trees around the old house, even the modern parts of which have a venerable appearance owing to the ivy which covers it so profusely. The extensive grounds are now used as golf-links, and the old Hall itself has recently become the club-house.

The neighbourhood is even more changed than the house itself. Now, as one walks from Manchester by Chorlton-cum-Hardy towards Didsbury and Cheadle, one is never out of sight of houses. The once desolate moor has become a busy and populous suburb; miles of streets have sprung up in the immediate vicinity of the ancient home of the Barlows, and there are now more than ten thousand people living near the old house which was once so isolated.

Yet, even to this day, Barlow Hall is fairly secluded. Situated close to the banks of the river, the wide fields surrounding it give it an air of aloofness from the busy hive of men.

Barlow Hall in ancient days was situated in the parish of Didsbury— the parish church being more than two miles distant across the moor. In the reign of Edward I. it was owned by Sir Robert de Barlow. During the two hundred and fifty years that succeeded, the Barlows steadily increased in wealth and importance in the county, and their honourable name and position was equalled by their fidelity to the Catholic faith, a fidelity

BARLOW HALL.
*Photo by James Watts*

*To face page 210*

that was to be put to a rude trial in the days that were coming. "An intensely conservative family," says Mr. Fletcher Moss, "more than one of whose members sacrificed everything, even to life itself, for their faith."

The Hall was rebuilt in or about the year 1574 by Alexander Barlow, Esquire, the then Lord of Barlow. This date is inscribed on the old sundial in the quadrangle, together with the beautiful and significant motto—*Lumen me regit, vos umbra.** It is very probable, as Mr. Moss suggests, that this motto may have some reference to the frequent changes of faith which had then become so common in England. But the Barlows at least were determined always to follow the light, even if their countrymen preferred the shadow.

Alexander Barlow was son and heir of Ellis Barlow of Barlow, and by his wife Elizabeth he had a son also called Alexander, and four daughters. His sister, Margaret Barlow, had married Edward, head of the house of Stanley, and third Earl of Derby. She died in February 1559, leaving a son and two daughters. This brilliant match may be said to mark the climax of the fortunes of the house of Barlow.

"In rambling through Barlow Hall only a short time ago," says a modern writer,† "we found a succession of tiny, silent bedrooms, each opening into its neighbour, and each also into a long, narrow, rickety corridor. From the corridor we could see, through square bits of coloured glass, traces of a quaint timbered court-yard, and learnt that this was the oldest part of the house, and these bedrooms were probably used by the four daughters of Alexander Barlow."

Mr. Barlow had sat as member for Wigan in at least six Parliaments between 1547 and 1555, his devotion to the old Faith explaining his absence from the early Parliaments of Elizabeth. It was to his safe and faithful keeping that Laurence Vaux, the last Warden of the College at Manchester, and himself a glorious confessor for the faith, handed over the leases and other charters relating to the College lands, that they might be preserved until better times. Here, too, at Barlow, he spent many of the later years of his life.

As the times grew steadily more dark, and the position of Catholics, even in faithful Lancashire, more precarious, the Barlows had their full share of the cup of suffering. It is touching to read in the stained glass of the splendid oriel window of the Great Hall, the mottoes, *Prist en foyt* and *Respice finem*, together with the initials, A.B., and the date 1574. No doubt Mr. Barlow chose them as guides in the darkness, and as encouragement to be constant to the end. This oriel window, in the

---

* "The light rules me, the shadow rules you."
† *Fallowfield,* by Mrs. W. C. Williamson. London, 1888.

half-timbered quadrangle, has often been erroneously called the Chapel window. It is, of course, merely the usual bay-window in the banqueting hall. This courtyard is small, but very beautiful, and this part of the house is almost all that has survived the lapse of centuries and the devastation caused by the fire.

In 1576, for prudential reasons, Mr. Barlow conveyed his estates in trust to his son-in-law, Edward Scarisbrick, of Scarisbrick, and five other feoffees. Not long after, the pursuivants descended upon Barlow Hall, and the peaceful home became the scene of all the horrors of a search for Popish priests. This took place on January 17, 1583. No priests were found, but the master of the house was seized and carried off to Salford gaol, although at the time he was too ill to sit upright on his horse. Here he was still, with many Lancashire Catholics, gentlemen, ladies, priests, and others, at the end of January 1584. He died in confinement, a valiant confessor of the faith—an inscription on the portrait of his son, Sir Alexander, stating that he " died in pryson for the Catholyck religion." *

His eldest son, our martyr's father, was knighted, together with his eldest son (both Alexanders), at the coronation of James I. in 1603. Mr. Gillow says of this Sir Alexander Barlow, that he was perhaps the most notable representative of the family honours, and is recommended in the records of Douay as " that constant Confessor of Christ."

A strange custom of our ancestors is exhibited in the story of his marriage. When only four years old, he was taken to church and solemnly espoused to an heiress, one Elizabeth Bellfield. However, twelve years later, the young man testified that he had never ratified the alleged marriage, for being so young he could remember nothing about it. It was therefore dissolved, and he afterwards took to wife one of his own choosing, Mary, daughter of Sir Uryan Brereton of Handforth, County Chester, Knight, by whom he had a large family. And of these Edward Barlow, the subject of this memoir, was the fourth son.

Sir Alexander had his full share of persecution on account of his faith. " A true and perfect Recusant Catholic " as he styled himself in his will, in spite of royal honours, his name, together with those of his wife and children, occurs constantly on the Recusant Rolls, and after paying for many weary years the extortionate fine of £20 a month for his refusal to attend Protestant worship in the desecrated parish church, he actually came within the iniquitous Act by which James I. was empowered to refuse this monthly fine, and to take two-thirds of the Recusants' estates.

* In a list of Recusants brought up before the Ecclesiastical Commissioners (dated February 14, 1584) Alexander Barlow's name occurs among those who had " conformed," but also among those who were " bound for their appearance." C.R.S., vol. v. pp. 70, 71.

THE QUADRANGLE, BARLOW HALL
*Photo by James Watts*

*To face page* 212

What was even more intolerable soon followed. On January 19, 1609, the "benefit" of Sir Alexander's estates was granted to two of the King's needy favourites, William Markey and Thomas Webber, that they might get what they could out of them for themselves.

This system, worthy of the unspeakable James, worked out as follows : Each individual favourite who grew clamorous for the royal Scot's bounty, was ordered to search out as many Catholics as possible, and to select from the more opulent those who were most likely to answer his purpose. The King, in his bounty, then "bestowed" these persons upon him, *i.e.* he made over to him whatever claims the Crown possessed, or might afterwards possess on them for the fines of recusancy ; and authorised him either to proceed at law for the recovery of the penalties, or to accept a grant of money by way of compensation for the amount. The "hungry Scots" and their fellows fastened like vampires on their prey. The State papers are full of these grants of "the benefit of Recusants."

Sir Alexander Barlow died April 20, 1620, and was buried by torch-light in the Collegiate Church of Manchester. It is not known why his wish as to his funeral expressed in his will (dated April 14, 1617) was not carried out. For in this testament he directed, "Yf yt fortune I die within twentye miles of my house of Barlowe, that my said bodye be leyde in Didsburye Churche as neere unto my father as may be."

In this will he bequeathed to his wife, "my owne picture to keepe during her lyffe," with an injunction that it should afterwards remain as an heirloom at Barlow Hall. Here, indeed, it remained till the last of the Barlows died in 1773, when it was sold, but happily passed into the hands of Dr. James Barlow of Blackburn, who claimed to be descended from a junior branch of the family, and among his descendants it still remains. It has been engraved on copper, and the print that used to hang in Barlow Hall, when it was occupied by the late Sir William Cunliffe Brookes, Bart., is now in the possession of Mr. Joseph Gillow. He thus describes the picture : " A half-length portrait, holding a Primer or Manual in his left hand with the other uplifted, the words *Tute si me et te* apparently proceeding from his lips, and *Ecce* from the glory in the corner, with the supplication, *Jesu Fili Dei miserere mei, Sancta Maria Mater Dei ora pro me.* On the left-hand side is a curious inscription, the lines in red and the lettering in gold.

"It states that Sir Alexander was then sixty years of age (about 1616 therefore, the year that his martyr son made his vows at Douay), and that he was the son of Alexander Barlow, Esq., who died in prison for the Catholic religion. The names of his eight sons and six daughters, with some additional particulars, are also recorded, and after the names of

William and Edward is the letter A, or some private mark, probably intended to note their religious profession."

We may now leave Barlow Hall for the present to pay a visit to the "Old Church" at Didsbury, where Alexander Barlow, the elder, had been laid to rest. As Barlow was, in those days at least, situated in the parish of Didsbury, it was natural that the family should be buried there, even after the change of religion, for Catholics had then no graveyards or churches of their own in which they could be interred. And so "a true and perfect recusant Catholic," like Sir Alexander, found resting-place in the Protestant churchyard.*

But something more serious still was the fact that his children had to pass through the form of "christening" in Didsbury Church. Even now, in the register, we may read the entry of the "christening" of Edward Barlow, our martyr, on the 30th of November Anno Domini

*Anno Domini. 1585.*

*Edward the sonne of Alex Barlowe yeut 30°*

1585—"Edward the sonne of Alex. Barlowe gent." This was a necessary formal matter, but, no doubt, the children of such devout Catholics as Alexander and Mary Barlow had previously been baptized at home by a priest in accordance with the usual practice of Catholics in those penal days.

It is a pleasant walk from Barlow Hall through the meadows by the Mersey banks to Didsbury Church. The Church itself is most dis-

---

* Most probably without any funeral service, as an "excommunicate Recusant." Dr. Cox in his *Parish Registers of England* (1910) p. 106, says : "The persecution of the Recusants, that is, of those who clung to the old unreformed faith, was carried on relentlessly even to the grave throughout the reign of Elizabeth ; though their burial at night without any rite was winked at in various parishes, particularly where they were numerous." He gives many instances, *e.g.* at Hathersage, where four were buried in 1629, four in 1630, and five in 1631—all by night ! "At Norbury, Derbyshire, there are three entries in the parish register, for the year 1723, of interments without service. In two of these instances it is specified that the deceased were 'papists.'" (*Ibid*, p. 108). At Tamworth, 1644, we have the entry, " *Cast into the ground the body of Ellen wife of Richard Ensor, a popeling.*" (*Ibid*. p. 99.)

PORTRAIT OF THE MARTYR'S FATHER
*From the print in possession of Mr. Joseph Gillow*

*To face page 214*

appointing. Successive " restorations " and rebuildings have destroyed almost every vestige of antiquity, and nothing but the old tower seems to speak of the times when an Alexander Barlow was Chaplain of Didsbury, or even of the later days when another Alexander was buried there beside his Catholic ancestors.*

Fortunately, there are now keen and competent antiquaries living close to the poor old church, who will see that nothing more is destroyed of its few remaining relics of the past, and will lovingly gather together everything that industry, devotion and skill can discover of the history of the days that are gone.†

## HANDFORTH HALL

Edward Barlow, as we have seen, was the fourth son of the fourteen children whom Mary Brereton of Handforth bore to Alexander Barlow. Among these children were two, who, like Edward himself, were destined to wear the Benedictine cowl : William (the third son, well known to history as the famous Doctor and Canonist, Dom Rudesind) and Robert, of whom little is known, save that he was professed at St. Gregory's, Douay, in 1630, and died in England some three years later.

When Edward went abroad he had, according to the usual custom, to take another name, in order to escape the unwelcome attentions of the Government, and the name he chose to be known by was his mother's name of Brereton.

It will be interesting to visit Handforth Hall, part of which, happily, still stands, and forms yet another shrine for the pilgrim of the martyrs.

There is a ford with a ferry over the Mersey just below Barlow Hall, and thence it is about six miles, as the crow flies, in a south-easterly direction to Handforth Hall. We cross the fields and pass along the slopes of Northenden Moor, and then by Kenworthy Lane (past the

---

* Didsbury Church, which dates from 1352, was rebuilt in 1620, and again in 1770, and was extensively " restored " in 1855 ! It can well be imagined how much of the ancient building remains.

† To Mr. James Watts, of Abney Hall, and Mr. Fletcher Moss, of the Old Parsonage, Didsbury, the antiquaries to whom we refer above, we owe more than we can ever adequately acknowledge. Their delightful series of books entitled *Pilgrimages to Old Homes*, illustrated with Mr. Watts's magnificent photographs, are a joy to all who love the ancient houses of England. Their devotion to our martyr is as great as if they shared the faith for which he died, and without their assistance this record must have lost more than half its interest. We have already acknowledged the illustrations which they have so kindly lent us.

215

modern Catholic Church of St. Hilda) to Northenden. A short walk brings us to Cheadle, and the London road, which we take for three or four miles more, until we come to Handforth Church. The Hall is a little to the east of the railway station (the London and North-Western Railway line here runs parallel to the road) and stands in dignified seclusion aloof from the modern houses, the Nonconformist Chapel, and the deplorable bleaching and dyeing works which have recently disfigured the charming valley of the Dean.

Handforth Hall itself, like so many ancient and dignified manor houses, is now a farm. The old avenue still leads to it, and hard by is a pleasant stream and what was once the village green.

It is a grand old half-timbered house, but the portion to the left of the porch is a modern imitation. All to the right is ancient. Two noble gables remain, with magnificently carved barge-boards. The oak carving throughout the house is really magnificent. Curiously enough (though we have noticed the same phenomenon elsewhere), the woodwork has weathered far better on the north side than on the south.

The half-timbered work is very beautiful, and makes Handforth Hall worthy to find a place among the many fine old Cheshire manor houses built in this style.

But the unique glory of Handforth is the porch. This is a splendid piece of oak work, most elaborately carved, and still in an extraordinary state of preservation. On either side of the doorway the great oak posts are carved with arabesques, surmounted by the coat of arms of the family, on which the Handforth (or Honford) star is still prominent. The crest is a bear's head, muzzled, for Brereton.

The star borne by the Handforths commemorates the Crusades, when, according to the legend, a star fell from heaven in front of the armies of Saladin, which Handforth of Handforth instantly seized and fixed to his shield, and thus it became the cognisance of his race. Above, along the lintel of the doorway, is carved in Gothic lettering the following inscription :

*This haulle was buylded In the yeare of*
*Oure Lord God m.ccccc.lxii.*
*by Uryan | Breretoun Knight Whom maryed*
*Margaret daughter and heyre of Wyllyam*
*Handforth | of Handforthe Esquyer and*
*had Issue vi. sonnes and ii. daughters*

Below the inscription is some charming scroll-work, which shows a briar and a tun (or barrel), and thus forms a rebus of the name Brereton. This ornament is continued all round the jambs of the doorway.

216

THE PORCH, HANDFORTH HALL
*Photo by James Watts*

*To face page* 216

# THE SKULL OF WARDLEY HALL

The most striking feature of the interior is a magnificent oak stair-case, far more elaborate and beautiful even than that at Wardley. In the side of this stairway is a hiding-hole.

The history of Margaret Handforth, whose marriage to Sir Uryan brought Handforth and all its broad acres to the Breretons, is a strange and romantic one.

Her father, William Handforth, the last of his race, fell at Flodden Field, September 9, 1513. His twelve-year-old daughter and heiress was immediately married to the gallant young knight, Sir John Stanley, who, though only seventeen years of age, had commanded at Flodden the forces of his father, James Stanley, Bishop of Ely and Warden of Manchester. He had won his spurs at the great battle, and it may well be that he won his bride there too. Two years later the Bishop died, and Sir John completed the building of the great Derby or Stanley Chapel, on the north side of the Collegiate Church at Manchester, which his father had begun. Over the door of this Chapel may still be seen the shield of arms of Sir John (the stags' heads and eagles' feet of the Stanleys, impaled with the seven-rayed star of the Handforths) and the half-defaced inscription in Latin : *Vanitas vanitatum, omnia vanitas.*

"We beseech you that you aid us, James, Bishop of Ely, John Stanley, knight, and Margaret his wife, and the parents of them, with your prayers to Jesus Christ, who built this Chapel in His name and in honour of St. John the Baptist, in the year of the Incarnation, 1513."

The date of the battle is given, probably because the Chapel was built in fulfilment of a vow made during the campaign.

Later on Sir John fell into disgrace with Cardinal Wolsey, who had him imprisoned in the Fleet. But he does not seem to have needed this reminder that all earthly pride and wealth was vanity : at any rate, he determined to bid farewell to this world and all it could offer him. He therefore made his will (it is dated June 30, 1527) in which he disposed of all he had, making many donations to the churches of Manchester and Cheadle, among others, and leaving "penny doles to be given to poor widows, poor maidens, and poor persons who would say a paternoster, ave, and a credo for him, or pray for the souls of his father, himself, and his wife, and for William Handforth, Ellen and Anne Stanley." A priest was to sing Mass daily for the repose of their souls. He then obtained letters of fraternity for himself and wife and children from the Abbot of Westminster, whereby they became entitled to the prayers of the Convent for ever, and to have their names enrolled among the obits read out after the Martyrology in Chapter ; and then he and his wife petitioned for a divorce that they might devote themselves to the religious life.*

* See Fletcher Moss, *Chronicles of Cheadle, Cheshire* (1894), pp. 35 *et seq.*

# FORGOTTEN SHRINES

On June 25, 1528, their case was examined by the ecclesiastical authorities in the sacristy of St. Paul's Cathedral, London. They having made their petition to be permitted to separate in order to enter holy religion, this was accorded to them, and Sir John Stanley forthwith became a monk at Westminster.

He had literally fulfilled the counsel of Our Blessed Lord, and given up home and wife, children and lands for Christ's sake and the Gospel's, and we cannot doubt that he received the promised reward. The religious houses of England were soon to be destroyed by the tyrant, and their inmates driven forth from their peaceful retreats, but it would seem that Sir John had the happiness of dying before the evil day dawned.

"What a strangely chequered life he had," observes Mr. Moss. "He was a noble scion of a distinguished race, emphatically a warrior and a saint. After charging like a whirlwind round the Scottish hosts on Flodden, he was married to a little child, and after his unjust and arbitrary imprisonment, he surrendered all that he had at the early age of thirty-two, and became a poor monk, and died quietly in a cloistered cell."

His young wife had a very different fate. We may suspect that her vocation to the religious state was not altogether spontaneous, but rather the outcome of the influence of the stronger will and more fervent faith of her husband. No doubt she must have entered the cloister, but it is very possible that she never made her vows. In any case, within ten years or so, she must have been thrust again into the world, through the Dissolution of the Religious Houses. A widow now, still young and an heiress, she was not likely to be permitted long to remain single.

At any rate, we know that she married, as her second husband, Sir Uryan Brereton, ninth son of Sir Randle Brereton of Shochlach and Malpas Hall, who thereby became the new Lord of Handforth. She, who was the widow of a monk, was to become the grandmother of three more Benedictines, and her life forms an interesting link between the old monasticism of England and its revival in the teeth of the penal laws.

At Cheadle Church, the parish to which Handforth belongs, the Chapel at the end of the south aisle is known as the Handforth or Honford Chapel. It is screened off to the west and north by admirable Perpendicular screen-work, which is evidently the work of Sir Uryan Brereton. The breast-summer is in fact carved with his rebus, the briar and the tun, and the initials V.B. also appear on it. The Chapel itself seems to have been built by Sir John Stanley. Two fine recumbent alabaster effigies of knights that lie within are believed by Mr. Moss,

HANDFORTH HALL
*Photo by James Watts*

*To face page* 218

with good reason, to be those of Sir John himself, and of his father-in-law, William Handforth. In the east window of the Chapel Sir John Stanley's arms may still be seen, though the inscription that begged for prayers for his own soul and those of his relatives, in similar terms to that at Manchester, has unhappily disappeared. The roof of the Chapel is exceedingly fine, and on it the star of the Handforths still glows resplendent. While lingering in Cheadle Church (which seems to have been entirely rebuilt between 1520 and 1556), we cannot omit to mention that the chancel was built by another Benedictine, no less a person, in fact, than the Lady Katharine Bulkeley, last Abbess of Godstow, near Oxford. She built the chancel and glazed the window at her own expense in the year 1556, during the brief restoration of Catholic worship under Queen Mary, and was buried there on February 13, 1559, just after the accession of Elizabeth, but happily before that queen had succeeded in effecting the change of religion, so that the good old Abbess was laid to rest with the ancient rites that she so dearly loved. She was a daughter of Rowland Bulkeley, Esquire, of Cheadle.

Alas! the stained windows that commemorated her family, the fair high altar, the holy images and sacred ornaments that she had provided, were soon broken down " with axes and hammers," and even her humble request for prayers for the repose of her soul was not spared by the heartless fanatics who profited by her charity.

But to return to Handforth Hall. As we have seen, the present house was built in 1562, twenty-three years before the birth of Edward Barlow. From this very house then his mother passed forth as a bride, and to this house her martyr son must often have made his way, as a boy, to pay a visit to his kinsmen there. We have approached it, as he would have done, by ford and field and ancient highway from Barlow Hall, but the modern pilgrim will find it easier to visit it from Manchester by rail, as it stands close to a railway station.

It is strange that Sir William Brereton, the great-grandson of Sir Uryan, was a notable Roundhead General, and the last person likely to sympathise with " Popish Recusants." He was born in 1604, the year that Edward Barlow entered the English College at Valladolid, and, judging by his subsequent career, it seems extremely improbable that our martyr can ever have visited Handforth Hall after his return to England as a priest. Certainly, we must dismiss as quite impossible the theory that has been put forward as to this old house having been one of his " stations " as a missionary. We are, indeed, expressly told by his contemporary biographer that he confined his priestly labours to the Lancashire side of the Mersey, and refused to work in Cheshire.

Sir William Brereton, the famous Parliamentary General, died shortly after the Restoration, April 7, 1661. He was a strong Puritan, with an intense dislike for prelacy, and the Royalists reported of him that he was "a notable man at a thanksgiving dinner, having terrible long teeth and a prodigious stomach, to turn the Archbishop's Chapel at Croydon into a kitchen, also to swallow up that palace and lands at a morsel." *

His son, Sir Thomas, who succeeded him, was the last of the Breretons of Handforth. There is a monument to him in the Handforth Chapel in Cheadle Church, just west of the two alabaster figures already referred to.

The Barlows, on the other hand, were as loyal to their King as to their faith, so that it was more than the Mersey that separated Barlow Hall from Handforth in the days of Charles I.


## DOUAY

THERE is an old saying, "In Cheshire Leghs are thick as fleas," which, though not very refined nor very respectful to a great family, has the merit of being true. Our martyr was closely connected with the chief stem of this family-tree, since his paternal grandmother was Elizabeth, daughter and co-heiress of George Legh of High Legh Hall, the very centre and heart of the Legh country. The Hall lies half-way between Warburton and Arley, the seat of the Egerton-Warburtons, and about three and a half miles from either. Here, embowered in trees, is an ancient chapel standing in the grounds of the Hall. In one of the old stained-glass windows there is a representation of Thomas Legh of High Legh, the founder, and his wife, Isabella Trafford, with their arms emblazoned on their mantles. The date is 1581.

At the age of twelve Edward Barlow was taken from school to be a page in the house of his kinsman, Sir Uryan Legh of High Legh, in Cheshire. It was the common practice of the time for the sons of gentry thus to serve their apprenticeship, as it were, in the hall of some nobleman or gentleman of note, but, in this case, it would seem that the custom might have led to disastrous consequences. For Sir Uryan was a Protestant, and the influence of a conforming household could not but have a pernicious influence on the faith of the Catholic boy who was exposed to it. Why his parents should entrust their son to a Protestant lord we cannot tell; possibly, they had little or no choice in the matter. In 1597 the persecution was at its height, and one of the favourite plans of the Government was to tear Catholic children from their homes, and to hand them over to Protestants to be brought up in the State religion.

* *The Myesterees of the Good Old Cause* (1663), p. 3.

220

THE STAIRCASE, HANDFORTH HALL
*Photo by James Watts*

However this may be, we learn from an intimate friend who wrote *The Apostolical Life of Ambrose Barlow,* that our martyr himself told him of his conversion, which, he says, "I had more cause than ordinary to remember ; for he said that a certain lady who was the widow of Sir William Davenport, and mother of the now Lord Chief Baron of the Exchequer, was the cause of his conversion and my father's about the same time, her residence being then near unto his sister Talbot's,* which I think is not many miles from the place where he suffered for his conscience."

This good lady, who was thus instrumental in bringing back the future martyr to the practice of his holy faith, was Margaret, daughter of Richard Assheton of Middleton in Lancashire. She was the wife of Sir William Davenport of Bramhall, Cheshire ; her third son was Sir Humphrey Davenport, the famous judge. Middleton is just north of Manchester, so that the Asshetons and the Barlows were near neighbours. Her name deserves to be held in benediction, since but for her the noble army of Christ's martyrs might have lost one of its bravest knights.

Edward Barlow was not content with returning to the faith : he longed to give himself more perfectly to God. "As he grew up, and considered the emptiness and vanity of the transitory joys of this life, and the greatness of things eternal, he took a resolution to withdraw himself from the world, and to go abroad, in order to procure those helps of virtue and learning which might qualify him for the priesthood, and enable him to be of some assistance to his native country." He was approaching manhood, if indeed he had not already passed his twenty-first year.

Dr. Dee records in his diary that in 1597 he lent to Mr. Barlow a Spanish grammar for the use of his son. This son will probably have been William, who was then preparing to complete his education on the Continent, but possibly it was Edward himself.

The place he naturally turned his eyes to was Douay, the College of his fellow countryman, William Cardinal Allen, the training-ground of so many valiant athletes and the seed-plot of so many martyrs. Thither his brother William, only nine months his senior, had gone before him, and after making his studies there, had been professed

* Margaret Barlow married John Talbot of Salesbury, County Lancaster. These Talbots were a younger branch of the Talbots of Bashall, who had a martyr of their own, the Venerable John Talbot, who suffered in 1600. Salesbury Hall is about a mile east of Ribchester, and about two and a half miles south-west from Stonyhurst. Salesbury formerly belonged to the Clitherows, and passed by heiresses to the Talbots. John Talbot, our martyr's brother-in-law, was born in 1608. His daughter and heiress, Dorothy, born in 1650, married Edward Warren of Poynton, County Chester.

a Benedictine monk at Cella Nuova in Galicia, under the name of Dom Rudesind. He was already, it would seem, ordained priest, and was studying for his Doctor's degree at Salamanca.

To Douay, then, Edward Barlow made his way: a journey not without peril in those days, when to seek Catholic education abroad was as great a crime as to provide it at home. "Here," says Challoner, "meeting with two other young gentlemen of equal age, and of the same inclinations, he chose them for his chamber-fellows, and with them frequented the humanity schools at Anchin College, under the Fathers of the Society, as the alumni of the English Seminary all did during Dr. Worthington's presidency."

We do not know the date of his arrival at Douay, and so cannot tell how long he stayed there. No doubt his Latin had grown very rusty, as he had left school at so early an age, and a young man of twenty-three does not find it so easy to set himself again to the study of grammar and syntax. But he persevered, and in 1610 he was sufficiently advanced to be able to begin his philosophy. He was sent by Dr. Worthington to make these studies at the English College at Valladolid, where the Benedictine martyrs, Barkworth and Roberts, had studied before him. He was admitted there, with a companion, on September 20, 1610. His age was put down in the College register as twenty-three, but he was in reality nearly twenty-five. He was known by the *alias* of Brereton, his mother's maiden name. Here he studied philosophy for two years, and then was sent back to Douay, "partly," says the Register, "on account of ill-health." The "partly" is interesting, for it suggests that there was another reason, and we cannot doubt that this was his Benedictine vocation. The Benedictine revival was in the air, and was greatly exciting the minds of all who were interested in the future of English Catholicism. We have recounted in the life of the Ven. John Roberts the conflicts which it engendered in the College at Valladolid. The echo of those conflicts can hardly have died out in 1610, and even if they were almost forgotten, the martyrdom of Dom John Roberts, on December 10 of that year, must have aroused new enthusiasm among the students for the ancient Order to which England owed her faith.

Already in July 1609, the theological faculty of Salamanca, where Dom Rudesind Barlow was studying, had given its formal opinion that the English monks could undertake the work of the Mission in their country, as there was nothing in their state to hinder such a work. Pope and King had alike sanctioned the establishment at Douay of a Benedictine House, dedicated to St. Gregory the Great, Apostle of England, where the English monks who belonged to the Spanish Congregation of the Order could find a home, which was to be at once a monastery, a college, and a training-school for those of their number who desired to follow in the steps of the first missioners to the English race. In the October of the year 1611 the monks were able to move into the monastery built for them by the generosity of Abbot Cavarel of St. Vedast's, which was to be their home until the Great Revolution drove them back to their native shores.

It was, then, to the new monastery of St. Gregory at Douay, already illustrious through the martyrdom of its first prior and founder, that Edward Barlow directed his steps when he left Spain. Thither, his brother, Dom Rudesind, had preceded him in 1611. He was not, however, originally destined for the Monastery of St. Gregory.

In 1611 Dom Gabriel Gifford, afterwards Archbishop of Rheims, a very notable man, who had been Head Chaplain to Cardinal Allen and to St. Charles Borromeo, and also Dean of Lille, before he took the Benedictine habit, was sent by his Superiors to Spain to solicit help for the English monks. Tarrying at Saint Malo for a ship, he and his companion were induced by the Bishop of that town to settle there. Dr. Gifford was appointed theologian to the Bishop, and attached to this position was a house which would serve for a temporary monastery. Thus a new English foundation was made ; and to this monastery, which was placed under the invocation of St. Benedict, Edward Barlow went from Douay, early in 1614, to beg the monastic habit. He was clothed in due course, and became a novice under the name of Br. Ambrose. But for some reason or other, after nine months' stay at Saint Malo, he asked to be permitted to return to Douay, on the plea of completing his theological studies. Perhaps one reason for this change was that his brother, Dom Rudesind, had been made Prior of St. Gregory's in 1614. At any rate it appears that he was again clothed with the habit by his brother on January 4, 1615, and that the Convent of Saint Malo gave up their right to him as a member of their house on September 20 of that year.

Dom Ambrose (as we must henceforth call him) made his solemn vows as a Benedictine monk on January 5, 1615, and was afterwards incorporated into the monastery of Cella Nuova, in Galicia, where his brother had been professed. We learn these facts from the MS. collection of Dom Athanasius Allanson, the annalist of the Congregation.

The monastery of Saint Malo was not destined to endure, at least as an English foundation. Owing to various difficulties it was sold to the Maurist Fathers in 1672. During its uneventful history of sixty-one years, only fourteen choir monks were professed. Thus it seems providential that the future martyr should have been transferred to a community which still endures, and cherishes his memory as one of its chiefest glories.

223

## THE MISSION

DOM AMBROSE BARLOW was ordained priest in 1617, and soon afterwards was sent to labour on the English Mission.

Of his wonderful apostolic life we have many precious details written down by some of those who knew him best. Challoner's moving account of our martyr is taken from two MS. relations which were in the hands of his brethren at Douay, one of them being a letter of his brother Dom Rudesind to the Abbot and monks of Cella Nuova, dated January 1, 1642. The materials for much of Dom Rudesind's letter are taken from a MS. now in the library of Manchester College, which has lately been printed by the Chetham Society.* It is entitled *The Apostolical Life of Ambrose Barlow*, and is written by a friend and penitent of our martyr's, in the form of a letter to his brother, Dom Rudesind. There is no clue to the identity of the writer, except that he says that his father was converted about the same time as the martyr, through the instrumentality of the same lady, Margaret Davenport. The little book (it consists of only 38 MS. pages in small quarto) is extremely touching and interesting, and we shall make no apology for quoting largely from it.†

Father Barlow naturally turned to his native country, and it was in Lancashire that he spent the last twenty-four years of his life. He was now over thirty years old, the age when our Blessed Lord began His Ministry, and was " well qualified both by virtue and learning for the apostolic calling." Knaresborough says that " his memory is held in great esteem to this day in Lancashire, for his great zeal in the conversion of souls and the exemplary piety of his life and consecration."

He went home to Barlow Hall at first, as was natural. We have a characteristic story of his home-coming. His biographer writes to Dom Rudesind : " He was such a lover of the purity which he professed, that upon his coming home, when your deare mother and his went towards him, as if she would have saluted him, he told me that he did runne backe till he came to the wall, by which she understood that he had received holy orders and the Sacred Kisse of Our Saviour : no more to be toucht by any creature."

But he did not intend to remain in comfort among the loved ones at home, and it was not long before Divine Providence opened to him a field for his labours, which, though in the neighbourhood of his home,

---

* Edited by W. E. Rhodes, M.A., 1908.

† A MS. copy was kindly given to the writer by Mr. Sutton, Librarian of the Free Library, Manchester, some time before its publication.

gave him the independence which was necessary for his apostolic labours. No doubt he often visited his home ; and we may be sure that he consoled the last moments of his good father, who died full of years and merits in 1620.

The principal place of his residence was the old hall of Morleys, in Astley, in the parish of Leigh, about seven miles from Manchester and about as far from Barlow. The owner of Morleys was Mr. (afterwards Sir Thomas) Tyldesley, the famous knight, *sans peur et sans reproche*, who was Major-General in the royal army, and Governor of Lichfield. He was slain at the Battle of Wigan Lane in 1651. Sir Thomas was a devout Catholic, as all his forbears had been. His grandfather, Thomas Tyldesley of Morleys Hall, and Myerscough Lodge, Preston (near Claughton-on-Brock) was himself a grandson of Thurstan Tyldesley of Wardley Hall, where Father Barlow's kinsmen, the Downes, now resided.

This older Thomas Tyldesley was specially obnoxious to the Elizabethan Government, and Lord Burghley has placed a cross against Morleys Hall on his famous map of Lancashire, to signify that its owner was a specially stiff Papist and would require extra coercion.* In a report presented to the Privy Council in 1591 it is said that " his children and family are very greatly corrupted, and few or none of them come to the church." His widow, Elizabeth, daughter of Christopher Anderton of Lostock Hall, was reported to Lord Burghley in 1598 as "one of the most obstinate" Recusants ; and so she continued till the day of her death. She survived until our martyr came on the Mission, for we are told that he assisted her at her death, and she left a pension of £8 a year to a priest that would take the charge of the poor Catholics in the neighbourhood of her residence. This charge was undertaken by our martyr himself, and he, therefore, with the consent of Sir Thomas, took up his abode at Morleys. Of the £8 a year he gave £6 to the poor man with whom he lodged, for his diet, though he was almost always absent for a fourth part of the year.

"For his custome was to be three weekes at home, the fourth in circuit, excepting onely the weeke in Advent. At two places of his circuit I have beene with him ; the one was a widdow's house (who is a tenant of my Lord Stranges) some twenty miles from Morleys where there was a great number of people. That widdow's house is very near a parke of my Lord Molineux,† whose good father (though then a Protestant) gave his horses leave to feed in that parke of his."

* C.R.S. *Miscellanea*, vol. iv. pp. 162, 172, 207.
† Sir Richard Molyneux of Croxteth Hall, and of Sefton Hall. His son, Richard, was created Viscount Molyneux of Maryborough in 1628, and the family remained Catholic till 1769.

Another station of his must have been Wardley Hall, the residence of his kinsman, Roger Downes, where, as we have seen, his head is still preserved. Even at Morleys he was by no means left in peace. He incurred the odium of some rich heretics who sublet the estate of Morleys for Tyldesley (who himself lived far away at Myerscough Lodge), by informing him of their extorting exorbitant rents from the poor Catholic tenants. This he did partly for the sake of the poor, partly out of gratitude to the gentleman who lent him his house gratis. "After that, those heretickes, as well for this, as for their hatred to Religion, laboured (as he conceived) the more, by threats and devices to fright him from thence, or to get him thrust out of doores or taken ; so that upon a time when their rage was great, he desired me to go to Mr. Tyldesley from him, to inform him of the treuth of some things. Which I did, who thereupon was so well satisfied with our martyr's real dealings and fidelity, that he promised (and like an honest gentleman performed) that he would not bid him begone ; although (as he said) that they had informed him that Mr. Barlow was a man obnoxious to the State. Our martyr, in great gratitude, had much repaired his house, and at that time he promised by me to bestow at least 40 shillings a yeare in the repaire of it. He lived in the worst part of it by farre, leaving the other for his guests, for whom he had furnished (as I thinke) four roomes with beds."

Unhappily, Morleys Hall has been pulled down, and nothing now remains to remind us of the martyr.

"Once when some of the gentry came to him for help, and to lodge with him, his words of entertainement I must not forget, which were, ' You must not be offended with our clownishness, for we are all clowns.' Now indeed there were still (besides his servant and the poore man that tabled him), some one poor Catholicke or more that wanting services he gave lodging into, working there for his living. But surely he though apparelled in their fashion, was not so esteemed, but for a devout follower of his maister, a true lover of poverty, who would be poore in his clothes, poore in his lodging, accompanied by the poore, whom he served againe, and whose poore diet he chose to eat : for although God had put into his hands (as I thinke) enough wherewithal to have played the housekeeper, he chose rather to subject himselfe, and become a sojourner with a poore man and his wife to avoide thereby (as I did conceive) distractive sollicitude and dangerous dominion, and to expose sensuality to be curbed with the simple provision of poore folkes, and this I thinke was no small matter ; at least, I and many others (I assure myself) were much edified with it, knowing his poore and patient manner of living, and so will that partie be (I hope) whom wee heard to say that he could have plates enough if he would live upon curds and buttermilke. Which milke our martyr oft was contented with insteed of drink, when the poore folkes thought their beer (which was small as could be made) was too new. . . . His diet was for the most part white meat ; yet as he did not use to ask for this or that, but contenting himself with whatsoever they provided, so he did not refuse to eate a litle of their flesh meates when God sent it ; and thereupon he said unto me once, that if God should send a venison pastre, he would not refuse to eat of it. Indeed the best part of his sustenance was usually of spoone-meat, that if it were not for some other reason, that perhaps was a cause that he did drinke so little. which for quantity was the least that ever I knew a man to live with. Once after dinner, he used those words unto me : 'You see that I have eaten well, yet verily I rise as hungry as when I sat downe.' Of bread he had his choice, for commonly there was a fair browne loafe and a ionacke. He fasted Advente, and because of that (as he said unto me) he kept home that moneth.

"Notwithstanding his infirmities, I never knew him to tamper with the physicians ; surely he was to himself Dr. Diet, Dr. Quiet, and the onely Dr. Merriman that ever I knew. I remember he told me that when he returned into England (being then either weake with austerity or of a consumption), he went to Dr. More, and desired him out of charity to tell a poore priest what course he had best to take to be recovered of a consumption ; and his answer was, 'Goe into your owne country and for your physicke drinke a morning a messe of new milke and eat a roasted apple at night, which physicke now and then he used. How many yeares above twenty he lived after that, till he yielded to die of the consumption of charitie, I did not know, . . . but by a notable thing which he told me at Easter was two yeares, I knew it to be above twenty, and it was this : That he had bin above twenty yeares in England and no one day thereof omitted to celebrate, and I beleeve that many daies besides Christ-masse he had occasion to celebrate oftner than once, for the help of his charge ; for so one Christopher Bate (who for diverse yeares out of devocion had served him) told me and somewhat more which was this, saying : 'That so long as Mr. Barlow was able he would not ride, but still went on foot with a long staffe on his backe like a countryman ; and then (quoth he) he tooke mightie paines ; for he would have gone sometimes to severall places in a morning to say masse ; and after that to another, I know not how farre off that night, and (as I think) he also said that our martyr was too hard for him at that time ; yet he was broughte so weake againe, that with but riding a foot-pace a short day's journey, he found himself very weary at night, as he told me himselfe."

It is very interesting to hear that our martyr sometimes said Holy

227

Mass several times in one day, but this does not seem to have been so uncommon in England in the days of persecution, where priests were few and the harvest very plenteous. The discipline of the Church of our own day is against it on account of the abuses to which such a practice might give rise, and if we may believe a report made by a Roman envoy of the state of religion in England during the reign of Charles II., these abuses were already a subject of complaint.

However, there can have been no such suspicion of avarice in the case of so apostolic a man as Dom Ambrose Barlow. But to continue the narration :

"Whereas I said that our martyr was a sojourner and no house-keeper, so I say he was never without a servant, yet would be no maister, God providing servants for him, who out of devotion would waite on him, and thus he had all the good offices done for him better than for others that provide for themselves, and for their domineering give wages ; yet he gratis used to bestow on his man yearely as much frise as would make him a suite, and though (as I have said) he was so well served by them when they did serve him, yet it was no litle (I think) that God mortified him therein ; for they doing it voluntarily, and at their owne charges, in a manner, by paying for their diet, so they did often leave him, and I am sure it was so since I came acquainted with him ; for I have knowne two within a litle space to hold this course, as now the one and then the other againe, the former and then the latter ; and this changing and inconstancy of theirs that usually makes others angry, made him merrie ; for as the old man said, he turned all that came to a jest. Certainly God had given him the perfect habitt of indifference, which I might perceive in his carriage towards me, for when I had beene with him for some time, and the humour had taken me to goe home, he would never have persuaded me to stay, but asking when I thought to come againe he bad me farewell merrily, and as merrily welcome when I returned, with pretty jest. . . .

"Our martyr was so mild, witty and chearefull in his conversation, that, of all men that ever I knew, he seemed to me the most lively to represent the spirit of Sir Thomas More. His infirmities and labours were often great, but did not alter him, nor robbe him of his cheerefulness. Neither did I ever see him mou'd at all upon occasion of wrongs, slaunders or threats which was frequently raised against him : but as one insensible of wrong, or free from choller, he entertained them with a jest, and past over them with a smile and a nod. A certaine grave man and an old Penitent of his being present, when there was told him of the threats of some neighbouring Heretickes ; which he received after his wonted fashion, making himself and us recreation with it. The old

228

man, rownding with me, said : In sooth, I have knowne Mr. Barlow a great while, and this has beene still his custome, to turne whatsoever happened unto him to a jest, using other words to this purpose, as arguing him of invincible patience. How long it was from the time of their acquaintance I do not remember, nor is it materiall, but sure it was on one of St. James's days, when they were both prisoners in Lancaster. I certainly remember he showed that old man the way to heaven, and took him into the Church."

For it must not be supposed that even in this faithful part of Lancashire the priest of God had no persecutions to undergo. Once when he was describing his many adventures and hair-breadth escapes to his biographer, the good man said to him : " I wonder how you escaped from being a martyr," to which he replied : " I have bidden as fair for it as another." And then he told him that he had been no fewer than four times in prison, and that when he was in Lancaster Castle the ministers flocked about him, and he told them thereon. As a matter of fact he lived for more than thirteen years in calm and certain expectation of the destined crown.

On Thursday, August 28, 1628, there suffered at Lancaster the glorious martyr, Father Edmund Arrowsmith, a priest of the Society of Jesus. And that very night he appeared in glory at the bedside of the monk who was to follow in his steps. When Father Barlow lay under sentence of death in Lancaster Castle, he wrote to Dom Rudesind : " I believe I shall suffer, for Mr. Bradshaw " (this was one of the names used by Father Arrowsmith for concealment), " the last that suffered martyrdom, the night after he suffered, whereas I knew nothing of his death, spoke thus to me, standing by my bedside : ' I have suffered, and now you will be to suffer ; say little, for they will endeavour to take hold of your words.' "

And so our martyr lived in the daily expectation of the martyr's crown. When his biographer visited him for the last time, at Easter, 1639, two years before he was apprehended, he told him plainly, as he had often done before, " that they would not leave till they had him to Lancaster." His friend was astonished at these words, as all seemed quiet at the time, " and there were great hopes of better and better, and no danger that the heretics could prevail to have him imprisoned." But the martyr knew well what was coming ; and then going on to speak of the conversion of England, he expressed what was a constant thought with him, in the following words, " Indeed, it must be by the sword."

By this he meant, we suppose, that the blood of many martyrs must be shed, before the sin of our country should be atoned and God restore her to His favour.

He then went on to tell his friend of Father Arrowsmith and his prediction, and of his warning to have a care of his words when he came before the judges. "To which, I answering in these words, 'I am sure, Sir, that you will talke to them' (my meaning was that he would speake boldly to the honour of God and confusion of heresy), at my blunt reply he did laugh heartily : and now our merrie martyr is merrie indeed, and his joy shall never have an end."

So anxious was he for the promised crown that it would seem that this was the reason why he refused to leave the county of Lancashire, where it had been revealed to him that he was to glorify God by his death. Thus his biographer tells us the following story :

"Once a friend of mine, who lived in Cheshire, desired me to procure a priest to come into his house, but he must be such an one as was of exemplar life. Whereupon I propounded our martyr, and describing his life and conversation he liked well thereof. I went then and delivered my petition with no diffidence at all of being denied : but after some hours were past, he answered me first in these words : 'In good deed Lancaster is my prison,' which now I understand ; and he likewise said that priests 'did alwaies much goode in Lancaster Castle, but in Chester jayle he never heard of any good that they did.' I thought it strange (and so I was bold to tell him), that he talk't of prisons, the times being then so quiet. In conclusion, he wish'd me to procure some other and excuse him, for he must not goe out of Lancaster ; and he hath bin as good as his word."

Nor did he take the least trouble to conceal himselr.

"When he travelled abroad he went the ordinary way, and even through the towne of Leigh when his businesse was that way, and I thinke he was as well knowne to many there as their Parson. Some talke much of discretion, but his fortitude hath sure brought out good fruit. Upon a time, speaking of some of the gentrie that would not be seene by any at Masse, he said, 'I like not those that will be peeping at God.' And indeed two of these peepers have give no good example of late."

Here is a delightful picture of the simple, homely life our martyr led, mingled as it was with so many perils :

"At Christmasse will be five, six, or seven yeares, I cannot tell which, I being then at Morleys with him, there came upon the eve (as usually there did at that good time), very many Catholickes far and neare to watch and pray. Among the rest there came a young man from behind Manchester, where, in his passage, he understood, as he told us, that there was a pursevant (and his name was Cartwright as I remember), who had commission to have taken Mr. Barlow, and for

230

THE VENERABLE AMBROSE BARLOW, O.S.B.

*To face page* 230

that purpose intended to have beene here upon Christmasse day in the morning, as he had told to some in the towne ; 'but he hath (quoth he) fallen downe the staires at Holiwels the innkeeper but yesterday, and broken his necke.' And so our martyr's day being not yet come, wee had the happinesse to heare his three Masses and his sermon ; and the poore folkes having every one of them received the feast of feasts at our martyr's hands, had his feast at last, and did praise Our Lord. But I must returne againe to speake of the fervour of his pœnitents. The foulest winter weather was no hindrance to them ; old folkes as well as young came, and those that could not well come by day came by night.

"Being come, they hasted to the chappell, where the men having their hats upon a round table altogether (representing the unity of their hearts), they past by a faire cole fire to the altar which upon the eve was ready drest with cleane linnens ; and a venerable old vestment laid thereon, which came out but upon great daies, with all other things poore and cleane. The old picture before the altar was the araignment of Our Blessed Saviour. Against that good time, he used to prepare great wax candles, which he did helpe to make himselfe. I have still had a great desire to express how much I was edified in that place by the Pastour and his pœnitents, who seemed to me to represent the good Catholickes in the primitive Church. They so truly united in Charity, rejoyced coming (from severall places) to meet one another in that holy exercise ; they spent the night modestly and devoutly, sometimes in prayer before the altar, other whiles singing devout songs by the fireside in another roome where they had another fire, that their singing might not disturbe those that would be praying in the chappell. . . .

"Upon all great Holidays and most Sundays (as I thinke) he used to preache, and (as I conjecture) in every place that he lodged at in his circuit. Surely he had a singular talent therein, and could performe it with great facility without penning it. His stile phrase in preaching as it seemed to me was the likest unto the Scripture phrase of any that ever I heard, briefe, plaine, and pithy ; using therein also many pretty parables, in citing of the Holy Scriptures very ready. Oft have I called to mind, how (upon the first Good Friday I heard him preach) so movingly he did mention unto us the Passion of Our Saviour, and those words of St. Paul, which I had not taken notice of before, he made me ever to remember, and highly to reverence, viz. *Jesum Christum prædicamus Judæis scandalum, gentibus autem s.ultitiam.* ("But we preach Christ crucified, unto the Jews indeed a stumbling-block, and unto the Gentiles foolishness." 1 Cor. i. 23.)

But his example was more potent than any preaching. "When he talkt with women I observed that he was either sitting and then he look't another way, or he walk'd casting his head downwards." He never forgot he was a monk, and so either he stayed at home where he was not troubled with the company of women, or when he was forced to go among them for charity's sake, he went but as a passing traveller, and never stayed longer than was necessary.

" Upon a time, I came with my mother to Morleys to spend a good time with him in devotion. But it so fell out that I was called away upon some businesse, and so for some weekes absent. In the interim at Masse and meate, our martyr and my mother did meet, but no oftner. When I returned he told me what a solitary time my mother had had on it, and I thinke it was the solitariest that ever she had in her life. He wished me to excuse it if need were, but she was much edified with it."

And yet, with all his love of solitude, our martyr's hospitality was truly Benedictine.

"Our martyr's man alwaies sat at meat with him, unlesse there were better guests than myselfe. Our ordinarie was three pence, our martyr paying for priests and poore folkes, and on all in the winter that lodged he bestowed a good cole-fire in their chamber. His house was the onely sure refuge that I knew for poore folkes and pœnitents. For other folkes use to stand upon their nice termes, which he did not.

"His solemne daies of invitation were three, viz. : Christ-masse, Easter, and Whitsunday ; and then he entertained all that would dine with him. Their cheare was boil'd beefe and pottage, minched pies, goose and groates, and to every man a gray coate at parting. He served them, and his example made some others of his richer guests to doe the like. In fine when the poore were risen, he sat downe at their table, and made his dinner of their leavings : and then the residue that was left was divided among the poorest to take home with them."

We have some precious details of his personal appearance and dress.

" Remembering how Sir Thomas More jested at his beard, it put me in mind that our martyr was ever careless of his ; for he did not trouble him selfe nor other with the trimming or shaving of it, but let it alone as nature had framed it. It was forked and not long, much haire about his cheekes. The haire of his head curled naturally, which sure was sometimes cut, for it was never long." Hair, of a chestnut colour, was still adhering to the skull when found at Wardley Hall.

" His cloathes were still of gray-frise, the fashion thereof for the oldness might be the same, that was in use when he first did leave or return into England ; a long-waisted jerkin and doublet, his breeches tied above

232

knees.   The best hatt that ever I saw him weare, I would not have given two groates for ; the band about his neck of the country folkes fashion, as poore a one as is ordinarily worne by any, tied with a round threaden point, as I remember : no cuffes at all.   Instead of pantofles, a pair of scurvy old slip-shoes, which continually he wore within doores.   I adventuring once to find fault with those slip-shoes said unto him : 'Alas, Sir, why doe you not get a paire of warme slippers ? besides, you goe uneasily in those trashes.'   His answer was, 'We must have somewhat to looke at.'   Although it be a common thing amongst many good men that would be loath to fight, to weare swords, yet our martyr would wear none ; and thus merrily he answered me when I tooke notice thereof, saying, 'Indeed, I dare not weare a sword, because I am of a cholleicke nature.'   And then he told me in these words, that he had like once to have gone together by the eares with one that would have taken him, but in the end his heeles proved his best weapon.

" He loved to observe how time passed, but he had no pocket watch : and once I asked him why he had not a watch to take abroad with, as it was usuall : and he answered me that it was pride, pride. He had a clocke at home for that purpose, which nobody kept but himselfe."

One more personal detail, and we have finished with this precious document.

" He desired me very earnestly once to teach him to make pictures, at which I confesse I did then much wonder ; but now I am much comforted therewith.   Indeed I thought it was unlikely that he should reape any profit to himselfe or others by it, and that he knew how to make better use of his time in some other thing : yet he had a further project which was, that in teaching of him, I would make a picture for his altar : which I did, and it was of Our Saviour crowned with thorns. All things considered, I did much wonder that it was performed so well.   But in the meane time my goode scholler made three for one with me, which I thought then would have beene in no esteeme, because they were no better than the letters that young scribes use to make at first : but verily even then his poore ghostly children beg'd them, and (as he told me) were very glad of them.   After this he fell seriously to his worke, and made many more : which I believe will be now in more esteem than artificiall [*i.e.* artistic] pictures, and will remaine as deare memorialls of Christ's martyr."

It is quite possible that the picture of our martyr, engraved on vellum, and now in the possession of Mr. Gillow, may be taken from a portrait painted by this worthy man.   A copy of it is reproduced in these pages.

2 G

# FORGOTTEN SHRINES

It bears the inscription :

*Vera Effigies Rdi. P. Ambrosii Barlow, presbyteri, et monachi congregationis Anglicanæ, ordinis Sti Benedicti, qui pro Christi fide sanguinem fudit Lancastriæ in Anglia, 10 Septembris, 1641, ætatis suæ 56.*

(The true likeness of the Reverend Father Ambrose Barlow, of the English Congregation of the Order of St. Benedict, who for the faith of Christ shed his blood at Lancaster in England, 10th September, 1641, aged 56.)

## THE LAST YEARS

BEFORE describing the martyr's arrest, we may add some further particulars of his holy life, gathered by Bishop Challoner from the Knaresborough MSS.* and from other authentic sources.

" Such was the fervour of his zeal that he thought the day lost in which he had not done some notable thing for the salvation of souls. Night and day, he was ever ready to lay hold of all occasions of reclaiming any one from error ; and whatever time he could spare from his devotions, he employed in seeking after the lost sheep, and in preaching the Word of God.   But then he never neglected the care of his own sanctification : he celebrated Mass, and recited the office with great reverence and devotion, had his fixed hours for mental prayer, which he never omitted, and found so much pleasure in this inward conversation with God (from which he received that constant supply of heavenly light and strength), that when the time came on which he had devoted to this holy exercise, he was affected with a sensible joy, as much as worldlings would be when going to a feast.   He had also a great devotion to the Rosary, which he daily recited and recommended much to his penitents ; and was very tenderly affected with the sacred mysteries of the Incarnation, Passion, and Resurrection of the Son of God (which he there contemplated), and was much devoted to His Blessed Mother.   He often meditated on the sufferings of his Redeemer with his arms extended in the form of a cross, and these meditations enkindled in his soul a desire of suffering for Christ, a happiness for which he daily prayed.

" He had a great contempt of the world and its vanities, and a very humble opinion of himself, joined with a great esteem, love and veneration for the virtue of others.   He was always afraid of honours and preferments, and had a horror of vain glory, which he used to call ' the worm or moth of virtues,' and never failed to correct in others,

* Now in the possession of the Lady Herries.

234

sometimes in a jocose way, at others seriously, according to the temper of the persons. He industriously avoided feasts and assemblies and all meetings for merry-making, as liable to dangers of excess, idle talk and detraction. . . . He always abstained from wine, and being asked the reason why he did so, he alleged the saying of the wise man, *Wine and women make the wise apostatize.* . . . He was sometimes applied to exorcize persons possessed by the devil, which he did with good success. He had a great talent in composing of differences, and reconciling such as were at variance; and was consulted as an oracle by the Catholics of that country in all their doubts and difficulties.

"Yet he was very severe in rebuking sin, so that obstinate and impenitent sinners were afraid of coming near him. Nothing more sensibly afflicted him than when he saw any one going astray from the right path of virtue and truth, more especially if it were a person of whom he had conceived a good opinion or had great hopes; upon these occasions he would at first be almost oppressed with melancholy, till, recollecting himself in God, and submitting to His wise Providence, (justly permitting evil to draw greater good out of it), he recovered again his usual peace and serenity."

We can imagine how he wept over the terrible fate of an unhappy apostate in the town of Leigh, who perished some two years before his own death. This man had not only fallen from the faith, but had become "a notorious sport-master to the Protestants," greatly scandalising the faithful by his blasphemous parody of the ceremonies and gestures used in celebrating Holy Mass. Whether he was doing this at the time is not clear, but, in any case, as he was standing in the tower of the Protestant Church at Leigh, a rope suddenly broke, and the clock-weights fell upon his head, killing him on the spot. The Catholics of Leigh who came to Mass on Easter Day, 1639, told this to our martyr with great awe, as a manifest judgment of God.

Some months before his last arrest, he was again afflicted by hearing that some persons whom he loved as his own soul, had resolved to do something very wicked, which was likely to lead to the ruin of many souls. He was so affected by this sudden and unlooked-for blow that it brought on a stroke of paralysis, which took away the use of one side, and put him in great danger. What added very much to this cross was the fear that his poor children would thereby be deprived of spiritual consolations. He suffered so much that he was brought to death's door, and to add to his affliction, no priest could be found to administer to him the last Sacraments. In this extremity he was comforted by God Himself, for after falling into a sort of ecstasy, he was heard to break forth into words like these, "Lord, Thy will be done! A due conformity of our will to Thine, is to be preferred to the use of the Sacraments, and even to martyrdom itself. I reverence and earnestly desire Thy Sacraments, and I have often wished to lay down my life for Thee in the profession of my faith ; but if it be pleasing to Thine infinite wisdom by this illness to take me out of the prison of this body, half dead already, Thy will be done !"

Thus he was willing to resign, if God so pleased, even that very crown for which he so ardently sighed. To reward such dispositions, God was pleased to send to him a priest of the Society of Jesus, who administered to him the consolations of our holy religion. According to Challoner, he was thus rewarded for having himself twelve years before administered the last Sacraments to the illustrious Jesuit martyr, Father Edmund Arrowsmith, as he lay in prison awaiting his last conflict. Though the biographers of Father Arrowsmith do not mention this incident, Challoner's authorities are so good that we may well accept it as a fact. Perhaps this is the reason why this holy Jesuit appeared, after his martyrdom, to our Benedictine, as already related.

Before proceeding to recount the last act of the tragedy, it may be well to give a glance at the political aspect of affairs in England at this troublous time, as this will greatly help us to understand the story. Father Barlow's missionary life lasted, as we know, from 1617 to 1641. These years witnessed the growing power of the House of Commons, and of the Puritan sect, till the movement culminated, during the later years of Charles I., in open rebellion and civil war.

Charles I. came to the throne in 1625. He was naturally averse to persecution, and being married to a Catholic wife, did his best (in the feeble sort of way that was characteristic of him) to protect the most faithful and devoted of his subjects from the utmost rigours of the penal laws. But the Parliament was ever urging upon him to execute the laws against them, and the unhappy prince gave way again and again to their insolent demands.

However, Father Arrowsmith was the only priest to suffer under Charles I., till the summoning of the Long Parliament in November 1640, and the impeachment of Lord Strafford on a charge of high treason, brought the struggle for supremacy between King and Commons to the point of open rupture. The execution of Strafford, May 12, 1641, was the virtual proclamation of civil war, and henceforward the Parliament became ever increasingly powerful. Hating Catholics with a double hatred both for their loyalty to the Pope and their fidelity to the King, they vowed a relentless war against the "Popish Malignants." The Venerable John Goodman had been thrown as a victim to the malice of the "Short Parliament," but his own generous plea that he might be sacrificed rather than live to be the subject of discontent between the King and his people, softened even Puritan hearts, and he was permitted to die in prison. But the Long Parliament thirsted still more for blood ; and the Venerable William Ward, who was martyred at Tyburn on St. Anne's day, two months after the execution of Strafford, was its first priestly victim. Our martyr was to be the second.

"The political manoeuvres," writes Charles Butler,* "which persuaded the multitude to believe that the sovereign was a favourer of popery, and which left him, as he too readily supposed, no means of repelling the charge, except that of causing the laws against them to be executed with due vigour, may be dated from the beginning of the reign of James I. Frequent resort to this unjustifiable but effective measure was had, during the contests between Charles I. and his Parliament : the religion of the Queen was too often used as a pretext to give the insinuation credit and currency. Stories the most absurd and ridiculous were, at the same time, propagated, to inflame the multitude against the Catholics by rendering them objects both of hatred and alarm."

Thus, at this time, the celebrated Hampden actually introduced to the House of Commons a tailor of Cripplegate, who pretended that he had overheard the details of a plot to assassinate one hundred and eight leading members of Parliament at the rate of £10 for every lord and 40s. for every commoner so murdered !

This preposterous story lashed the House into a frenzy : the trainbands and militia of the kingdom were ordered out, and the tailor's report was printed and circulated throughout the kingdom.

Proclamation after proclamation was issued against the unhappy Catholics. On March 7 a royal decree ordered that all priests should leave the kingdom within the space of a calendar month. Those who did not obey were to suffer the penalties prescribed for traitors. When this proclamation appeared, Father Barlow's friends besought him, at least, to conceal himself. But he steadily refused. "Let them fear that have anything to lose which they are unwilling to part with," he said. For himself, he most earnestly desired to lose his life in so good a cause. He was beginning to recover from his illness, and his hopes of martyrdom had revived. Nor was he to be disappointed.

* *Memorials of English Catholics*, vol. ii. p. 397.

## LANCASTER CASTLE

EASTER-DAY, that year, fell on April 25, so that it was already more than a fortnight after the date fixed by the royal proclamation.

On this the queen of all Christian feasts, the Protestants of Leigh were gathered together in their old parish church, to take part in the Anglican service and listen to the exhortations of their Vicar. Meanwhile the faithful were gathered round their beloved priest at Morleys Hall, to assist at the adorable sacrifice of the Mass. The Lamb of God whose Pasch they were celebrating was offered up by the trembling hands of the half-paralysed priest, who was so soon to offer his own blood in union with that of his Lord and Redeemer. Well he knew that since the time of grace had expired, the hour of his sacrifice was close at hand. Yet even he can hardly have anticipated such an interruption of the Paschal solemnities as was destined to take place.

For at Leigh Parish Church a strange scene was being enacted.*

The Reverend James Gatley, the Vicar, was a man of zeal for the Anglican religion, and it seemed to him that he could not celebrate so great a feast more worthily than by striking a blow against the hated Catholics. There was a numerous congregation gathered round him, and he was so fired with the idea, that he proposed to them to omit the usual service, and to proceed in a body to Morleys Hall, where they would be sure to find the Papists assembled at their idolatrous Mass, and could help him to apprehend Barlow, that noted Popish priest, in the very act; and thus they would perform a work more worthy of their zeal for the Gospel, than if they were to have their sermon and prayers, and risk the chance of missing the priest by delaying till after the service. No sooner said than done. The proposal was accepted with enthusiasm, and the whole congregation, about four hundred in number, armed with clubs and swords, followed the parson, who marched in front in his surplice, to Morleys Hall, where our martyr, having finished his Mass, was making an exhortation to his people on the subject of patience. There were about one hundred gathered together before the humble altar, with its picture of the arraignment of Our Blessed Saviour. We can imagine their panic, as the shouts of the rabble outside were heard, drowning the priest's voice. The minister began to thunder at the house doors, and the faithful within crowded round their beloved Father, urging him to take shelter in one of the hiding-holes in the house. But, like St. Thomas

* It has frequently been stated, in error, that this happened at Eccles. Morleys is in the parish of Leigh, and this church is much nearer to the Hall than that of Eccles.

HANDFORTH HALL
*Photo by James Watts*

*To face page* 238

of Canterbury, he refused to save himself and leave his sheep to the mercy of these wolves, and, after briefly exhorting them to constancy, he ordered the doors to be opened.

The mob immediately rushed in, crying out, "Where is Barlow? Where is Barlow? He is the man we want!" Even now he might have escaped in the crowd, but no such thought crossed his mind. Calmly and patiently he gave himself up into their hands, feeling that at last his hour was come.

The faithful were permitted to leave unmolested, after their names had been taken, and they had given caution for their appearance before the justices. In the meantime the mob searched the whole house, broke open the martyr's chest, and rummaged and turned over his clothes; but by God's providence did not discover a considerable sum of money which had lately been given him for the poor. Father Barlow was full of gratitude for this, and was able, later on, to give directions for the disposal of the money according to the directions of the donors.

The martyr was now carried off by the minister and his mob (who, it seems, had acted in this whole affair without any warrant), and brought before a Justice of the Peace named Risley, probably (says Mr. Gillow), a member of the family seated at Risley Hall in the parish of Winwick. He sent him, guarded by sixty armed men, to Lancaster Castle. Some of his flock would have attempted to rescue him on the road, had not the martyr earnestly entreated them not to think of it.

He was carried to prison in a sort of triumph by his armed mob, who treated him with every species of insult and contempt, though he was still so weak that he could not sit on horseback without one behind to support him. But all this he bore joyously for the love of Christ.

The old towers of Lancaster Castle still frown upon the town at their feet, as they did in our martyr's day. As he entered the great gateway he must have thought of Father Arrowsmith, whose quartered limbs had been exposed on the summit of John of Gaunt's Tower but a few years before. To those who came to him in prison he loved to speak of his Jesuit forerunner, and of the vision which assured him that he too would win his palm.

A priest of his own Order, who had interest at Court, wrote to him to ask what he desired to be done for him. Would he prefer to be sent into banishment, or to be removed to London? He replied that he desired neither, but that he wished him not to concern himself about him, since to die for this cause was to him far more desirable than life.

In prison he found much comfort in the book of Boëtius, *De Con-solatione*, till the jailor, noticing this, had the barbarity to take it away from him.  But the martyr only said with a smile, " If you take this little book away, I will betake myself to that great book from which Boëtius learned his wholesome doctrine, and that book you can never take away from me " : and by this he meant mental prayer, which indeed he continually practised.  When any one came to visit him in prison, he would not suffer the time to be lost in vain or worldly talk, but spoke only of spiritual things.

After more than four months' imprisonment the trial came on September 7, before Sir Robert Heath.  Information of his capture had been despatched to the Council, and on Friday, May 20, 1641, the following resolution had been passed by the Lords :

" Whereas this House was informed that a Romish priest was appre-hended on Easter-day last past at the Hall of Morleys, in the County of Lancaster, called by the name of Edward Barlowe, who upon his examination confessed himself a Romish priest, and has received orders at Arras ; he being now committed to the common gaol of Lancaster, it is ordered that the said Edward Barlowe shall be proceeded against at the next Assizes for the said county, according to law."

The Judge had received instructions from the Puritan Parliament to see that the extreme penalty of the law was executed upon any priest convicted at Lancaster, " for a terror to the Catholics who were numerous in that county."

The indictment being read, Father Barlow freely acknowledged him-self a priest, and that he had exercised his priestly functions for above twenty years in the kingdom.  This, of course, sealed his fate.

Asked why he had not obeyed the royal proclamation and departed the realm before April 7 last, he pleaded first that the edict only specified " Jesuits and Seminary priests," whereas he was a Religious of the Order of St. Benedict ; and secondly, that as was well known to those who had brought him to prison, he had been so weakened by his recent severe illness, that it was quite impossible for him to have undertaken the journey at that time.

The Judge, perceiving that the people were moved with compassion towards him, and that every one said that his sickness was a legitimate excuse for him, turned the subject, and asked him what he thought of the justice of those laws by which those of his profession were put to death.

" I esteem them unjust and barbarous," replied the martyr.  " For what law," he continued, " can be more unjust than this, by which priests are condemned to suffer as traitors, merely because they are Roman, that is, true priests ? For there are no other true priests [in England] but the Roman ; and if these be destroyed, what must become of the divine law, when none remain to preach God's word and administer His Sacraments ?"

"If such be your opinion," retorted the Judge, "what do you think of our kings who have made these laws ?"

Perceiving the malice of this question, the martyr only said that he prayed God to pardon the authors of such laws, and those who carried them into execution.

The Judge then told him that his sickness excused him in some measure, and that he would set him at liberty, provided he promised not to seduce the people any more. "It will be easy," said the servant of God, "to pledge my word to this, since I am no seducer but a reducer of the people to the true and ancient religion. I have laboured all along to disabuse the minds of those who have fallen into error, and I am in the resolution to continue until death to render this good office to these strayed souls."

The Judge, as he afterwards acknowledged, was astonished at the constancy of his answers and his courage, and said to him : "You speak very boldly to a man who is master of your life, and who can either acquit or condemn you as he shall judge proper."

"It is true," replied the martyr, "that you have power given to you over me through a wicked policy, but be aware, although I appear before you in quality of a criminal, being, as I am, a minister of Jesus Christ and a priest of the New Law, in spiritual matters, I am judge, and I declare to you that if you continue to condemn the innocent, and remain in the darkness of heresy, you will have no part in the happiness of the children of God."

"I shall have the advantage of you," concluded the Judge in anger, "since my sentence will be executed first." *

Upon this the Judge directed the jury to bring him in guilty, and the next day, the Feast of the Nativity of Our Blessed Lady, he pronounced sentence upon him in the usual form.

He seems sincerely to have regretted the martyr's fate, but pleaded that his hands were tied by the express orders of the Parliament, and that once the prisoner had confessed his priesthood, he could do nothing to save him.

Father Barlow heard with great serenity and cheerfulness the dreadful sentence pronounced, exclaiming, "Thanks be to God." He then prayed with all his heart that the Divine Majesty would pardon all who had in any way been accessory to his death.

* Allanson MSS. (Ampleforth Abbey) *Biography*, i. pp. 82-85.

2 H

The Judge applauded his charity, and granted him what he petitioned for : that is, a chamber to himself in the Castle, where for the short remainder of his time he might without molestation apply himself to his devotions, and prepare for his end.

Meanwhile, his religious brethren were met together in General Chapter. Dom Rudesind Barlow resigned the Cathedral Priorship of Coventry,* and his brother, Dom Ambrose, was elected in his place on September 3. But before this information could reach him, he had passed into eternity. Yet it was a last testimony on the part of his brethren to the affection and reverence in which they held this great servant of God, who was fighting his Lord's battles in England.


## THE MARTYR'S CROWN

Father Barlow had the happiness of shedding his blood for his Lord on a Friday. It was only two days after his condemnation that he was led out to die—*i.e.* September 10, 1641.

The hurdle was ready at the foot of John of Gaunt's Tower, and the martyr was laid on it. We do not know if he was permitted to wear the Benedictine habit on this his day of triumph. When a monk is professed, he lies prostrate beneath a funeral pall to typify his death to the world, till at the Communion of the Mass the deacon comes to him and sings : " Awake, thou that sleepest, and arise from the dead ; and Christ shall give thee light." He then arises and goes to the altar to receive Holy Communion.

Our martyr's thoughts must have gone back to that day, five and twenty years before, when in the prime of his manhood he made his holocaust to God. Now he was about to consummate the sacrifice, for he had been, like his great Exemplar, "obedient unto death."

As he was drawn on the hurdle from the Castle gateway to the place of execution hard by, he held in his hand a little cross of wood which he had made. When he was come to the place, he was loosed from the hurdle, and went three times round the gallows, reciting the *Miserere*. Some of the ministers were for disputing with him about religion, but he told them that it was an unfair and unseasonable challenge, and that he had something else to do than to hearken to their fooleries. Surely, he had

---

* By the Bull of Urban VIII., *Plantata in agro Dominico*, the restored English Congregation of the Order received the rights and privileges of their predecessors, and among them the right to the nine cathedrals which had belonged to the Benedictines in times gone by. Priors were appointed to these Cathedral Monasteries, and these titular dignities survive to our own day.

242

suffered enough already from the zeal of parsons! As to this, Mr. Fletcher Moss quaintly says, "Some 'ministers of religion' persisted in trying to 'convert him.' Perhaps they thought they were kind and good. An old Lancashire proverb says, 'There's nowt so queer as folk.'"

He suffered with great constancy. According to the sentence, he was hanged, dismembered, disembowelled, quartered, and boiled in tar; but, as another martyr said, as he listened to the dreadful details at his condemnation, "All this is but one death." And as he had said himself, when they tried to persuade him to petition for mercy, he "must die some time or other, and could not die a better death."

There is something extremely touching in the contrast between the tragedy of such a death, and the sweet, homely details of the good monk's life. But he died as simply as he lived, without ostentation or parade, rejoicing "to be dissolved and to be with Christ."

"There is a tradition among the Catholics of Lancashire," says Dodd, who derived his information from Edward Barlow, *alias* Booth, the martyr's godson, "that Mr. Barlow, before he suffered, foretold that he was to be the last that should die at Lancaster upon account of Holy Orders, which has hitherto been verified. For though several priests have been condemned since at Lancaster, none have suffered, excepting Mr. Smith, *alias* Harrison, who was maliciously indicted and taken off upon another account."

When the news reached Douay, Dom Clement Reyner, the President-General, sent round a circular "Mortuary Bill" to the brethren in the various monasteries, of which a copy is still preserved. It begins *Te Deum Laudamus*, and is, of course, in Latin. We append a translation :

*Te Deum Laudamus.*

"At Lancaster in England, after a holy life, daily labours endured in cultivating the vineyard of Christ for four and twenty years, and an abundant harvest of souls offered to God, our Reverend Father in Christ, (by us to be honoured with all reverence),

"FATHER AMBROSE BARLOW

suffered a glorious martyrdom, for the defence of the faith of the Holy Catholic and Roman Church, the Mother of all who have God for their Father. He was a priest and monk of the English Congregation of the Order of St. Benedict, professed in the Monastery of St. Gregory at Douay, and was in the 55th year of his age, the 25th of his profession, and the 24th of his priesthood. We desire, therefore, that this should be made known to all, especially to the monks of our English Congregation, and to others of the same Order, that the

Masses and other prayers which they are bound to recite for their departed Brethren should be changed into Masses of the Most Holy Trinity, the Hymn *Te Deum Laudamus,* and into other acts of thanksgiving, for to pray for a Martyr would be to offer wrong to Jesus Christ, the King of Martyrs. But let these and all other the faithful of Christ praise God together with us, and pray that this Benedictine tree of the English Congregation should so ever grow in virtues that it may merit frequently to offer to God fruit of this kind. And oh ! would that he, who with immense joy of heart signs this letter, might be the next ! By God's mercy, a fuller account of the life and death of the aforesaid Martyr shall follow on this notice.

" (Signed)     Fr. CLEMENT REYNER,
" Unworthy President-General of the English Congregation of the Order of St. Benedict."

It would seem that a large portion of the holy relics of our martyr came into Catholic hands.

His head, as we have seen, was rescued by Francis Downes of Wardley Hall, and is still preserved in that historic house, which is about five miles distant from Morleys Hall.

At Stanbrook Abbey, near Worcester, the Benedictine nuns religiously preserve the martyr's left hand, which was formerly kept at the Mission of Knaresborough, in Yorkshire. The appearance of the hand, as regards colour and texture, is much like old parchment. The furrows of the skin are very conspicuous, the thumb and index-finger are pressed together, the little finger rests against the ring finger, but its point is drawn inwards across the inner side of the latter ; the middle finger stands apart from the others. The nails are almond shape, the " free edge" is broken and uneven. The points of the fingers are shrunken and contracted. We give an illustration of this precious relic. The nuns have also a portion of one of the fingers of the right hand, and a small piece of bone.

At St. Gregory's Abbey, Downside, the martyr's own Monastery, there is a piece of a rib about four inches long. At the Franciscan Convent, Taunton, is a bone about two inches long. Lastly, at our Abbey of St. Thomas the Martyr, at Erdington, are preserved two relics. One is a bone about two inches long, one of the metacarpal bones. It bears the inscription in seventeenth-century handwriting :

" *Beati Ambrosii Barlow sacerdotis et Martyris ex ordine Sci Benedicti in Anglia.*"

This relic was preserved in St. Mary's Convent, York, for many many years, but was given to the writer in 1899. The other Erdington

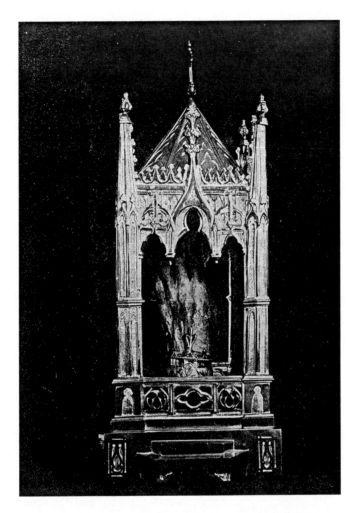

THE HAND OF VEN. AMBROSE BARLOW,
O.S.B., AT ST. MARY'S ABBEY, STANBROOK

*To face page* 244

relic is a piece of one of our martyr's ribs. This was in the possession of the late Miss Blundell of Little Crosby, in Lancashire, and was kept with other relics in a silver reliquary, which has in the front a crucifix incised, and on the back the inscription

" MRA    A relique of B. Fr. Sutton."

The reliquary, with the other relics, is now at Taunton, but the relic of Father Barlow, which is about one and a half inches long by three-quarters of an inch wide, is at Erdington Abbey. It still has some skin adhering to it. On the paper that enfolded it is written in a contemporary hand, " Mr. Barlow's Rib."

The small portrait of Father Barlow, which we have reproduced, was engraved immediately after the martyrdom. A copy printed on vellum, in possession of Richard Morse Carr, Esquire, has attached to it a piece of the martyr's bone.

Let us now return to the martyr's family and its fate. On Sunday, May 26, 1644, that is, in less than three years from the tragedy at Lancaster, Prince Rupert and his army encamped on Barlow Moor on their rush to succour Bolton and Lathom House, and it is most likely, says Mr. Moss, that the Prince and his officers would rest in Barlow Hall, for the Barlows were loyal to the King, though he had let their brother die. In 1620 all the family had been inscribed as Popish Recusants, but it was among these that the King in his need found his most faithful friends.

In the next century, when Prince Charlie came to Manchester in the famous '45, Lord Elcho and his cavalry went south by the Barlow Ford, close to Barlow Hall. The main army built, and crossed by, the first bridge over the Mersey, between Didsbury and Cheadle.

The troubles and persecutions of the family thickened through their devotion to the Stuart cause. In 1734 there is mention of a dispute about " the consecrated goods or ornaments in the Popish Chapel at Barlow."

Our martyr's eldest brother, Sir Alexander Barlow of Barlow, died in 1642, the year after the martyrdom, and was buried in the Collegiate Church of Manchester, by the side of his father, on July 6.

Dom Rudesind died at Douay, September 19, 1656, aged seventy-two. He had been President-General of his Congregation, Prior of his Monastery, and was for forty years Professor of Theology in the College of St. Vedast. He was a profound scholar, and one of the foremost Canonists of his age.

Sir Alexander was succeeded by his son Alexander, the fourth in succession of the name recorded in the pedigree of the family. He died without issue in 1654, and was succeeded by his half-brother Thomas,

245

who died in 1684, and was succeeded by his son Anthony. The name of Anthony Barlow appears in the list of Papists who, in conformity with the Act 1 George I., registered their estates with the respective values thereof. The yearly value of the Barlow Hall estate is returned at £171 9s. He died in 1723, and the estate descended to his eldest son, Thomas, who died of gaol-fever in Lancaster Castle in 1729. He was succeeded by his eldest son, Thomas, the last male heir of the family, who died in March 1773, at the age of fifty-four, without issue, and was buried in the Collegiate Church, Manchester. In him a lineage of over seven hundred years ended.

The arms of the Barlows of Barlow were *sable*, a double eagle displayed *argent*, membered *or*, standing on a limb of a tree raguled and trunked of the second.

The estate was sold by auction, according to Act of Parliament, in 1785, and was purchased by Samuel Egerton of Tatton.

"There are to-day," writes Mr. Moss, "men of the name and lineage of Barlow of Barlow toiling as day labourers on the land which bears their name, and of which their fathers once were lords."

Earthly honours and wealth pass away, indeed, but the glories of the aristocracy of heaven only increase with the centuries. Ambrose Barlow is now numbered among the Venerable Servants of God; soon, we hope, he will be raised to our altars as one of the beatified martyrs of England. Some day he will, doubtless, be honoured as a Saint by the Vicar of Jesus Christ and the Church Universal. Already pilgrimages are made to his birthplace, and Barlow Hall is regarded as a shrine for his sake.

Let us conclude this sketch in the words of his ancient biographer.

"F. Ambrose Barlow having led an Apostolicall life in England for above twenty years, done all the good offices of a Prelate, converted many to the Catholicke faith, faithfully following his Maister to the last, hath now concluded his daies with the maister-piece of charitie, and so sealed his doctrine with his owne innocent blood, to the great honour of God's Church and St. Benedict's Order, to the confusion of Hereticks, the ædification of all Catholickes and to the extraordinary comfort of all his Ghostly brethren and children in Christ Jesus. Surely, *Digne in memoriam vertitur hominum.*"

# THE SECRET TREASURE OF CHAIGLEY

IN a little secluded farm-house, approached by winding lanes and field paths, far away from that smoke of chimneys and that throb or machinery with which Lancashire is mainly associated in one's mind, there lies a hidden treasure, known to very few even of those who inhabit the rural hamlets which lie nearest to the spot. The name of the place is Hill House, Woodplumpton; and it is a typical old English farmstead, white and low, roofed with thatch in the good old fashion, lying isolated from its neighbours, embowered in orchards, as though it were anxious to keep its hidden treasure safe from prying eyes. For this little farm-house contains relics of very pathetic interest : relics which take us back to the cruel old penal days, when the faithful Catholics of Lancashire had to celebrate the rites of their holy religion in secret places, in the dead of night and at peril of their liberty, sometimes even of their lives.

An old lady and her daughter inhabit the place, and at the time of our visit they were busy making cheeses. We entered this humble home with a reverence far greater than would befit many a more stately dwelling ; for the mistress of the house is the representative of a grand old Lancashire family, who were staunch to the old Faith through dark days. And if they are no longer in their old high position in the county, this is due, no doubt, to the fidelity with which their forbears had clung to a proscribed religion in spite of the cruel fines and exactions which had gradually devoured their estates—yes, and in spite of crueller things than confiscation of property ; for this old farm-house is, in fact, a sanctuary where repose the relics of a martyr-priest, and we had come on pilgrimage to visit these sacred treasures.

Our errand was soon explained, and we were led into a small inner room. Here was produced an oak chest, evidently of great antiquity. The lid is now broken off, and the lock keyless. The chest is about a yard long by a foot wide, and curiously carved. The contents of this chest were what we had come to see. But before describing them it will be well to say something of their history.

On the fell-side that rises behind the famous Jesuit College of Stonyhurst, there stands an old farm-house called Chapel House, in the grounds of which formerly stood a chapel dedicated to St. Chad. The Mercian Saint has given his name to the village of Chaigley, or Chadgley, near which Chapel House stands. Now, at Chaigley Hall there lived for many centuries, down to the year 1637, a family named Holden. They were of gentle blood, and allied to some of the best-known families of the county. John Holden, of Chaigley Hall, died in 1637, leaving no male heir. His daughter and heiress, Mary, married Thomas Brockholes of Claughton, Esq., the representative of one of the oldest of the Catholic families of Lancashire. One of John's brothers, Henry, became a priest and a Doctor of the Sorbonne. Another Henry Holden, probably a cousin, also became a priest, and returned to Lancashire to exercise his sacred functions. He is said to have lived to a great age, and to have died about the time of the Revolution, in 1688. But though the Holdens of Chaigley died out in the direct male line, numerous scions of their family remain, and are still flourishing in various parts of Lancashire ; and, what is more, still constant to the old religion. Nor is this wonderful when we know that there has ever been a tradition in the family that they had given to God a martyr, a priest of their own stock.

The old oaken chest which we were shown at Woodplumpton contained this martyr's relics. But who was he, and when did he suffer ? Very little is known for certain as to the facts, but these are the family traditions which form a very touching story. It would appear that during the times of persecution (probably during the Commonwealth, when Cromwell's soldiers were let loose on the "Papists" of Lancashire) a priest was saying Mass in the old chapel of St. Chad at Chapel House, Chaigley. The house was then in possession of a member of the Holden family, and the priest is supposed to have been a son of the house. While he was engaged in the Holy Sacrifice, the soldiers burst in upon the little congregation, tore the celebrant from the altar and slew him as he stood, clad in his sacred vestments, which were deluged with his blood. His head was cut off, and it rolled down the altar steps.

According to one account, the soldiers were carrying this off as a trophy upon a pike, when the martyr's mother, who had been present at the fearful scene, ran after them and implored them to give it to her. One of the men tossed it to her, and she caught it in her apron. From that day to this the family has kept this relic, together with the vestments of the altar and everything that had been used at the martyr's last Mass, and has handed them down from father to son as a most sacred treasure. For many generations—in fact, down to the year 1812— these precious relics were kept with the greatest possible secrecy. Only the head of the family knew of their existence, and shortly before he died he confided the secret as a sacred trust to his eldest son. As far as we know, there is no other instance of a family treasure of such sacred and poignant interest. Wherever the Holdens moved they bore their treasure with them ; and they still preserve it, as we ourselves saw, at Woodplumpton.

# THE SECRET TREASURE OF CHAIGLEY

In 1812 the relics were in possession of Thomas Holden, at Crawshaw Farm, near Stonyhurst. His father, Richard, seems to have settled there in 1727. It happened that one of the Stonyhurst Jesuits, Father John Fairclough, came one day to see the Holdens at Crawshaw. He was shown (I quote from the *Stonyhurst Magazine* of 1888) an old Mass-book with some German writing on the fly-leaf. He asked Holden how he came by the rare old volume ; and then was confided to him, doubtless with a good deal of hesitation, the family secret. The Mass-book was one of a collection of relics handed down for generations past.

Then the Father was taken to see the treasure, carefully kept under lock and key in an oaken chest at the top of the house. He found what we are about to describe, and, above all, the martyr's head " still covered with its flesh, as soft and fresh as if it had but recently been severed from the body." The Father told Holden that there was no longer any need to keep their secret, now that the storm of persecution had blown over ; and from that day many were the pilgrims who came from Stonyhurst and from the country round to see the relics of the martyred priest.

Many years after Father Fairclough's visit, Richard Holden, the oldest surviving member of Thomas Holden's family, used to tell how he had, as a small boy, discovered the existence of the mysterious chest, before the secret had been divulged. He and his sister had heard his parents speak of the hidden treasure ; " and each independently, finding the key while their parents were absent, had stolen upstairs and peeped into the old box. But the unexpected sight of a human head within it made them hurry down again, with a scare which they never forgot to the end of their lives."

Before he moved to Crawshaw, the father of Thomas Holden lived at another farm-house in the same neighbourhood, called Lambing Clough. Here he used sometimes to take the relics and carry them down to a quiet place on the river bank, and lay them out to be aired in the sunshine. Thomas Holden's eldest son, Henry, inherited the relics, and from him they passed to his youngest son, Ralph, as his elder brothers had died without children. Ralph moved to Woodplumpton, where he died at Hill House, in 1885. It is his widow who now guards the sacred deposit. Their son is a priest, and is now Rector of Claughton, the old seat of the Brockholes family.

The reader may imagine with what emotion we gazed at the contents of the venerable oaken chest, as they were spread out before us. Here were the vestments and altar linen still stained with the martyr's blood ; here the chalice, the Missal, and the small silver crucifix which he had been using in the sacred function. Here was the treasure that had been guarded with such care and fidelity by generation after generation of this old Catholic family : the one possession they had clung to and preserved, while houses and lands and goods gradually melted away under the pressure of the cruel penal laws. But we must describe some of the contents of the treasure-chest more minutely.

There is, first of all, the Missal. It is a small octavo volume, printed by Plantin, at Antwerp, in 1570. In it is written the inscription, "*Ex lib. Hen. Johnsone.*" Now, Johnson was the alias of Dr. Henry Holden of the Sorbonne, so no doubt the book belonged to him. Then, on a slip of paper gummed to the fly-leaf are written two lines of German in English characters, with the English translation beneath each line, as follows :

> " Dieses gehört unserm marter,—
> This belongs to our martyr ;
> Und unserm lieben Pfilp,—
> And to our dear Philip."

This writing is not old. It was written by one of the Stonyhurst Fathers for the Holdens, who could not read or translate the old inscription, which has now, unfortunately, disappeared. It is a very singular fact that it should have been written in German ; it was probably done to avoid the attention of Protestants, in case they should ever see the book.

Then there is the altar-stone. It is just a small piece of slate, with crosses scratched in the centre and at the four corners, but with no place for relics. There are several of these old altar-stones of persecution days remaining, and they are all much alike. They had to be small and light ; for the hunted priests had to carry them about with them, and, by a special privilege, they were allowed to be consecrated without the usual relics which it was almost impossible to get in England during the persecution.

And then there is the chalice. St. Chrysostom says that in the early days of the Church the priests were of gold and the chalices of wood ; but that in his time the case was reversed, and the priests were wood, while their chalices were gold. And so in the days of persecution in England, the chalices used by these golden priests, these true-hearted servants of Jesus Christ, who ministered to their brethren at the peril of their lives, were, as a rule, like this one, merely of pewter. The chalice is of the old Gothic shape, six inches high, with a large bowl, four inches in diameter. The paten just covers the top of the chalice.

The altar-cloth (3 ft. by 4 ft.), with a narrow lace border and fringe, is stained with blood. In one corner two letters are embroidered in black silk ; apparently they are P.H., and they would seem to stand for

THE RELICS OF THE CHAIGLEY MARTYR

*The skull, blood-stained alb, missal, chalice of the martyr, together with the old oak chest in which the relics have been preserved*

*To face page 250*

# THE SECRET TREASURE OF CHAIGLEY

Philip Holden. Then there are : a linen sheet (about 6 ft. by 8 ft.) ; a Communion cloth (about 10 ft. by 1 ft.), which is deeply stained with blood ; some fragments of candles, evidently home-made, of unbleached beeswax, with plain cotton wicks ; a small silver crucifix, corporals, palls, a purificator, amice, and large alb. This last article has a large stain of blood in front. There are two chasubles : the first Gothic, and very much faded and mutilated. It was of green silk, embroidered with fleurs-de-lis, and the pillar of red silk has in its centre the chalice and Host and the sacred monogram.

But the other chasuble seems to have been the one worn at the martyr's sacrifice ; for it is stained with his blood. It is made of ribbed white silk, embroidered with flowers. On the cross behind is embroidered in old Gothic letters the inscription :

> " Orate p. aiabs Oliveri Wastlei
> Et Ellene uxoris ejus."

Finally, we come to *the* relic—the martyr's head. It is still partly covered with flesh, and part of the neck remains. It is no longer in the state of preservation in which Father Fairclough found it nearly a hundred years ago. "The flesh is brown and shrivelled and sunk into the crevices of the bones, and in some parts fallen away into dust. The right side is more perfect than the left. Here you can distinctly see the close-shaven hairs of the whiskers, and the place where the ear has been cut off. The neck has not been separated from the body at the joining of the vertebræ, but cut straight through with a sharp instrument. All the teeth are now missing, and a considerable portion of the flesh has been cut away from the neck." This was done in order to give relics to the pilgrims who came to Crawshaw after the existence of the relics was made known. But one day, the story goes, as some one was cutting the neck, the head uttered, or seemed to utter, "a kind of whistling noise" ; and the Holdens were frightened and resolved to let no more of it be cut away. But it is a great pity that these pious depredations were ever permitted.

It seems sad to think that we shall probably never know more as to the identity of this martyr priest. The family tradition is that he was Philip Holden, but no priest of this name is known. The inscription in the Missal hardly suggests that " our dear Philip " and " our martyr " were one and the same person. The learned writer in the *Stonyhurst Magazine* to whom we are so much indebted, and from whose minute account of the relics and their history we have freely quoted, suggests that it may have been Henry Holden the younger, whose death about the time of the Revolution of 1688 is chronicled by Dodd the

251

historian.   But it seems strange that Dodd had not heard that he died a martyr.

The mystery will perhaps never be fully solved.   In any case, the story of these relics is well worth putting on record, on account of the touching fidelity with which they have been treasured by the Holden family.   The family is said never to have been without a priest among its members, and it looks upon this fact as a sign of God's blessing through the intercession of its own martyr.   That there is foundation for the family tradition, the relics bear eloquent witness ; and though we may never learn all the truth, we know enough to honour the Chaigley martyr as one of that white-robed army which bear the victor's palm before the Throne of God.

INTERIOR OF THE COURT, HARVINGTON HALL

*The* x *marks the crevice in the beam which communicates with the priests' hiding-place.   Photo by Thomas Lewis, Birmingham*

*To face page* 253

# A FRANCISCAN APOSTLE
## HIS HOME AND HIS FLOCK

IT was one of those exquisite days of "St. Luke's little summer," when the English climate seems to relent for a moment in its headlong progress towards wintry gloom, and turn back with regret towards the vanished glories of summer, a day flooded with golden October sunshine, mild and mellow as the apples that gleamed scarlet and gold upon the laden branches of the orchards, when a little band of pilgrims set out for North Worcestershire, to visit the scenes consecrated by the life and labours of a martyred priest, a son of the Poor Man of Assisi, known as the Venerable John Wall ; in religion Father Joachim of St. Anne of the Friars Minor.

The party consisted of a man of science, who acted as our guide ; a young Rhodes Scholar from Oxford, whose home was in distant Natal ; and the present chronicler. It was our aim to visit a group of houses which had sheltered the martyred priest during his apostolic labours, and to glean what traditions we could of his life and sufferings in the district which had been his home.

We started from the ancient town of Bromsgrove, after having paid a visit to the fine old parish church, magnificently situated on a hill-top overlooking the town at its feet. The fabric has indeed greatly suffered both from the iconoclasm of Cromwell and his soldiers, and also from the well-meant but disastrous zeal of the modern architect who restored it. It still, however, contains many features of interest for Catholics, notably the fine fifteenth-century tombs of the Talbots of Grafton, lords of this country—a grand old Catholic stock that came to so sad an end, a generation back, in the person of the last Catholic Earl of Shrewsbury. It was in fact owing to a half-obliterated inscription on one of these tombs that the present Protestant holders succeeded in making good their claim to the Shrewsbury title and to the broad lands of the Talbots. Grafton Manor itself is hard by, and its beautiful old chapel, Catholic within living memory, but now desecrated, tells its own sad tale.

But we were not bound for Grafton on this occasion, but for Harvington. Six miles along the Kidderminster Road brought us to Chaddesley Corbet, a typical old English village, full of the most delightful black-and-white houses, with one splendid old Elizabethan inn, with quaint porches approached by flights of steps at either end, and in the midst a fine old signboard bearing the Talbot arms. But the glory of Chaddesley Corbet is the church, a structure of intense

253

interest, with a nave of Transitional Norman, and a chancel of the richest and most exquisite Decorated work, far surpassing in beauty what is usually found even in our favoured land of fine parish churches.

Reserving, however, the church and its monuments for detailed inspection on our return, we hastened on our way to Harvington Hall, about a mile farther on. As we entered the lane leading to it, the leader of our little company, who had known every inch of this country from his boyhood, broke out with the exclamation : " I always think, when I come along this road, of the words, ' Take off thy shoes from off thy feet, for the place where thou standest is holy ground.' " It was the more striking an utterance as the speaker, alone of the pilgrims, had not the happiness to be a Catholic.

In a few minutes more we were standing, in silence, upon a green common, facing the moated mansion we had come to seek. How majestic it was even in its decay ! It rose before us, its old brick-work wreathed and crowned with ivy, the wide, encircling moat green with sweet sedge and water-lilies, the desolateness of the whole striking a note of sadness as it spoke of an heroic time now passing away. As we stood there gazing, almost awestruck, a loud whirr of wings above our heads startled us, as two great swans flapped slowly past us, and splashed into the moat beyond. No other sound of life there was, though the Hall does not stand altogether isolated. On our right as we faced it, across the green, was the Hall farm, where kindly Catholics welcomed us as pilgrims to the shrine they loved, while on our left was the cheering sign that the Faith planted here by the martyred son of St. Francis had not died out, for here in this lonely spot was a pretty Catholic church, with its churchyard around it, and hard by, the presbytery, embowered in a walled garden teeming with fruit trees.

In the midst of the churchyard stands a large crucifix. To this we first directed our steps and, on its base, we read the following inscription :

" DEUS MEUS ET OMNIA.
IN MEMORY OF
FATHER JOHN WALL, O.S.F.,
IN RELIGION FATHER JOACHIM OF ST. ANNE,
WHO, OBEYING GOD RATHER THAN MAN,
FOR TWELVE YEARS MINISTERED THE SACRAMENTS TO THE
FAITHFUL
IN THIS AND OTHER PARTS OF WORCESTERSHIRE
IN DAILY PERIL OF DEATH."

On the back of the cross was the following :

THE BANQUETING-ROOM AND STAIRCASE
HARVINGTON HALL
*The* x *high up in the centre marks the position of the hiding-place under the stairs. Photo by Thomas Lewis*

*To face page 254*

# A FRANCISCAN APOSTLE

" HE WAS BORN 1620,
ORDAINED PRIEST 1646,
WAS TAKEN AT RUSHOCK COURT, DECEMBER, 1678,
AND PUT TO DEATH FOR THE FAITH
AT WORCESTER,
ON THE OCTAVE OF THE ASSUMPTION, 1679."

Here, then, the note was struck, for this visit of ours was no vulgar excursion, but a pilgrimage.

This touching monument was erected in 1879, when the bicentenary of the martyrdom was celebrated at Harvington with great solemnity. Its erection was chiefly owing to the zeal of a member of the martyr's order, and the example set by this good Franciscan in thus commemorating the labours and passion of the martyr in the chosen place of his abode, is one that it would be well to follow in the case of other martyrs.

Father Wall has indeed never been forgotten amid these beautiful pastoral scenes of fruitful Worcestershire, any more than Father Postgate has been on his own wild Yorkshire moors. But though enshrined in the hearts of the people, it is surely fitting that our martyrs should also have some visible, tangible memorial amid the scenes of their heroic labours for God.

We entered the little church to spend a few minutes in prayer before the Tabernacle, where the King of Martyrs held His court.

It was time to turn to the old Hall. Our photographs will describe it better than any words can do.

Three centuries ago it was one of the finest and most substantial of the many moated mansions of the Worcestershire gentry. It is majestic even now. Though the greater part of the present building would appear to be Elizabethan in date, the middle portion of the principal front between the eastern " tower " and the western noble pile must undoubtedly have been standing in all its picturesque beauty more than four hundred years ago.

We pass over the stone bridge which has replaced the ancient drawbridge that once spanned the moat, as our guide points out to us the sweet sedge (*Acorus calamus*), a rare plant in Worcestershire, and still growing luxuriantly in its waters. It was formerly used for strewing the floors of hall and chapel, yes, and for making a pallet for the hunted priest in the secret hiding-places of the old Hall.

The old oaken doors of the gateway still hang on their hinges, and still bear traces of the stormy days they have witnessed. We were shown a hole made in them by a bullet aimed at the heroic mistress of the house, the martyr's hostess, Mary, Lady Yate, when a howling mob of Protestant fanatics came over from Kidderminster to search the Hall for priests. What an eloquent story that hole seems to tell!

On entering within the oaken doors you pass, under the gateway, a deep square tunnel, leading to the inner court. On the left, as you enter under the gateway, is a large beam lying crosswise as a support to the upright woodwork of which each side of the gateway is formed. That oak beam must be noted, for it has a hole pierced through it obliquely (but which is now plastered over) large enough to admit a man's hand, and this hole communicates with a secret hiding-place within. Through this orifice letters or food could be passed to the priest concealed in the little chamber, access to which is gained, as we shall see, from within the mansion.

On entering the courtyard we have the main body of the Hall on our left. It is a very noble pile, built of old brickwork, with square-headed mullioned windows and facings of cut stone. The main part of this front is recessed within a huge arch, which gives a very striking character to the whole design. There are doors in the angles of this arch, one of which communicates with the grand staircase.

Though in a very tottering and dilapidated condition, the old Hall, with its massive walls and many passages and turnings, still presents an admirable specimen of the ancient Catholic mansion of the penal days. A huge mass of ivy covers the greater part of this front and roof, and threatens the whole Hall with speedy destruction. Though the front facing the moat is still inhabited, this principal wing is in a sad state of decay, with roof half gone and windows broken, so that its final destruction can only be a question of a few years. It is very melancholy to think that so precious a relic of the days of persecution should thus be doomed to inevitable ruin.

On entering the door at the farther angle of the recessed front, we come at once on the grand staircase. This is indeed a noble feature of the house. It is all of solid oak, with massive turned balusters and uprights of sixteenth-century date. It goes up two stories of the house. An American gentleman, we were told, had wanted some months ago to carry it off bodily, and erect it in a fine new mansion he was building. But, fortunately, he gave up the project. This is the more satisfactory, as it is by this very staircase that entrance is gained to one of the three priests' hiding-holes for which Harvington Hall is famous.* At the top,

* Since our last visit to Harvington, we have heard that Sir William Throckmorton has actually removed this grand old staircase and set it up at Coughton. This deplorable act of vandalism will naturally hasten on the complete ruin of Harvington Hall, and it is to be feared that before long this historic house, with all its Catholic associations, will have disappeared. The staircase has been completely remodelled and now forms a double approach to the tribune of the ancient chapel at Coughton Court, which is now converted into a ballroom.

ENTRANCE TO THE HIDING-HOLE IN
THE STAIRCASE, HARVINGTON HALL
*Photo by Thomas Lewis*

*To face page 256*

on the landing, is a passage approached by two or three steps. One of these, a three-cornered stair, moves down on secret hinges and discloses, when removed, a small hole about sixteen inches square, which is, in fact, the entrance to the principal hiding-hole. Within is a chamber 5 ft. 9 in. long, by 5 ft. wide, its height being 6 ft. On its floor, until quite recently, was the self-same thick sedge mat-bed, on which had lain the venerable Franciscan martyr (and, no doubt, many another martyr and confessor of the Faith) when a sudden visit by magistrate or pursuivants forced him to fly for refuge and concealment. This has mostly now disappeared, carried off by pious visitors as relics. Air is admitted by a singular contrivance in the roof.

The reader can imagine with what interest our Rhodes Scholar gazed on this relic of the days when his Catholic forefathers had to suffer so much for the Faith in the old country. He would not be content without slipping through the narrow entrance into the close, confined chamber, which had once held the martyr priest, perhaps for days at a time. It was, in fact, a spot upon which few could gaze without emotion. We pictured the martyr lying silent and patient in his confinement. He had secured himself against intruders by closing and bolting a strong little oak door across the narrow entrance. The pursuivants must often have passed within a few inches of their victim without being able to detect his hiding-place. In the banqueting hall close by, a door admits to a small cupboard or pantry, the low ceiling of which conceals the priest's retreat. From this cupboard a small chink communicates with the hiding-place, through which, at a moment when the attention of the enemy was called elsewhere, a word could be whispered, or some small portion of food passed through for the captive's refreshment. The existence of this hiding-place has been most carefully concealed, and though now the entrance to it is visible, at the time when it was in use it would have needed a very practised eye to detect it. It is probable, too, that the captive could hear, through tiny holes pierced in the brick-work and concealed beneath the decorated plaster of the frieze, what was passing in the banqueting hall below him.

Let us now descend to the first story, and enter the banqueting hall. It is a room of stately proportions, once panelled in oak and hung with costly tapestry. The tapestry has been carried off to Coughton, the seat of Sir William Throckmorton, the owner of Harvington, and the panelling has, alas! also disappeared. We were told that it now adorned the drawing-room of an Anglican clergyman in Oxford. On entering, we have at our left the door of the little pantry of which we have spoken, which is, in fact, immediately under the hiding-hole already described. Next to this door is a fine mullioned window of great size.

# FORGOTTEN SHRINES

From the banqueting hall opens another room of great interest. It is known as Lady Yate's bedroom, although in some accounts it is styled the reception-room. It is still panelled in oak, painted green, and has a coved ceiling. This room runs along the front of the house, facing the moat. It has recently been put in repair, and is now inhabited by an old lady, who most kindly permitted us to examine it minutely. On either side of the fireplace is a door. The one on the right, that is on the side facing the moat, leads to a china-closet. The left-hand door opens on a long corridor which runs across the gateway, and connects this part of the Hall with the tower on the other side. (These doors were, it would seem, originally sliding panels.) In this corridor is the second hiding-place. Thus, if at the time the pursuivants arrived the priest was with the family in the banqueting hall, he had two means of escape. He could fly to the staircase on the left, or to the right through this room to the corridor beyond, which communicates with the tower. But the hunted priest had no need to hasten along this corridor, for, just inside the sliding panel, he could stoop down and raise up three thick boards from the flooring, which form a trap-door to the hiding-place. The original ladder, with its broad oaken staves, still remains fixed against the wall. The priest could quietly descend the eight strong steps, and, before reaching the bottom, close and bolt the trap-door over his head. Even if the pursuivants discovered the sliding panel, they would be baffled here, for the boards are thick and give no hollow sound, however hard you kick them. The only way of reaching the priest would be by tearing up this floor, and there is nothing whatever to show that the three planks which form the trap-door are any different from the rest of the flooring. When one is in this hiding-place, a chink is visible near the outer corner of the chimney-stack, which goes up several feet high to the floor above ; and it was this hole that communicated with the oak beam under the gateway, to which allusion has already been made. In this second hiding-place the poor priest could only manage to stand upright. It has no floor but the loose, dry earth. This hole is 8 ft. deep and 4 ft. by 2 ft. wide. As one who for many years was priest at Harvington has written : "When you stand in it, making your devout meditation on the sufferings and joys of the martyrs, you feel as if you were encased in a venerable, saintly relic."

But we must leave this spot, and return through the banqueting hall to the staircase landing. Here a door on our left leads to a passage which communicates with more rooms. We pass through this door, and take the first door to our right, down the passage. Five steps lead us up into a narrow room panelled in oak. It is about 12 ft. long by 8 ft. broad. This is called Dodd's Library, because it is the room where the

STAIRCASE SHOWING POSITION OF HIDING-HOLE
*Photo by Sir Benjamin Stone*

LADY YATE'S BEDROOM
*On the left, through the doorway, is seen the open trap-door leading to the hiding-place by the gateway.   Photo by Thomas Lewis*     *To face page 258*

famous church historian and controversialist, Hugh Tootel (known as Charles Dodd), kept his books. The old bookcases still remain, though in a sadly dilapidated condition, but the books (each bearing the inscription " *Bibl. Harvin. Cler. Sæc.*")—and a very valuable and fascinating set of rare old books they are—have been removed for safe-keeping to St. Mary's College, Oscott. This was done in the time of Bishop Milner.

At the end of the room opposite the window is a large cupboard in the panelled wall. It is about 5 ft. from the floor, and it needs some agility to pull oneself up into it. This, how-ever we did, and found that we were easily able to stand upright in it. The cupboard, in fact, is about 7 ft. high by 4 ft. broad. On the left side, as you face the window, is a huge oaken beam embedded in the brickwork of the wall, apparently one of the main beams of the house. But all things are not what they seem, especially at Harvington. Our guide proceed . to show us that this huge beam is hung on a pivot, and when the lower end is pressed it yields to the pressure, swings back into the wall, and discovers a hole through which a man can creep. The pivot is an iron rod which passes right through the middle of the beam and sticks out about two inches on either side into holes made in the brickwork. Once you have crept through you find yourself in a large hiding-hole about 8 ft. long, 2 ft. broad, and 6 ft. high. Inside the movable

Hiding place in Harvington Hall

beam, at the lower end, is a strong iron staple, through which, once within the hole, you can pass a bolt, and so secure yourself from intrusion. It would need a very skilful pursuivant to discover this hiding-place. Indeed, it was so skilfully made that the Catholics of Harvington had no idea of its existence till quite recently, when during some alterations it was accidentally discovered by a priest who was staying there. It had probably remained forgotten and unknown for some two centuries.

At present there is another means of access to this hiding-hole. If you leave the library and go along the passage, you soon come to a winding staircase, which is known as the chapel stair. Mount this and you come to a small closet, opening from a landing. Inside this closet a hole communicates with the hiding-place. But it is doubtful whether there was any original access to it from this side, though it is probable

259

that there was a chink of communication through which, as in the other two hiding-places, notes or food could be passed. Possibly it would be only liquid food, such as broth or milk, which the imprisoned priest could take through a straw.

It is very interesting to notice the ecclesiastical designs roughly stencilled in black and red on the open rafters of this winding staircase. These were, no doubt, intended as a guide to the faithful to the place where Mass was celebrated, and they would pass unnoticed by those not initiated.

At the top of the staircase is a large room known as "Lady Yate's Nursery." It has windows in every direction, so that those on watch here could see if any one were approaching the house from any side. For this is indeed the ante-room to the secret chapel. Three steps lead up from it into the little sanctuary where the martyr was wont to offer up the Adorable Sacrifice. The door is latticed, and beside it is an opening of lattice-work, so that the watchers kneeling in "Lady Yate's Nursery" could yet assist at the holy mysteries within.

The walls of the chapel were, at some early date, carefully decorated in good Gothic style, with foliage, vine stems, pomegranates, pots of lilies, and scroll-work in red. There are three windows in the chapel, but those by the altar have been blocked up. We were touched to see two swallows' nests built in the angle of the wall over the place where once the altar stood, recalling to the mind the psalmist's words: "The swallow hath found her a nest where she may lay her young, even Thine altar, O Lord of Hosts."

We had to tread with great caution on the floors, for the boards were very rotten, and the whole place seemed fast going to ruin. Looking out of the windows of the "Nursery" towards the front of the house, we found the roofs below covered with a luxuriant drapery of polypody fern, which made a beautiful harmony of colour with the old red tiles.

A few steps up to the narrow doorway leads us on to the roof, from which we get access to various lumber-rooms and closets, fitted in among its ponderous and complicated timbers. These rooms communicate with each other in most bewildering confusion, and seem admirably adapted for the purposes of concealment or escape.

I have come across an old account of Harvington Hall, printed a good many years back, from which I have gleaned the information that follows:

"The priests' rooms were at the top of the house, at the farther end of a dimly lighted passage. Near by is a large room which has always gone by the name of 'the chapel,' in which still hang tatters of the tapestry. This is supposed to be the room used as a chapel in the

260

**"LADY YATE'S NURSERY"**

*The steps in the corner lead to the secret chapel.   Photo by Sir Benjamin Stone*

THE LABYRINTH OF PASSAGES AROUND THE
SECRET CHAPEL
*Photo by Sir Benjamin Stone*

*To face page* 260

darkest days, when the other room was not considered secure. Guard could be safely kept by persons standing in the long passage, for it was thought well to have more than one room set apart for Holy Mass, so as to baffle the pursuivants more effectually. Doubtless Father Wall often said Mass in either room.

"A third chapel within the precincts of the moat was built in 1743, and is also very interesting, though it has, of course, no connection with the martyrs. Outside, it appears like two cottages. Within, a handsome oak staircase leads to the 'upper room,' where the divine mysteries were celebrated for the Catholics of Harvington, Kidderminster, and the neighbourhood.

"At the farther end of this room is still standing the quaint old altar step, a very shallow one of oak, overpassing the rider, and worked round at each corner. The sacristy was behind the altar and is approached by a small door. But the chief interest of this chapel, to us, lies in the fact that it was the depository for many years of some priceless relics of the days of persecution.

"These consisted of sundry small chalices that would fit inside each other, a long candle, sacerdotal vestments, books, including the old register, and a curious box strongly clamped with brass. These most precious relics of our martyrs were placed under the old altar in this chapel. They were in course of time forgotten, and priests of later days were not aware that the altar could be opened. However, the late Mrs. Anne Parkes, who in the early part of the nineteenth century was entrusted by the priest with the care of the altar, one day, when dusting behind it, observed through a chink in the panelling some glittering objects inside the altar. She specially noticed the chalices, the gold lace of the vestments, and the large book. Unfortunately, Father Marsden, the priest in charge, was just leaving home, and when he returned very weary on Friday night, he decided to inspect the treasures next day. But, alas! that very night a fire broke out in the room beneath, and the chapel and altar were soon in flames. Before it could be extinguished the whole of these hidden treasures of bygone days were in ashes. In the confusion, some one threw the smouldering heap into the moat, and when this was emptied some years later, tiny bits of gold lace and a mass of molten metal were found there.

"Who knows what treasures perished in that fatal fire of 1823 ? Very likely the clamped box held relics of the martyrs. In any case, the books, vestments, and chalices were of themselves most precious relics, whose loss we can never sufficiently deplore."

But it is time that the reader learned something of the life of the glorious martyr for whose dear sake Harvington Hall has become a shrine of pilgrimage, yes, and of the noble lady, his hostess, who risked her life to give him shelter, and thus secure the sacraments of God's Church for herself and the little flock of the faithful round about.

Mary, Lady Yate, was the elder of the two daughters and co-heiresses of Humphrey Packington, Lord of Chaddesley Corbet, who died in 1631. She married Sir John Yate of Buckland, County Berks, Bart. Her portrait, of which we are happily able to give a reproduction, now hangs at Coughton Court, the seat of her descendants, the present owner of Harvington. Lady Yate's father was a Protestant, but her mother belonged to a good old Catholic family which had suffered much for the faith : she was Abigail, daughter of Henry Sacheverell of Morley, County Derby. Lady Yate seems to have been born and brought up at Harvington, until her marriage. Her husband belonged to another family illustrious for their fidelity to the old religion. It will be remembered that Blessed Edmund Campion was taken in 1581 at the house of a Mrs. Yate at Lyford, and Lyford is close to Buckland. Thus Lady Yate was closely connected with two families of tried fidelity, and she was herself not unworthy of them. By her father's death the manor of Chaddesley Corbet fell to her share, but her mother had a life interest in it, and so the latter lady resided at Harvington Hall till her holy death in 1657. Next year Sir John Yate also died, and his widow retired to Harvington, which she henceforth made her home. She gave up her life to good works, and especially to the maintenance and propagation of the Catholic religion in the district in which she lived. It must have been soon after her return to Harvington that she took the holy Franciscan, Father Joachim of St. Anne (otherwise John Wall), under her roof, for he came on the English mission in 1656, two years previously, and we know that the greater part of his missionary career was spent at Harvington.

John Wall was a Lancashire man, and was born in 1620, probably at Chingle or Singleton Hall, in Goosnargh parish, being the fourth son of Anthony Wall, the first of the name to hold Chingle. His younger brother William became a Benedictine monk at Lambspring Abbey, and was also tried and condemned to death, for his priesthood, during the Oates plot frenzy. He was, however, subsequently reprieved. John had a happier lot : he was to gain the martyr's crown and palm.

His early life is soon told. Educated first at the English College of Douay, and then at Rome, he was ordained priest in the Eternal City in 1645, his name being entered in the College lists as John Marsh. At the age of thirty-two he took the Franciscan habit at the Convent of St. Bonaventure at Douay, that convent which has been the nursery of so many glorious martyrs ; and there he made his holy profession on January 1, 1652.

HARVINGTON HALL

The bridge across the moat leads to the gateway. In the door a bullet-hole can still be seen. From a photograph by Thomas Lewis, Birmingham

He took the name of Joachim of St. Anne, on account of his tender devotion to our Blessed Lady, and perhaps, as Miss Stone suggests, in memory of a pilgrimage which he had made on leaving Rome, to our Lady's house at Loreto, where he seems to have received the grace of his religious vocation. After serving as Vicar and Master of Novices in his convent, he was sent on the English mission in 1656. Here he laboured for over twenty years chiefly, if not entirely, in North Worcestershire, under the assumed names of Francis Johnson or Webb.

Our martyr did not come to England alone : he was one of a little band of friars, of whom he himself and the energetic Father Leo Randolph were the leaders. They first made their way to the old Manor House of Wood-Bevington, in the parish of Salford Priors in Warwickshire. This was the home of Father Leo, and was at that time in possession of his father, Ferrers Randolph, Esquire.

The Manor House of Wood-Bevington, which is still standing, was even then an old building. It seems to have been erected about 1490, by the Austin Canons of Kenilworth Priory, for their first lessee, William Grey. It is in the half-timbered style, though it has now, unfortunately, been modernised and covered with rough-cast.

The manor passed to the Ferrers of Baddesley Clinton by the marriage of Elizabeth, granddaughter of William Grey, to Edward Ferrers, second son to Sir Edward Ferrers of Baddesley. He died September 16, 1578, leaving only daughters, of whom the eldest, Elizabeth, married Thomas Randolph of Codrington, in Buckinghamshire, and became Lady of the Manor of Wood-Bevington. Their eldest son, Ferrers Randolph, was in possession of the manor when Dugdale wrote his history of Warwickshire in 1656. He was not, however, the owner, for in 1636 he had sold the manor to St. John's College, Oxford. The same year the College granted him a lease of it for three hundred years, at the annual rent of £200.

It was thus to his father's house that Father Leo led the little band of Franciscan missionaries, and here they received a warm welcome and a safe shelter, while they discussed their future plans. It was decided that Father Joachim Wall was to have charge of Worcestershire, that his companions were to go north to labour in Yorkshire, while Father Leo took Warwickshire and Staffordshire as the sphere of his apostolate.

Before we leave this holy and zealous friar, we may add that a very interesting relic of him still remains in the old register belonging to St. Peter's Church, Birmingham, which records the results of his missionary labours, and is now preserved at St. Mary's College, Oscott.

The first entry in this register, under the heading of those " admitted into the Confraternity of the Cord of St. Francis," is " Elizabeth Randolph of Bevington, County of Warwick, 15th of September 1657." This was probably the friar's own mother. In October 1657, we find him registering the marriage of Thomas Wheatley and Margaret Walden of Tanworth, as celebrated "in Bevington." In the same autumn he is baptizing a child at Solihull, and giving the last rites of the Church to three dying persons at Edgbaston. It was Father Leo Randolph who built the first public church in Birmingham, in Mass-house Lane, in 1688 ; it was dedicated to his own patroness, St. Mary Magdalene, though its present successor bears the title of St. Peter. In the list of benefactors who contributed to the erection of this church, King James II. has the first place, with a gift of timber to the value of £180. The Dowager Queen Catherine gave £10 15s.

It was Father Leo Randolph who obtained the head of his martyred *confrère* after the cruel execution at Worcester, and sent it over to Douay. His apostolic labours recorded in the precious register give us an idea of what Father Wall's must have been, which is the more valuable, since the records of our martyr's apostolate have so unhappily perished. We read that Father Leo reconciled his kinsman, Edward Ferrers of Baddesley Clinton, on December 10, 1660, and that he buried him at Baddesley on January 7, 1664. At Bevington, Salford Priors, Alcester, Tamworth, Baddesley, Edgbaston, Birmingham, and many other places we find the Franciscan drawing souls to God's Church. With his life in his hands, he never wearied in doing God's work ; until in 1695, at the close of his long ministry, he could thank God that he had been instrumental in converting no fewer than six hundred and eighty-nine souls to the Faith of their fathers.

One of these converts has a special interest for us. One day when Father Wall was engaged on his perilous ministry, not very long, indeed, before his capture, he happened to be at King's Norton, near Birmingham. Here he had a very narrow escape of being arrested, and was only saved by a Protestant gentleman who took pity on him, and, at his own peril, concealed him in his house. The good Franciscan could not find words to express his gratitude, but before leaving his benefactor he said to him : " If it please God that I have to die for the Faith, I will offer my life's blood for your soul." The gentleman's name was Thomas Millward. The martyr's holocaust was accepted by God, and five years after the tragedy at Worcester we find recorded in Father Randolph's register, among those reconciled to the Faith : " A.D. 1684. *Thomas Millward of King's Norton, County of Worcester, 19th January.*" " Amen, Amen, I say to you, he that receiveth whomsoever I send, receiveth Me, and he that receiveth Me, receiveth Him that sent Me."

The room can still be identified in the old Manor House of Wood-

DAME MARY YATE
*From her portrait at Coughton Court*

*To face page 264*

Bevington where these Franciscan apostles first said Holy Mass and administered the Sacraments. It was called the "great parlour." No other room would be so suitable for the purpose, as it was in a retired situation, and had a secluded doorway into the garden. It is a large room, wainscoted with fine old Tudor panelling, which has been painted, probably in the early part of the eighteenth century. The doorway into the garden has been long stopped up, and the space between the outer and inner doors is now a small closet, where you can still see the remains of the old panelling which lined the little passage through the wall.

In the old-fashioned garden, with its ancient walnut-trees (planted, according to tradition, by five sisters), we may still imagine we see our holy martyr pacing up and down, saying his office, and pleading before God for the souls of his countrymen.

But it is at Harvington, above all, that we find him. Almost do we catch sight of him, in his russet robe and bare feet, passing swiftly along the dim, mysterious passages that lead to the hidden chapel in the roof. Still is his memory green among the descendants of his little flock, who cherish with a holy pride their traditions of "Blessed Father Johnson," their martyred pastor.

For it is as Johnson that he was known at Harvington, and under this name his beloved memory was handed down to generation after generation of faithful Catholics, as ever on his anniversary the priest reminded the little flock of the glorious martyrdom of him who had once been their shepherd. Still at East Bergholt Abbey, in Essex, is reverently preserved a large piece of the rope with which the "Blessed Mr. Johnson" was hanged at Worcester, August 22, 1679, in the same month that saw good old Father Postgate die for the same holy cause at the York Tyburn. It is for his sake that Harvington is and ever will be so dear to every Catholic heart.

On our way back from Harvington we stayed at Chaddesley Corbet to refresh ourselves in the picturesque old inn, and to visit the very beautiful church hard by. The church contains a very curious Saxon, or early Norman, font, carved with strange, interlaced dragons. The chancel is in the Middle Pointed style, and as fair a specimen as it would be possible to find of that most beautiful period of English Gothic. The exquisite Decorated tracery of the windows, the enriched buttresses, the sedilia and piscina, and other features breathe a refinement of artistic feeling such as is rarely surpassed even in our noblest ecclesiastical buildings.

But what attracted us most in the church was the tomb of Lady Yate, the brave hostess of our martyr, and those of her family around it. They are in the North Chapel, which is the family chantry and was, of old, dedicated to St. Nicholas.

# FORGOTTEN SHRINES

We copied the epitaph of the Lady of Harvington Hall :

" Here lies the Eldest Daughter and Coheire of Humphrey Pack-ington, Esqre., Lord of ye Manor of Chadesley Corbet, and the incomparable Widow of Sir John Yate, of Buckland, Knight and Baronett, the Lady Mary Yate, of pious memory, whose loss is too great to be forgotten.

" She lived for the common good, and died for her own.

" She lived too well to fear death, and could not have died if the prayers of the poor had prevailed. Her prudence in ye management of a bad world was alwaies aiming at a better.

" Her justice was more than exact in paying all she owed, even before it was due.

" Her fortitude was built upon her faith, a rock which no storm could move.

" Her temperance was grounded on her Hope and Charity, wch raised her heart so much above ye world that she used it without enjoying it.

" She bestowed it liberally upon those who needed it, lived in it as unconcernedly as if she had never loved it, and left it as easily as if she had allwaise despised it.

" Ripe for Heaven, and as full of vertue as of daies, she died in ye 86th year of her age, the 12th day of June in the year of our Lord 1696, after having been lady of this manor 65 years.

" REQUIESCAT IN PACE

" This is a dutyful tribute erected by her daughter, Apolonia Yate."

" *Her fortitude was built upon her faith, a rock which no storm could move.*"

How touching those words sounded when one thought of the hiding-places and the secret chapels of the old Hall we had just left, and realised that they meant a life of constant peril, for it was death to harbour a priest : a life exposed to continual terrors, sudden invasions and attacks : a life crushed beneath the burden of cruel fines and iniquitous exactions ! Daily to see the estate grow more impoverished, daily to endure some fresh injury, daily to live in a home that had no sanctity, no privacy ; to be the object of hatred and suspicion ; to see the priest you loved and venerated torn away from you to a cruel death, and to be able to do nothing to protect or save him—this was all summed up in these few words of her epitaph, every line of which breathes a daughter's love. This daughter, Apollonia, it may be noted, remained unmarried, and was distinguished for her filial piety and virtuous life. The elder daughter, Abigail, married Charles, Viscount Fairfax, of Gilling Castle, in Yorkshire.

EXTERIOR OF THE CHANCEL, CHADDESLEY CORBET CHURCH
*Photo by the author*

*To face page 266*

# A FRANCISCAN APOSTLE

Lady Yate has left many marks of her charity and benevolence. She built and endowed in perpetuity at Harvington three almshouses for poor widows. She also founded and endowed a permanent charity for the purpose of putting out poor children into respectable apprenticeships. At the accession of James II., when Catholics began to breathe again after the cruel persecution, she founded and endowed a charity by which a priest might be supported at Harvington, and another at Buckland ; and another charity she similarly originated and secured in favour of Douay College. These last benefactions were unhappily engulfed in the new wave of confiscation which accompanied the landing and usurpation of Dutch William. A well-known and learned priest, the Rev. Silvester Jenks, owed his education to her bounty. He was ordained priest in 1684, and on account of his great abilities was called by King James II. to London. After the revolution he escaped to Flanders, but returned and died in London in 1715. He was appointed to succeed Bishop James Smith, Vicar Apostolic of the Northern District, but died before his consecration. He was the author of a number of learned and devout works.

During the reign of James II. some of the Catholics had ventured to build public chapels, but no sooner had the king taken flight than mobs were incited in many parts of the kingdom to destroy these chapels on a fixed day, which was afterwards known as "Running Thursday." Among others, a mob from Alcester demolished Sir Robert Throckmorton's chapel at Coughton ; the Franciscan chapel in Birmingham was burnt, and a mob from Kidderminster came to Harvington, and finding the bridge over the moat withdrawn, shot through the large oaken doors at Lady Yate. As we mentioned, the bullet-hole is still visible.

> "When nobles forced the king to run
> And took away his crown ;
> Then running mobs enjoyed the fun
> Of knocking Popish chapels down."

At the decease of good Dame Mary Yate, in 1696, her estates passed to her granddaughter, Mary, for both her son, Sir Charles, and her grandson, Sir John Yate, had died before her. Mary Yate, who was the sister and sole heir of Sir John, married Sir Robert Throckmorton of Coughton, Bart. Thus Harvington and Buckland passed into the hands of the Throckmorton family, in whose possession Harvington still remains, though Buckland was alienated but a year ago. And thus it is that up to this day the home of the martyred Franciscan has ever been in the hands of Catholic owners, and has ever continued to shelter a priest to minister to the faithful of the district.

# FORGOTTEN SHRINES

It was in 1743 that the new chapel, formed out of the garrets of two adjoining cottages standing within the safe enclosure of the moat, was opened, with infinite precautions. Special care was taken to secure facilities for the escape of the officiating priest to one of the hiding-holes within the mansion, in case of the approach of danger.

This plain and lowly room continued to be used as the chapel until in 1825 the new church was publicly opened, this time outside the moat.

Chaddesley Corbet and Harvington have many another tale to tell, but we pilgrims could not linger to hear it. We had yet to visit other spots consecrated by the memory of the martyr. A couple of miles brought us to Rushock, where he had been captured in the house of his friend, Mr. Finch, in December 1678.

There are few lovelier spots in Worcestershire than this orchard-covered hill, on which the Manor House and little church of Rushock stand. The orchards at the time of our visit seemed literally afire with the bright scarlet apples with which the trees were loaded, and the autumn tints of the leaves glowed in the October sunshine, as we mounted the picturesquely winding lane, set deep in hedgerows, which leads to Rushock Court. Of the old house in which the martyr was taken, little or nothing remains. There is one old wall in the garden which probably formed part of it, and that is all. But the view of the smiling valley around remains the same as when he gazed on it for the last time as he was hurried off in triumph by his captors. A fair spot, indeed,—few fairer, perhaps, to be found in all England! From the hill we gazed southward towards Droitwich, and saw at our feet an old farm-house, which was to be the next stage of our pilgrimage. A mile or so, through winding lanes and grassy fields, would bring us there. But before leaving Rushock we must recall to mind these scenes of our martyr's life.

His capture here was really an accident, for the sheriff's officer with six or eight men came here in the middle of the night in order to arrest a gentleman for debt. Breaking down the doors, they entered a bedroom in which they found Father Wall in bed. They soon guessed who he was, and they carried him off in triumph. He was first taken before Sir John Packington at Westwood Park. This magistrate, though the brother of our martyr's noble hostess, committed him to Worcester gaol, where he lay imprisoned for five months.

While in prison he wrote a narrative of his sufferings, which still exists, and in which he bears unconscious testimony to the heavenly dispositions with which he endured them. He writes:

"Imprisonment in our times, especially when none can send to his friends, nor friends come to him, is the best means to teach us how to

RUSHOCK COURT AND THE WITCHES' POOL
*Photo by Sir Benjamin Stone*

put our confidence in God alone in all things, and then He will make His promise good, 'that all things shall be added to us' (Luke xii.), which chapter, if every one would read and make good use of, a prison would be better than a palace, and a confinement for religion and a good conscience more pleasant than all the liberties the world could afford. As for my own part, God give me His grace, and all faithful Christians their prayers! I am happy enough. We all ought to follow the narrow way, though there may be many difficulties in it. It is an easy thing to run the blind way of liberty, but God deliver us from all broad, sweet ways."

It was with such thoughts as these stirring in our hearts that we threaded our way among the orchards and over the pleasant pasture-land to Purshall Hall.

This fine old house is situated about a mile from the high road leading from Kidderminster to Bromsgrove, and is about four miles from the latter town. The exterior is not so attractive as that of Harvington Hall, and its comparatively modern appearance and large sash windows belie its real antiquity. Indeed, there is little to attract one in the front of the house, except the fine porch, near the apex of which is seen a large stone cross let into the brickwork. It seems to be merely a large farm-house shorn of much of its ancient grandeur, and gives no promise of the extraordinary treasure that lies concealed within.

For in very truth, Purshall Hall contains one of the most touching shrines that the Catholic pilgrim will find throughout the length and breadth of England. From the time of Richard II. down to the eighteenth century, it belonged to the family of Purshall, and from convert members of that family it passed in the later years of that century into the hands of a Catholic priest. And here was provided for the little flock a shrine of refuge, where they might worship their God in comparative safety, and meet together at dead of night to be strengthened with the Bread of Heaven. Though Purshall, Rushock, and Badgecourt hard by were, with other centres of Catholicity in North Worcestershire, nominally under the charge of the Fathers of the Society of Jesus, still it is evident that while our Franciscan martyr lived at Harvington, he must often have ministered to the Catholics in these places. As we have seen, it was at Rushock that he was captured. And at Purshall it was possibly he himself who erected the humble altar that we are now about to visit, though this cannot be considered certain. Until comparatively recent times, very few people knew any-thing of the existence of this hidden sanctuary. Indeed, it is due to our guide that it has become known at all to the outside world, and that its priceless value has been realised. And it is in his own words that I should wish to describe what but for him I might never have seen at all :

"If, with the kind permission of the tenant, we ascend the staircase, and still further continue our ascent up a rickety flight of stairs, we shall see an entrance to what appears to be a lumber-room or large attic immediately underneath the roof, with no window or aperture to admit the light, and which still enshrines a ruined altar, with the remains of its tattered altar-cloth crumbling to dust. The altar-rails and kneeling-bench are still almost perfect, preserved to us through the centuries by successive occupants of this lonely farm-house, and telling the story most eloquently of the midnight meetings of devout worshippers, who, by lonely lanes and field-paths, had assembled here to receive the consolations of their religion from the hands of the heroic Father Wall. We can picture it all, the kneeling worshippers in the upper room, lit with candle or rush light, and we can scarcely doubt that this was the scene of his labours, for we know that in the month of December 1678, he was arrested at Rushock Court, a farm-house about a mile distant, where he had gone to spend the night.

"Who knows the sighs, the tears, the supplications to Heaven, that this room has witnessed—that again in peace and safety these poor Catholics might publicly worship God, and that their priests be no more homeless outcasts, and that the privileges of a restoration to their former religious liberty might be granted to them !

"For more than two hundred years that upper room at Purshall Hall has been kept sacred by successive occupants; no desecrating hand has removed its mouldering altar, and to-day it speaks most eloquently of the time

"'When man pent up his brother men,
Like brutes within an iron den,'

and of the noble martyrs who

"'Proud of Persecution's rage,
Their belief with blood have sealed.'" *

If a non-Catholic could write thus (and all honour to him for these moving words !), it may well be imagined with what emotion we Catholic pilgrims knelt before this humble altar. To our Rhodes Scholar it was a revelation. It brought home to him, as nothing else could have done, what a price his English forefathers had had to pay to preserve the Faith which he had learnt at his mother's knee. And who could wonder if he

* John Humphreys, F.L.S, *Chaddesley Corbet*, a paper read before the Birmingham Archæological Society, December 9, 1903, p. 15.

270

PURSHALL HALL

*To face page* 270

knelt there, overcome by the memories of the place, feeling nearer to God, perhaps, in this dark garret than in the stateliest cathedral he had ever visited! Indeed, it seemed to us as if we knelt in the Cœnaculum itself, and it was very sweet to be there.

There is little, indeed, to describe, for the photograph gives an excellent impression of the place. Only, as it had to be taken by flash-light, it gives a quite erroneous idea of light. As a matter of fact, the place is pitch-dark, and when we visited it, it was only lighted by one flickering candle. The altar-stone has been removed, but the hole made to receive it in the *mensa* of the altar-table is still plain to see.

It seems that there could be no better place than this in which to open once again the Acts of the Martyrs, and read by the faint light of our taper the last scenes in the life of the Franciscan who by his apostolic toil and the generous sacrifice of his blood has hallowed for ever this peaceful spot.

It was on April 25, 1679, that Father Wall was brought to trial before Judge Atkins, at the Worcester Assizes. The usual charges were brought against him, that he, an English subject, had gone abroad, taken Orders in the Church of Rome, returned to England to promulgate the doctrines of the said Church, and had refused to take the oath of allegiance and supremacy, whereby he was guilty of high treason, under the Statute of 27 Elizabeth, ch. 2.

Besides this, there were other counts against him, alleging that he had said Mass and heard confessions, that he had reconciled converts to the Church, and finally, that he was a Jesuit.

Only one witness appeared voluntarily against him, and this man, named Rogers, was a native of Stonebridge, who, having been reprimanded by the martyr for his vicious life, took this opportunity of revenge. Dodd says " he became a vagabond, in testimony that heaven was not pleased with such kind of sacrifices."

Three other witnesses were compelled to appear. The condemnation that followed was a foregone conclusion. On hearing the sentence pronounced, the martyr bowed to the judge, and said aloud : " Thanks be to God ! God save the King ! And I beseech God to bless your lordship and all this honourable bench."

The judge was moved, and he replied courteously :

" You have spoken very well. I do not intend that you should die, at least, not for the present, till I hear the King's further pleasure." It does not appear, however, that he exerted himself to obtain a reprieve.

The martyr's own account runs as follows :

" I was not, I thank God for it, troubled with any disturbing thoughts, either against the judge for his sentence, or the jury that gave in such a

271

verdict, or against any of the witnesses; for I was then of the same mind, as by God's grace I ever shall be, esteeming them all as the best friends to me, in all they did or said, that ever I had in my life. And I was, I thank God, so present with myself, whilst the judge pronounced the sentence, that without any concern for anything in the world, I did actually at the same time offer myself and the world to God.

"After the judge was gone from the bench, several Protestant gentlemen and others who had heard my trial came to me, though strangers, and told me how sorry they were for me. To whom with thanks I replied, that I was troubled they should grieve for me or my condition, who was joyful for it myself; for I told them I had professed this faith and religion all my lifetime, which I was as sure to be true, as I was sure of the truth of God's word, on which it was grounded; and therefore in it I deposed my soul, and eternal life and happiness. And therefore, should I fear to lose my temporal life for this faith, whereon my eternal life depends, I should be worse than an infidel; and whosoever should prefer the life of their bodies before their faith, their religion or conscience, they were worse than heathens. For my own part, I told them, I was ready, by God's grace, to die to-morrow, as I had been to receive the sentence of death to-day, and as willing as if I had a grant of the greatest dukedom."

The martyr was sent back to prison, and after some time sent up to London, to be examined by Oates and Bedloe and their accomplices, to see if it were possible to fix upon him some of the odium raised by their pretended plot. Bedloe, he wrote, told him publicly that if he would but comply in the matter of religion, he would pawn his life for him, and that though condemned, he should not die. This was not the first offer of the kind. "But I told them I would not buy my own life at so dear a rate, as to wrong my conscience. . . . God's will be done. The greater the injury and injustice done against us by men to take away our lives, the greater our glory in eternal life before God. *This is the last persecution that will be in England: therefore I hope God will give all His holy grace to make the best use of it.*"

Four months elapsed, from the time of Father Wall's condemnation, before he was told to make ready for death. When it became known that his hour was drawing near, a brother Franciscan, Father William Levison, contrived to visit him in prison. He wrote a touching account of the interview to his brethren at Douay.

"Of late I was desired, and willingly went, to visit our friend, . . . prisoner at Worcester, whose execution drew near at hand. I came to him two days before it, and found him a cheerful sufferer of his present imprisonment, and ravished, as it were, with joy, with the future hopes

272

of dying for so good a cause. I found, contrary both to his and my expectation, the favour of being with him alone ; and the day before his execution I enjoyed that privilege for the space of four or five hours together ; during which time I heard his confession and communicated him, to his great joy and satisfaction. I ventured likewise, through his desire, to be present at his execution, and placed myself boldly next to the under-sheriff, near the gallows, where I had the opportunity of giving him the last absolution, just as he was turned off the ladder. During his imprisonment, he carried himself like a true servant and disciple of his crucified Master, thirsting after nothing more than the shedding of his blood for the love of his God ; which he performed with a courage and cheerfulness becoming a valiant soldier of Christ, to the great edifi-cation of all Catholics, and admiration of all Protestants, the rational and moderate part especially, who showed a great sense of sorrow for his death, decrying the cruelty of putting men to death for priesthood and religion. He is the first who ever suffered at Worcester [*sic*] since the Catholic religion entered into this nation, which he seemed with joy to tell me before his execution. He was quartered, and his head separated from his body, according to his sentence. His body was permitted to be buried, and was accompanied by the Catholics of the town to St. Oswald's churchyard, where he lies interred. His head I got privately and con-veyed it to Mr. Randolph, who will be careful to keep it till opportunity serves to transport it to Douay."

The day of the martyrdom was Friday, August 22, 1679, the Octave day of the Assumption of our Blessed Lady. It was a fitting day for so devout a client of Mary to enter his heavenly home.

The place of execution was on Red Hill, overlooking the city of Worcester. The exact spot was pointed out to me by the late Mr. Robert Berkeley, of Spetchley. It is marked by a pear-tree, standing in the garden of a modern house on the summit of the hill, close to the roadside.

A copy of his last speech in MS. is preserved in the library of St. Mary's College, Oscott, near Birmingham.* There is also printed : *A True Copy of the Speech of Mr. Francis Johnstons*, alias *Dormore*, alias *Webb*, alias *Wall*; *a Priest of the Church of Rome (who was convicted before*

---

\* It is headed :    MY LAST SPEACH
It Please God for my
RELIGION.

At his execution, he said : "I would have said more, but that I gave my speech to a friend to be printed." The "Animadversions" at the end of the printed copy referred to above are very bitter. "And thus this Popish Faction design to delude the world by pretending that they die only as Martyrs for their Religion," &c. &c.

# FORGOTTEN SHRINES

*Mr. Justice Atkins, at Worcester, last Lent-Assizes, upon an Indictment on the Statute 27 Eliz. cap. 2). Which he spake upon the Ladder immediately before his Execution, on Fryday last, August 22, 1679 : with Animadversions upon the same."*

It should be noted that though these two versions agree in substance, they differ widely in phraseology, and the advantage lies evidently with the manuscript copy, which is no doubt transcribed from the martyr's own autograph, for he composed the speech in prison shortly before his execution.

It will be sufficient here to quote his last words :

" I will offer my life in satisfaction for my sins, and for the Catholick cause : and I beg for those that be my enemies in this my death, and I desire to have them forgiven, because I go to that World of Happiness sooner than I should have gone. And humbly beg pardon from God and the world, and this I beg for the merits and mercy of Jesus Christ.

" I beseech God to bless his Majesty, and give him a long Life and happy reign in this World and in the World to come.

"I beseech God to bless all my Benefactors and all my Friends, and those that may have been any way under my charge " (and here his thoughts must have dwelt tenderly on his beloved flock at Harvington), "and I beseech God to bless all the Catholicks and this Nation.

" I beseech God to bless all that suffer under this Persecution and to turn our Captivity into Joy : that they that Sow in tears may reap in Joy."

\*       \*       \*       \*       \*

As we left the darkness of that hidden sanctuary, carrying in our hearts a memory that would never fade, we found the old hall flooded in the golden light of an October sunset. And with the glory of the dying day there seemed to fall upon our hearts some foretaste of that peace which passeth all understanding, that peace which God has promised unto those who love Him to the end.

> " The golden evening brightens in the west.
> Soon, soon to faithful warriors comes their rest :
> Sweet is the calm of Paradise the blest."

And is not the martyr's last prayer being fulfilled before our very eyes ? Truly, "they that sow in tears shall reap in joy."

\*       \*       \*       \*       \*

We had yet one more place to visit before our pilgrimage was done On our way through the fields to Purshall Hall, we had noted on our

MONUMENT IN MEMORY OF VENERABLE
JOHN WALL, O.F.M., IN THE CATHOLIC
CHURCHYARD, HARVINGTON. *Photo by the*
*author*                                    *To face page 274*

right an imposing Elizabethan house, not a quarter of a mile away. This was Badge Court, once the seat of the Wintour family, notorious for their connection with the Gunpowder Plot. It is not, however, in connection with this unhappy plot that our interest in Badge Court lies. In Father Wall's time it was the home of a devout and faithful lady, who had in her youth passed through the deep waters of sorrow, and now found her consolation in works of charity and devotion. Mistress Helen Wintour was daughter of Robert Wintour, of Huddington, who was executed in London for his share in the plot. Her mother was Gertrude, daughter of Sir John Talbot of Grafton. Doubtless in her hidden, solitary life she found her chief consolation in her visits to the chapel, and in ministering to the priests who came from time to time to seek refuge beneath her roof. Her days were largely spent in embroidering church vestments, and some most gorgeous and elaborate specimens of her skill have, happily, come down to us. It is with almost a shock of contrast that we realise that the splendid Wintour vestments, now preserved among the chief treasures of Stonyhurst College, were made for and were first used in such a poor and humble sanctuary as that we had just visited. But Helen Wintour knew that what makes the temple glorious is the presence of the King, and that the Holy Sacrifice of the Mass was not less worthy of honour when celebrated at dead of night in a garret, than when offered on the High Altar of St. Peter's Basilica by the Vicar of Christ himself. And so in most striking contrast to their surroundings, the holy priests who said Mass at Purshall or Badge Court were clad in vestments exceeding magnifical, stiff with gold embroidery, and covered with pearls.

The chasuble and cope of Pentecostal red are profusely adorned with cloven tongues of gold, while below we find the Wintour arms (a falcon alighting upon a tower), and the legend, *Orate pro me Helena de Wintour.*

The white vestments, embroidered with tulips and other flowers in richest colours, bear a representation of angels adoring the Lamb of God, and in the adornment of the two sets of vestments there are used no fewer than four hundred and seventy-one large pearls. Another chasuble is worked with pomegranates in silver and gold.

This devotion to the material beauty of divine worship is indeed no unfrequent phenomenon throughout the days of persecution. In spite of the daily peril of robbery and confiscation, devout Catholics were never tired of making rich offerings to the sanctuary ; and, indeed, it was fitting that the " golden priests " of that period of martyrdom should be vested in the richest sacrificial robes.

The waning light warned us that we must lose no time in visiting the interior of this old Catholic house.

The moat is mostly filled up, and the modern front of timber and lath and plaster which marks the venerable fabric does not prepare one for the interest of the interior. There is a wealth of carved oak panelling of the richest kind, both in the hall and the reception-rooms below, and in the best bedroom above. The hall is noticeable for a magnificent representation of the Wintour arms, emblazoned on the ceiling, with a proud array of quarterings, among which we recognise the bearings of the Talbots, the Staffords, the Huddingtons, and many others. The great shield is surmounted with the Wintour crest, a falcon surrounded by a coronet. A second escutcheon of the Wintour arms, splendidly carved in oak, is displayed over the dining-room mantelpiece. One of the most interesting features of the house is a set of encaustic tiles surrounding the fireplace of the best bedroom. These tiles are enamelled with the arms of the Wintours and their various alliances, among them being the hound of the Talbots, surrounded with the words, " Sir John Talbot."

This Sir John succeeded to the Talbot estates in 1529, and was, as we have seen, the maternal grandfather of Mistress Helen Wintour. We had already seen his tomb at Bromsgrove Church. The tiles may therefore suggest the probable date when Badge Court was built.

All these features were pointed out to us by our learned guide, who had made a special study of this part of North Worcestershire, and in particular of its Catholic associations. It is to him we owe very much of the information contained in these pages.

The Wintour vestments were left by Mistress Helen to the Jesuit Mission in Worcestershire (or to the " College of St. George," as it was called), with the stipulation that they should not be sent for safety beyond the seas, lest they should never return. In 1854 they were transferred from Grafton to Stonyhurst College, save for the chasuble embroidered with pomegranates, which is still in possession of the Jesuit Fathers at Worcester.

As we wended our way home in the twilight we talked of the wondrous change that has come upon England with the blossoming of the Second Spring. We marked how the first dawning of a brighter day synchronised so strangely with the agony of the Church of France during the Great Revolution. In 1791 a Bill passed the British Parliament tolerating the schools and religious worship of Catholics, and repealing certain of the most cruel statutes still in force against them. Almost immediately we find John Baynham of Purshall Hall, Richard Cornthwaite of Harvington Hall, and Andrew Robinson of Grafton Manor, together with other Worcestershire priests, subscribing certificates that they had set apart rooms in their respective houses for Catholic worship. In 1829 came Catholic Emancipation, and then only did our fathers begin to breathe freely. From 1558 they had endured the long agony of a cruel persecution, but now at last the night began to pass away, and joy came in the morning. In 1850 the restoration of the Catholic hierarchy was, as it were, the harbinger of the Second Spring. Then John Henry Newman arose amid the Fathers of the First Council of Westminster, to hail, in deathless accents, its coming, and as that august assembly listened to his words, tears fell fast from their eyes, sweet tears of thankful joy. " And they sung together hymns and praise to the Lord : because He is good, for His mercy endureth for ever towards Israel."

Since the above record of our pilgrimage to Purshall was written, facts have been brought to my notice by Mr. R. H. Murray, of Worcester, which throw great doubt on the theory that would connect our Franciscan martyr with the secret chapel at Purshall Hall.

Mr. Murray is an expert on old woodwork and furniture, and in particular on ancient Communion Tables. He has convinced himself (and after a second visit to Purshall, made in his company, he has convinced me) that the old altar and rails were originally a Lord's Table and Communion-rails put up in some Anglican church in the time of Archbishop Laud. As the annexed plan (which we owe to his kindness) clearly shows, the table itself has been somewhat clumsily altered to suit its new purpose.

It is clearly a Laudian table, not an Elizabethan one, for the latter were made after the same pattern on all sides, whereas this is evidently made to stand against a wall. Only the front legs are turned, at the back are mere plain supports. The original size of the table is shown clearly by the old rail, which has not been lengthened, and by the old nail-holes and other marks still remaining. The present top is of deal, two feet longer and twelve inches wider than the original one. The tattered piece of printed calico which partly covers the table has tack-holes all round, which also show the original size of the top. One of the present supports at the back of the table is carved on one side, and resembles other pieces of carving still to be seen about the house.

The balusters are of a pattern of which other examples may still be found in churches where the old arrangements have not been disturbed nor replaced by modern fittings from the Church-furniture shop. They are of oak, but have at one period been coloured green. The rails in front have their proper sill, but the side rails are held at the base by two

277

strips of wood. The top rail is perfect all round, but the pillars at the angles have disappeared and been replaced by a baluster sawn in two.

The kneeling is of English soft wood, and is almost all worn away with dry-rot. The original kneeling was probably of stone, when the whole thing was in a church.

The table has been converted into an altar not merely by enlarge-

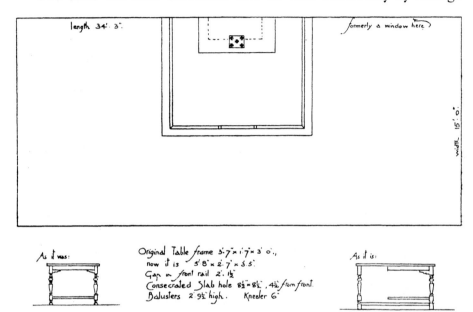

ment. In the centre of the new top a hole has been made for the consecrated altar-slab.

The history of this converted Communion Table is not certain. It will be remembered that Archbishop Laud ordered the Communion Tables to be fixed at the east end of the chancels, altar-wise, and railed round, to preserve them from desecration. Up to his time the tables were usually kept in the chancels, but at the time of the administration of the Lord's Supper they were moved down into the nave, and put lengthways, the minister standing in the middle of the north side, facing south. (The ends faced east and west.)

The tables in Elizabethan days were made like other tables that have to stand in the centre of a room; it was only in or after Laud's time that the carving was often omitted at the back, where it would not be seen against the wall.

Now it appears that the Purshalls of Purshall Hall were not Catholics in the seventeenth century. Edmund Purshall, who died in 1650,

278

*To face page 278*

THE SECRET CHAPEL, PURSHALL HALL

aged 96, was churchwarden of Elmbridge (his parish church) in 1622, and in all probability till he died. He was buried in Elmbridge Church, May 21, 1650.

Two children of John Purshall (Edmund's great-grandson) were baptized at Elmbridge—Jonathan in 1696, and Elizabeth in 1699. (The said John Purshall was married in the same church in 1694.) This does not look as if they were Catholics at the time, especially as the note, "a Catholick," is appended to certain names in the register, but not to theirs. Catholics had, of course, to be buried in Protestant churches, and even their baptisms were often registered there.

It seems probable, then, that the Table and Communion-rails in question were fixed in Elmbridge Church during the height of Laud's power, and that when the "Ordinance of Lords and Commons" was passed in 1643, ordering all chancel floors to be reduced to their former level and all rails removed, Edmund Purshall, as churchwarden, removed the table and rails to his own house. It is possible that during the Commonwealth, when the Prayer-Book service was proscribed, and the "Directory" took its place, that he and his family and friends may have used the secret chapel in the roof for the Anglican form of worship.

Be that as it may, the chapel certainly became Catholic in 1750, when the estate was purchased by the Rev. John Baynham, S.J., and the mission of Badge Court was transferred to Purshall. Father Baynham also served Grafton Manor, near Bromsgrove, the seat of the Talbots.

It was probably he who transformed the old Anglican Communion Table into a Catholic altar. He may have received the last Purshall of Purshall Hall into the Church, but of that we cannot be certain. Unless the Purshalls had become Catholics, Father Baynham could hardly have acquired the property.

He registered the place as a chapel for Catholic service in 1791, according to the terms of the first Catholic Relief Act, but no doubt he used, after the need of secrecy was gone, a larger and more commodious chapel.

Father Baynham died February 24, 1796. He left his property, says Foley,* to a Mr. William Collins, whose first wife was the Father's niece, on condition that if he had no children the property should devolve to the Church. (As an ex-Jesuit, he had, of course, the right to dispose of his property as he wished.) "St. Mary's College, Oscott, and various missions of the diocese of Birmingham are indebted to this good Father for the enjoyment of his real and personal estate, Mr. Collins having died childless."

It also appears from more careful inspection, that there was originally

* *Records*, vol. v. p. 854.

a small window in the chapel, to the right of the altar. It has been blocked up with bricks, at what date does not appear, but probably not more than a century ago. It is seen from the back of the house, but is almost hidden behind the great chimney-stack. This window is very small, but there may possibly have been light in the roof, as the present roof is new. If not, the chapel must always have been very dark, though not pitch-dark, as it now is.

These facts, though they throw doubt on our martyr's connection with the chapel, make it of great and unique interest. I do not know of any other instance of an Anglican Communion Table being converted during the penal days into a Catholic altar.

PURSHALL HALL FROM THE GARDEN

*The secret chapel lies behind the central stack of chimneys*

*Photo by R. H. Murray, Worcester*

*To face page 80*

# A MARTYR OF THE YORKSHIRE MOORS

ONE of the most touching figures in the glorious roll of the martyrs of England is undoubtedly that of the old priest, the Venerable Nicholas Postgate, D.D., who laid down his life at York, at the patriarchal age of eighty-two. His memory is held in singular veneration to this day, even among non-Catholics. The great work he accomplished for souls, during his long and laborious ministry, still bears abundant fruit amid those wild moors which cover the north-east portion of Yorkshire, and there are few of our martyrs about whom so many traditions still exist among the people. This is, of course, partly because he was one of the latest of the martyrs, having suffered at York on August 7, 1679. But of other contemporary victims of this persecution very little is known, and it is evident that Father Postgate, by the sanctity and simplicity of his life, and the pathetic circumstances of his cruel death at so advanced an age, made an impression upon the minds of his generation which is all but unique, and left a memory behind him which the lapse of more than two centuries has failed to efface.

Nicholas Postgate was born at Kirkdale House, in the parish of Egton, near Whitby, in the North Riding of Yorkshire. His father was apparently the son of William Postgate of Kirkdale, and his mother, Jane, was living there a widow in 1604. His father's mother was by birth a Watson, a name which the martyr assumed while working on the mission. His widowed mother was returned as a Recusant in 1604. "Jane Postgate doth keep in her house William Postgate, her father, a Recusant who teacheth children, and also Marmaduke Petch and Jane Smallwood, Recusants." * It was further stated that she had been a Recusant for at least eight years past, and of late years had had children baptized privately. The future martyr was no doubt one of these children, baptized by some Catholic priest, who at the risk of his life ministered to the faithful of the district. There were many Catholics in these inaccessible parts of Yorkshire, and more than sixty Recusants were returned from Egton parish in 1604. Of these, about twenty had become Recusants since Lady Day, 1603, which shows that zealous priests were at work in the district. This is indeed an instance of what was going on all over England when the death of Queen Elizabeth and the accession of the son of Mary Stuart gave new hopes to the persecuted Catholics, and were the immediate occasion of a great increase among professed Recusants.

* Peacock's *Yorkshire Catholics*, p. 97.

The martyr's parents were great sufferers for their Faith. Their relatives were also Catholics, for we find "George Postgate and Isabel, his wife," "William Postgate, the younger," and "Katheren Jeffrason," their servant, presented as Recusants, belonging to Eskdale Chapelry; and they are reported to have had three children privately baptized From Ugglebarnby Chapelry in the same year were presented as Recusants for the past eight years, James Postgate, Margery, his wife, and two members of their household. It is further stated that James and Margery "were not marryed at the church, but secretly not known where," and also that their children were "none of them baptized at church, but privately." *

Kirkdale, or Kirk House, our martyr's birthplace, stood near Egton Bridge. A writer describes it in the year 1838 as "now literally a cattle-shed." It must have been but a poor cottage, in spite of its high-sounding name.

In 1621 Nicholas was sent abroad, to be educated for the priesthood, and was admitted to the famous college at Douay on July 11. He was already a man, and so he became a convictor, not an ordinary student. It was the custom of those days for the students to take another name, since it was a penal offence for Catholics to be educated abroad, and if known by their names they might bring trouble upon their parents at home. Nicholas accordingly took the name of Whitmore. In later years, as we have seen, he sometimes used the *alias* of Watson.

He was ordained priest March 20, 1628, and sang his first Mass on April 1, at which date he must have been about thirty years old. We do not know why he began his ecclesiastical studies so late. He was sent to the mission in his native country on the feast of SS. Peter and Paul, June 29, 1630.

And now began a long ministry of nearly fifty years, in which he laboured with such devoted zeal that he is said to have reconciled near a thousand persons to the faith of their ancestors. The diary of his college records the extraordinary reputation he has gained there for piety and zeal, and this reputation was not belied by his subsequent career.

At first he made his home at Saxton, with the Hungate family, who were devout Catholics and loyalists. Sir William Hungate, knight, married Jane, daughter of George Middleton of Leighton, County

---

* A Ralph Postgate, born in Oxfordshire in 1648, was ordained priest in 1674, became a Jesuit, and was subsequently twice rector of the English College, Rome. He was the son of William Postgate and Joanna Mylott, both Catholics, and, like the martyr, was educated at Douay. He died at Rome in 1718. It is not known if he were a relative of the Yorkshire Postgates (Foley, vol. v. p. 757).

# A MARTYR OF THE YORKSHIRE MOORS

Lancaster, and he died without issue in 1634. Father Postgate lived o
with his widow until her death, about 1638.

Saxton is near Tadcaster in the West Riding of Yorkshire. The
famous battle of Towton, in the Wars of the Roses, was fought close to
the village. After leaving Saxton our martyr became chaplain to "the
old Lady Dunbar." She was the widow of the first Viscount Dunbar,
Sir Henry Constable of Burton Constable, the head of a well-known
Yorkshire Catholic family : he was created Viscount in 1620, and died
in 1645.

Subsequently the martyr served Kilvington Castle and Hall (the
seat of the Saltmarsh and Meynell families) and other places widely
apart. Kilvington is a little north of Thirsk, near the Hambleton
Hills. Thomas Meynell of Kilvington was born in 1564, and for four
years, from 1600 to 1604, was imprisoned for the Faith, first at Hull,
and then in York Castle. A Mrs. Meynell of Kilvington, probably
his son's wife, was among the martyr's visitors in prison, as we shall
hear.

But the martyr's chief abode was a thatched cottage at Ugthorpe,
two miles from Mulgrave Castle, and about five from Whitby, in the
midst of a wild moor known as Cleveland Blackamoor. Here he lived
as poor among the poor, conforming himself in dress, diet and lodging
to the flock which he zealously tended.

Thomas Ward, the well-known controversialist, who was born and
lived at Danby Castle, some seven miles from Father Postgate's
hermitage at Ugthorpe, knew our martyr intimately. He has paid him
a tribute of love and admiration in the fourth canto of his Hudibrastic
poem, " England's Reformation." After describing the Oates plot and
recounting the faith of the Catholics who suffered from that orgy of
panic and fanaticism, he continues :

> " Nor spar'd they Father Posket's blood,
> A reverend priest, devout and good,
> Whose spotless life, in length was spun,
> To eighty years and three times one.
> Sweet his behaviour, grave his speech,
> He did by good example teach ;
> His *love right bent, his will resign'd*,
> Serene his look, and calm his mind ;
> His sanctity to that degree,
> As angels live, so lived he.

> " A thatched cottage was his cell,
> Where this contemplative did dwell ;
> Two miles from Mulgrave Castle 't stood,
> Sheltered by snowdrifts, not by wood ;

# FORGOTTEN SHRINES

Tho' there he lived to that great age,
It was a dismal hermitage ;
But God placed there the saint's abode,
For Blackamoor's far greater good.

"The holy lives of those bless'd saints should I
Presume to write, and had a thought could fly
Beyond the limits of the vaulted sky,
Yet would my verse ten thousand times fall short
Of their due praise.   Let angels in consort
Sing forth their virtues on celestial lyres ;
They are exalted to these peaceful choirs.
Stop, then, my pen, and to this period come :
*God saw them worthy of martyrdom.*"

Father Postgate had another retreat in his own native parish of
Egton, about four miles away.   Here he would often come to celebrate
the Divine Mysteries in a small dark loft, which is to be one of the
shrines of this pilgrimage.   His devoted labours were felt all over the
surrounding country.   Egton, Sleights, Whitby, Pickering,—all were
scenes of his apostolate.   Though he lived in such utter poverty,
deprived of all comforts, he was yet a man of gentle nurture and refinement, a Doctor of Divinity, possessed of no mean literary attainments,
and no small practical talent.   The touching hymn which he composed,
it is said, in his dungeon in York Castle, is a proof of this.

The old man would probably have gone to his grave in peace, had
not the popular mind been driven into frenzy by the supposed discoveries
of the so-called Popish plot.   "These falsehoods," says Peacock, "stimu-
lated the persecuting zeal, not only of those misguided people who sincerely
thought that they did God service by hunting Catholic priests to death,
but also of every unprincipled ruffian who did not shrink from swearing
away a man's life for a reward."

Thus we find that beside the immediate victims of the infamous
informers—Oates and Bedloe and their crew—priests were at this period
hunted out and done to death all over the country ; not indeed that they
were accused of having had any share in the pretended plot, but merely
for their faith and priesthood.   Thus at Cardiff, Ruthin, Worcester,
Hereford, York, and other places, innocent servants of God were put to
death amid scenes of atrocious ferocity, for the sole offence that, having
been ordained Catholic priests by the authority of the Holy See, they
had dared to return to their country, and remain in it for more than forty
days, in order to minister to souls.

On December 8, 1678, our martyr was called to baptize a child at the
house of one Matthew Lyth at Ugglebarnby, a village some miles from
Whitby in the valley of the Little Beck.   While he was in the house he

THE HAND OF FATHER POST-
GATE AT ST. CUTHBERT'S,
DURHAM

*To face page 284*

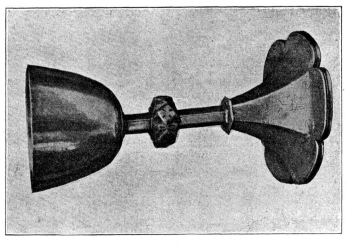

ONE OF FATHER POSTGATE'S
CHALICES AT UGTHORPE
*By kind permission of Mr. T. M. Fallow*

was apprehended by an exciseman, named John Reeves, an implacable enemy of Catholics, who hoped to gain the reward of twenty pounds promised to such informers. He associated with himself in this piece of villainy one Henry Cockerell.

The house in which the martyr was taken is said to be still standing. It is called Redbarns, and I much regret that I was not able to visit it. Ugglebarnby, it may be noted, is about three miles from Sleights, the station next to Whitby on the line from Pickering. It is at Sleights that the Little Beck, a stream that takes its rise in the high moorland of Sneaton, flows into the river Esk.

The old man was carried off to Brompton (a place between Pickering and Scarborough, some twenty miles south of Sleights as the crow flies) to be examined by Sir William Cayley, the resident justice of the peace. Canon Raine, in his *York Castle Depositions*, has printed the official record of the examination which took place on December 9, before Sir William Cayley and his son, William Cayley, Esquire, Junior.

"John Reeves, his Majesty's surveyor or gauger for the town of Whitby, saith that upon the 7th instant he was informed that Matthew Lith of Sleights, being at a wedding, should speak these words: 'You talk of Papists and Protestants; but, when the roast is ready, I know who shall have the first cut.'

"Upon notice whereof this informer thought himself obliged to search the said Matthew's house, which accordingly he did upon the 8th instant, supposing that some arms or ammunition might be found there, the said Matthew and his family being all Papists. And he saith that though he was interrupted by the said Matthew, he did find a supposed Popish priest there (called Postgate), and also Popish books, relics, wafers, and several other things, all which the said Postgate owned to be his. The said Postgate said that he was called Watson, but afterwards being called by others by the name of Postgate, he owned that to be his right name.

"Nicholas Postgate, about the age of fourscore years, saith that about forty years since be lived at Saxton, with the Lady Hungate, until she died. And since then he hath lived with the old Lady Dunbar, but how long it is since, he knoweth not. Of late he hath had no certain residence, but hath travelled about among his friends. Being demanded whether he be a Popish priest or no, he saith, 'Let them prove it,' and would give no other direct answer. Being demanded how he came by, and what use he made of the books, wafers, and other things that were found with him and which he owned, he saith that some were given him by Mr. Goodricke, a Roman Catholic, and other some by one Mr. Jowsie, a supposed Romish priest, both which are dead; and that he made use of them by disposing them to several persons who desired them for helping their infirmities.

285

Being demanded why he named himself at the first Watson, he saith that he hath been sometimes so called, his grandmother on the father's side being so called, and he being like that kindred."

It will be observed that the venerable priest took good care to name no one, except those who were already dead, and out of the power of the persecutors. On the same day, December 9, 1678, Andrew Jowsie of Egton was charged with being a priest, before Edward Trotter and Constable Bradshaw, Esquires, justices of the peace. He denied the fact, but refused to take the oaths of allegiance and supremacy. He was acquitted. He cannot have been the Mr. Jowsie to whom the martyr referred, but was no doubt a relative. From Brompton the venerable confessor was carried off to York, no doubt *via* Rillington and Malton.

He was placed at the bar at the York Assizes, and indicted for high treason, not as connected with the plot, of which he was obviously innocent, but, under the old penal Statute of 27 Elizabeth, for being a Catholic priest. Three witnesses appeared against him : Elizabeth Wood, Elizabeth Baxter, and Richard Morris. These deposed that they had seen the old man baptize, and exercise other priestly functions. Upon their evidence he was convicted and condemned to death, a sentence by no means unwelcome to one who had all his lifetime been learning to die. The trial seems to have been conducted with more than the usual want of humanity and even of justice.

An old account says :

" The Judge, like a scarletted huntsman, cheered on the pack, and their feeble prey was run down by acclamation. He stood like a victim bound to the altar, and never lost his composure except once, while hearing the evidence of one of his own converts, one to whom his charitable hand had often been extended, but who now witnessed against him. His lips then quivered for a moment, and his eyes shed tears, for who can withstand the force of ingratitude ? His simple statement in his own defence did but vex his persecutors the more, for they were bent upon his destruction, and by outrageous clamour they silenced a witness who had ventured to speak in his behalf. All the evidence of his guilt was that he had baptized a child in the Catholic faith : its mother testified this truth ! . . .

" Whilst there remained a hope of his acquittal—for what human being could be thought so fiendish as to condemn him ?—the old Father felt a desire for justification ; but no sooner was all hope denied by the verdict of the jury, than he resigned himself to his fate. It seemed a voice calling him to heaven, and he thanked God. The lawyers left the court and went to glory in their triumph over a bottle of wine, while the poor prisoner was conducted back to his cell. He was visited by the woman whose testimony had been most material; she came with remorseful tears to beg his pardon; he blessed her and gave her money to bear her expenses home—money that had been given him to provide comforts with, in this, his hour of need." *

"The day allotted for his triumphant exit," continues another old account, "was the 7th of August, 1679; on which day in the morning, amongst other visitors, went to see him, Mrs. Fairfax, wife to Mr. Charles Fairfax of York, and Mrs. Meynell of Kilvington. These ladies having done their devotions, went together to his room to take their last leave of him, and to crave his blessing.

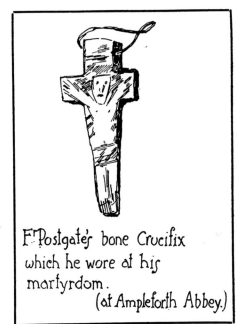

F<sup>r</sup> Postgate's bone Crucifix which he wore at his martyrdom.
(at Ampleforth Abbey.)

"The confessor seeing them in great concern, whereas he was cheerful, came up to them, and laying his right hand upon the one, and his left upon the other, said: 'Be of good heart, children, you shall both be delivered of sons, and they will both be saved.' Immediately after, he was laid upon a sledge, and drawn through the streets to the place of execution, where he suffered with great constancy. The two ladies soon afterwards gave birth to sons, who were both baptized and both died in their infancy. Thus the prophecy was fulfilled." This was told to Mr. Knaresborough, the martyr's biographer, by Mrs. Fairfax herself, in 1705.

His dying speech is still preserved. He said but little, the substance of his words being as follows: "I die in the Catholic religion, out of which there is no salvation. Mr. Sheriff, you know that I die not for the plot, but for my religion. Be pleased, Mr. Sheriff, to acquaint his Majesty that I never offended him in any manner of way. I pray God give him His grace and the light of truth. I forgive all who have wronged me, and brought me to this death, and I desire forgiveness of all people."

The unhappy man who had apprehended him never had the reward which he looked for, but, after having suffered for some time an extreme

* *Catholic Magazine*, A.D. 1838, p. 300.

torture in body and mind, was found drowned in the Little Beck, the stream we have already mentioned, which flows by Ugglebarnby to empty itself into the Esk at Sleights. The place where the informer was found —"a pool hollowed out by the concussion of a mountain cataract," is still pointed out, and it bears the significant name of "the Devil's Hole," or "the Devil's Dump." The country people declare that no fish are ever caught there, and they believe it to be still an accursèd spot. The good old priest at Egton Bridge told the present writer that a colleague of his had desired to test the truth of the tradition, and had fished the Devil's Hole for a whole day, but without seeing a single fish rise. It is indeed a weird, uncanny spot. The continual hiss of the cataract seems to sound the knell of the wretch who there perished in his despair.

A pilgrimage to the places sanctified by the labours of the dear old martyr is an extremely interesting one, and the wild romantic scenery of the Cleveland moors greatly adds to the attraction, for one who is a lover of nature. The wooded glens which descend from the moors inland are often of great beauty, and the exhilarating air of sea and moorland is delightfully invigorating. Many of the scattered farms are inhabited by faithful Catholics, who have lived in their old homesteads for generation after generation, clinging to their holy Faith with admirable tenacity.

Thus it is no small pleasure to the pilgrim to visit a spot so blessed by God. And owing to the kind co-operation of Catholic residents in the neighbourhood, we have been able to gather together many an interesting tradition. On a fine summer afternoon we drove out from Whitby northward, along the coast, until at the picturesque seaside hamlet of Sandsend—with its cottages perched up on either side of the ravine through which runs a little rippling beck—we turned inland and, leaving on our left the wooded park of Mulgrave Castle, soon arrived at Lyth Church. It was curious to see the trees stunted and warped in their growth by the force of the strong sea-winds, and the old church seemed as if it too had felt the buffeting of the tempests, for it was propped up by as strange and massive a series of buttresses as it has been our fortune to meet with. Within, "restoration" of the most drastic kind had worked more harm than ever storms could do, and had left nothing of interest remaining.

And now, by rough steep roads, through numerous gates, we approached Ugthorpe, which was for many years the home of the dear old martyr, Father Nicholas Postgate. The village stands on the brow of a hill, one long straggling street—if street it can be called—with a new Protestant church, built as if in protest against the far more

288

imposing Catholic one, which claims the allegiance of the majority of the inhabitants of the district. It is indeed cheering to see that the Faith has not died out in Ugthorpe. How could it, indeed, when it was watered by a martyr's blood? Foley speaks of the "extraordinary religious fervour which still exists in the district." The presbytery is of unusual size and spaciousness, which is explained by the fact that the late priest, "Mr. Rigby," had started there a secondary school.

This priest, from all accounts, was one of the old school of "Garden-of-the-Soul Catholics" : a fine old school it was ! formed in the traditions which had been handed down by the martyrs, of solid, genuine English piety, not so demonstrative in outward expression of devotion as is the custom nowadays, rough and uncouth perhaps to modern notions, but sterling, true and faithful, through evil report and good. Many years he had ruled his Ugthorpe flock, and every day after Mass he would recite with them the beautiful and touching hymn which tradition has handed down as "Father Postgate's hymn." Whether it were really composed by the old martyr or not does not seem certain, but it is at any rate attributed to him and no doubt was constantly recited by him. The tune to which it is sung is also traditional. Our readers may like to have it.* At Catholic funerals in this district it was also the custom to sing the hymn. It was begun as the corpse was carried across the threshold of the house, and was given out—two lines at a time—by an old Catholic of the place, John Gallon, who then raised the tune, and the people sang it as the funeral procession went on towards the church. It is unfortunate that in late years this pious custom should have been dropped.

Father Rigby, it may be added, was a physician of bodies as well as of souls. He worked miracles in the way of removing the bigoted prejudices of Protestants by means of his "Black Bottles, White Bottles, Pills for human beings, Pills for Turkeys to prevent their feathers falling off," and other remedies for man and beast. Once, indeed, to his high glee, the Protestant parson, having been taken ill in the night, was obliged to send for him, as no doctor could be got. "I did what I could for him, poor man!" said he, with a sort of pitying contempt, very characteristic, but indescribable. His powerful and eloquent sermons completed the good work begun by his remedies. Up to his advent, the Protestant feeling had been very bitter, and Catholics were afraid even to speak of their religion before outsiders. No doubt it was in this way that so many of the precious traditions of the penal days were lost. The faithful feared to be overheard by their bigoted neighbours, and thus expose themselves to being tabooed and persecuted.

* See p. 303.

Peace be to the memory of the aged priest who did so much to over-come this bitterness!

It was disappointing to find no certain relics of the martyr in the present beautiful church at Ugthorpe. However, in the sacristy we were shown two old chalices, both of which, probably, and one of which was certainly used by him. They are figured in a paper, printed in the *Archæological Journal* (vol. lxi., No. 241), by Mr. T. M. Fallow, F.S.A., on "Yorkshire Plate and Goldsmiths."

Mr. Fallow says: "Both these chalices are interesting as having been those ordinarily used by the well-known Nicholas Postgate, who at the age of eighty-two was barbarously hanged at York, in 1679, for saying Mass." The smaller, and apparently the older chalice is a silver one of Gothic design, with wavy flames round the bowl. It is pro-nounced by Mr. Fallow to be of French origin. (A very similar one is shown as a "Persecution Chalice" in the Museum of St. Mary's College, Oscott.) It unscrews in three places for the purpose of being carried about. This chalice seems certainly to have been used by the martyr. The other chalice is somewhat taller. "It is probably English, as it corresponds with similar chalices having English marks elsewhere." Mr. Fallow gives its date as *c.* 1630. It has a Gothic knob (pierced). On the foot, below a crucifix, is engraved the inscription *Ora pro D.M.F.*

It would be very interesting to identify the donor of this chalice. May it have been Mrs. Charles Fairfax of York, who was so great a friend of our martyr? However that may be, this chalice belonged at one time to Bishop Matthew Gibson, Vicar Apostolic of the Northern District and founder of Ushaw College, who resided, from time to time, in a house opposite the present Catholic Church at Ugthorpe.

In a hollow below the hill on which the village stands, lies Ugthorpe Old Hall, which was for many generations the seat of the Radcliffes, a Catholic family which suffered much for the Faith. They were formerly owners of Mulgrave Castle, but their adherence to the old religion cost them this estate and many other broad lands as well. The house, now fallen from its ancient dignity, is still interesting.

It is of Tudor date, with mullioned windows, and there are some curiously carved stones built into the walls. The oak door, at which our martyr must often have entered, still exists with its quaint old knocker and latch. In an out-building to the left of the Hall, which is now used as a cow-byre, there is a curious priests' hiding-place made in a chimney. The Radcliffes were among the staunchest of the old Catholic gentry, and must have often sheltered priests. In 1641, "William Radcliffe of Ugthorpe, Gent," is among the Recusants presented to Quarter Sessions. And in 1637 we find the names of "Thomas

# A MARTYR OF THE YORKSHIRE MOORS

Poskett, Tailor, and Margaret his wife of Ugthorpe," as Recusants. "Poskett" is "Postgate," written phonetically, and even now all old Yorkshire folk pronounce the martyr's name "Poskett." These good people were probably his near relatives.

Another cow-byre close to the old hall (on the right hand as you face the front door), was once a Catholic chapel. People still living remember their parents speaking of the time when they used to hear Mass regularly in this humble sanctuary. There is little enough now to tell of its former sacred character, though there still can be seen what is called a holy-water stoup, but which is perhaps more probably an aumbry. It is sad to see this building, which once witnessed the Sacred Mysteries, now the home of the beasts of the field. But, after all, it was in such company that the Saviour of the world was born.

A short walk from Ugthorpe Hall brings us out on "the lingy moor" where Father Postgate made his humble home. ("Ling," it may be noted, is Yorkshire for heather.) This forms part of the great moors that cover this Cleveland district, stretching from Scarborough northward almost to Middlesbrough, and from Whitby eastward to the Hambleton Hills. The great moor was called the Cleveland Blackamoor, and its wild romantic beauty is still the delight of the traveller, though of course in many places it has been encroached on by enclosed and cultivated land. Here the old apostle of the moors had his retreat.

The thatched cottage in which he lived was standing within living memory, but some forty years ago it was unhappily pulled down. Fortunately the site is preserved, and its memory still cherished. It stood near the high road that leads across the moor from Guisborough to Whitby. Its site is now occupied by a small farm-house, hidden in a clump of trees, and known as the Hermitage or Postgate House. The old house was a very humble dwelling, a hermitage in fact as well as in name. It consisted of two rooms only, both on the ground floor, and paved with what are locally called "cobble-stones"—undressed stones rounded unevenly by wear or by the action of water. (They are generally brought from the beach or from the beds of streams.) It was thatched, and there was no upper room nor any ceiling, the roof being open under the thatch. There was a small porch outside, from which one entered directly into the kitchen or living-room.

There was a little garden in front, and my informant, a good Catholic, seventy-six years of age, who was born at Ugthorpe, said that she had been told by her grandmother that Father Postgate was the first to bring the daffodil to that part of the country. From another source I learned that for many generations the site of the martyr's garden was fragrant with white lilies, which grew there in profusion.

291

# FORGOTTEN SHRINES

Of the little house, there is still one wall standing. This, which is now the outer wall of the farm-house, on the right as you face the entrance, is plastered to a certain height, and this part was, in fact, the inside wall of the martyr's kitchen. The plaster still shows the height and width of the building, though the wall itself has been heightened. There is now an open shed for carts built up against it, and in the pavement of this shed are still remains of the old cobble-stones which formed the kitchen floor. Catholics still live in the house and are proud to show what is left of the martyr's home. When the old house was pulled down, part of the oak beam which went across Father Postgate's bed-place was taken to Egton, and crosses were made of it, which are still preserved by the pious Catholics of the district. The present writer possesses one of these little crosses.

In the *Catholic Magazine* for 1838 there is an interesting paper on "Nicholas Postgate, the Old Catholic Priest," by a writer who signs himself "J. W." and dedicates his work, with great affection, to Father Nicholas Rigby. He, too, bears testimony to that priest's influence in breaking down prejudice against the Faith. "I was born in the Church of England," he writes, "and bred in all its prejudices against the Church of Rome; but having lately read several sound expositions of Catholic doctrines, with the loan of which I was favoured by you, I have conceived a respect for the priests of that persuasion, both as men and Christians, and am proportionately disgusted at the misrepresentations that have been imposed on me by Protestant preachers." His account of Father Postgate, he goes on to say, is designed to be an act of reparation for the wrong which he had unwittingly done to the Church by prejudices, "which, however, can only have injured myself."

The most valuable part of his paper is an account of the martyr's hermitage, as it then was. This I will quote at length :

"He lived in a little cell in the midst of a wide moor. I have visited that cell, for it still 'stands where it stood.' It is one of the poorest huts of the poor—a mere cattle-shed in appearance—its little chimney alone denoting it to be a human habitation. There are two or three old ashen trees that bend their blasted forms, and point, with their bare branches, like the witches on the heath, as if to indicate the spot to the by-way traveller. Looking towards the north, the west, and the south, a black moor presents its desolate aspect ; but on the east, a long tract of cultivated land stretches like a promontory before whose brow a small sea-bay is visible. Vessels, diminished in the distance to the size of birds, seem stationary, as they skim with white wings across. After the eye has wandered like a dove seeking in vain for a green oasis, it rests with pleasure on the fields, the woods, the

FATHER POSTGATE'S HERMITAGE, UGTHORPE

*The figures are standing just in front of the wall of the martyr's kitchen.   Photo by **Miss A. Jackson***

*To face page 292*

park of Mulgrave, with its castle crowning the ridge that bounds the horizon. . . .

"I stooped to enter the lowly hut where pride must be put off with the hat. It consists of two small apartments, one emphatically styled 'the house,' in which the domestic duties are done ; the other a place for rest : both are on the ground floor, which is paved with uneven stones. The thatched roof is just overhead ; the latticed windows are very narrow, and deeply indented in the clumsy walls ; there is a hearth for a peat fire. Yet piety dwelt peacefully in this humble abode, and the sunbeam that shed a ray of glory within was a heavenly halo round its head. I was shown the spot where 'once the garden smiled,' but no garden flowers remained ; a few daffodils had long survived the rest, but the mistaken reverence of some visitors had led them to transplant those perennial relics into their own gardens.

"No sounds, no sights, now denoted that a 'reverend hermit' had passed his patriarchal days in this lonely cell, and yet there was a time when he was seen and heard by many children who were blessed by him. Many pious persons, who clung closer to their religion because it was proscribed by the rulers of this world, oft came in secret pilgrimage to this cell, and revered the good Father more because he was content to render himself obnoxious to persecution for their sakes. . . . He had made a vow of poverty, and his path of life, though so lowly and lone, was a glorious path, for it led towards heaven. The alms which he received he gave to these poor penitents who confessed that poverty had led them into sin. He imposed a heavy penance upon the guilty, but made it light by paying the greater portion himself, and he was rewarded by witnessing the compunction of the sinner who felt remorse on seeing the innocent old man a voluntary sufferer for his sake. He encouraged the diffident by confessing to them his own sins. Those disagreeable duties which others shrank from doing he did for them, and sometimes seemed to go with the sinner, that he might insensibly lead him from the error of his ways. His crucifix was a better peacemaker than the constable's staff. The humanity of the man overcame the prejudices against the priest, and he first made strangers friends and then Christians. Bad men he treated as though they were good, and those who injured him as though they had benefited him. This was his method of re-claiming them ; and it generally succeeded. He regarded the persecutions against his Church as judgments sent for the amendment of her children, and he conducted himself with a more perfect resignation, because he was under the ban of the law. . . . Such was his benevolent zeal, that some say he made above a thousand converts. However that may be, the majority of the people in that district are Catholics to this day."

# FORGOTTEN SHRINES

The Hermitage is about six miles from Whitby; and a beautiful drive of about three miles more, across the moor, brings us to Egton, which is also closely connected with the dear old martyr. It was at Kirkdale House in this parish that he was born. And at Egton stands still the most interesting little Mass-house, where he used to offer the Holy Sacrifice in a humble loft.

Near this old house is a grass field which was pointed out to me as having an interesting history. It rises high above the road, and its green slopes are visible for many miles round. My guide told me that old men tell how, in the evil days, on Sunday mornings, sheets were laid out to dry, and the Catholics knew where Mass was to be said that day by the number of the sheets. My recollection is that the places named were Egton, Newbiggin in Eskdale side (once a home of the Salvins), and Sleights, all places within about six miles of Father Postgate's hermitage on the moor. Mr. Fallow, in his account of the Ugthorpe chalices, says: "Some linen sheets are preserved at Ugthorpe which used to be spread (as if to air) on the hedges, as a signal that he was in a neighbouring house and was about to say Mass."

Another interesting tradition was told me. We have seen that the martyr was taken at the house of Matthew Lyth at Redbarns, Ugglebarnby, whither he had gone to baptize a child. (There is still a Catholic Matthew Lyth living in the neighbourhood.) With Lyth were imprisoned two other Catholic yeomen, named Redman and Roe.

They remained staunch for some months; but when harvest-time came round, and their presence was sorely needed at home to look after their crops, Roe and Redman yielded, at least externally, and were released. Lyth, however, remained firm. And the old people say that ever since that day, while a Redman or a Roe has occasionally been known to go astray from the Faith, the Lyths have always remained faithful. I fear that in these days this is not absolutely true, but there are still many faithful Catholics of the name living in the neighbourhood. As the present venerable Bishop of the diocese testifies: "The Catholics of Egton really have the Faith": they are no degenerate descendants of the martyr's flock.

The principal interest at Egton centres round the old house, where Father Postgate had his little oratory, in which he seems at times to have reserved the Most Blessed Sacrament. It is an old thatched cottage which may date back to the sixteenth century, standing near the modern Anglican schools, on the summit of the hill. Through the kindness of a friend I am able to give an excellent photograph of the back or eastern side of this old Mass-house.

The house is very low, with small windows in the low stone walls,

THE OLD MASS-HOUSE, EGTON

*Photo by Sutcliffe, Whitby*

*To face page 294*

and gabled roof of thatch. There is a lean-to porch in front which is comparatively modern. The martyr's secret oratory is in the thatched roof to the right of the picture. Its position is marked in the photograph by the upper window under the thatch.

The pilgrim cannot but regard this humble oratory with deep veneration. Here a glorious martyr celebrated the Holy Mysteries year after year, at peril of his life. Here he retired to pray and to gain strength for his arduous labours from the presence of His Divine Master, Who condescended to dwell here in His Adorable Sacrament. From this loft the humble priest carried Him to His faithful persecuted children, to console them in sickness, and to be their Viaticum.

The place is so tiny that there is hardly room for any one but a server to assist at the Sacrifice. At most, two or three could have knelt behind. Probably the worshippers were content to kneel in the kitchen below, from which they would hear the sound of the sacring-bell (if, indeed, the use of a bell were compatible with safety), and the voice of the priest, though they would hardly be able to see him. The loft is very dark. There is, however, one tiny window, at the end of a kind of tunnel through the thatch, on the level of the floor. It seems to be of later date, and it is probable that nothing but the tapers of the altar ever cast a light there, in the martyr's time. It was in sanctuaries such as these that the English Church kept vigil in the days of her sorrow. The darkness and stifling air of so confined a space must have recalled vividly to the martyr priests those sanctuaries of the Roman Catacombs in which the Christians of the first ages met to celebrate the same Divine Mysteries, and to gain strength from them to endure a persecution not more cruel.

The very existence of this oratory was long unknown. No doubt, at the time of the martyr's arrest, the entrance to it was carefully closed, and in the lapse of time it became forgotten. It was only discovered by accident in the early years of the nineteenth century, probably in the thirties. The story of the discovery, as related by a member of the family who lived in the house at the time, is a very interesting one. A girl, mounted on a ladder, was employed in cleaning the upper part of the kitchen wall, when she found the plaster give way under her hand, and she broke into the long-hidden doorway to the loft. To her amazement, she found herself looking into an oratory, with the altar prepared for Mass, with the vestments lying spread out upon it, with the missal, crucifix, candlesticks, and all that was necessary for the Sacrifice. She hastened to apprise Mr. Harrison, the tenant of the house, who was himself a devout Catholic. The welcome news was at once conveyed to the Vicar-Apostolic of the Northern District, Bishop Penswick, who soon afterwards came to see for himself. He found that everything remained as it had been left by Father Postgate when he last said Mass there. The Bishop left the altar-stone, tabernacle, two crucifixes (one with relics in it), and other treasures in the charge of the Harrison family, but most of the relics he took away with him.

The altar-stone and other furniture of the altar were finally removed to the chapel at Egton Bridge in 1850 by the Rev. Andrew Macartney, then priest-in-charge. The tabernacle framework and door still remained, however, in their original position, under the charge of old Mr. John Harrison. Shortly before his death, the door was carried off by a well-known Anglican clergyman, now deceased, who visited the house, garbed in cassock and cloak, as though a Catholic priest, and persuaded Mr. Harrison to let him take this relic away with him. The Catholics of Egton, whose good faith was thus deceived, have been hitherto unable to recover the lost treasure; though I have been fortunate enough to secure a photograph of it. The framework of the tabernacle, however, remained in place until the death of Mr. Harrison, at the age of ninety-nine. It was then removed by Canon Callebert, the Catholic rector of Egton Bridge. The oak step-ladder, which the martyr used to mount to his little oratory, has been removed and cut up for relics. Canon Callebert has a large piece of the wood, and at St. Mary's Convent, York, there are preserved several small crosses made out of it.

Before leaving the Mass-house, a few minutes may be spent profitably in studying the structure with the aid of the plans here given, which I owe to the kindness of Father Storey, the present rector of Egton Bridge.

The east elevation, it should be noted, is the back of the house, i.e., the side turned from the road. The road to Egton Bridge runs at the foot of the garden on the west side of the house. The structure is a very simple one, just a thatched cottage of one story, with a loft under the thatch. Since my photographs were taken, a new building has been added to the primitive structure, but we need take no account of this. Its position is marked on the plan.

The interior consists of a kitchen or living-room and two bedrooms, A and B. The small dark loft, C, in which our martyr celebrated the Divine Mysteries, and in which the Most Holy made His sacramental dwelling, is situated above the two bedrooms. Till quite recently access to it was gained by a ladder, which was set up in the kitchen, and led direct to the loft through a low door (marked C in the section). However, since the present occupants took the house, they have, unfortunately, altered the entrance to the loft. They have boarded up the door C, and

To face page 296

FATHER POSTGATE'S SECRET ORATORY
IN THE OLD MASS-HOUSE AT EGTON

J. R. BAGSHAWE

have removed the ladder to bedroom B, so that now you gain access to the loft through a trap-door in the ceiling of this bedroom.

The loft is a very singular place in its way, and it has most touching interest for the pilgrim. It is very small, only 15 ft. by 10 ft.,

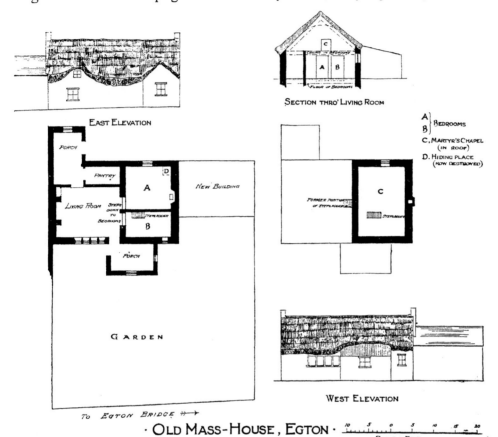

EAST ELEVATION

SECTION THRO' LIVING ROOM

A } BEDROOMS
B }
C, MARTYR'S CHAPEL (IN ROOF)
D. HIDING PLACE (NOW DESTROYED)

PORCH
PANTRY
LIVING ROOM
STEPS DOWN TO BEDROOMS
A
B
D
NEW BUILDING
PORCH

GARDEN

FORMER PORTION OF STEP-LADDER
C
STEP-LADDER

WEST ELEVATION

To EGTON BRIDGE →

· OLD MASS-HOUSE, EGTON ·

SCALE OF FEET.

and not more than 5 ft. 6 in. high in the middle, below what is called in Yorkshire the "rigging-tree," the main beam of the roof. At the end in the wall opposite the old entrance is a hole, now boarded up and papered over, which served as the tabernacle.

There is yet another indispensable feature of this hidden sanctuary. In the ground plan of the cottage the part marked off (D) was a hiding-place (now thrown into the room), which communicated with a trap-door in the floor of the loft. It was down this hole that the priest could escape, in case of need, by means of a ladder. It appears that

2 P

originally there was an exit from this hiding-place into some houses adjoining which are now pulled down. The new addition to the house now takes the place of this old building.

It would be difficult to find more romantic and beautiful scenery than that which meets the pilgrim's eyes, as he gazes from the top of Egton Hill down into the valley of the Esk at his feet. In complete contrast to the wild lingy moor behind him, here is nature in her softest mood : splendid woods, green pastures, the rippling river, framed by the distant moors and hills around. There are few spots, even in this favoured county, more romantic and beautiful than Egton Bridge and Glaisdale. The paradise of the tourist and the angler, it has also special joys for the Catholic pilgrim. The Catholic church of St. Hedda is a really noble building, worthy of its high purpose, and forming the greatest possible contrast to the humble little Mass-house of the martyr priest on the hill above. It has been furnished with loving and artistic care by the venerable Belgian priest who has spent over forty years of his sacerdotal life in this remote Yorkshire village ; and the elaborate Stations of the Cross, the carved-oak pulpit, the sculptured " Mysteries of the Rosary," let into the external walls, the Grotto of Lourdes and Stable of Bethlehem erected in the presbytery garden, speak to him of the art and devotion of his native land, while they teach to Yorkshire Catholics the truths of the one Faith more vividly than was possible in the days of Father Postgate.*

Here are preserved some relics of the old martyr that are of deepest interest. In the altar of the Lady Chapel is inserted the altar-stone from the Mass-house at Egton, on which the old priest must so often have offered the Holy Sacrifice. This altar-stone, like most of those that have been preserved from the times of persecution, is a small square piece of slate, without any receptacle for relics, but with the five crosses rudely scratched upon it. In the sacristy is a piece of oak framework in the shape of a triangle, with some carving on the sides. This is the pent-house roof to the door of the tabernacle, which we have already seen in the loft of the Egton Mass-house. The tabernacle itself was a mere hole in the wall ; and we have already learned the fate of the door.

In the presbytery are preserved still more relics. There are two pyx-bags which the martyr is said to have used in carrying the Blessed Sacrament to the sick. One is heart-shaped, made of old blue and white brocade, with little flame-like tassels of yellow silk at intervals round the edges, which are bordered with yellow silk

* Canon Callebert has now retired from active work, but happily still lives on at Egton Bridge.

298

DOOR OF FATHER POSTGATE'S TABER-
NACLE, FROM THE OLD MASS-HOUSE
AT EGTON.                        *To face page 298*

braid. This was till lately at Whitby, in the possession of Jane Harrison, a staunch Catholic, who was descended from the woman who " did for " Father Postgate, and was, no doubt, a relative of old Mr. Harrison, who inhabited the Egton Mass-house. She gave it to the present Bishop of Middlesbrough, who gave it to the church at Egton Bridge. The second bag is made of green silk, lined with red; it is of the usual shape, and is much worn and frayed. It is fastened at the neck with cord and tassels of green silk. This was given to Canon Callebert by an old woman, named Ann Redman, who cherished it during her lifetime as a very great treasure. She belonged to a very old Catholic family, the Hodgsons of Bigginhouse, and lived at Egton.

There is also a crystal cross of delicate workmanship, ornamented with silver filigree, containing a relic of the true Cross. This came from old Mr. Harrison's house at Egton, where the martyr used to say Mass. The crucifix which now hangs on Father Postgate's rosary, preserved at St. Hilda's, Whitby, also came from this house. It belonged to Bishop Briggs, who, on his death-bed, left it to Canon Callebert. He, knowing it to have belonged to the rosary, gave it to the priest at Whitby, who had possession of the beads. These beads form a complete chaplet of five decades and are made apparently of bone, strung on a piece of cord. They are large beads, and at the end of the chaplet is a large boss or ball of what is apparently leather (unless, indeed, it be some Oriental bean), to which is attached a tassel of red silk. The metal crucifix already mentioned is attached to this tassel.

Another place connected by tradition with our martyr is the quaint old town of Pickering, which was his market-town. Here, it is said, he used to come, disguised as a gardener, to minister to the little flock which had remained faithful throughout the persecution. In a garden, adjoining the present Catholic church, a pear-tree is shown which it is said that he pruned.

While ministering to the Catholics in and around Pickering, Father Postgate is said by tradition to have inhabited a small thatched cottage, built on the site of the gardener's house in the quarry just outside the town, on the Whitby side. The site of this little sanctuary is very romantic and beautiful, though so near the town. It is in full view of the frowning old castle, whose ruined towers overshadow it. Here, then, the aged priest lived in the gardener's cottage, and here, too, his memory remains in benediction.

It is said that the mode of intimating to the people that the priest had arrived, and that Mass would be said in the cottage on the following morning, was just as at Egton, by spreading sheets on the hedge adjoining the cottage. This practice was not, indeed, confined

299

to Father Postgate; we have met with traces of it in other parts of the country.

The old man seems to have been fond of gardening; the flowers that blossomed round his hermitage were a proof of it, and as we saw, tradition credits him with the introduction of the daffodil. And what character would be more suitable for the saintly labourer who, in the sweat of his brow, toiled in the vineyard of his Lord, from the earliest to the eleventh hour, bearing the burden and heat of the day? His task was to root up the weeds and briars that heresy had sown so thickly in the garden of the Lord, and to cultivate the flowers and fruits of virtue. Thus he was made like to Him who was taken for the gardener as He stood by His empty grave, who Himself tells us with what care and love He digs round and manures the sterile tree, hoping against hope that it will at last bring forth fruit unto eternal life.

The pilgrim cannot refrain from adding that the spirit of the aged martyr priest is still alive at Pickering. The devoted priest who, in spite of the most abject poverty, has laboured there for the last seven years, has still an uphill task before him. When he was sent there, things were at their lowest ebb; there were but two Catholics left in the old town where the mural frescoes and the very stones of the grand old parish church still speak so eloquently of the faith of bygone days; but by dint of suffering and labour equal surely to that of any missionary in a heathen land, borne with silent heroism and offered up as a sacrifice for his people, Father Postgate's successor at Pickering is gradually breaking up the hard and frozen soil, and causing it to flourish once more with the flowers of faith and devotion. His vineyard is still but a little one, yet there is promise in Pickering of the Second Spring, and hope that the wilderness will once more flourish and blossom as the garden of the Lord. He sadly needs help and encouragement in his difficult and laborious task, and may God grant that, for His martyr's sake, help may be given to him generously!

Already Father Bryan has earned one rich reward. In answer to his prayers and entreaties, an altar-stone, which the blessed martyr used to carry about with him, has been given to his little sanctuary, and is now let into the altar of St. Joseph's Church, at Pickering. This altar-stone, of the kind already described, has an interesting history. It was given by the martyr to Mrs. Fairfax, wife of Mr. Charles Fairfax of York, who, as Challoner tells us, was a great friend of Father Postgate's, and who visited him in prison. She gave it to her friend, the Rev. John Knaresborough, who is so well known as a chronicler of the lives of many of our martyrs. She also gave him "a piece of cloth dipped in Mr. Posket's blood by Thomas Garlick (present at the execution), a

300

RELICS OF FATHER POSTGATE

1. *Rosary*; 2. *Relic of the true Cross*;
3 and 4. *Pyx-bags. Photo by Sutcliffe, Whitby*

*To face page* 300

servant of Mr. Tunstall's of Wycliffe." Both Garlick and Tunstall, it may be noted, are martyr names. Mr. Knaresborough left the altar-stone to the Rev. Ambrose Witham of Cadeby, who left it, with the residue of his property, to the Rev. Thomas Daniel, who gave it to the priest of Dodding Green, where it remained till the year 1908, much venerated as a precious relic. But the incumbent of that mission, with the kind consent of his Bishop, has now generously given it (under certain conditions) to Pickering.

We must not close without giving a description of the other precious relics of the dear old Yorkshire martyr which still remain.

Alas! we have not succeeded in discovering where his sacred body lies. Challoner tells us that "his quartered body was given to his friends," and that "the following inscription was put upon a copper plate and thrown into his coffin" :

*Here lies that reverend and pious divine, Dr. Nicholas Postgate, who was educated in the English College at Douay. And after he had laboured fifty years, (to the admirable benefit and conversion of hundreds of souls), was at last advanced to a glorious crown of martyrdom at the city of York, on the 7th of August, 1679, having been priest 51 years, aged 82.*

One of his hands, we are told, "is preserved in Douay College." This is, no doubt, the right hand, which is now preserved at St. Cuthbert's, Old Elvet, Durham. It is the small hand of an old man, the skin desiccated and brown. The little finger is missing. But it is said to be preserved in some other church, the name of which is not known to the present custodians of the hand. Portions of the skin have been pared off down to the bone for relics, especially between the thumb and forefinger. The nails are intact. The fingers are contracted towards the thumb. The hand has been severed from the arm at the wrist. Another touching relic preserved here consists of two locks of silky white hair tied together crosswise with red silk. There is also the entire lower jaw-bone of the martyr. The teeth are all missing. Yet another relic is a vertebra of the backbone. All these relics of Father Postgate were examined and certified by Bishop Hogarth in 1853.

Our martyr's left hand is in possession of the Benedictines of St. Lawrence's Abbey, Ampleforth, near York. The thumb and fore-finger of this hand are missing. The paper that contained it is inscribed in a contemporary hand. "This Paper contains ye Hand of ye Rev. Mr. Postgate Priest who dy'd for his Faith, in suffering Martyrdom at ye City of York Anno Domi 1680 togeather with a cloath that was diped in his Blood. As alsoe certain very valluable & well attested Reliques of Saints. Therefore whoere thou art be very careful of thy

FORGOTTEN SHRINES

conduct herein." (Endorsed, "The Rev. Mr. Postgate's Hand with
several Reliques &c.") It may be conjectured that this relic also came
through the Fairfax family. At Ampleforth, too, is treasured the little
bone crucifix, already figured in these pages, which the old martyr wore
at his death. It is very rude, almost grotesque in its simplicity.

The present Bishop of Middlesbrough cherishes a precious little
book which belonged to Father Postgate, and still has his autograph
inscribed on the fly-leaf. It is a little book of moral theology for the
use of priests, *Aphorismi Confessariorum*, by the famous Jesuit theologian,
Father Emmanuel Sa. It is a product of an Antwerp press and is dated
1599. Opposite the title-page, the name, *Nicholaus Postgayt*, is written
in a bold firm hand. His Lordship very kindly lent me the book, so
that I was able to photograph the signature.

At St. Mary's Convent, York, is preserved a piece of the rope with
which he was hanged, while "the Blod of the Gloreses marter father
Poscatt" may be venerated at Downside Abbey; St. Benedict's Priory,
Colwich; Stonyhurst College; and elsewhere.

At St. Mary's College, Oscott, is preserved a very interesting
collection of the martyr's relics. One is a piece of linen stuff,
lined with canvas, with a buttonhole in one corner; it is labelled
"*Mr. Posket's cape he woore 30 years.*" Besides this little cape
there are a lock of hair, a piece of his "backbone when quartered,"
a piece of the rope, and a cloth stained with his blood. These
relics belonged to Mrs. Juliana Dorington, a pious Catholic lady,
who lived at Old Oscott for many years, and died there in 1731. She
seems to have acted as housekeeper to the Rev. Andrew Bromwich, a
venerable priest who was condemned to death for his faith, at Stafford,
August 13, 1679, during the same persecution which proved fatal to
Father Postgate, but who escaped death, and may be considered the real
founder of Oscott. No doubt he knew Father Postgate personally, and
thus these touching relics have the best of pedigrees.

Finally, an altar crucifix and a candle, which come from the Egton
Mass-house, are now in possession of a member of the Harrison family
at Scarborough.

I have done my best to gather together notices of all these scattered
treasures, and here to put them on record, lest through the lapse of
time any be lost sight of or forgotten. It only remains to give the
text of Father Postgate's hymn.

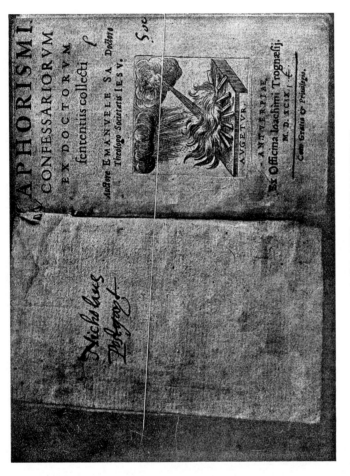

BOOK WITH THE AUTOGRAPH SIGNATURE
OF FATHER POSTGATE
*In possession of the Bishop of Middlesbrough*

*To face page 302*

# A MARTYR OF THE YORKSHIRE MOORS

*Father Postgate's Hymn.*

"O gracious God, O Saviour sweet,
  O Jesus, think of me ;
And suffer me to kiss Thy feet
  Though late I come to Thee.

"Behold, dear Lord, I come to Thee,
  With sorrow and with shame,
For when Thy bitter Wounds I see,
  I know I caused the same.

"O sweetest Lord, lend me the wings
  Of faith and perfect love,
That I may fly from earthly things
  And mount to those above.

"For there is joy both true and fast,
  And no cause to lament,
But here is toil both first and last,
  And cause oft to repent.

"But now my soul doth hate the things
  In which she took delight,
And unto Thee, the King of Kings,
  Would fly with all her might.

"But oh, the weight of flesh and blood
  Doth sore my soul detain ;
Unless Thy grace doth work, O God !
  I rise but fall again.

"And thus, dear Lord, I fly about
  In weak and weary case,
And like the dove that Noe sent out
  I find no resting-place.

"My wearied wings, sweet Jesus, mark,
  And when Thou thinkest best,
Stretch forth Thy hand out of the ark,
  And take me to Thy rest ! "

# WOODCOCK HALL AND
# THE MARTYR'S ALTAR

ONE of the most venerable relics of the persecution still remaining in Catholic hands is the old missionary altar, which has been the treasured possession of the Burgess family since the early days of Queen Elizabeth. It is now the property of Mr. Thomas Clarkson, of Bolton-le-Sands, who kindly allowed me to photograph it some years ago.

The late Rev. Thomas Abbot, of Monmouth, a venerable old priest, whose mother was a Burgess, inherited the altar; and in his last years of retirement at Lancaster used to say Holy Mass on it every day. He gave me the following account of the family traditions concerning it, which had been handed down to him by his uncle, Bishop Burgess of Clifton, who died in 1854.

The altar is in the shape of a wardrobe or bureau, and when closed gives no indication of its true character. In Mr. Pike's beautiful drawing, which we reproduce, it is represented both open and shut up. It was made in 1560 by the Mr. Burgess of the day, who was at that time acting as agent and bailiff to the Townleys, near Burnley in Lancashire. (It will be remembered that by Elizabeth's Act of Uniformity, Holy Mass became an illegal act on St. John's Day, June 24, 1559.) The object was that the Townley family and their dependents should be able to hear Mass in secret in Mr. Burgess's house, which was situated close to the family mansion, and thus avoid the danger of having their estates confiscated, which would have occurred had the altar or priest been discovered in the mansion.

As it was, Mr. Townley had to undergo a life-long persecution for his adherence to the ancient Faith. According to an inscription beneath his portrait in the gallery at Townley Hall, he was imprisoned in no fewer than nine prisons, and, at the age of seventy-three, when he had become blind, " was bound to appear and keep within five miles of Townley his house. Who hath paid into the Exchequer twenty pounds a month and doth still (1601), so that there is paid already above five thousand pounds."

After Mr. John Townley's first imprisonment, about 1564, the neighbourhood of Burnley became too dangerous for Mr. Burgess and his family to remain there. They therefore removed to a large farm under the Hoghtons of Hoghton Tower. The farm, called Denham Hall, was in the parish of Brindle, and about three miles distant from Hoghton Tower. Mr. Burgess placed the altar in a large room in the old farm-

WOODCOCK HALL

2 Q

house, for the convenience of the numerous Catholics living there under the protection of the Hoghtons.

In Easter-tide, 1581, Blessed Edmund Campion said Mass at this altar, and remained at Denham Hall until the Worthingtons carried him off, in the disguise of a groom, to Blainscough Hall.*

When the Hoghton family lost the Faith, *i.e.*, about the year 1611, the Burgess family found it necessary to remove to a more distant and sequestered farm called Woodend, in the neighbouring parish of Clayton-le-Woods. They, of course, took the altar with them.

It is very unfortunate that Woodend has been pulled down, as two illustrious martyrs visited the house, and said Mass on the old altar there.

The first was the Venerable Edmund Arrowsmith, who, after his release from his first imprisonment for the Faith, said Mass here in the year 1622. The other was the Franciscan martyr, Venerable John Woodcock, who said his last Mass here on the Feast of the Assumption, 1644, being apprehended the same day. We are able to give some interesting details of this memorable event, and also a beautiful drawing of Woodcock Hall, the martyr's birthplace, which is, happily, standing, and is only about two miles from Woodend.

Woodcock Hall stands near Lostock, on the road from Leyland to Bamber Bridge.† It has now fallen from its former state, and is divided into two tenements. When we visited it the smaller portion of the house was inhabited by Catholics. The fine oak doors, staircase and panelling in the main part of the house are tokens that it was once a residence of some importance. There are said to be traces of a hiding-place, but the place shown us was not very convincing. The old house is very picturesque, and has about it something of the air of mystery and aloofness which one looks for in a forgotten shrine. For it is chiefly venerable as a martyr's birthplace.

John Woodcock (in religion Father Martin of St. Felix, O.F.M.) was, in fact, born in this house in 1603. His father had conformed to save his estate, which had been in the family above four hundred years,‡ but his pious mother (an Anderton by birth) kept firm to the Catholic faith. She sent her son to the English College at St. Omer's, and from thence he went on to that of Rome, where he studied for the priesthood. But he felt himself irresistibly drawn to a more penitential life, and

* See *In the Brave Days of Old*, by the present writer, "The Worthington Boys" (Burns and Oates).

† We are informed that there is another Woodcock Hall at Newburgh, about four miles distant, which belonged to the same family.

‡ In the Free Library at Wigan are a number of deeds connected with the family and its property, some as old as the reign of King John. They were presented by the present squire, Colonel Farrington, of Worden Hall, Leyland.

therefore, leaving Rome, he sought admission among the Capuchins at Paris.

Dr. Oliver says * he saw a letter from him to Father Thomas Fitzherbert, S.J., the Rector of the English College, dated September 25, 1630, thanking him for the many kindnesses he had shown him, and telling him that he had worn the habit, he "thanks sweet Jesus, almost now a year." It was not, however, God's will that he should spend his life in France, and, to his great sorrow, he was dismissed by the Capuchins as unsuitable. After many difficulties, rebuffs, and internal struggles, he was finally admitted, at his most earnest entreaty, to the English Convent of St. Bonaventure at Douay, and clothed with the habit of St. Francis by the future martyr, Father Heath, in the year 1631.†

He became the model of the novitiate, excelling all his fervent companions in strict observance and mortification, while his wonderful gift of prayer brought him into close communion with God and His angels. In 1632 he made his vows in the hands of another future martyr, Father Francis Bell. Two years later he was ordained priest.

He was consumed with the desire of martyrdom, especially after the glorious death of Father Heath at Tyburn in 1643, and implored his Superiors to permit him to go to England, although so feeble in health that it was feared he was stricken with mortal disease. He wrote: "I beseech you, by the tender love of the most sweet Jesus, to send your consent without delay. Reverend Father, the season admits of no delay; winter approaches, and my health through this anxiety and even others that are greater, is not strengthened and confirmed as your Reverence, and even myself, could expect. Wherefore, for the love of God (kneeling now in my cell), I ask you on my knees to say Amen and to send me your consent as soon as possible."

This letter touched the Guardian's heart, and brought the long-desired permission. As Father Woodcock was hurrying on his preparations for departure, the news of Father Bell's martyrdom reached him (December 11, 1643). Thus both he who had clothed him and he who had received his vows, were now with the martyrs of Christ in heaven. The news inflamed his ardour still more. Thirsting to be united to Christ by the same sufferings, he set out in the spring of 1644, and, after some perils, landed at Newcastle-on-Tyne. His first thoughts were for his family and friends, many of whom needed reconciling to God; but it was not till the Vigil of the Assumption (August 14), that he finally reached his home. He at once made arrangements to say

* *Collections*, p. 563.
† For the details of Father Woodcock's life, see *Certamen Seraphicum*, by Father Angelus Mason, O.F.M. (New Edition ; Quarrachi, 1885), p. 183 *et seq.*

Mass during the night on the missionary altar at Woodend, for the Burgess family and the neighbouring Catholics.

But just as he had finished hearing confessions and was standing in his vestments to commence the Mass of the Assumption when the clock should strike twelve, one of the Catholics came rushing in to beg all to disperse immediately, as the pursuivants were coming! Father Woodcock immediately took off his vestments, closed up the altar, and got into the priests' hiding-hole, before the pursuivants arrived.

When they came up to the room, Mrs. Burgess, who had thrown herself into a rocking-chair, protested against their rude intrusion into a sick woman's room at that time of night. But they said they had come with a warrant to apprehend the popish priest. She said, "You will not find a man in my room at this time of night." They asked, "What are all these people assembled here for, if it be not to meet the popish priest?" She said, "They are some neighbours who have come to sit up with me."

They searched the farm-house, but happily could find no trace of the hidden priest, and left, disappointed of their prey. As soon as the pursuivants were gone, Father Woodcock came out from his place of concealment, and the few Catholics in the immediate neighbourhood returning, he said Mass, gave them Holy Communion and then hastened away before daybreak to his father's house.

Early the next morning the traitor who had summoned the pursuivants hastened to them again, saying: "I had quite forgotten. There is a hiding-hole in that house, for I once went there courting the servant-maid when the mistress was absent, but she came back earlier than was expected, and I was put into the hiding-place. I think I can find it again, behind a certain panel." The pursuivants returned with the traitor to the house at Woodend, and he went immediately to the hiding-hole and withdrew the panel, but found the place empty.

Mr. Woodcock, hearing this, was afraid if the priest was caught in the mansion that he would lose his estate, and therefore gave his son his breakfast, and ordered him out of the house as quickly as possible. The holy priest had not got a mile away from his father's house when the traitor and the pursuivants overtook him on Bamber Bridge, arrested him, and brought him before the magistrates, who ordered them to convey him to Lancaster Castle. There he was kept in prison for two years, and was put to a cruel death, with two secular priests, on August 7, 1646.

Owing to the trouble brought on them through this tragic event, the Burgess family removed once more with their precious altar, now dearer to them than ever. They put themselves under the protection

THE OLD MISSIONARY
ALTAR—OPENED AND
CLOSED

of the great Catholic family of Gerard of Brynn, in the parish of Ashton-in-Makerfield, near Warrington. They remained there till they were able to secure a tenement lease for three lives, according to the custom of those times, of a farm called the Hawkslough, in Cuerden, situated near Bamber Bridge.

Here, in a large parlour, the altar was placed, and was much frequented by the numerous Catholics of that neighbourhood. Upon the expiration of the lease, Mr. Thomas Burgess (father of Bishop Burgess of Clifton), the penal laws not being then so stringently enforced, was able to purchase from the Booth family a plot of waste land at Clayton Brook, adjoining the old farm of the Hawkslough, upon which, in 1784, he built the present brick house. He placed the altar in a large room at the back of the house, until the Chapels of Brownedge, Clayton Green, and Leyland were opened.

Upon the death of Mr. Thomas Burgess, which occurred in 1843, the house being let to a Protestant, the altar was removed to a private oratory in the house of the Bishop's sister, Mrs. Ann Abbot, at Brockholes, near Preston in Lancashire; and after her death, to the house of her daughter, wife to Mr. Henry Clarkson, of Bolton-le-Sands, for the commencement of that new mission in 1886.

Upon Mr. Clarkson's death, his widow, Helen Clarkson, retired to Lancaster, and by the permission of Bishop O'Reilly, the altar was removed from Bolton-le-Sands, and set up in a little oratory in Dale Street, Lancaster, by the Rev. Thomas Abbot, Mrs. Clarkson's brother, on June 30, 1891. Here Bishop O'Reilly often used to visit it and make his meditation in the little chapel, in veneration of the glorious martyrs who had offered the Holy Sacrifice upon it. Here, too, we visited it in June 1906, not long after the death of the venerable priest who took such a holy pride in it.

A detailed description of the appearance of the old altar is unnecessary, as the drawing shows it well. Various pious ornaments added in modern times have here been omitted. The oak is very dark, though part of the woodwork has been spoilt by paint. There are curious iron hinges to the upper doors, which cannot be seen in the drawing. The carved panel at the back, which serves as a reredos, is of very black oak; it may possibly have been used for another purpose before the altar was made. The pillars which divide the upper doors from the centre of the altar, are covered with a scale-like ornament; they are detached, and really belong to the lower half of the altar. They formed the supports of a plain front which is now kept separately. The pediment at the top, carved with the sacred monogram surrounded with rays, and very rude cherub heads, is held in position only by a couple

310

of pegs, so that it could be easily removed when the altar was not in use. It is made to slip conveniently into the lower part of the altar.

The original altar-stone is very small, but Father Abbot used a larger one. He also fitted to the old projecting ledge of the bureau, which was the original *mensa*, a much larger slab of wood, so that Mass could be more conveniently celebrated.

The little tabernacle contains an old silver chalice and paten. On the chalice is engraved, " When Him you see, remember me," with I.H.S. and A.S. on either side of a heart. In the long drawer beneath the modern *mensa*, are two small altar-stones and a missal of 1609, which formerly belonged to the English Benedictine nuns of Our Lady of Consolation of Cambray, now at Stanbrook. In other drawers are the vestments, some of which date from penal times. Those used by Venerable Father Woodcock are still to be seen, and the *palla*, described later on among the relics, was given by Father Abbot to the present writer.

Father Woodcock's vestment is much worn with age. It could be used for either red or white, as it is composed of these two colours. The old alb is very handsome, of cambric, with old point-lace let in. There are three chalice-veils with old embroidery, one of which is exquisitely worked, and is now framed and hung on the wall. Several other old vestments had to be destroyed, they were so moth-eaten.

The altar has now been taken back to Bolton-le-Sands, and set up in a private oratory in the house of Mr. Thomas Clarkson.

# THE OLD CHAPEL AT MAWDESLEY

MAWDESLEY is in the very heart of that blessed land where the Faith still flourishes, where farmer, labourer and squire are united in one holy bond, and where the large plain Catholic chapels have extensive stabling attached to them for the sake of the faithful who drive or ride, sometimes from long distances, to Holy Mass.

Mawdesley lies in a rural district, about seven miles south-west of Chorley, in the midst of pleasant, undulating country, so that the pilgrim fancies himself farther away than is in fact the case, from the chimneys and collieries which make Lancashire what it is to-day.

Mawdesley stands high. From the great "Town Field" behind the Hall, the surrounding district for miles can be seen. Harrock Hill, which overhangs the village, is a famous beacon. From its summit one enjoys a complete sweep of scenery, stretching on the western side from the dimly towering hills of Wales to the grey mountains of Cumberland. On the north, the intervening ground, belted at the outer rim with the waters of the Irish Sea, opens out before one like a gigantic panorama, embracing some dozen towns and above twenty villages. Eastward the eye ranges over Wigan and Chorley to the belt of hills beyond them.

In the hall at the foot of the hill, the glorious martyr, Venerable John Rigby, was born in 1570, when beacon-fires were blazing on the hill above to announce the Catholic Rising in the north. As he was dragged to die at St. Thomas's Waterings in South London, he answered an inquiry thus: "I am a poor gentleman of the House of Harrock in Lancashire; my age about thirty years; and my judgment and con-demnation to this death is only and merely for that I answered the judge that I was reconciled, and for that I refused to go to Church."

He then disclosed the divine secret that he had preserved his virginal purity to the end, forcing his questioner to cry out in admiration: "I see that thou hast worthily deserved a virgin's crown; I pray God send thee the kingdom of heaven, and desire thee to pray for me."

The Hall itself is disappointing, as the greater part of it is modern. But there is one portion which may be as old as the date of the martyr's birth, and here we were shown the position of a priests' hiding-place.

The great house has long been untenanted, and it is very desolate. Grass has grown over the gravel drive, and the rain streams in through more than one gaping hole in the roof. Our footsteps echoed dismally through the large empty rooms and corridors where there was little to remind one of the brave young man who was born and brought up there three centuries ago.

# THE OLD CHAPEL AT MAWDESLEY

But at Mawdesley there is a forgotten shrine, which has far higher interest for the pilgrim. Lane End House is the home of the Finches, a family which boasts not only of its own martyr, Venerable John Finch, a young layman, who suffered at Lancaster, April 20, 1584, but is also closely connected by marriage with the Haydocks of Cottam Hall, and therefore with the Venerable George Haydock, priest, who shed his blood at Tyburn, February 12, 1583-4. His thrilling story has been so vividly told by Mr. Gillow * that we need not recount it here.

The quaint old house was erected in the sixteenth century, and had more than one hiding-place for priests. The chapel is at the top of the house, under the roof, and is unusually spacious. Till the church was built in 1831, it was, indeed, the only chapel which the numerous Catholics of the district could attend. When the last Squire Haydock of Cottam Hall died, outlawed, for his share in the Jacobite rising of 1715, the treasures till then preserved at Cottam were transferred to Mawdesley. Thus in the house hang portraits of the Haydocks, and a great hatchment with their armorial bearings. Mary Haydock, sister of the last Squire, had married Thomas Finch of Mawdesley, and to Mawdesley in 1714 came the Rev. Cuthbert Haydock, a younger brother of the Squire,† to act as chaplain and minister to the faithful of the neighbourhood. He devised his estate to his great-nephew, James Finch, and some of his books are still preserved in the little sacristy adjoining the chapel.

But the greatest treasure of Mawdesley is the martyr's skull, which had been religiously preserved at Cottam till the estate passed into other hands. It was kept in a faded red velvet bag, and after it was translated to Mawdesley, was concealed in the priests' hiding-place adjoining the chapel. Now, however, it has been enclosed in a glass box, and placed on the altar of the old chapel.

It is, unfortunately, not certain whose skull it is. The tradition of the family has ever been that the skull is that of the Venerable George Haydock, the supposition being that the martyr's cousin, William Hesketh, when discharged from the Fleet prison in 1582, obtained possession of the skull and brought it to Cottam. It was specially fitting that this relic should be preserved by the family who cherished the legend of "The Gory Head of Mowbreck Hall."

This is thus told by Mr. Gillow, who himself claims descent from the Haydocks. ‡

* *The Haydock Papers* (London, 1888), *passim.*
† He had three brothers priests, Gilbert, Cuthbert, and Hugh.
‡ *Haydock Papers*, p. 25.

It must be explained that Vivian Haydock, the martyr's father, became a priest in his old age.

"On the hallowe'en preceding the arrest of his son George, Vivian Haydock stood, robed in his vestments, at the foot of the altar in the domestic chapel at Mowbreck, awaiting the clock to strike twelve. As the bell tolled the hour of midnight, the 'fugitive' beheld the decapitated head of his favourite son slowly rising above the altar, whose blood-stained lips seemed to repeat those memorable words: *Tristitia vestra vertetur in gaudium.* Swooning at the horrible apparition, the old man was carried to his secret chamber, and when the little children called on All Souls for their somas cakes, to their customary acknowledgment of 'Pray God be merciful to the suffering souls in Purgatory,' they added: 'God be merciful to the soul of Vivian Haydock.' His body was borne to its last resting-place and laid beneath the chapel at Cottam Hall by his son, Dr. Richard Haydock."

In recent years, however, some doubt has been cast on this identification of the skull. The late Bishop Goss of Liverpool thought it to be the skull of an older man than George Haydock (who was only twenty-six at his martyrdom), and believed that it was the skull of William Haydock (a great-uncle of Vivian) who was a Cistercian monk of Whalley Abbey, and, for his alleged share in the Pilgrimage of Grace, was hanged in a field adjoining the Abbey, March 12, 1537, two days after his Abbot's execution. He was one of the senior monks of Whalley, and was aged about fifty-four.

His body was allowed to hang on the gibbet, and was subsequently rescued by his nephew and secretly removed to Cottam Hall. Here it was preserved with great veneration. When the house was pulled down at the beginning of the nineteenth century, the skeleton was found concealed in the priests' hiding-place. We, however, are inclined to believe the family tradition that this skull is that of George Haydock, the young Seminary priest who laid down his life so blithely for the prerogatives of Peter.

While in his desolate dungeon, he had consoled himself by carving on the wall the name and ensigns of the Roman Pontiff with the inscription, "*Gregory XIII on earth the Supreme Head of the whole Catholic Church,*" and though severely taken to task by the warder, he stoutly refused to efface it.

At his martyrdom he rejected the advances of the Protestant clergyman, but begged all Catholics to pray for him.

"There are no Catholics here present," cried one of the crowd.

"Nay, we be all Catholics!" shouted another. The holy man must have smiled as he gently replied: "Catholics I call them which cherish the faith of the Holy Catholic Roman Church: God grant that from my blood there may accrue some increase to the Catholic Faith."

"Catholic Faith," cried the Sheriff, "the devil's faith! Drive on with the cart, hang the traitorous villain!"

When we made our pilgrimage to Mawdesley, we were permitted to photograph the old chapel and its treasures.*

The picture given here shows our fellow pilgrim, the Very Rev. Dom Hilary Willson, O.S.B., now Prior of Fort Augustus, vested in one of the old vestments preserved in the Chapel sacristy, together with the martyr's skull, the old Gothic processional cross, the chalice and other treasures. I owe to him the following inventory of the chapel furniture, which is exceedingly interesting, as these old vestments and other furniture have come down to us almost intact from penal days, and some of them even from Pre-Reformation times.

It was, indeed, a delightful experience to burrow in the old oak box which contains these treasures, and draw out, one by one, the sacred vestments which had been worn by generations of confessors, and doubtless by many a martyr of Christ.

There is a most interesting little library of old books also preserved here; but we content ourselves with giving the inventory of the " Church stuff," as our fathers called it.

## INVENTORY OF CHURCH GOODS AT
## LANE   END   HOUSE, MAWDESLEY

MASS VESTMENTS

*All kept in old oak chest 4 feet 6 inches ×
2½ feet, 2 feet deep, solid ends to ground.*

1. *Chassuble, yellowish green ground,* blue cross and pillar about 9 inches broad, worked with conventional Gothic flower pattern in silk and gold thread. French shape, lengthy; lining of coarse blue canvas or buckram; cross square-edged; pale blue binding round chasuble. Stole and maniple of brownish yellow velvet, very much worn, only 2 inches broad; canvas lining. Burse of same colour with green edging, quite limp; no veil. A pall of brown stuff on upper side, linen below.

2. *Chasuble, dull blue,* with green cross and pillar 9 inches broad; material seemingly cotton silk with Gothic flower pattern; conventional.

* This photograph of the Chapel forms the frontispiece to my *Tyburn Conferences,* second series, "Oxford, Douay, Tyburn." (Burns and Oates, 1906.)

An effective binding all round of braid in brown, green and red; lined with stout blue canvas as No. 1. French shape, but broader than No. 1 —quite 3 feet broad and 4 feet 6 inches long; cross square-edged. Stole and maniple—former of dull green silk lined with yellow canvas, latter of lighter green and very long, lined with blue canvas; silver tinsel crosses on both. Veil of very bright green silk with I.H.S. surmounted by cross and heart with three nails, surrounded by rays all in bright yellow silk; a flower pattern is worked all round the outer edge of veil about 1 inch in breadth. The veil would seem to have belonged to some other set. No burse.

3. *Chasuble of pale salmon-coloured silk*, very much worn; the cross and pillar square-edged, of well-worn silver tinsel about 1 inch broad, worked on to ground material. A plain white tape-binding round edge of chasuble seems to have been added later. Lining of salmon-coloured canvas. Stole and maniple of same silk lined with yellow canvas; white tape crosses, perhaps later. Veil small, 14 inches square, with small silk tassels at corners, and binding of gold braid one-eighth of an inch broad. No burse.

4. *Red chasuble*, pale Gothic red flower on yellowish diaper ground, square-edged cross of white binding, with green and salmon-coloured silk pattern throughout, lined with yellow canvas. Long stole and maniple with shovel ends of same material as chasuble. Veil of same; no burse. Marked B. All in good preservation. Generally effective.

5. *Bright red chasuble* of serge, reversible; black serge on other side; square cross on either side of different gold tinsel braid. Stole and maniple to match; black and red veil, red side of duller shade than chasuble; a burse, black on one side with broad silver tinsel cross; reverse side is of red velvet made out of old vestment or cape with (sixteenth century?) fleur-de-lis and cherubim worked in silk and gold thread, about 1 foot square. Chasuble much moth-eaten. Additional red velvet stole and maniple, narrow; also red burse, and two red stuff palls with Gothic patterns; linen below.

6. *Older black cotton-velvet chasuble*, with silver tinsel cross 2 inches broad, cut square; narrow white braid edging round chasuble. Stole and maniple to match. Veil of same material, with I.H.S., cross, and heart, in rayed circle. Burse of stuff not velvet; pall of black one side and red stuff on the other; the whole, save burse, reversible for red of magenta shade; white edging of narrow tape, very worn and moth-eaten on red side. Additional pall, black silk one side, linen below with thin cardboard; other old cardboard stiffenings.

7. *Old black serge chasuble*, stole and maniple, burse and pall; no old veil. Newer veil, stole, maniple and burse of black cloth edged

THE RELICS AT LANE END HOUSE,
MAWDESLEY
*Photo by the author*                    *To face page* 316

with white braid seem to have been added. Burse very large, 11 inches square, fastened with buttons.

8. *Purple chasuble* (of brownish tint) with flower pattern on ground, cross square, 7 inches broad, of white water-lined narrow silk, braided edge in silk; coarse brown buckram lining. Stole and maniple (narrow) and burse, all of same material with green crosses. Veil of thin silk, pale purple, with cross of red silk on three steps of same.

9. *White chasuble* (marked B in red silk) of silky material with small flower pattern, in good preservation; square cross of narrow silver braid, and a single-line cross down centre and arms of cross, and pillar on front. Long narrow stole and maniple of same material; no veil or burse; thick lining of linen.

*Albs :* one, 6 feet 6 inches long, very ample, made of four breadths of yard-breadth linen, homespun. Neck gathered on a strong tape with strings, wrists also gathered on tape; very narrow hem below; not much worn, only a few small holes. (See illustration.)

*Alb of homespun*, 6 feet long, ample, four breadths of yard-broad linen, fastened at neck with tape, button like a shoe-button and linen loop, and frilled. The arms of both are long, ample and shaped, being much broader down to elbow; not much worn.

Remnant of a third alb which has been cut up; apparently shorter; arms short but very broad, 1 foot 6 inches at arm-hole, repaired at hem below with piece 4 inches deep. Lighter quality of linen, same ample breadth, four of one yard broad.

*Girdles : two very long girdles*, one of thin double cord about thickness of strong window-blind cord, the other of triple cord of same strength with large tassel. One very short girdle, only 3 feet 6 inches, of plaited linen with small tassels. One of plain tape, 4 feet 6 inches, with tassels one inch long.

*Amice :* one, worn and soiled, short strings.

*Purificators :* two pieces of linen, apparently purificators.

*Corporal :* one linen corporal with lace edge and embroidered edges within, 1½ inches broad; on lower portion a very quaint figure of Crucifixion, with Our Lady and St. John worked in silk of dark brownish green. The whole is 7 inches by 4 inches. This is, perhaps, the most interesting and valuable piece of work in the whole collection.

*Chalice and paten* of pewter, very roughly made and much battered; chalice 6 inches high, 2¼ inches broad; paten 3 inches in diameter; no cross on foot. (See illustration.)

*Altar stones :* one of brown sandstone 8 inches by 7 inches, crosses well incised, four 1½ inches and centre one 2½ inches each way. No sign of a relic chamber anywhere—not even in front edge, as sometimes. No

317

signs of cere-cloth, but centre cross seems to have had something like wax adhering to it at some time.   No sign of same elsewhere.

Second altar-stone of green Cumberland slate, 8½ inches long by 5½ inches broad, set in old oak frame.   Crosses square, with holes at points, and below centre cross a larger hole apparently for relics ; signs of wax all over stone, but little left.   Stone contained in old linen cover.

The altar in chapel has a larger modern altar-stone.

*Processional cross*, head only.   Very quaint figure of Crucifixion, three Gothic foliated ends, with emblems of four Evangelists, eagle above, angel below, lion on left, ox on right ; very quaint figures of Our Lady and St. John in separate pieces fitting into socket with cross ; above, a six-lobed knot with Gothic four-leaved flowers on facets ; short stem, chased, and back of cross also.   All apparently regilded.   The left arm of cross has been broken and roughly repaired—no staff.   (See illustration.)

*Cruets :* four large glass cruets with double arms, would hold half a pint.

*Large supply host-box,* 10 inches by 4 inches, with sliding lid, and marks of cutting hosts on lid ; two round host-boxes of boxwood and walnut, with I.H.S. and three nails inlaid.

*Altar-cards :* one set of paper mounted on wood in deal frame painted black, worm-eaten and worn.   Second set of paper mounted on cardboard with print in colours in centre card ; a triptych, the Nativity, Crucifixion, and Resurrection, 9 inches by 5 inches each.   Initial letters on blue and red ground, blue border round the whole, plainest print. Below : *à Paris chez Jacques Houervoc* (?) *Rue Saint Jacques à la ville de Cologne.*

*Altar table,* of oak, 5 feet broad, supported by two pillars 3 feet 9 inches high, 4 feet apart.   This and the back below are of old oak. A new front of oak with cross and gilded rays seems to have been added. Has two steps or gradines, 2 feet by 4 feet.   Old deal tabernacle ; oak credence, 3 feet high, 2 feet 6 inches by 1 foot top.

# BADDESLEY CLINTON

THE moated Hall of Baddesley, near Warwick, seat of a branch of the Ferrers family from 1517, has been so frequently pictured and described that we need not give it more than a passing notice.

The writer feels that he cannot omit it altogether, for of all these forgotten shrines, Baddesley is, to him, the most familiar and the most dear. None is more romantic in its studied isolation, none more beautiful with the poetry of age. The old grey walls, reddened with lichen, rise from the waters of the moat with a simple dignity unsurpassed elsewhere; the mullioned windows, blazoned with innumerable heraldic shields, give light to rooms panelled in blackest oak, in whose dim recesses seem to lurk mysterious spirits of the past; the dark winding corridors, broken by unexpected flights of slippery oaken steps, lead here to a priests' hiding-place, there to a banqueting hall, here again to a ghostly room, where the blood of a murdered priest still stains the floor. But the heart of the house is the old chapel where the Master of the house deigns to dwell in His tabernacle, and the haunting legend is inscribed above the door:

> Transit gloria mundi:
> Fides Catholica manet.

Here at Baddesley that Faith has ever had a stronghold; never did this beautiful old house belong to any but a Catholic. Through the dark days of persecution, hidden chaplains—like the "Sir William the priest at Badsley" revealed to us in Elizabethan documents—ministered to the faithful, hidden away in the recesses of the great Forest of Arden. Here for thirteen generations of unbroken line, the Ferrers of Baddesley have worshipped God in the old Catholic manner during nigh four centuries, three of which were ages when no Catholic was suffered to serve his God in peace.

The diary of Henry Ferrers, who lived more than eighty years at Baddesley (1549-1633), is still preserved among the Rawlinson MSS. at the Bodleian, and in it are to be found minute and vivid details of the life of a typical Catholic country squire during the fiercest period of the persecution. Needless to say, he did not escape arrest and imprisonment, though for the greater part of his life he managed to live quietly at Baddesley.

From the middle of the sixteenth century till the first quarter of the nineteenth, the Franciscans served Baddesley, and even yet the spirit of St. Francis broods over the place, for hard by the present Catholic church, the cloistered daughters of St. Clare live their hidden life of penance and perpetual intercession, and shed the fragrance of their virtues around.

But there are even holier memories at Baddesley. It has one little link with the martyrs of Christ, which, so far as we know, has never yet been recorded. Rowington, the nearest village to the manor-house, was the home of one of the most attractive and heroic of the many laymen who gave their lives for the Faith in this country.

Robert Grissold, or Greswold, was born at Rowington, probably about 1575. He came of a family very numerous in the district, which settled at Kenilworth about 1400, and spread into the neighbouring parishes. Robert seems to have belonged to the elder branch of the family, though the Greswolds of Solihull Hall were the richest and most distinguished. They were armigerous, and important people in the county.

Robert was the son of John Grissold of Poundly End, Rowington, whose will, dated 1586, was proved at Worcester, April 20, 1587. In this will he names seven sons (including our martyr), and a daughter, Christian. He leaves three pounds to William Skynner, Lord of the Manor of Rowington, who was an ardent Catholic, and five years later got into trouble for harbouring a priest. At his examination one "Thurstan Tubbs deposed to seeing an old man in Mr. Skynner's orchard reading a Latin Portesse (Breviary), and he met him with his Challice and Book going towards Baddesley."

This is just where we should have expected to find him going.

John Grissold also mentions in his will his three brothers, Robert, Henry, and Ambrose, with whom our martyr seems to have been staying when he was arrested. They were " three unmarried brethren, Catholics, for many years living and keeping house together."

The will continues : " I give unto Robert my sonne 40s. I give and bequeath unto my sonne John the table-board in ye Hall with ye sitinge benches." This is the John who in 1606 was so " ill-used in the Tower, that at one time he was reported to have died of torture." *

The name of Grissold frequently occurs in the Recusant Rolls. In 1592–3 we find Robert Grissold de Rowington, yeoman, fined £40; Robert Grissold (perhaps our martyr), £80; Richard, Christian, Henry, William, and Robert Greswold, husbandmen, each, £80. This was for four months' recusancy. It would seem incredible, had we not the documentary evidence before our eyes, that men in this humble position should have been fined these immense sums simply for conscience' sake. Their cattle and goods were carried off, and sold to pay the debt.

* Gillow, *Dictionary*, vol. iii. p. 53.

The Moated Hall of Baddesley Clinton
E. Pike. 1910.

2 S

"Isabel Griswolde, widow," the martyr's mother, also appears in the Recusant Roll for 12th James I., and she is fined £40 for not attending church. She appears in the "Court Roll" for 1605 as holding "one messuage and one yarde * land by estimation 25 acres, and payeth rent yearlie."

John Grissold was a friend of the famous Jesuit, Father John Gerard, who tells us that he was " an honest faithful man " who had the keeping of the house where Mrs. Anne Vaux lived, near London, and where it was supposed Father Gerard himself lodged.

"This honest man, being taken in the beginning of the troubles, was first committed close prisoner to the Gatehouse, and there lodged in a dungeon, upon the bare ground, for the keeper (though he was earnestly entreated by the other prisoners) would not allow him so much as straw to lie on, pretending that if he had any straw to lie on, he would set on fire the house.

"This man did both endure his affliction with great constancy and fidelity, but afterwards, when Father Gerard was taken prisoner in the Tower, the Commissioners, desiring to get matter against him, removed this man to the Tower also, and there put him to the torture with great extremity, and very often almost every day for a long time together, as we did confidently hear reported, with which and other bad usage in his diet, he was for a long time after like to die, and it was thought by many that he was dead ; and doubtless he escaped very hardly."

Robert and John, as boys, must often have heard Mass at Baddesley, and their memory still seems to linger round the old house.

Of Robert we learn from an old MS. that " he was single and upright in his actions, unlearned, but enlightened with the Holy Ghost. Feared God, hated sin, led a single life and chaste, was kind to his friends, mild in conversation, devout in prayer, bold and constant in professing the Catholic religion, and heartily loved and reverenced Catholic priests."

He was to give, indeed, a signal proof of this.

One of the priests who said Mass at Baddesley towards the end of the reign of Elizabeth was doubtless the venerable martyr, John Sugar,† of Merton College, Oxford, once Protestant Vicar of "Cank" (Cannock ?) in Staffordshire. There is no more beautiful story in the Acts of the Martyrs than this of the old convert parson and the young man who served him so lovingly, and laid down his life so gladly rather than desert him.

It was on July 8, in the first year of James I., on the Sunday

* A yarde appears to mean a virgate, *i.e.* the fourth of a hide—about thirty acres.

† The Sugars had some interest in Rowington, where even yet a field is known as "Sugar's Close." But our martyr was a Staffordshire man.

322

known to our fathers as Relic Sunday, that a neighbouring magistrate, Mr. Burgoyne of Wroxall Priory, was stirred into unwonted activity. He sent a constable with a warrant to search a Catholic house (probably Mr. Skynner's) in Rowington for a priest who was supposed to be hiding there. The constable failed in his search, but probably having heard that Robert Grissold had been seen about with a stranger, who from his demeanour was supposed to be a priest, the man went on to the house of the old bachelor uncles, which he also searched. Here, too, he drew a blank, but on the road home he was more fortunate. For, on the high road, somewhere in the neighbourhood of Baddesley, he came upon Robert Grissold and the priest.

Mr. Sugar had been making an apostolic journey in Staffordshire, Worcestershire, and Warwickshire, "to serve, help, and comfort the meaner and poorer sort of Catholics with the holy Sacraments." It may be that at Broadway, in Worcestershire, he had come across Robert Greswold, who was servant to a Mr. Sheldon there, and that Robert had brought him back with him to his old home. In any case, he was a faithful and devoted companion and guide.

And now we come to the most touching feature of what was only too common an event. The constable was accompanied by Clement Grissold, our martyr's first cousin,* who lived at Henley-in-Arden. Though this young man was an apostate and informer, he had no quarrel with his kinsman.

"Cousin, if you will go your way, you may," he said to him.

"I will not," answered he, "except I may have my friend with me."

"That you shall not, for he is a stranger, and I will carry him before Mr. Burgoyne."

"Then," said he, "I will go with him to Mr. Burgoyne ; for he knoweth me very well, and I hope he will do my friend no wrong when he heareth me speak."

This hope was unfulfilled, for both were committed to Warwick gaol, where they lay a year and more. Here, again, Robert might have escaped, had he wished, but "for the love of Mr. Sugar and zeal for martyrdom, he would not."

At his trial a justice cried to him, "Grissold, Grissold, go to church, or else, God judge me, thou shalt be hanged."

"Then God's will be done!" quoth he. As sentence was pronounced it was the judge who faltered and trembled.

On the morning that they were to die (it was July 16, 1604), the

---

* He was a son of George, brother of John Grissold, Robert's father. George Grissold's will is dated 1599 ; he left his lands to Clement. Clement's will is dated 1611.

priest said to his weeping friends : " Be ye all merry, for we have not occasion of sorrow but of joy ; for although I shall have a sharp dinner, yet I trust in Jesus Christ I shall have a most sweet supper" : words that, in our own day, have inspired the poetic genius of Francis Thompson :

> " High in act and word each one.
> He that spake—and to the sun
> Pointed—'I shall shortly be
> Above yon fellow.'   He too, he
> No less high of speech and brave,
> Whose word was : ' Though I shall have
> Sharp dinner, yet I trust in Christ
> To have a most sweet supper.'   Priced
> Much by men that utterance was
> Of the doomed Leonidas :
> Not more exalt than these, which note
> Men who thought as Shakespeare wrote." *

Robert Grissold uttered words not less memorable : " Good woman, why do you weep ?   Here is no place of weeping but of rejoicing ; for you must come into the bridegroom's chamber not with tears but with rejoicing."   And when the mourner answered, " I hoped you should have had your life," " I do not want it now," said he, " for I should be loath to lose this opportunity offered me to die ; but yet God's will be done."

And as he bade farewell to the prison, he left to the Catholics who crowded round him one last legacy of love : " Look that ye all continue to the end."

The incident that follows, told by an eye-witness of the scene, has been painted on canvas by the present Lady of Baddesley Clinton, and the picture now hangs in our Abbey.

" As he was going on foot to the gallows, one willed him to go a fair way, and not to follow through the mire Mr. Sugar, who was drawn on the sledge before him : to whom he made answer, ' *I have not thus far followed him to leave him now for a little mire.'   And so through the mire he went after him.*"

And thus, praying for the King, and for all who had brought them to their end, the two blissful martyrs shed their blood at Warwick for their Lord.

* *To the English Martyrs,* by Francis Thompson.   By a play upon words, characteristic of Shakespeare's time, the Venerable John Sugar was known on the Mission as Swete. He was also sometimes called Cope.   Rowington is in the heart of the Shakespeare country, and has a " Shakespeare Hall," which is said to have belonged to a near relative of the poet.

# BADDESLEY CLINTON

"Lovely and comely in their life, even in death they were not divided." *

This is the story that we dream of at Baddesley as we sit under the cedars and gaze at the old grey house, with its black oak gables, sleeping in the sunshine. It is all so tranquil now, the swans in the moat seem to be the only sign of life; and it seems difficult to associate this "haunt of ancient peace" with memories of strife and blood. Yet across the moat we can still discern the narrow loopholes which light the subterranean passage by which the hunted priest escaped, and in which one famous Jesuit hid for three days, knee-deep in water. Even now we can visit the strong-room at the foot of the well-staircase in the tower, where the massive door can be barricaded from within, and a pulley lifts a great stone which gives access to the moat.

Baddesley is now a house of memories, a shrine of golden deeds, forgotten by the world, but dear to the angels of God. And, sometimes, perchance, from the battlements of heaven, there look down with love and blessing upon the old house, still the abode of their King, two at least of that martyr army who stand in their white robes before the throne of God.†

We add some lines inspired by a visit to Baddesley, and the legend inscribed in its chapel.

> "TRANSIT GLORIA MUNDI
> FIDES CATHOLICA MANET."

> "Home of an ancient race—no prouder name
> Lives in our annals, gleams on any page—
> And yet more glorious for His Love who came
> To make in thee His lowly hermitage.

> "Reared in the days of chivalry, thy halls
> Rang to mailed feet, thine oaken stairs were trod
> By knights who manned thy battlemented walls,
> And in thy chapel bowed before their God.

> "Fortress of peace, deep-planted on the rock,
> And laved with living waters evermore,
> Dear refuge of the little hunted flock,
> Who hear the Shepherd's voice, His Will adore!

---

* 2 Kings, i. 23.

† For Baddesley, see the monograph by the late Rev. Henry Norris, F.S.A. (London, 1897). For Venerable Robert Grissold, see J. W. Ryland's *Records of Rowington* (Birmingham); Gillow's *Dictionary*; Challoner, whose account is taken from a MS. written by an eye-witness of the martyrdom. For John Grissold, see Morris, *The Condition of Catholics under James I.*, p. 181.

# FORGOTTEN SHRINES

" The swans gleam white upon thy lonely mere
 Girdled with golden lilies : not less white
 The souls who, spurning wealth and honours, here
 Fled from defilement, faithful to the light.

" O worn grey stones, that yet are splashed with red
 As though with martyrs' blood, a lesson high
 Ye teach, of worldly glories long since dead,
 And of the faith of Christ that cannot die."

# WASHINGLEY HALL

AMONG the least known of our English martyrs is the Venerable Robert Apreece [or Price] of Washingley Hall, Huntingdonshire. So little is known of him that in the Decree of the Sacred Congregation (Dec. 4, 1886) which proclaimed him and two hundred and sixty others, Venerable Servants of God, his Christian name is left blank, and he is entered simply as

"—— Price, Layman."

The story of his martyrdom is thus given by Bishop Challoner :

" 1644. This same year also, as Mr. Austin writes (under the name of William Birchley) in his *Christian Moderator*, Mr. Price, a Catholic gentleman, was murdered at Lincoln, in hatred of his religion. The story he relates thus : ' I remember an officer of my acquaintance, under the Earl of Manchester, told me, that at their taking of Lincoln from the Cavaliers, in the year 1644, he was an eye-witness to this tragedy. The next day after the town was taken, some of our (the Parliament) common soldiers, in cold blood, meeting with Mr. Price of Washingley in Huntingdonshire, a papist, asked him, " Art thou Price, the Papist ? " " I am," said he, " Price, the Roman Catholic " ; whereupon one of them immediately shot him dead.' "

This is all that has been known till now. Thanks, however, to the untiring exertions of a devout client of the martyr, Mr. Joseph Fabian Carter of Kimbolton, we are able to add a few more particulars. In the first place, after a search of many years, Mr. Carter has discovered the martyr's Christian name, Robert. The Apreece family, according to Burke, settled at Washingley in the early years of the sixteenth century. Their name was originally ap Rhys, and they deduce their descent from Blethin ap Maenarch, Prince of Brecknock, who was slain in 1094 by Bernard Newmarch. The family continued in Wales till Einon ap Rees came to England, and served under Henry III. and Edward I.

Robert ap Rees, great-great-grandson of Einon, son of Isaack ap Rees by Joan, sister to Sir Reginald Bray, Chancellor to Henry VII., married (*circa* 1510) Joan, daughter and heiress of John Otter of Walthamstow, and thus acquired the Washingley estates, which had been inherited by the Otters from the Wassingleys.

His descendants were buried in the church of Luton, co. Northampton, in which parish Washingley is situated.

Robert Apreece, the martyr, was the son of Jeronimus ap Rhese, who set up in Luton Church certain monuments, bearing inscriptions to

327

the memory of his ancestors, one of them recording that fact, with the date, 1633.

Blessed Edmund Campion stayed at Washingley Hall in the winter of 1580–81. The Squire at that time was Robert Apreece, whose monument may be seen at Luton. He was the grandfather of our martyr. His name is constantly found in the Recusant Rolls, and he suffered greatly for the Faith.

This good man, with twelve other gentlemen, was imprisoned at Ely for recusancy, March 25, 1594. His sons also were put in prison for aiding three priests to escape from Wisbech Castle in March 1600. Two of the priests were future martyrs, Venerable Thomas Hunt and Robert Nutter.

The monument of white and black marble, with a canopy in the Renascence style, supported by two marble columns, is on the Gospel side of the chancel, and represents Robert Apreece kneeling with folded hands, together with his father, William, and his grandfather, Robert, the first Apreece of Washingley. The three figures are of life size, presumably portraits, as the features and beards differ in each case. Father Campion's host has a very long white beard. The three figures are coloured, and wear dark Elizabethan costume, with gowns and white ruffs. They face the spectator, with hands joined in prayer, and kneel on cushions.

Below are coats of arms, with the Apreece spear-heads, and three separate framed slabs of black marble, each bearing an incised inscription in Latin, one of which we quote in memory of the old confessor who received a martyr into his house, and had as a reward the grace of being grandsire to another martyr.

PIAE MEMORIAE
ROBERTI APREECE DE WASHINGLEY ARMIGERI, ROBERTI NEPOTIS, RELIGIONE ET MORUM CANDORE INSIGNIS, NULLI UNQUAM GRAVIS, OMNIBUS ACCEPTI ET EGENIS MUNIFICENTIA CHARI : DUCTAQUE IN UXOREM JOHANNA FILIA ET COHÆREDE ROBERTI WILFORD, EX QUA FILIOS NOVEM FILIASQUE SEX SUSCEPIT, PLENUS TANDEM VIRTUTIBUS ET BONIS OPERIBUS, ANNISQUE NONAGENARIUS SANCTISSIME E VITA NONO DIE APRILIS MIGRAVIT, 1622.

which may be Englished thus :

To the Pious Memory
Of Robert Price of Washingley, Esquire, grandson of Robert, remarkable for his religion and the lustre of his character, harsh to none, popular with all, and dear to the poor through his

liberality, who, having married Johanna, daughter and co-heiress of Robert Wilford, by whom he had nine sons and six daughters, at length, full of virtues and good works, and in years a nonagenarian, departed this life in the odour of sanctity, 1622.

Our martyr must have known this good old grandfather, whose death preceded his by only twenty-two years. He himself married into an illustrious house, for he espoused Marie, the daughter of the renowned Cavalier, Sir Henry Bedingfield, of Oxburgh, co. Norfolk. Marie was born in 1621, being Sir Henry's seventh child by Elizabeth, daughter of Peter Hoghton of Hoghton Tower in Lancashire.* Sir Henry Bedingfield, by the testimony of his grandson, the second Baronet, was "tall and finely shaped and a handsome man, a great sportsman and kept a great house."

His portrait shows that this account of his appearance was not coloured by the partiality of a relative, and his monument, in the Bedingfield chantry in Oxborough Church, declares his services to the royal cause.

"The 17th Knight of ye Family eminent for his Loyaltie to his Prince and Service of his Countrey. In the Time of the Rebellion he was kept three years Prisoner in ye Tower, and great Part of his Estate sold by ye Rebells, the rest sequestered during his Life . . . he dyed November 22 An° Dni 1657, Aet. 70 and 6 months."

The Bedingfields lost more than £45,000 by their devotion to the King. Not less loyal was Robert Apreece of Washingley. He was a Colonel in the loyalist ranks, and helped, in 1644, to defend Lincoln against the rebels.

The British Museum Library contains a very rare pamphlet, *A true Relation of the Taking of the City, Minster, and Castle of Lincoln—by the Right Honourable the Earl of Manchester on Monday the sixth of this instant May together with a list of the names of the Commanders. London, printed by R. Cotes for Job Bellamy*, 1644.† This shows us that the martyrdom took place on Tuesday, May 7, 1644.

In the list of prisoners we find the names of "Lieutenant-Colonel Benefield" and "Ensign James Aprice." The former was Thomas Bedingfield, our martyr's brother-in-law. In a petition to King Charles II. Colonel Bedingfield says:

* See C.R.S. *Miscellanea*, VI. Bedingfield Papers, pp. 2, 36, 228, &c.

† It is bound up in a Collection of Pamphlets, 4to, bound in sprinkled leather (sheepskin), with red edges. Lettered, *Gift of G. III.* They are known as "The King's Pamphlets," or the Thomason Tracts.

# FORGOTTEN SHRINES

"That your petitioner upon the advancing of your Royall Father's Standard, Did at his oune charge raise a Regiment of foot, and a troop of Horse for his service, and maintained them untill at the Storme of Lincolne hee was sorely wounded and taken Prisoner, and for two yeares suffered loathsome Imprisonment in the Common Gaole and was at lengthe Banished, his Father's whole estate being sold by the Usurped Power, soe as his Father and hee have been Damnified above three score thousand pounds." *

Ensign James Aprice was probably a younger brother, certainly a near kinsman, of our martyr. His own name does not appear in the list of prisoners.

The pamphlet gives a striking account of the assault, which took place about three o'clock on the Monday morning. Six pieces of ordnance being fired off as a signal, "within less than a quarter of an houre we got up to their workes, which the Foot with much gallantness performed, receiving all their shot which they poured out like haile, the Enemy being all ready to receive our charge, and expecting us when we came. Our Foot never left running till they came to the top of the Hill, which would have been enough to tier a Horse, being under their workes we set up the scaling ladders, which they seeing left their firing and threw mighty stones upon us over their workes by which we received more hurt than by all their shot; but all would not daunt our men, but up to the top of the ladders they got, which proved too short, most of them, to reach the top of their wals and workes, they being most of them as high as *London* Wal; but yet they shifted to get up, which the Enemy perceiving, they had no spirit left in them, but betooke themselves to their heels, and our men over their works shouting, and following as fast after them; but they not knowing whether to runne, cryed out for quarter, saying they were poor Array men; we slew about fifty of them, about twenty of them were slaine in the Castle yard, where they made the most resistance. We lost not more than eight men in the storming of it; whereof one a Captaine, Captaine *Oglesby*, another Lieutenant *Saunders*. We took of them as follows, a List of those Names I have here sent you, both of the officers and common soulders, as I see them taken, which is with the least, there being more found since in corners, whose names were not inserted into this list of Prisoners."

Our martyr must have been concealed at the first storming of the city, "when all the Pillage of the upper Town was given to the souldiers," since he was not murdered till the next day. The pamphlet does not mention him.

* There is a beautiful portrait of Colonel Thomas Bedingfield at Oxburgh. It is reproduced in the C.R.S. volume already referred to.

330

He left one little son Robert, then about nine years old. The child was brought up a Protestant by guardians appointed by the State. His mother was married again, to one Humphrey Orme. The Apreece family in the male line became extinct in 1842, at the death of Sir Thomas George Apreece, second Baronet, born August 17, 1791; died in 1842, aged fifty-one. He left all his property to St. George's Hospital. The baronetcy was created July 12, 1782. The arms of the

Washingley Hall

family are those of their ancestors, the Princes of Brecknock: *sable, three spears heads argent guttée de sang.* The crest is a spear's head, as in the arms.

The motto is a good one for a martyr:

*Labora ut in æternum vivas.** 

"Washingley Hall is still standing," writes Mr. Carter, "and to all appearance little altered since the martyr dwelt there. The spot is a very secluded one, situated about six miles from Oundle, where St. Wilfrid died, and some thirteen miles from Kimbolton Castle, the residence of the Manchester family. Edward, second Earl of Manchester, at whose men's hands our martyr met his death, was therefore his neighbour, and the men who slew him were also his neighbours, and recognised him at sight; and so it seems to me the martyrdom is unique. He was slain by his neighbours."

Washingley some years ago was in decay, almost a ruin; but since

* "Labour that thou mayest live for ever." Burke, *Peerage and Baronetage*, 1841.

then the place has been thoroughly restored, and it is now again tenanted.
The house is of brick and stone, and very secluded. There are fine yews
in the park, and a sheet of water. Year by year in the month of May
a family of faithful Catholics make a pilgrimage from Kimbolton to
Washingley to beg the martyr's intercession for the conversion of their
common country. Father and mother, brothers and sisters, they kneel
in the fields near the Hall and recite the Rosary, and rise to sing the
martyrs' hymn:

> "O Thou, of all Thy warriors, Lord,
> Thyself the crown and sure reward!
> Set us from sinful fetters free
> Who sing Thy martyr's victory."

Thus in a country where Catholics are few indeed, the memory of
this almost unknown martyr is kept green by faithful hearts.

# PEMBRIDGE CASTLE

THIS "forgotten shrine" yields to none in interest and in pathos. There is surely no figure, among all the heroic and devoted priests who fill the pages of England's martyrology, more attractive and delightful than that of old Father John Kemble, whose simple homely life and character endear him to us with a special charm.

The old man's dismembered body rests in the peaceful churchyard of Welsh Newton, about three miles away, but his spirit still seems to live

PEMBRIDGE CASTLE

at Pembridge Castle, and to welcome the rare pilgrim who finds his way to his old home.

The place is romantic and beautiful in the extreme. Webb, in his *Memorials of the Civil War in Herefordshire*,\* has the following description of it :

"The small Castle of Pembridge stands in the parish of Welsh Newton, about five miles from Monmouth, whence the road to it lies through the narrow pass of the Buckholt, remarkable for its wild romantic scenery, steep rocky banks, tall woods, and rapidly descending

\* London, 1879, ii. p. 114.

rill. After an ascent of more than three miles, a turning to the left, described in an ancient map, and probably not without reason, as 'the way to Chester,' passes by the spot in question. The form of the building is square, its foundation resting upon a rock, from which the stone for constructing it was apparently raised. It presents a fosse and gateway, with vestiges of a drawbridge and portcullis, and has four towers at the angles of its walls ; that at the north-east is in the form of a quadrant, its angle impinging upon the point at which the curtains meet.

"Pembridge Castle commands one of those noble prospects that an omnipotent hand has in so many instances spread out in situations little seen and known. Over a beautiful tract where the Monnow winds in the deep green vale below, the eye leaps, as it were, at once to the distant mountains. From a wide hemisphere including the Clee, Malvern, and Hatrel hills, the Blorenge, Graig and Garway, and the heights above Abergavenny, each beacon that blazed in the days of border warfare might have been visible here. The knightly race of the Pembridges were more than merely famous in the local annals of this county. Sir Philip, the 52nd Knight of the Garter, deemed worthy of that privilege by one of the most splendid of our kings, as a companion of his victories in France, lies entombed in the Cathedral of Hereford. Their castle passed in after times to the Pyes of the Mynd. Its resident possessor in 1644, to whom the latter had sold it, was George Kemble, a gentleman, among the branches of whose stock it is believed may be found the Kembles and Siddons of later days."

One greater than the famous actors, however, is still remembered at Pembridge Castle.

John Kemble was born at Rhydycar Farm, in the parish of St. Weonard's, Herefordshire, in 1599. He studied at Douay, and was ordained priest there February 23, 1625, and on June 4 following was sent to begin his long apostolate in England.

There were few more Catholic parts of England than the Welsh Marches at this period. The people of Hereford and Monmouth shires had never taken kindly to the new religion. Great nobles, like the Marquis of Worcester at Raglan Castle, and almost all the landowners—Vaughans, Blounts, Wigmores, Pritchards, Bodenhams, Moningtons, Beringtons, and many others—were faithful to the old Church, and protected the clergy who ministered to them. The Protestant Bishop Bennet wrote to Lord Salisbury in June 1605, of the numbers and " desperate courses " of the " rude and barbarous people." Three days before he had sent an armed party " unto the Darren and other places near adjoining to make search and apprehend Jesuits and Priests . . .

334

INTERIOR OF THE COURT, PEMBRIDGE CASTLE

THE LARGE WINDOW ON THE FIRST FLOOR IS THAT OF FATHER KEMBLE'S ROOM

and did make diligent search, all that night and day following, from village to village, from house to house about 30 miles compass, near the confines of Monmouthshire, where they found altars, images, books of superstition, relics of idolatry, but left desolate of men and women." He adds despairingly : " If we go out with few, we shall be beaten home ; if we levy strength, we are descried and they all are fled to the woods, and there they will lurk until the assizes be past."

At this time Father Kemble was only a little boy of six years old. Five years later his friend and spiritual Father, the Venerable Roger Cadwallader, suffered a cruel martyrdom at Leominster (August 27, 1610).

He knew then what he might expect when he, in his turn, came to take up his work among his own people, and yet for many a long year he was left in peace. This is not the place to recount his life; indeed, for the most part it was uneventful. He lived with his nephew, Captain Richard Kemble, at Pembridge Castle, and from that retreat made his missionary journeys over the wild and beautiful country all around.

Pembridge Castle is one of those old border castles, once of great strength and importance, but long since turned from a warrior's fortress into an abode of peaceful farmers. Three of the old round towers which guarded the inner ward still exist, as well as the old gateway in which the portcullis once hung. The moat still surrounds the walls, but only part of it is now filled with water. Within the enclosure of mediæval walls and towers a sixteenth-century house shelters the modern occupants as it sheltered the Kembles before them. The pilgrim is kindly welcomed by the farmer and his family, who, though they do not share his faith, are proud of Father Kemble and anxious to tell all they know of him.

Upstairs the martyr's room is shown, a large square room with windows looking on to the Castle court. Just outside this room is the old seat on the stairs, of which we give an illustration. It is known as " Father Kemble's seat," and is a curious relic of the old man, who was seventy-nine years old when he was arrested here at Pembridge and carried off to prison. No doubt in his old age he found the stairs a difficulty, and was glad to rest here on his ascent. Above, at the top of the house, is the old chapel. Here he celebrated Holy Mass on the altar now preserved in the Catholic church at Monmouth.*

Other glorious martyrs must often have come to Pembridge to visit

* This and his other relics there are fully described in the section on the " Relics and Memorials of the Martyrs."

336

the old man, especially Father David Lewis (or Baker), S.J., who had found a shelter at Raglan Castle. Not far distant was the Cwm (or Coombe) where the Jesuits founded an important college in 1662, which they held under the Marquis of Worcester. There were two houses, the Lower and Upper Cwm, " situated at the bottom of a thickly wooded and rocky hill, with several hollow places in the rocks wherein men may conceal themselves, and there is a very private passage from the houses into the wood."*

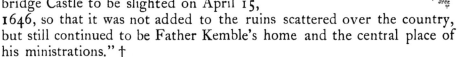

Here several future martyrs stayed, most, if not all, of whom must have known Father Kemble well.

When the Civil War broke out, the Catholics were all on the King's side. Monmouth Castle had succumbed to treachery, when Raglan fell on Wednesday, August 19, 1646. Raglan was the last castle to hold out for Charles I., and they say that when it fell at last, forty priests were found within its walls. Loyalty and Faith went hand in hand then as always.

" Colonel Birch had ordered Pembridge Castle to be slighted on April 15,

*Father Kemble's Seat Pembridge Castle*

1646, so that it was not added to the ruins scattered over the country, but still continued to be Father Kemble's home and the central place of his ministrations." †

In 1650, a year after the death of George Kemble, the martyr's elder brother, the estates were sequestrated for the Recusancy of Anne Kemble, his widow. But they were recovered from the clutches of the Parliamentary Commissioners, and Pembridge still remained to the family.

Captain Richard Kemble, the martyr's nephew, who succeeded, was Captain-Lieutenant to Lord Talbot at the Battle of Worcester, and did great service to the royal cause; for when Charles II. was nearly captured through his horse being killed, Captain Kemble gave him his horse, and rallying the troops with the aid of Sir James Hamilton, charged the enemy gallantly in Sudbury Street and High Street. Both Captain Kemble and Sir James were desperately wounded in the action, but succeeded in effecting his Majesty's safety and escape, so that for the

* Foley, *Records, S.J.*, vol. ii. p. 230.
† *Father John Kemble*, by R. Raikes Bromage, M.A. (London, 1902). I owe much to this excellent pamphlet.

FORGOTTEN SHRINES

future the Kembles changed their crest of a wolf's head on a coronet to that of a horse's head.

The Catholics naturally expected to receive better treatment when Charles II. came to the throne, as he was the son of a Catholic mother, had married a Catholic wife, and could vividly remember the loyalty of his Catholic subjects during the whole of the Civil War, and, besides, owed his life to their protection. At the Restoration, therefore, Captain Richard Kemble tried to regain the lands that had been taken from him, but Charles replied that it was impossible, and offered him a knighthood, which Kemble refused, saying : " Plain Richard Kemble I was, and plain Richard Kemble I will remain." His three sons were George, Richard, and Roger, and from these the different branches of the family are sprung.*

When the dreadful frenzy roused by Titus Oates and his pretended Popish plot seized the whole country—a mad fury of which some results have lasted to our own day—priests were arrested everywhere. Not the most proved and devoted loyalty, not the most obvious and striking innocence, could save them then.

The Cwm was sacked, of course, and though the Fathers had escaped with most of their altar furniture and vestments, the searchers found the altar-stone and a few sacred objects hidden in the woods. The records of the College were also discovered, together with many books, some of which are still to be seen in the Cathedral Library at Hereford. *Res clamat domino* is a principle that does not seem to be understood there.

The Bishop of Hereford at this time was Dr. Herbert Croft, who had himself been educated at Douay, where his father, Sir Herbert Croft, had in his old age joined the English Benedictines. Yet he was not a whit behind his Episcopal brethren in hunting down the unhappy priests in his diocese.

On December 7, 1678, he was ordered by the Council to search for priests, and he put the matter in the hands of Captain Scudamore of Kentchurch, who hunted down Father David Lewis, whom he sent to Monmouth Gaol, and then proceeded to Pembridge Castle to arrest Father Kemble.

The old man, being greatly beloved in the district, was urged to hide or escape, but refused, saying that as he had but few years to live, it would be an advantage to him to suffer for his religion. So when Scudamore's men came thundering at the gates of the old Castle, the aged priest calmly gave himself up.

He was carried off through the snow to Kentchurch Court, the fine old house of the Scudamores, which still exists in good preservation, and

* R. Raikes Bromage, *op. cit.* p. 13.

still belongs to the family. Here he was among friends, for Mrs. Scudamore and her children were Catholics, and were devoted to the old man. It must have been a bitter grief to them to see him thus made prisoner by their own nearest relative. Kentchurch Court is only six miles from Pembridge Castle.

Next day he was carried off to Hereford Gaol, a fifteen miles' journey.*

"The Governor of the Gaol evidently had a great respect for his prisoner and took a pen-and-ink sketch of him, which still exists. His devoted relatives and friends also determined to have a good picture of the martyr, and procured the services of one of the best artists of the time. This beautiful oil-painting is now in the keeping of Mrs. Clarkson of Highgate, who is one of the Catholic descendants of the family." †

Father Kemble, while patiently awaiting his crown, devoted himself to ministering to and encouraging the crowds of the faithful who flocked to the prison. Among them were Captain Scudamore's children, who often came to visit their old friend. He received them with special kindness, and treated them to the dainties which other friends had sent him. When asked why he so kindly petted his captor's children, he answered, "Because their father is the best friend I have in the world."

On April 23, 1679, the House of Lords ordered that the old priest should be brought up to London. On his journey to London and back he suffered terrible agony ("more than a martyrdom," Challoner says), from extreme old age and from a disease which would not permit him to ride except sideways. It is said that he was strapped like a pack to his horse on the way there, and that he was allowed to walk most of the journey back.

Nothing came of this cruel proceeding, for neither Oates nor Bedloe ventured to implicate him in the fictitious plot. In Newgate prison he met a crowd of confessors, for the gaols were full to overflowing with the victims of these infamous apostates. Probably he had the holy Jesuit, Father David Lewis, as his companion to and from London. This, at least, must have been a comfort to him.‡

At the Summer Assizes held in the old Town Hall of Hereford, before Chief Justice Scroggs, our martyr was indicted for saying Mass at Pembridge Castle, and was, of course, condemned.

No shadow of evidence connected him with any treason, and it seemed incredible that the cruel sentence could be carried out. Popular sympathy

---

* The story of Father Kemble is told in Archdeacon Coxe's *Monmouthshire*, and by Webbe, *Memorials of the Civil War*, vol. ii. p. 118.

† R. Raikes Bromage, *op. cit.* p. 26–27.

‡ From an excellent article on "Herefordshire Martyrs," by the Right Rev. Prior Ildefonsus Cummins, O.S.B. *Ampleforth Journal*, vol. x.

in Hereford went out to the innocent old man, whose blameless life and kindly disposition endeared him to all that knew him. Efforts were made to prevent the judicial murder, but the roused passions of the puritan mob demanded victims, and Father Kemble was left to his doom. . . . An anecdote which has a very modern sound will touch a sympathetic chord in many breasts. Father Kemble loved his pipe ! He is probably the only or the earliest Venerable Servant of God who indulged in the habit of smoking. Lovers of tobacco are badly in want of a patron saint : they may find one some day in the holy missioner who, tramping footsore among his scattered flock, or resting peacefully by some friendly fireside, must have often found solace in his pipe. During his last days in prison he and the governor of the gaol used to smoke their pipes together ; and when the hour of his death was announced and they came to carry him to execution, he requested time to finish his prayers, and then to be allowed one last pipe of tobacco. The request was readily granted, the Under-Sheriff (Mr. Humphrey Digges) smoking another. When the blessed martyr had finished his prayers and his pipe, he took a cup of sack, and said he was ready to go. The incident gave rise to a local custom, once common, of calling the parting smoke "a Kemble pipe." *

In the evening of August 22, 1679, the cruel sentence was executed. He was strapped to a hurdle and dragged out to the public race-course, called Wigmarsh, or Widemarsh, Common, just outside the city. The place of execution is traditionally handed down as near the trees at the north-west corner, where the Leominster road leaves the Common.

He met his fate with fortitude and dignity. His last words to the crowd were taken down, and were subsequently printed. They were like himself, simple, straightforward, and Christian :

"It will be expected I say something, but as I am an old man it cannot be much, not having any concern in the plot, neither, indeed, believing there is any : Oates and Bedloe not being able to charge me with anything when I was brought up to London, though they were with me, makes it evident that I dye only for professing the old Roman Catholick Religion, which was the Religion that first made this Kingdom Christian ; and who-ever intends to be saved must dye in that Religion. I beg of all that either by thought, word, or deed I have offended, to forgive me, for I do heartily forgive all those that have been instrumental or desirous of my death."

"Honest Anthony, my friend Anthony," he said to the hangman,

* In Hawkins's edition of Izaak Walton's *Compleat Angler* is a very curious account, in a note, of Father Kemble's last pipe. The writer confuses the martyr (who was a contemporary of Walton's) with the Protestants who suffered under Queen Mary Tudor !

THE SERMON AT THE PILGRIMAGE TO FATHER
KEMBLE'S GRAVE, 1909
*The martyr's grave is marked by flowers. The slab beside it covers the
grave of Catharine Scudamore, who was miraculously cured while
praying at the martyr's tomb. Photo by* G. C. Miers

*To face page* 340

"be not afraid ; do thy office ; I forgive thee with all my heart. Thou wilt do me a greater kindness than discourtesy."

And so the old man, after some quiet time spent in prayer, sweetly and patiently met his death. His last words were those of our Blessed Lord—*In manus tuas, Domine, commendo spiritum meum.* And thus he went to meet the Lord he loved.

The dismembered body of the martyr was buried in Welsh Newton churchyard by his nephew, Captain Kemble, who erected the flat stone over it with the inscription : " J. K., who dyed Augt. 22nd, 1679," and a large cross outlined on the full length of the stone. It seems certain that the holy body still rests in this humble grave. The late Rev. Thomas Abbot, for fifty years Catholic Rector of Monmouth, wrote as follows to the author :

" I attended an aged Catholic named Watkins of Slangrove Common, who was born in 1752, and used to go to Mass at Pembridge Castle, and visit the tomb on his way, and he never heard any talk of the body having been removed. I also attended another of the name of Hull who had looked after the tomb, and had repaired it, when broken, with an iron clamp ; and after his death, for about fifty years, I have looked after the tomb and kept it in repair. It has been, and is, visited annually. I attended an old woman, a Mrs. Stead, who told me she remembered Mrs. Siddons (*née* Kemble) at Monmouth with her company of play-actors, in 1805. She went to visit the tomb with her brother, and said she claimed to be descended from the Kemble family, and was more proud of the holy Father Kemble than if she had been descended from Royalty. She composed a poem on her visit to the tomb. A recent version of these verses was published with some three or four stanzas added to Mrs. Siddons' composition."

Welsh Newton is situated on the Hereford Road, three miles from Monmouth and about the same distance from Pembridge Castle. The church is a tiny structure dating from Norman times, though most of its walls above the foundations now belong to the Early English period. It has a dwarf spire of stone. The interesting stone rood-screen of three arches still remains, and beneath it, at the entrance to the chancel, lies an old altar-stone. The martyr's tomb is bright with flowers, and is surrounded by the resting-places of old-time Catholics, who longed when living for the assurance that their bodies after death should be laid to rest close to the relics of the old Douay priest. Father Kemble's tomb has been cleansed a little of late, and the stonework beneath the slab has been repointed, but all the original features remain intact. It is close to the churchyard cross. Here, year by year, a devout band of pilgrims comes in procession to keep the martyr's anniversary and invoke his intercession. For two hundred years and more this pilgrimage has continued, and the strange sight may then be seen of Catholics kneeling in a Protestant churchyard, reciting the Rosary and other prayers. A sermon is often preached from the steps of the churchyard cross (in 1909 the present writer had the honour of preaching it), which overshadows the martyr's grave.

Beside his tomb is a slab which covers the body of Catharine Scudamore, a near relative of the martyr's captor, who recovered her hearing as she prayed at the grave on the occasion of one of these pilgrimages. This miracle was testified to by Bishop Matthew Pritchard, O.S.F., Vicar-Apostolic of the Western District, who " with three or four of the family of Perthyre " (*i.e.*, of the Franciscan Community there), was present on the occasion, as he wrote to Bishop Challoner. The daughter of Captain Scudamore had previously been cured of a malignant sore throat by putting to her neck the cord with which the martyr had been hanged.

The other relics of Father Kemble are described elsewhere. Father Abbot informed me that the chalice was stolen at the time of the martyr's apprehension, but the altar, and the small missal, bearing the date 1623, with some of his handwriting in it, remained at Pembridge Castle till 1839, and were used by his predecessors, at the eight Indulgence times, for the convenience of the neighbouring Catholics, till the Townley family of Burnley sold the old castle and estates to a Welsh ironmaster. Father Abbot then removed the precious relics to Monmouth.*

The reredos which now surmounts the altar was made by Father Abbot out of an old oak bedstead from Perthyre† on which Bishop Matthew Pritchard died in 1750.

Let us close this account of the venerable martyr with the words of his old biographer :

" The Protestants that were spectators of the exit acknowledged that they never saw one die so like a gentleman, and so like a Christian."

* Webbe has a note as follows :

"An annual midnight Mass is still celebrated at the grave of the Rev. John Kemble (!) It has been reported that Captain Scudamore committed suicide. . . . When Morgan, the last Roman Catholic tenant of Pembridge Castle, left the farm, he took with him the key of the chapel, to be delivered to none but a priest. The altar and candlesticks are still at Scatterford near Coleford. Many Herefordshire houses were provided with a fish-pond : there were several at the Castle which were not drained till the present century (*Memorials of the Civil War in Herefordshire*, vol. ii. p. 428).

† Perthyre is about one and a half miles from Welsh Newton, and three from Pembridge Castle. In 1758, we find that a Franciscan from Perthyre said Mass one Sunday in the month at Pembridge Castle. (Thaddeus, *The Franciscans in England*, London 1898, p. 175).

342

THE ALTAR, CHALICE, MISSAL, AND MISSAL-STAND
OF THE V. JOHN KEMBLE
*Now preserved in the Catholic Church, Monmouth*                    *To face page* 342

# THE CHAPEL OF ST. AMAND AND ST. JOHN BAPTIST AT EAST HENDRED

THIS chapel, which, like that of Stonor in the adjoining county, has never been alienated to Protestant uses, stands in the Manor of Arches at East Hendred, in Berkshire.

East Hendred is one of those charming old-world villages which lie in the neighbourhood of Wantage, at the foot of the Downs.

" With its Manor House in the heart of the village, elms that have grown to an extraordinary stateliness in that sheltered nook, streets that have ancient names, the virgate of land that is still called Paternoster,* grass terraces testifying to the linen industry of days gone by, its half-ruined wayside chapel of the Carthusians, its grand Anglican church, an ' Elizabethan farm-house ' (once doubtless occupied by Benedictine monks and farmers), and a modern Roman Catholic chapel in pure and severe Gothic, East Hendred is a village of no ordinary attraction to the mere passer by. For its history, too, East Hendred is well worthy of a monograph. . . . The private chapel, which is the glory of the house, has stood there since the thirteenth century at least. There it stands still, having an entrance for the congregation from the grounds, and a private entrance from the squire's library, with the sacred lamp burning in front of the altar, as it has continued to burn for more than six hundred years. There, every day, is held such office of prayer and praise as the Roman Catholic Church prescribes, and there the considerable Roman Catholic population of East Hendred attends with a regularity that might put professing Protestants to shame. A very plain building is this, with walls of enormous thickness, a gallery for the Eyston family, and a few fragments of ancient glass carefully preserved, besides some stone figures in the vestry. Still, on him who shall enjoy the rare privilege of entering it, even though he should be of another form of faith, the simple dignity of the edifice must needs impress a feeling of reverence deeper than comes from presence within many a more majestic church. Six hundred years at the least—that is a long time ; for six hundred years and more, through good report and evil report, in the days when Rome was all-powerful and persecuting, in the time of her humiliation and of her persecution ; when the Squire of Hendred was the unquestioned head, so far as layman might be, of a Roman Catholic community ; when the Squire of Hendred must flee to remote Catmore for safety and the consolations of his religion ; and now

---

* Because the tenant held it on the terms of saying, so many times a day, a Paternoster for the souls of the King's ancestors. Another instance is at Pusey in the same county.

in happier times of toleration, this little chapel has stood, inviolate, to be the centre for a religious life of varying intensity and volume. It has never, say the Eystons, I am told, been 'desecrated,' that is to say, no Protestant service has ever been held in it; and there are those who resent the word; but surely to know all is to pardon all, and Eystons, who have grown to manhood in the atmosphere of this chapel, who have heard how their forefathers suffered for their Faith, may well be pardoned for using such a word in such a connection, because it is so very easy to understand their attitude. . . .

"Surely, then, it must be a small mind—for that matter, there is no lack of such—that fails to perceive something of dignity and of pathos in this survival of a Roman Catholic family, and of no inconsiderable Roman Catholic community of good citizens, in the very heart of rural England; and there will be many to whom it will be joy to learn that the little and ruined chapel [of the Carthusians] in the middle of the village has been acquired by Mr. Eyston, and will be treated with due reverence."

This long extract from a charming modern book * will, we hope, be forgiven us, in consideration of the extraordinary interest of the subject. If not entirely accurate in every detail, it gives a sympathetic and touching picture of a place that to Catholics is a very holy of holies.

The Eyston family have been settled at East Hendred since the fifteenth century, but they derive their title by marriage from the ancient Lords of the place, the de Turbervilles, who owned the Manor in the thirteenth century, if not earlier.

On May 10, 1256, Sir John de Turberville, Knight, obtained permission from Pope Alexander IV. to build a chapel on his estate at East Hendred, provided the Bishop of Salisbury (then Giles de Bridport) should consider it expedient.†

The Chapel must have been built very soon after, as it had been in existence some time previous to 1291, when it was entered in the *Taxatio Ecclesiastica* of Pope Nicholas IV. Two years later Bishop Nicholas Longspée of Sarum granted his consent to annexing the tithes of the Manor of East Hendred (afterwards known as the Manor of Arches), for the use of the Chapel and the support of the Chaplain.

The Chapel is usually known as the Chantry of St. Amand (or St.

---

* *Highways and Byways in Berkshire*, by James Edmund Vincent (London, 1906), pp. 217–21.

† The Pope's Bull is copied on the margin of the Register of Bishop Hallam (1408–1417), f. 33. A dispute as to the tithes having arisen in this Bishop's time between the Chaplain and the Rector of the Parish, Bishop Hallam investigated the origin and foundation of the Chapel.

HENDRED HOUSE IN 1661

*Drawn by Joseph Pike from an old print*

Amen), but sometimes as the Chantry of St. John Baptist. St. Amand is nowadays little known in England, but is very popular in Belgium. He was a Benedictine monk, who founded a famous Abbey which still bears his name, near Tournai, where he died, A.D. 675. He is known as the Apostle of Flanders, and the chief field of his missionary labours was the city of Ghent. Here he founded two abbeys long famous in Belgium: St. Bavon, which subsequently became the Cathedral, and St. Pierre de Mont-Blandin. In 649 he was created Bishop of Maestricht, but resigned his see a few years later in favour of St. Remaclus. The Sarum Breviary kept his feast on February 6, together with St. Vedast.

It is strange that St. John Baptist should be put second to St. Amand, in the dedication of this Chapel.

From the Turbervilles the manor passed to the Arches family at the end of the thirteenth century, by the marriage of Amice, daughter of Sir Richard de Turberville, to William de Arches. It then became known as the Manor of Arches. Ralph de Arches of "Esthenrette" (who died between 1418 and 1422) left an heiress, Maud, who married John Stowe of Burford, co. Oxon, Esquire; he died 1436–7, leaving also an heiress, Isabel, who married John Eyston, ancestor of the Eystons of the present day. Thus the Eystons are descended, in the female line, from the original builder of the Chapel. In the reign of Edward VI. the glebe and tithe of the Chapel were seized by the Crown, and after a time annexed to the King's Manor of East Greenwich; subsequently they passed through various hands, and have been permanently alienated from the service of the Church. A house called St. Amand's still stands on the old glebe-land, and proclaims by its name its real and lawful possessor. The Chapel, however, was never seized, although, from the reign of Edward VI., it remained for a long period desolate and unused, and in process of time was even converted into a wood-house.

We have the following account of it from a MS. of Mr. Charles Eyston (who died November 5, 1721). He wrote these notes in 1718; they are still preserved in the family.*

"... The Chappell before it was repaired had a broaken Pavement w^ch by the remainder one might see were a sort of Dutch Tyle. Some part of the Altar was left till then also standing, but it was onely of small moultering stones, on which the Reall altar stone stood, and not above a foot and an halfe high, so this remainder being lookt upon to bee worne out and uselesse, it was thought necessary to make the altar quite

* Mr. Eyston was a great friend of the eminent antiquary, Thomas Hearne of Oxford.

anew of wood and to pave it quite anew; for I saw some of the Stones w<sup>ch</sup> belonged to the Altar and some of the Pavements when handled moulter to Earth and Sand.

"There was a Partition in the Chappell before it was repaired, the bottom of it was oaken wainscot, and the Topp was in ye same nature as the windowes now are in the Chappell Chamber."

Mr. Eyston also gives a most interesting account of the restoration of the Chapel to Catholic worship in the reign of James II. We give it in his own words, for he was an eye-witness of the events which he chronicles. It is indeed touching to think of these brave Catholics, once they were granted a moment's breathing-space from cruel persecution, proceeding with joy and jubilation once more to consecrate to God the beloved Chapel in which their fathers had worshipped. Strange, too, it is to read of a Catholic Dean of Christ Church being present at the unique ceremony, when the sons of St. Francis, so many of whose brethren had been martyred during that very century, met once more in peace to hallow the house of God and St. Amen. Stranger yet to think of the quiet courage with which, even after the usurpation of the Prince of Orange had dashed Catholic hopes, the Eystons met day by day within those hallowed walls to offer the sacrifice of peace.

"My father, George Eyston, Esquire, began the Repaire of this Chappell on Wednesday in Easter weeke in ye yeare 1687, w<sup>ch</sup> happened to bee that yeare on the 30th of March. And it was completely finisht on the 17 of September yt yeare, one Andrew Bartlet painted and guilded it and had 42 pounds for doeing it as appeares yet by his Bill and acquittance w<sup>ch</sup> are to be found amongst the Papers which belong to the Chappell.

"Saturday, September 24, 1687, Father Pacificus, alias Philip Price (who then lived in the Family) a Franciscan Fryer, and one who after-wards was twice Provincial of his order, blessed the altar stone, being assisted by Father Francis, alias Wm. Hardwick, Father John Baptist, alias Wm. Weston, two of the same order. After that was done, vespers were said with as much solemnity as the Place would allow. The day following, being Sunday the 25th of September, there were seaven Priests who said Mass in it. The Priests were Mr. Price who said the first, Mr. Prosser and Mr. Evans two clergy Priests, Mr. Francis Hildesley, Soc. Jesu, Mr. Anthony alias Francis Young, Mr. Weston above named and Mr. Hardwick, the 3 last were Franciscan Fryers.

"The company who were here at the opening of the Chappell were Sir Henry More of Fawley and his Family, Sir John Courson and his first Lady, Mr. John Massey actually then Deane of Christ Church in Oxon, Mr. Robert Charnock, and one Mr. John Augustin Bernard, the former Fellow of Maudeline College, and the latter Fellow of Brazen-nose College in Oxford, Mr. Perkines of Ufton, Mr. Perkines of Been-ham, Mr. Hildesley of little Stoake and his brother Martin, Mr. Francis Hide Junior of Pangboan, Father to the present Mr. Hide, and some other Catholick gentlemen came hither for the service in the morning. But onely Sir John Curson and his Lady, and my uncle Bar. Winchcomb and his first wife were at the Consecration of the Altar Stone the day before.

" And the yeare following there were meanes found to have both the altar and the Chappell privileged : as may be seene by the Bulls w^{ch} are amongst the writings w^{ch} relate to the Chappell.

" From the time of its being opened till the Prince of Orange came in, and invaded the Nation, the Chappell was open to all Commers and goers. The Blessed Sacrament constantly kept w^{th} a Lamp burneing, Mass dayly celebrated in it. But when he and his army past over the Golden Myle,* some loose Fellowes (whether by orders or not I cannot tell) came hyther, went into the Chappell, pretended to mock the Priest by supping out of the Chalice, w^{ch} they would have taken away had it been silver, as they themselves afterwards gave out. However, haveing torne doune the JESUS MARIA from the altar, w^{ch} holy names were painted upon Pannels on the same Frames, where the JESUS MARIA are now wrought in Bugles, they retired, takeing an old suite of Church Stuffe with them to Oxford, where they drest up a mawkin with it and set it up there on the Topp of a Bon-Fyre.

" This happened on Monday December the 11th, 1688, and this is all the mischief they then did, besides breakeing the Lamp and carrying away the Sanctus Bell. Mass from that day ceast there till Monday June 24th, 1689, when Mr. Weston above mentioned by accident fortuned to bee here, and then he sayd Mass in it againe, and from that time till now i.e. August, 1718 wee have generally used it."

The chapel remained in this condition till the end of 1808, when some alterations were made by Basil Eyston, Esq., and stained glass was put into some of the windows.

In 1845 the Chapel, being found too small for the congregation attending it, was lengthened, an addition of about ten feet taken from the Manor House being thrown into it at the west end.

More extensive alterations were made in 1862, under the direction of Mr. C. A. Buckler, who left the Chapel in the state in which we now see it.

A new roof was made, and a new buttress on the south side added. The decorated east window and the two lancets, north and south, were

* The most eastern of the three roads in the parish which leads to the Downs.

THE CHAPEL OF ST. AMAND, EAST HENDRED

*Photo by the author*

*To face page* 348

left intact, but a new decorated window was added on the south side, and two new square-headed windows above it, in place of the former windows "which corresponded badly with the original architecture of the chapel." A small trefoil window was opened at the east end just below the roof. A new stone altar was erected, with oak reredos.

A recess was made in the north wall of the sanctuary in which an iron safe was placed for the safe-keeping of the Blessed Sacrament. This recess was fitted with outer door of oak and canopy of stonework, and thus forms a "Sacrament-house" such as are often met with in Germany and Belgium. It is rare to find one in England, though they exist in the old churches of Scotland. In the east window are figures by Hardman of St. Amand and St. John the Baptist. The most remarkable piece of stained glass is, however, in the north lancet. This represents the monogram H.F. and crozier of the Blessed Hugh Cook (or Faringdon), last Abbot of Reading, martyred by Henry VIII. The Abbots of Reading held lands at East Hendred, and there was a monastic grange or cell in the village.

The chapel was reopened and the new altar consecrated by Bishop Grant, of Southwark, August 30, 1862.

Besides the virgin chapel of "St. Amen," there are other precious relics at East Hendred. The Eystons are descendants of Blessed Thomas More, and have the joy of possessing relics of him, including a portrait, "a Holbein which there seems to be no reason to doubt," a copy of the great family group of which the original sketch is preserved at Basle, "and more than one rare print of the one Roman Catholic martyr to conscience who has an unquestioned place in the heart of every Englishman. Very curiously interesting it is to note in these portraits the difference between the expression of More's face in youth, and that of the same features in his sorely tried middle age. More's drinking-cup is there too, and a portrait of Cardinal Pole, and the stick on which Fisher, the Cardinal Bishop of Rochester, leaned as he walked to the scaffold at the Tower, exactly a fortnight before More met his fate at the hands of Henry VIII.'s headsman." *

We give an illustration of the drinking-cup. It is of dark wood bound in silver rims, with a lid. It has an inscription on one of the rims : " The drinking-can of Sir Thomas More, sometime Lord Chancillor of England."

The relics came to the Eystons in the following way :

The last male descendant of Blessed Thomas was the Rev. Thomas More, S.J. ; through him the More relics preserved at Stonyhurst came to the Society. He died May 20, 1795, aged seventy-one.

* Vincent, *op. cit.* p. 221.

His two brothers predeceased him. He had also three sisters, one of whom, Catherine, died unmarried; another, Mary (in religion, Augustina), became a nun, and subsequently Prioress, at the English Convent, Bruges, to which she bequeathed a very precious relic of the martyr, a vertebra of his neck. Blessed Thomas More's rosary-ring, now in possession of Mr. Charles Trappes, also belonged to her. The third sister, Bridget, was twice married, and her descendants now represent the More family. By her first husband, Peter Metcalfe of Glandford Briggs, co. Lincoln, she had a son, Thomas Peter Metcalfe. He had a son and a daughter by his marriage with Teresa Throckmorton. The son, who assumed the name and arms of More, died unmarried; the daughter, Maria Teresa, married Mr. Charles Eyston of East Hendred, the grandfather of the present Squire.

She brought him not only the relics, but also the More estate of Barnborough, which came to the martyr's son by his marriage with the heiress of the Cresacres. The estate was, however, sold at Mr. Eyston's death.

Thus we leave with reluctance the beautiful and romantic village of which there is still much that deserves to be told. It is, indeed, a place of pilgrimage to all who love the past.*

* I have to express my gratitude to Mr. Eyston for the loan of his father's MS. history of the Chapel of St. Amand, from which I have taken most of the facts here set down.

THE DRINKING-CAN OF BLESSED THOMAS
MORE, PRESERVED AT EAST HENDRED

*To face page* 350

# BURGHWALLIS HALL

ANOTHER home of the ancient faith connected with a martyr is Burghwallis Hall, near Doncaster, the Yorkshire home of the Annes. The Venerable John Anne (called Amyas on the Mission) suffered at York, March 15, 1588-9.

Dr. Champneys, who was a witness of the martyrdom, was very greatly impressed by the meekness and constancy shown by the blessed man and his fellow martyr, Venerable Robert Dalby. At their trial "one Bramley, a felon, saw hanging over their heads a great round

Burgh Wallis Hall

The Drive

light which every time they spake would, as it were, move itself, and at the end of their speeches vanish away." This converted the man, and he died with the martyrs, a good Catholic and sincere penitent.

John Anne "had been a married man and dwelt in Wakefield, a great occupier of cloth; and when his wife died he gave his children portions and placed them well, and then went over sea to his book, and so profiting in virtue took holy orders, and then returning into the vineyard did much good."

When the judge taunted him at the trial with being "a bankrupt and an inferior man" the martyr gently answered: "Not so; I am a gentleman by birth, of an ancient house, and when I gave up my trade I was able to live with the best." *

John Anne was born at Frickley, some five miles from Burghwallis, then the residence of the Annes. His father was Martin Anne, and his mother Elizabeth Nevile, widow of Thomas Bosvile of Ardsley, Yorks.

* From Father Grene's MS. "F." quoted by Foley, vol. iii. p. 45.

351

# FORGOTTEN SHRINES

The Hall at Frickley no longer exists. It was a moated dwelling, destroyed by fire some hundred and fifty years ago. The ancient family chapel has also very nearly disappeared, only very insignificant ruins now marking the place where, for some hundreds of years, Mass had been offered up.

But Burghwallis, where the martyr's sister lived, still happily remains. The present lady of the house, Mrs. Anne, has kindly furnished the following account of her home:

"Burghwallis Hall (anciently Burgh Wallis) was built in the fourteenth century, and has been added to from time to time. It has been the property of the Annes for more than 400 years, and has had a Catholic mission attached to it ever since the venerable parish church was taken out of the rightful owners' possession, in the sixteenth century.

"The Hall was formerly a picturesque gabled manor house with the large Hall and heavily timbered roof found in those early days, and the fine old ceiling with its oak beams is still to be seen running through the main part of the older portion of the building.

"Sir William Gascoign was living at Burghwallis in 1440, and, in the sixteenth century, Francis Gascoign married Elizabeth, daughter of Martin Anne of Frickley, while about the same time George Anne, son of the same Martin Anne, married Margaret Fenton, only child of Richard Fenton, then resident at Burghwallis. This Elizabeth and George Anne were half-sister and half-brother to the Venerable John Anne.

"By inquisition post-mortem of John Anne (36 Henry VIII.) it was found that he held the manor of Frickley of William Gascoign as of his manor of Burgh Wallis. In Bernard's survey, 1577, Martin Anne is returned as holding the manor of Frickley of Leonard West, Esq. (who was a younger son of Lord De la Warr, married to Barbara Gascoign) as of his manor of Burgh Wallis.

"From that time onward Burghwallis has belonged to the Annes, and when Michael Anne sold Frickley in the eighteenth century it finally became the family residence.

"It is believed that there was a chapel in some sequestered spot at Burghwallis, erected almost immediately after the ejection of the Catholics from their churches, for an old door, now belonging to one of the cottages on the estate, is still spoken of as 'the door of the old chapel.' No vestige of any building, however, remains. In the hidden chapel, wherever it may have been, the Venerable martyr will often have celebrated Mass, and we may suppose that he wore those very vestments which now lie tattered and stained with age in the drawers of the Sacristy, and used the old Missal printed at Antwerp in 1576.

# BURGHWALLIS HALL

" In Hunter's *Deanery of Doncaster* we find : ' The family of Anne never complied with the terms of the Reformation of Religion, and have borne their share of the losses and disabilities to which the professors of the Roman Catholic faith have been exposed. There was an ordinance of Parliament, November 18, 1652, for the sale of the estate of Philip Anne of Burgh Wallis, for treason against the Parliament and people. But if the Annes' attachment to a profession of Christianity which was dis-countenanced by the Court and unpopular with the multitude, may have prevented them from being advanced to honours and distinctions, to which their fortune, and still more their high ancestorial pretensions, might be said to entitle them, it may have contributed also to keep them out of the way of accidents, to which families mixing more in public affairs are exposed. It is a remarkable fact that this Catholic family is the single instance of the male line being maintained in its ancient port and rank, out of all the gentry of this deanery summoned to appear before the Heralds in 1584.'

" In the house are many treasures relating to the past. One is a portrait of George Leyburne, President of Douay College from 1652-1670; the other is a beautiful oil-painting of Bishop John Leyburne, the first Vicar-Apostolic, who on being sent by the Pope to England, lost no time but went at a gallop through the northern counties, and confirmed 20,000 people in two months. These portraits came to the Annes through Miss Elizabeth Anne, whose mother was related to the Leyburnes— Elizabeth Anne being the last representative of that ancient family. In the library the furniture dates back hundreds of years, and some fine specimens of oak carving belonging to the fifteenth and sixteenth centuries are to be found among the high-backed chairs. There is also a quaint old fifteenth-century table. The book-shelves contain a great number of old missals, breviaries, and books of piety, in whose fly-leaves may be read such names as Gage, Fitzherbert, Killingbeck, Clifford, Cholmeley, Needham, Vavasour, Brackenbury, Philip Hamerton (the father of the founder of the Pontefract mission), Father James Meynell, and many of the Annes.

" In 1907, in taking some measurements in the attics, a small chamber was discovered to which there was no access except by crawling along a very narrow space under the roof for a distance of some twenty yards. This chamber measures seven or eight feet square, and was empty, but it was so constructed that any one in the room would think that the space was the well of the staircase adjoining. A builder who has seen it can give no explanation why it was made, as it is not in any way necessary to the construction of the building.

" Burghwallis is the mother mission of the whole neighbourhood : in fact Burghwallis has always been Catholic. The date of the present chapel, an unpretentious addition to the house in red brick, is uncertain, but its very unecclesiastical appearance outside, and its unobtrusive public entrance—up a narrow flight of stone steps in the back yard—point to its having been built in penal times, probably some time early in the eighteenth century. It is evident that Catholicism was flourishing in Burghwallis in 1732, for we find in the parish register of that year, in Latin, an entry which, translated, reads: 'Dedicated to posterity, 1732. Dec. 23rd, Marm: Downes, S.T.B., Fellow of the College of St. John the Evangelist at Cambridge, most willingly resigned this rectory. May better treatment await my successors whilst they dwell in this parish, but I consider this rather to be hoped for than expected, papist fury not being yet extinguished, nor, as there is likelihood to judge, is it soon to be so.' " *

* We give the original Latin :

*Posteris Sacrum* 1732.

*Dec.* 23^tio. *Hanc rectoriam lubentissime resignavit Marm. Downes, S.T.B. Socius Coll. D. Johannis Evang. apud Cantab.: Successores meos meliora fata maneant, dum in hoc pagello moram traxerint ; sed hoc sperandum potius quam credendum censeo ; furore papistico nondum extincto neque, uti proclive est judicare, jamjam exstinguendo.*

# RELICS OF THE ENGLISH MARTYRS

**F**OR some years I have been trying to chronicle and describe, in as complete a manner as possible, the scattered relics of our glorious martyrs which have been preserved by the faithful, in remembrance of a period of persecution (1535–1681) almost unparalleled for length and ferocity.

Though still incomplete, my collections have now swelled to a large folio MS. volume of nearly three hundred pages, and it may not be without interest to Catholics if I give some brief account of them here. The list would indeed have been far longer and more important were it not for the terrible ravages of the French Revolution. In this sad period the sacred relics which had often been snatched at the risk of life from the persecutors, or bought perhaps by pious Catholics from a venal hangman at the very foot of the gibbet, or distributed by the martyrs themselves on the eve of their agony, were torn from the religious houses and colleges on the Continent where they had long been preserved, and were scattered, lost, or destroyed.

Thus, of the many holy relics preserved till then at the English College of Douay, the *alma mater* of the majority of our martyrs, nothing, or scarcely anything, remains to us. The body of the Venerable John Southworth, in its leaden coffin, still lies hidden, no doubt, somewhere in the grounds of the College, which is now transformed into barracks. It used to rest under the altar of St. Augustine of Canterbury in the College church, and was buried, for safety, at the outbreak of the Revolution. Strange that while the hidden plate was afterwards, at least in part, dug up and recovered, we find no more trace of the martyr's relics.*

At the adjoining English Benedictine Monastery (now alas! desecrated) were formerly venerated the quarters of Dom John Roberts, O.S.B., and of his companion in martyrdom, the Rev. Thomas Somers, which Dom

---

* At Downside is a piece of tape in a paper bearing the following inscription : "The enclosed is part of some tape which I, Richard Southworth, found tied round the leaden coffin in which is enclosed the body of the Rev. John Southworth, who suffered death for his priestly character under Oliver Cromwell, June 28th, in the year of our Lord 1654. This I brought with me to England in the year 1786 when I first came over on the mission. I took it from the coffin above-mentioned, which at that time lay under St. Augustine's Altar at Doway College, but was afterwards, during the trouble in France, removed and buried deep in a private place within the precincts or premises of the said College. It still remains there.

"Brockhampton, June 22nd, 1816.

"RICHD. SOUTHWORTH."

Endorsed outside—

"Taken from under St. Augustine's Altar at Doway College in 1786."

Augustine Bradshaw tried to get leave to place upon the altar on high feast days. For many years these sacred treasures were lost sight of, and were supposed to have perished at the Revolution. Shortly, however, before the expulsion of the monks from Douay (to be precise, in May 1902), Abbot Gasquet was led to examine a chest of unknown relics which for many years had lain beneath the high altar of the monastic church. Together with the relics of a St. Fabian, a martyr from the Roman Catacombs, he found several large bones "all comparatively recent, heavy, and well preserved." They consist of a leg quarter (right) with a part of the foot, a right and left humerus, and two small ribs—four large bones and six small. They all, apparently, belong to the same body. On the tibia a paper label was fixed. It was torn, and only the following words were legible :

. . . l ho . . .
Vide Arnoldum Raiisium In C. . .
Martyriu . . . Anglo Duacensiu . . .
pag 73
(The paper is torn at the dots, but is quite easy to read.)

Reference to Arnold Raisse's little *Catalogus Christi Sacerdotum, qui e nobili Anglicano Duacenæ civitatis Collegio Proseminati præclarum fidei testimonium in Britannia præbuerunt* (Duaci, 1630) shows that these are the relics of the Venerable Thomas Wilson (*alias* Somers), though Abbot Gasquet at first supposed that they belonged to his more famous companion. These relics were translated to Downside on Tuesday, August 18, 1903. It is a very great disappointment that the relics of the Venerable John Roberts, founder of the Community now at Downside, are apparently lost without hope of recovery. Gone, too, is the head of that glorious martyr, Dom Mark Barkworth, which Arnold Raisse beheld and venerated there, wrapped in silk and gold.

Though the Jesuits have still preserved portions of their treasures, they are as nothing compared with those which were once preserved at their Colleges of St. Omer, Liége, Watten, Valladolid and Rome. There may yet, indeed, be bodies or relics of the English martyrs hidden away in Spain, but, even there, many have been lost owing to the Revolution and the suppression of the religious houses. Thus, for instance, the arm of the Venerable John Roberts, O.S.B., once preserved at his own monastery of Saint Martin, Compostella, was a relic which the late lamented prelate, Don Rudesindo Salvado, Abbot *nullius* of New Nursia, himself the last survivor of that ancient house, told me that he distinctly remembered.

We must, however, be thankful for what still remains to us ; and the fewer are the treasures, the more precious have they become. Arnold

356

# RELICS OF THE ENGLISH MARTYRS

Raisse, in his *Hierogazophylacium Belgicum*, has left us a catalogue of the principal relics preserved before the Revolution in Belgium, which makes us conscious of many of our losses. But there were very many which he does not mention, some of which are still happily preserved.

The Acts of the Martyrs constantly speak of the efforts made by the faithful to obtain their relics. Here, as in many another trait, these acts seem to take us back to the times of the primitive Church. Again we see a Lucina or a Praxedes gathering up the torn members of the martyrs of Christ, and preserving them for the veneration of the faithful. The touching story of the rescue of the bodies of Dom Maurus Scott, O.S.B., and his companion, made from under a heap of festering corpses, by a band of devoted Spanish Catholics, is well known; and the filial devotion of Margaret Roper, who rescued the head of Blessed Thomas More from its spike on London Bridge, was rivalled by the piety of Donna Luisa da Carvajal, that noble Spanish lady who devoted her life to ministering to the martyrs of Christ. We read how she had their sacred relics rescued at dead of night, and how she went with her companions in devout procession to receive them when they were brought to her house. Twelve of them, wearing white veils and carrying lighted tapers in their hands, would stand at the entrance of the house, and after venerating the holy treasure, would conduct the brave bearers through the passages, strewn with sweet-smelling flowers and decked with green branches, to the door of the oratory. Tenderly, and with mingled feelings of joy and sorrow, would they lay them there, while all night long prayerful vigil was kept around those glorious trophies. Luisa herself next day would wrap them in winding-sheets and embalm them in spices, and there they would remain in safety until it was possible to send them over to the Continent.

The Spanish Ambassadors themselves frequently showed the greatest zeal in collecting these sacred treasures. There are still venerated at Gondomar the relics of Venerable Thomas Maxfield (Tyburn, July 1, 1616), and Venerable John Almond (Tyburn, December 5, 1612), priests, which were obtained for the Duke of that name, then Ambassador in England, by his son, Don Antonio Surmiento, who was himself present at the martyrdoms. A still more ardent client of the martyrs was another Ambassador, the Count Egmont (afterwards Duke of Gueldres), whose long list of relics obtained during his sojourn in England (1640–1645) still exists in the Archives at Lille, and was published by the late Mr. Richard Simpson in the *Rambler*.* It is so little known, and it throws so vivid and so terrible a light on the details of the persecution that it may not be amiss to reprint it here in full:

* New Series, vol. viii. (1857), p. 114.

# FORGOTTEN SHRINES

"Louis, by the grace of God, Duke of Gueldres, Julliac, and Cleves, Count of Ormund, and Zutphen, Prince of Ghent, Count of Bures, Liege, &c., Lord of the cities and territories of either Mechlin, &c. &c.

"Whereas the English Catholics, who had been allowed some little repose for a few years, were, after the opening of the parliament in 1640, oppressed with a new and most bitter persecution; and whereas the utmost care and diligence were employed against priests, that when they were driven off, the flock, deprived of its pastors, might be more easily devoured,—therefore, besides the resumption of the laws made by Queen Elizabeth against priests and Catholics (which had been a short time dormant), new and most savage acts were passed against the servants of God, forbidding a priest to minister to Catholics in England under pain of death. But as when the ancient faith and religion were first expelled from England, no fear of a cruel death, nor threats of agonising tortures, could remove the faithful and watchful pastors from the flock committed to them, but rather gave many inhabitants to heaven, many martyrs to the Church, many patron saints to the Christian world; so also, during this persecution, England has beheld her most constant champions, her bravest heroes, enduring the most cruel torments for Christ and the Catholic faith. And as at that time our own business detained us in England, we were, by a sovereign grace of Almighty God, an eye-witness of the incredible constancy of divers martyrs; and out of the fifteen who, from the year 1640 to the end of the year 1645, gained the palm of martyrdom in different places, we saw eleven suffer in London, of whom were four secular priests, William Ward, Arnold Green,* John Morgan, John Duckett; three of the Society of Jesus, Thomas Holland, Ralph Corby, Henry Morse; one Benedictine, Bartholomew Rho [Roe]; and three Franciscan Minorites, Bolliquer [Thomas Bullaker], Francis Bell, and Paul of St. Magdalen [Henry Heath]. When these men, for God's cause and the Church's, were led like sheep to the slaughter, were hanged, were cruelly bowelled before they were half dead, were burnt, and were cut into quarters, we, in order that the memory of such noble persons might be for ever preserved among the faithful, and desirous of having, so far as it lay in our power, some relics of their bodies, by the aid, the devotion, and the diligence of our servants, did procure certain relics, which, on our departure out of England into France at the end of the year 1645, we carried with us, and have preserved to this day in our treasury; wherein as we intend to shut them all up, we have judged it necessary to publish abroad this testimony, lest devouring oblivion should ever erase the name of these venerable men, and the glory of these most renowned martyrs.

* Called by Challoner, Thomas Reynolds.

358

# RELICS OF THE ENGLISH MARTYRS

We, therefore, desiring more and more to promote the worship of God and the honour of the saints, and since we have no dearer wish than the aforesaid venerable martyrs should be worshipped, venerated, and honoured as they should be,—have made known to all to whom this present testimonal shall come, that the said venerable martyrs did, at London, in England, contend with the greatest constancy for the ancient faith, and, so to say, for their altars; did overcome, and did obtain the crown of martyrdom; and that we, by means of the aid of our servants and their devotion to the martyred saints, did recover the relics of the said martyrs here underwritten, namely: Of the venerable martyr William Ward, secular priest, who suffered at London, July 26, in the year 1641: his heart, drawn out from the fire wherein it had lain about five hours; the handkerchief he had in his hand when he died; his ring, and his diurnal. Of the venerable martyrs, Arnold Green, secular priest, and Bartholomew Roe, of the order of St. Benedict, who suffered at London, January 31, in the year 1642: of Father Bartholomew Roe, his Breviary, a thumb, a piece of burnt lung, a piece of kidney burned to a cinder, the *interula* with which he was martyred, and a towel dipped in his blood; of Mr. Arnold Green, a thumb, a piece of burnt liver, a towel dipped in his blood, and a night-cap which was drawn over his eyes when he was hanged, a sponge, a piece of linen, and a towel dipped in their blood, and the apron and sleeves of the torturer. Of the venerable martyr, John Morgan, secular priest, who suffered at London, April 26, 1642, certain papers containing pieces of altered and burnt flesh, three pieces of his præcordia, some of his hair, four towels dipped in his blood, the straw on which he was laid to be embowelled, some papers greased with his fat, the rope wherewith he was hanged. Of the venerable martyr (Thomas) Bolliquer, of the Order of the Friars Minor of St. Francis, who suffered at London (October 12, 1642), a little piece of his heart, some pieces of his bones and flesh, his liver, his diaphragm, some of his præcordia, two fingers, some hair, four towels dipped in his blood, the straw on which he was laid to be embowelled, some papers greased with his fat, the rope wherewith he was hanged. Of the venerable martyr, Paul of St. Magdalen, guardian of the Convent of English Minors at Douai, who suffered (April 17, 1643), a toe, three small bones, a piece of the windpipe, some of his burnt flesh, the straw on which he was laid to be embowelled, four napkins dipped in his blood, the rope wherewith he was hanged. Of the venerable martyr, Francis Bell, guardian of the English Friars Minor at Douai, who suffered December 1, 1643, a right-hand quarter of his body, six pieces of his flesh and fat, three napkins dipped in his blood and melted fat, with the remains of flesh, two fingers, and other small bones,

359

his *thyrotheca*.   Of the venerable martyr, Thomas Holland, priest of the
Society of Jesus, who suffered at London, December 22, 1642, one
bone, some pieces of skin, a nail, some hair, two napkins stained with
blood, a little box of fat, some papers greased with his fat, the shirt in
which he suffered.   Of the venerable martyrs, Ralph Corby, of the
Society of Jesus, and John Duckett, secular priest, who suffered at
London, September 17, 1644 : of Mr. Duckett, the right hand, a piece
of his neck, one vertebra and a half, with three other small pieces ; of
Father Corby, some vertebræ, with a piece of flesh, a tooth, a few napkins
stained with blood, two handkerchiefs that he used at his martyrdom, the
girdle wherewith he was then girdled, and his hat, some remains of burnt
viscera, some hair and skin of both.   Of the venerable martyr, Henry
Morse, of the Society of Jesus, who suffered on February 1, 1645, a
right side quarter, the right hand separated from the same, his liver
pulled out of the fire, a handkerchief stained with his blood, ashes of his
burnt intestines, the rope wherewith he was hanged, his hat, shirt, collar,
breeches, stockings, the apron and sleeves of the torturer.   Some part of
the skin, with hair upon it, of a certain Benedictine Father, who, with,
his companion, suffered at York when Charles, king of England, was
there.*   Which relics we testify that we did recover by the assistance of
our said domestics, who, with our knowledge and command, and in our
sight, and under the very eyes of the heretics, with no small risk of their
lives, did snatch part of them out of the midst of the flames, and the
other part did purchase of the executioner at the very time of the
execution ; of which thing, as of all the premises, were witnesses ;
Peregrine Abbot of Carlen, Abbot of St. Mary's, our chief councillor ;
Mr. Charles Cheney, missionary from the Holy See to propagate the
faith among the English, our domestic prelate and almoner ; Mr. Robert
de Mortimer, also a missionary priest ; Mr. Aymond de la Tour,
captain of a troop of an hundred cavalry under the most Christian king,
and our councillor ; M. Daniel de Bertair, our chief steward and a
councillor ; M. Philip de Circouve, the first gentleman of our chamber ;
M. Amé de la Rivière, our shieldbearer ; M. Peter de Belluart ;
Mr. John Morgan ; Anthony du Bois, of our bedchamber, and our
secretary ; Peter Garret and Louis Noel, also of our bedchamber ;
Edward Locke, surgeon of our chamber ; Peter of Lyons, who after-
wards suffered martyrdom for the faith in Ireland ; Simon du Bois ;
Gabriel Tirion ; James Beaucourt ; Quentin . . . . . . ; Alexander
Hocart ; Francis Daniel ; and others our servants, official and other.
In witness of all which, we have signed with our own hand, and sealed

* Venerable John Lockwood, York, April 13, 1642.   He was a *confrater* or oblate
of the Order of St. Benedict.

with our own seal, this present testimonial, valid for future as well as present times; and have ordered our said almoner, in his official capacity, to sign it in the name of all our domestics. Given at Paris, in our house at St. Victor, July 26, A.D. 1650." *

A truly ghastly list! but one which tells us more significantly than pages of description, the kind of fate which our martyrs looked forward to with so much joy. I do not know if these relics collected by the Duke still exist, but it is greatly to be hoped that they may yet be found. Challoner (quoting De Marsys) gives a long and most interesting account of the manner in which the heart of the Venerable William Ward was saved.

" . . . A person of great quality, Count Egmond by name, hearing by a servant of his who was present at the action, that an holy priest had suffered martyrdom that morning, asked his servant if he had brought any relic of the martyr away with him, who told him Yes, and gave him (as he said) the very handkerchief which the saint had cast out of his pocket. The Count, taking it with reverence, kissed it ; but finding no blood upon the same, gave the servant his own handkerchief, commanding him to run back instantly to the place of execution, and to dip that in some of the martyr's blood, if he could find any. The servant posting away came back to the gallows, made diligent search for some of the blood, but finding it was all scraped up by the zeal of other pious Catholics who had been before him, takes his stick, and rubbing up the ashes where the bowels of the martyr had been burnt, finds a lump of flesh all parched and singed by the fiery embers wherein it lay covered, and hastily wrapped up what he had found in the handkerchief which his lord had given him, not having time to shake off the fiery coals or hot ashes by reason that some malicious persons that stood by, and saw this fellow stooping and taking somewhat out of the fire, demanded of him what he took thence. . . ."

The account then goes on to describe how the man " nimbly slipped over a park pale " and ran for his life, hotly pursued by the enemy, both on horse and foot. Resolved not to lose the relic, he hastily dropped it, as he ran, into a bush, taking care to mark its position so that he might return to find it when the hue and cry was over. " And this he did with such dexterity, making no stop at all, but feigning a small trip or stumble, and yet seeming suddenly to recover himself, ran on, drawing

---

* Endorsed in French : " *Act of his Highness touching the relics of England.*" Simpson truly remarks : " These relics were not the less venerable on account of the disgusting processes they had gone through ; the horror does not attach to them, but to the brutes who presided over the butchery."

his pursuers after him, to delude them, and thereby to save the relic. In brief, this poor man recovered the outskirts of the town ere he was over-taken." He was of course apprehended, but the ambassador's influence was sufficient to get him speedily released, and early next morning he found the relic where he had left it in the park. It turned out to be the martyr's heart, and it was considered miraculous that the handkerchief which enfolded it had not been burned nor singed by the hot embers which clung to it, while the heart itself remained untainted and incorrupt for fifteen days, when the Count had it embalmed, " not to preserve it from corruption, which it seemed no way to incline to, but for reverence and religion to so rich a relic." " *Quia pretiosa in conspectu Domini mors sanctorum ejus.*"

There is at Downside a large piece of coarse sacking thickly clotted with blood, which is stated to have been dipped in the blood of the Venerable Alban Roe, O.S.B. It has been suggested that it may possibly form part of the " apron of the torturer," which was among the relics of this martyr secured by the Duke, as it is of precisely the material which one would expect such a garment to be made of.

The Duke's catalogue is, however, a very fair specimen of the kind of relics which are still preserved. They mostly consist of pieces of flesh or bone, linen dipped in blood (the most common of all), and pieces of straw also stained with blood. In the case of these martyrs we constantly find the Catholics dipping their handkerchiefs in the blood of the sufferers. Thus a contemporary ballad, describing the martyrdom of the Venerable John Thulis:

> " A hundred handkerchiefs
> With his sweet blood was dight,
> As relics for to wear
> For this said blessed wight."

Again, in the Acts of the martyrs already referred to, V. Thomas Reynolds and V. Alban Roe, O.S.B., we read : " The Catholics piously vied with each other in taking away relics of the martyrs. Many dipped handkerchiefs in the dismembered bodies ; others carefully collected the blood-stained straw from off the ground ; while some snatched from the flames the intestines, which, as usual, had been thrown into the cauldron, and carried them home." * It is interesting to note in connection with this passage that the relics of these martyrs preserved to this day at Lanherne, Colwich, and Erdington, consist precisely of pieces of linen soaked in blood, and little bits of straw.

At the martyrdom of the Venerable Edward Morgan, a more singular phenomenon was witnessed :

* Pollen, *Acts of English Martyrs*, p. 343.

# RELICS OF THE ENGLISH MARTYRS

" The officers calling for the people's handkerchiefs and gloves to wet in the blood, which they did, and delivered them again to their owners, and one got almost his whole heart out of the fire." *

This was very different from the scenes at earlier martyrdoms, where every effort was made to prevent the people getting hold of any relic, and where those who were detected trying to do so were frequently sent to prison. Here, again, we are reminded of the martyrs of the primitive Church, and the penal days in England recall the highest memories of those days of early fervour. Thus, at the martyrdom of Blessed Edmund Campion and his companions, a youth secured the martyr's thumb, which was handed over to the Society, and is probably the relic now treasured at the Gesù in Rome. It has of late years been divided, and half is in the hands of the Fathers of the English Province. But, as a rule, the precautions taken by the authorities to prevent these pious thefts were only too successful. It will be remembered how everything stained with the blood of Mary Queen of Scots was burned in the Great Hall of Fotheringay Castle, immediately after the execution. In the same way the relics of many of our martyrs were destroyed. Their heads were usually put up on spikes on London Bridge, or on the gateways of the towns where they had been martyred ; and when room was wanted for more, they were thrown into the river or other inaccessible places. Thus were treated the heads of the Carthusian Priors, to make way for those of Blessed More and Fisher. The head of Father John Cornelius, S.J., was used as a football by the bigoted mob at Dorchester, before it was placed over the town gate. That of Venerable James Bird, a lad of eighteen, was placed over a gateway of the City of Winchester, where his aged father, passing beneath one day, fancied he saw it bow reverently to him.

One of the most precious relics that still remains to us is the head of Blessed Cuthbert Mayne, the protomartyr of the Seminary Priests, now preserved at Lanherne. The square hole made by the spike on which it was exposed on Launceston Castle can still be seen in the skull. A pathetic story in the York records tells how a female prisoner, Mrs. Hutton, and her children, got into trouble for rescuing the heads of two

---

* I believe this heart is still preserved at St. Scholastica's Abbey, Teignmouth. It is 2¼ in. in length, nearly 2 in. in breadth at the widest, and 1½ in. thick. It is preserved in a curious cardboard box in the shape of a heart, just large enough to hold it. The box has intricate patterns on it made in very fine straw. The tradition handed down in the convent is that it is " the heart of one of the martyred missionary priests, which jumped out of the fire into which it had been thrown." In 1751 a lay-sister named Sister Agnes Morgan was professed in the English Benedictine Convent at Pontoise, and at the dissolution of that monastery joined the Teignmouth Community, then at Dunkirk. The relic is known to have come from Pontoise, and it is very likely that it belonged to Sister Morgan.

363

martyrs which were exposed on the leads over the prison in which they were confined. The children were interrogated in vain, and stood their whippings with a fortitude above their years; while the heroic mother was thrust down into the frightful underground dungeons of the Lower Kidcote on Ouse-bridge, where in a few days she died. These heads may possibly be the same as those that were discovered in recent years walled up in the old church of the Vavasours at Hazlewood, though it is more probable that these are the heads of the aged martyr, Venerable John Lockwood, and his younger companion, Venerable Edmund Catherick, who suffered at York, April 13, 1642. Others, martyrs in the same cause, were Thomas Monday and Thurstan Hickman, who, as Wriothesley's Chronicle * informs us, were arrested, tried at the Guildhall, and condemned to death for endeavouring to carry over to France the arm of the Blessed John Houghton, Prior of the London Charterhouse, and other relics. This arm, as will be remembered, had been fixed up over the very gate of the Charterhouse—a hideous piece of barbarity intended to strike terror into the hearts of the heroic monks. One day it fell down at the feet of two of them, who hastily concealed it. Unhappily, they were unsuccessful in their attempt to send it oversea. Those entrusted with this precious relic suffered the death of traitors, and doubtless were welcomed to Heaven by the martyrs they had sought to honour on earth.†

The main sources of the sacred treasures still preserved are, of course, the old religious communities which were founded on the Continent during the times of persecution, and settled in England at the French Revolution. Many of these communities succeeded in bringing over at least a portion of their treasures. Thus at Taunton, Lanherne, Darlington, Chichester, and Colwich are still preserved the relics once venerated at Nieuport, Antwerp, Gravelines, Hoogstraet, and Paris. At Downside are collected the treasures of Lambspring, while at Newton Abbot the Canonesses of St. Augustine still venerate the hair-shirt of Blessed Thomas More, which formed their chief treasure at Louvain. The English Canonesses who still inhabit their old convent at Bruges

---

* Wriothesley (Camden Soc.), 1875, i. 184–85 (July 1, 1547). Monday was parson of St. Leonard's, Foster Lane, and Hickman, a monk of the London Charterhouse. John Foxe, parson of St. Mary Magdalene, in the ward of Queenhithe, and one of the expelled Carthusians, had managed to escape overseas to the Louvain Charterhouse. Monday and Hickman had promised to follow him and bring him " the left arm " of B. John Houghton, " with other baggage that they called reliques," but they were apprehended, tried at the Guildhall, and condemned to death as traitors. The fate of this relic, which has been much discussed, is thus made clear ; and it would seem that yet another martyr should be added to the ranks of the London Carthusians. See Stowe, *Annales*, London, 1631, p. 594.

† Unhappily, not a single relic of the eighteen Carthusians has been preserved.

have some notable relics, while many other communities which succeeded in reaching England in safety, unhappily lost their treasures. A story told in the annals of St. Benedict's Priory, Colwich (then at Paris), shows how difficult it was to preserve them :

"The man employed by the administrators to make the search said he knew how nuns did hide things, but he knew how to find them, for his wife had taught him. He therefore spent a long time in picking open pin-cushions, and at length found concealed in a very large one a great quantity of relics. He then seemed much diverted, and carefully took them out by parcells, and put them on the window-seat behind him, where a nun had placed herself, who kept her eye on what he did, and the other nuns were emptying down before him the contents of their drawers, work-bags, and other things, so that he was greatly bewildered with such variety, and as he was seated on the ground, he was almost, or half of him, covered with things. Thus they amused him until he forgot the treasures he had put in security, as he thought, and being carried away by another guard, he never more thought to look for what he had laid in the window; and the relics were saved by this means."

However, on the journey from the Convent to the Castle of Vincennes, they were very nearly lost again, as the bag containing them was let fall by a frightened nun under the wheels of the coach; but again they were providentially recovered.*

The Poor Clares of Ayre possessed the head of Venerable John Wall, O.S.F. (Father Joachim of S. Anne, Worcester, August 22, 1679.) They joined their sisters at Gravelines in 1834, but left two years later to join the Rouen Poor Clares at Scorton, near Darlington. Afraid, however, to encounter the English Custom House officers with the head

---

* They were, however, strangely enough, lost again in the convent itself, or, rather, lost to sight and memory. When the late Father Morris made his list of English Martyr relics he asked if the nuns of Colwich had any, and they replied they had not. However, later on it struck them to examine the contents of a bag, or rather cushion, of relics, which was in possession of the infirmarian, and used to be laid on the bed of a sick nun. In this they found sewn up, to their great joy, relics of no fewer than twenty-nine different martyrs, including one of Venerable Margaret Ward, which is supposed to be unique, and others almost equally scarce. These relics are all very small; they have been neatly mounted in test-tubes, and sealed by the Bishop of Birmingham. The nuns have generously given a portion of their treasures to Downside and Erdington Abbeys. They have, unhappily, lost the arm of Venerable Oliver Plunket, which they once possessed. They have, however, a large circular pewter dish which belonged to Blessed Richard Whiting, Abbot of Glastonbury, which bears in the centre his rebus—a whiting. This was given to them after their return to England by Lady Arundel of Wardour. The most remarkable of their English Martyr relics, besides that of Mrs. Ward, are those of Blessed Richard Thirkeld, Venerable William Harrington, Venerable Thomas Pickering, O.S.B., Venerable Richard Langhorne (which are all extremely rare), and some of Venerable Philip Powel, O.S.B., inscribed : "*Rd. fa Philipe ye m: his Reliques and cloth wett with his blood and tears.*"

in their possession, they buried it before leaving Gravelines in the cloister garden, near the kitchen, enclosed in a wooden box. Repeated searches have been made for the head by the Ursuline nuns, who now possess the old Convent of the English Poor Clares at Gravelines, but hitherto without success.

Besides the relics preserved in religious communities, others have been handed down in old Catholic families from time immemorial. Some time ago the writer was brought a little collection of relics which had been treasured for centuries in an old Catholic family in Warwickshire. Very pathetic were these memorials of the penal days. They mostly consisted of little slips of linen deeply stained with blood, enclosed in papers which bore, in quaint seventeenth-century handwriting, such inscriptions as "bishop plunkit's blood," "Mr. Johnson his blood." Besides the relics of our martyrs, were others of those not usually reckoned among them : for instance, Lord Derwentwater ; and, most interesting of all, several of King James II.

But it is time to describe the principal treasures which are still preserved amongst us ; and we naturally begin with *reliquiæ insignes.* Of whole bodies there are very few, if indeed the mutilated quarters can be given that name. The most famous are those of Archbishop Plunket, at Downside Abbey, and of Philip Howard, Earl of Arundel, in the Fitzalan Chapel at Arundel. Archbishop Plunket's relics were taken by his friend and fellow prisoner, Abbot Maurus Corker, to his abbey at Lambspring in 1685, and were translated to Downside in 1883. The head of the venerable martyr is at the Siena Convent, Drogheda ; one of the arms at the Franciscan Convent, Taunton ; while the other, as we said, is lost. There are said to be some large bones of the martyr at Rome, but I have not been able to discover where they are kept. One large relic was left at Lambspring, and several smaller relics detached in 1883. I have before me a list of the bones now at Downside, made by a medical man at the time of the translation ; it includes most of the skeleton, with the exceptions already mentioned. The body of V. Philip Howard is entire, save for a bone which was taken out by the late Canon Tierney, and given to the mother of the present Duke, who enshrined it in a gold reliquary. Each of the bones is separated and wrapped in silk.

There are bodies of other martyrs in Protestant hands, notably that of B. Margaret Pole, Countess of Salisbury, in the Chapel of St. Peter ad Vincula in the Tower (a thigh-bone of hers was shown as a curiosity to the King of Siam !) ; that of V. John Kemble, which lies in Welsh Newton churchyard, and of V. Charles Baker, S.J., just outside the west door of the old Priory Church at Usk ; while those of others are known to rest in various churches or churchyards, but the exact spot has been un-

THE RELICS AT SUTTON PARK, GUILDFORD
*Photo by the author*

*To face page* 366

happily lost sight of. Thus the bodies of B. John Fisher and B. Thomas More may possibly yet be found under the belfry in St. Peter's ad Vincula, unless the tradition of their having been moved to Chelsea be correct. (If so, they are hopelessly lost, for the tomb in Chelsea Church is said to be empty.) B. Thomas Percy lies somewhere on the site of the demolished Church of St. Crux, at York; V. Thomas Thwing in St. Mary's Church, Castlegate, York; and several other York martyrs in various churches and cemeteries of the city;* while Venerable John Wall was buried in St. Oswald's churchyard at Worcester. But it is very unlikely that their sacred relics will ever be recovered. More happy are V. Thomas Maxfield and V. John Almond, who, as we said, rest at Gondomar in Spain, though considerable portions of their relics have been translated to Downside.

Next in importance come the heads of the martyrs. There are many of these preserved. That of B. Thomas More is, I believe, still safe in its niche in the Roper vault in St. Dunstan's, Canterbury. I have a drawing of it which appeared in the *Gentleman's Magazine* in 1837. The vault was accidentally broke open in 1835, and the head was found enclosed in a leaden box, somewhat in the shape of a beehive, open in the front, with an iron grating in front of it. Margaret Roper, whose filial devotion preserved this precious treasure, was, strangely enough, not buried in this vault, but at Chelsea; so that Tennyson's beautiful lines in his *Dream of Fair Women* are not justified by facts. I believe that since the restoration of the church access to the vault has been rendered impracticable, the organ having been placed over it, and the vault itself filled up with earth.

Among the heads of martyrs in Catholic hands, besides the skull of B. Cuthbert Mayne at Lanherne,† there are those of V. Christopher Wharton (York, March 28, 1600) at Downside, V. Oliver Plunket at Drogheda, and V. William Andleby at Bruges. That of Archbishop Plunket is noteworthy in that it sometimes emits a supernatural perfume which

---

* *E.g.*, V. William Spencer and V. Robert Hardesty in Holy Trinity Church, Micklegate Street, or else in that of St. Martin close by. V. Thomas Watkinson in the churchyard of St. John's Church.

† It is the upper part of the skull. A large piece of the lower part (that under the right ear) is at Sutton Place, near Guildford, in possession of the Salvin family. It was found in this beautiful old mansion of the Westons, together with a large portion of the clavicle of St. William of York, a rib of V. Robert Sutton (Stafford, July 27, 1587), and a vertebra of one of the Fathers Garnet. I give an illustration of these relics together with the old tabernacle (said to be of Marian date), in which they were preserved; a chalice of the penal times; and a Pre-Reformation sacring-bell. All these treasures now belong to the Church of St. Edward, Sutton Place, and the relics have been recently enshrined in modern reliquaries by the Rector, the Rev. Dr. Hinsley, to whose kindness the writer owes the gift of certain portions of each relic.

lasts for some minutes after the shrine is opened, and has been observed by many persons of the highest credit. The flesh and skin are still upon the face, the skin being of a dark brown colour. Part of the left cheek and a little of the upper lip are burnt quite black, no doubt from the fire into which it was thrown at the martyrdom. There is a little hair on the back of the head, and there is the mark of a deep cut across the top, as if an attempt had been made to split the skull. The coffin-plate of the martyr is also preserved in the convent.

The skull of Father Andleby came to the English Convent at Bruges in a curious manner. We give a copy of the paper preserved with it, as a good illustration of the vicissitudes which many of the relics experienced :

"*Ad majorem Dei gloriam*. I well remember that when Madame Vandenbrouek presented me the skull of the Rev. Wm. Andleby, it was without the under jaw. She had taken from it a tooth, which she kept as a relic for herself and family. She brought the whole from St. Omer's at a time when the French Revolution was in the hight [*sic*] of its fury against the God of their fathers, religion, and everything that related to religious worship. It came to her by a young man who came to her house and had an eye on her daughter. He had been at the sacking of the English College at St. Omer, and brought away the venerable head, which he treated with the utmost scorn and indignity, placing it with dirty pigs' feet, guts of dead animals, and all kinds of filth, to prove by fact that all prejudices were done away, and that the new way of thinking cut off at once all restraint on the score of religion. Miss Vandenbrouek received the present, but took care to have no more to say to the gentleman. Mrs. Vandenbrouek brought the head to Bruges, and presented it to Rev. Mother Anne Moore, rightly judging that the Community would be glad to receive the venerable head of an English martyr," &c.

"ANNE MOORE, *alias* Sister MARY CLARE,
"*August* 21, 1834."

The name of the martyr has been written in ink, in a seventeenth-century hand, on the skull. Unhappily, this precaution has not been taken in other cases : there are, for instance, two martyrs' skulls preserved at St. Beuno's which cannot now be identified. One of them has a hole in the cranium made by the pike on which it was exposed ; with them are the bones of a leg which were found wrapped up in a child's jacket, in which they were evidently hidden when rescued by some pious and daring Catholic from the gate or public place where they had been exposed. Father Morris found the skeleton of a mouse inside one of the skulls ! It had apparently made a nest there, and when the skull was

368

The Hand of Father Kemble
at Hereford
Joseph Pike 1910.

*To face page* 368

placed in a box, the mouse could not escape.   These relics come from
Holywell, and it is probable that they are those of V. Philip Evans, S.J.
(Cardiff, July 22, 1679), and V. Charles Baker, S.J. (Usk, August 27,
1679.)

The hands of our martyrs still preserved are more numerous than the
heads, and are most interesting relics.   One of the most famous is that of
V. Margaret Clitherowe, venerated at the Old Bar Convent at York—a
most pathetic memorial of that valiant woman, so justly known as the
Pearl of York.   It is in a beautiful state of preservation, though its vigilant
guardians lament that since a joint of one finger was severed in order to
give it to the late Mr. Charles Weld, the donor of the precious reliquary
that now enshrines the hand, it has begun to show signs of decay.   The
contracted fingers speak most eloquently of the agony of the terrible *peine
forte et dure* which Margaret underwent so bravely that Good Friday of
1586.   Then there is the left hand of V. Ambrose Barlow, O.S.B., at
Stanbrook ; the right hand of V. Francis Ingleby (York, June 3, 1586)
at Taunton ; the right hand of V. Nicholas Postgate (York, August 7,
1679) at St. Cuthbert's, Durham ; and the left hand of the same martyr
at Ampleforth.   At Hereford is the left hand of V. John Kemble
(Hereford, August 22, 1679), which was gorgeously enshrined at the
expense of the late Mr. Monteith of Carstairs, on his recovery from a very
serious illness, when the hand was applied to his lips by Bishop Hedley.
Still more famous is the "Holy Hand" of V. Edmund Arrowsmith, S.J.

I will now endeavour briefly to enumerate the principal places where
English martyr relics are preserved.   The Archbishop of Westminster
has in his keeping relics of various martyrs, the most important of
which is a bone, about six inches in length (the left clavicle), "taken
out of ye neck of Mr. Southworth, who suffered under Oliver Cromwell . . . by Mr. James Clark, chirugeon, who embalmed the body."
There are some other very interesting relics in this collection which
have been recently discovered and set in order by Father J. H.
Pollen, S.J.   Some, mainly of the Oates Plot martyrs, were in a
box with the inscription "To Lady Belling."   This lady was the
wife of Sir William Belling, Chamberlain to Catharine of Braganza.
Among these is one labelled, "This is all the King's Blood," the King
being James II.   There is also a beautiful piece of cloth of gold which
the South Kensington authorities have identified as being a piece of tenth-
century work from Constantinople.   A pattern of eagles, &c., is woven
into the costly fabric.   Though still brilliant, it has marks on it which
show it to have been buried.   It bears the inscription, "This came out of
St. Edward's shrine—a great relic."   It is evidently part of the saintly
Confessor's royal robe, taken from his tomb at the last opening in

James II.'s reign. There are two large "pieces of Bishop plunkets handkerchief," and half a corporal soaked with the blood of Father Paul Heath, O.S.F.

A curious relic is a finger of a very hard leather glove, inscribed as follows :

"This is forefinger of the left handed Gloufe of Mr. Francis Ingelby, Martir martired at Yorke."

Another curious relic is a patch of skin, with no name, but the inscription, "For Crany to wear at the breast." It seems to be the skin of a leg, and has a hole in it, as if for a ribbon to wear round the neck. Let us hope that "Granny" found comfort, if not healing, from wearing it. This was among Lady Belling's treasures.

There are large pieces of linen soaked in Father Morgan's blood, three pieces of the heart of Venerable John Lockwood (one has a clot of blood now turned to dust in it), part of the upper jaw of Father Maxfield, a bone (the end of a toe) of Venerable Edmund Catherick, and some of his hair, &c. Some are enclosed in a silk heart, like an *Agnus Dei* case, with "English Martyrs" embroidered on one side, and I.H.S. on the other.

There is also some hair of V. Margaret Clitherowe and of V. Anne Lyne (Tyburn, February 27, 1601).

But the most interesting of all is a collection of relics of the dear old martyr, Father Kemble. They bear the inscription by Monsignor Moyes : "Relics of the Martyr Father Kemble, received from Miss Hall, Italian Villa, Manchester, who received them from a member of Fr Kemble's family. J. Moyes, June 12, 1907."

On the paper that encloses them is written, "Relics of Father Kemble's Martyrdom."

"A piece of the Coat, hair of the last priest who suffered for the Faith in England, also a bit of the rope with which he was hanged. F. Kemble."

The lock of hair is enclosed in a torn letter, on which we read :

"Honrd Sr

"When you weare in towen I did my utmost indeauers to haue seene you but could noe waye obtaine it, for I was with my mother ye next day after that shee had bin with you, but could not persuade the keeper to let us speak wth you, which was noe small truble to my mother to see you noe more, and to me not to see you at all : but all though I mist of yt hapines, I hope I shal obtaine yt of hauing a part of your good prayers soe along with my mother beging your blessing and prayers I rem[ain] Hond Deare . . . [MS. torn].

370

# RELICS OF THE ENGLISH MARTYRS

"I hope you will honour me w [id.] . . . of your owne hands to s . . . of your good health, my . . . presents our umble duty . . ."

[Written from here sideways in the margin.]

*Endorsed on the back :* "Mr. Kemble hare, cutt of
before he Dyed."

This is exceedingly interesting. It is clear that the lady who wrote this sent it in to the prison, and that Father Kemble cut off a lock of his hair, wrapped it in her letter, and sent it back to her. The relic of the old man's coat is brown in colour.

At Lanherne, the old seat of the Arundels, where the light of the sanctuary has never been extinguished, the Carmelite nuns treasure, besides the skull of B. Cuthbert Mayne, ten remarkable portraits * and relics of about thirty martyrs. At the Franciscan Convent, Taunton, are many very precious relics, including a rib and a leg-bone (tibia, 14 inches long) of V. Francis Bell, O.S.F. (Tyburn, December 11, 1643), who was chaplain to this community when at Princenhoff, Bruges. An autograph letter of the same martyr, a tibia of V. John Baptist Bullaker, O.S.F. ($12\frac{1}{2}$ inches long), the linen corporal which he used at his last Mass, during which he was apprehended, and another dipped in his blood. They have also a tibia of V. Martin Woodcock, O.S.F. (Lancaster, August 7, 1646), a vertebra of V. John Wall, O.S.F.; the cord with which that seraphic martyr, V. Paul Heath, O.S.F., was hanged; fingers of VV. John Roberts and Maurus Scott, O.S.B.; the jawbone of V. Thomas Whitbread (the Jesuit Provincial who suffered for the Oates plot); in all, twenty-nine important relics, including the left arm of Archbishop Plunket, given to them by Mrs. Monington, of Sarnsfield, Worcestershire.

The English Canonesses at Bruges have a yet more precious relic than any of these—a vertebra of the neck of Blessed Thomas More. This is the only relic of his body in Catholic hands (except a tooth and small piece of bone at Stonyhurst), and it came to them through Father Henry More, S.J. Half of this relic is now at Roehampton. They have also a finger of Blessed Thomas Ford (Tyburn, May 28, 1582), together with his portrait, which came through Sister Catherine Willis, who was professed at Bruges in 1742, and who was a connection of the family. They had been brought to Belgium by the martyr's brother, an exile for

---

* The portraits are those of VV. Fathers Ward, Bell (O.S.F.), Bullaker (O.S.F.), Heath (O.S.F.), Ducket, Corby (S.J.), Wright (S.J.), Morse (S.J.), Holland (S.J.), and Green (or Brooke). There is a legend that they were all painted by a Mr. Gifford, a fellow prisoner of the martyrs, in an almost miraculous manner. But the story, as told, will not fit in with the dates.

371

the Faith. The relic consists of the last two joints of the little finger. It is white as wax, and set in a sort of small silver handle. This relic is credited with some remarkable cures.

The Canonesses at Newton Abbot possess one of the most historically interesting of all the relics—the hair-shirt of B. Thomas More. Of this I give an illustration, kindly lent me by the nuns. The story of this relic is so well known that I need not repeat it here, save to remind my readers that it was sent by the blessed martyr, the day before he suffered, to Margaret Roper, from whom it passed to his adopted child, Margaret Gigs, who married Dr. John Clements, and whose daughter founded the Community of St. Monica's, Louvain, now at Newton Abbot. A sleeve of this precious relic was given to Mother Margaret Hallahan, and is now treasured at Stone. Small portions are at Downside; St. Mary's, Cadogan Street; St. Joseph's Church, Roehampton; Ushaw, &c. This community also possess two autograph letters of V. William Howard, Viscount Stafford, written to his daughter Ursula, who was one of the Canonesses of St. Monica's. They seem, unfortunately, to have lost Sir Thomas More's rosary, which was once in their possession.

At East Bergholt is part of the rope which hanged V. John Wall, O.S.F., and two relics of V. Robert Southwell (Tyburn, February 21, 1595), which are said to emit the beautiful odour which distinguishes this martyr's relics. Also a letter, I believe, of V. Francis Bell, O.S.F., describing his apprehension at Stevenage.

The Benedictines of Downside Abbey possess one of the grandest collections of English martyr relics. Besides those already mentioned. they have the mutilated quarters of V. John Lockwood, O.S.B. (a confrater), and V. Edmund Catherick (York, April 13, 1642). These were rescued by Mary Poyntz, the faithful companion and successor of Mary Ward, and carried over to her convent at Augsburg. Here they remained, hidden beneath the altar in the infirmary, and almost forgotten, until they were obtained from the nuns by one of the monks of Downside, and joyfully translated to their splendid church. They have also part of a rib of V. Ambrose Barlow, O.S.B., and many small relics of other martyrs, besides a crucifix that once belonged to Abbot Feckenham, and afterwards to V. Philip Powel, O.S.B. (Tyburn, June 30, 1646). One of their most interesting relics is that of the hair of V. Anne Lyne. This consists of " two beautiful little coils of fine hair which were found enclosed in separate papers, one of which had always been in possession of the community, while the other was brought from Lambspring. They were put together loosely in a glass tube by Dom Ethelbert Horne, O.S.B., and he afterwards found that the hairs had twined them-

372

To face page 372

[BACK]

[FRONT]

THE HAIR SHIRT OF BLESSED THOMAS MORE

selves together in the shape of 8, with a small band across the middle.
A single grey hair had taken the form of L." This is the more
extraordinary, as the hairs were extremely brittle, and broke at the slightest
pressure.

At Clare Abbey, Darlington, were two fingers of V. John Roberts.
The skin is of the colour of parchment, and it is in almost perfect
preservation. On one finger is a label with the inscription, in a seventeenth-century hand, "*Beati Joannis Mervenia digitus sacerdotis et martyris
Ordinis Sti Benedicti in Anglia.*" There is also a bone of the same
martyr, and some other small relics. One of the fingers of Dom Roberts
was given by the nuns to the writer, and the other was subsequently
given to the Benedictines of Downside.

At St. Mary's Convent, York, besides the hand of V. Margaret
Clitherowe, there are about twenty different relics, including a piece of the
rope (apparently only two strands) with which V. Nicholas Postgate was
hanged; and some large pieces of blood-stained linen belonging to a
martyr unknown. Most of these came from Oscott, and were given
by Father Haigh, of Erdington, to the Convent. Others were given by
Father Morris. It is strange that there are not more important relics
at this famous old convent, which weathered the storm of persecution in
the penal days.*

At Oscott there are still several relics of V. Nicholas Postgate and
V. Thomas Thwing, the most interesting of which is a piece of linen
stuff lined with canvas, with a button-hole in one corner, and with the
inscription, "*Mr. Posket's cape he woore 30 yeare.*" These relics belonged
to a Mrs. Juliana Dorrington, a pious Catholic lady, who lived many
years at Old Oscott, and died there in 1731.

At St. Cuthbert's, Old Elvet, Durham, besides the right hand of
Father Postgate, there are two locks of his white hair, his entire lower
jaw-bone, and one of the vertebræ of the spine. There is also the jaw-bone
of V. Thomas Thwing (which still has four teeth on the right side and
three on the left) and one of his vertebræ.

In the Catholic Church at Monmouth are preserved the chalice,
altar, missal and bookstand used for many years by V. John Kemble.
They have already been illustrated in these pages. The altar is made
of two carved oak tables, or, rather, wide benches, one on the top
of the other, so that, when not used for Mass, they could be separated
and placed as benches on either side of the attic which formed the chapel.
The altar-stone is fixed in an oaken case, and is of Bath-stone (oolite);

* One relic here is remarkable; as it purports to be the blood of N. Wilkes, secular
priest, who died in York Castle under sentence of death, 1642. I think there must be
some mistake here.

it is now let into the upper table. The bookstand was very ingeniously made by the martyr himself out of one single board. It closes up very small, in order to facilitate its being hidden. The chalice was recovered by the Rev. Thomas Abbot, then priest of Monmouth, from a Protestant farmer's family, in the neighbourhood of the Castle, in whose possession it had remained since the sack of the Castle at the martyr's apprehension, and who used it as a drinking-cup at their harvest-feasts. It was repaired by Messrs. Hardman and reconsecrated by Bishop Browne, O.S.B., in 1839. The missal contains some MS. prayers written in the martyr's own hand. There is also at Monmouth a fourteenth-century chasuble, embroidered with the Crucifixion and angels catching the Precious Blood in chalices. This has a remarkable history:

"It appears that during the fiercest strife of the penal times two priests, named Jones and Powell, took the "Cross Keys Inn" at Holywell; the one acting as landlord, the other as ostler. At this inn the faithful yeomen would pull up for the purpose of obtaining bodily refreshment (as their Calvinistic neighbours thought), but in reality to obtain refreshment for their souls, for on Sundays and other convenient times Holy Mass was said in that wayside inn. At length the two priests came to the conclusion that it was selfish for both to remain at Holywell when so many Catholics were struggling on in South Wales without the sacraments, and so Mr. Jones came to Monmouth, bringing this chasuble with him. The vestment, after his death, was cut up into small pieces and hidden away by some one who was afraid it might be found in his possession. Father Abbot found the fragments stowed away in a loft, and had it restored and repaired. This splendid old vestment is priceless." *

At West Grinstead are some relics of V. Francis Bell, O.S.F., who seems to have ministered there as missionary priest. They were found under the altar. They consist of a part of his backbone, a bit of the leather of his sandals, and some of his hair-shirt. But the most interesting of all is an autograph letter written from Newgate. It ends: "All that I aske of any is that St. Andrew begged of the people, ' *ne impedirent passionem*,' God's holy will be done *in æternum*.

"Your poor brother,

"November 12, 1643."              "FRANCIS BELL.†

\* *St. Peter's Chair*, October 1893.

† The late Mr. Grissell of Oxford had a little MS. book entirely written by this martyr. It contains an account of his family and of his own life, and some coats of arms painted by his own hand. The last entry is the most interesting: " *Anno 1634 missus sum in Angliam ad convertendum animas ad fidem catholicam.*" This with the other relics of Mr. Grissell's magnificent collection are now kept in a chapel in St. Aloysius' Church, Oxford. There are, however, but few relics of our martyrs.

374

PAGES FROM THE PRAYER-BOOK OF B. THOMAS PERCY

*Note that in the copy of the prayer from the primer, the martyr has inserted in the margin "in temporal matters" after the words "our soveraigne ladie and supreme hed"*

*To face page 374*

THE GEORGE AND A CRUCIFIX
OF BLESSED THOMAS MORE
*Now at Stonyhurst College*

THE WATCH AND WATCH-CASE WORN BY
THE VENERABLE WILLIAM HOWARD, VIS-
COUNT STAFFORD, AT HIS MARTYRDOM
*Now in possession of the Lady Stafford.   Photo by the author*

*To face page* 374

# RELICS OF THE ENGLISH MARTYRS

At Husbands Bosworth Hall, the seat of Mr. Oswald Petre-Turville, is preserved a very beautiful relic of the martyr, B. Adrian Fortescue (beheaded, Tower Hill, July 9, 1539). It consists of the Book of Hours constantly used by the martyr, and since his beatification it has been kept in a shrine in the church. On the front page Sir Adrian has written some beautiful maxims, a kind of rule of life, which he has signed at the end, "Adryan ffortescue." Curiously enough, not far off, at Newnham Paddox, there is the Book of Hours of another martyr, B. Thomas More. This most precious little book was used by the blessed martyr when imprisoned in the Tower, and it also has some autograph prayers written in the margin, which are of exquisite beauty and pathos. They begin thus :

> " Give me Thy grace, good God,
>   To sette the world at naught ;
>   To sette my minde faste upon Thee and not to hange
>     uppon the blaste of mennys mowthis."

*     *     *     *     *

> " Of worldly substance, frendys, libertie, lyfe and all
>     to sett the loss at right nowght for the wynning of Christ.
>   To think my moste enemys mye beste frendys
>     for the brethren of Joseph could never have done him so
>     much goode with their love and favour, as they did hym
>     with their malice and hatred."

The third great layman among the *Beati* has also left a MS. book of prayer, but this seems to be entirely written in his own hand. I refer to the prayer-book of B. Thomas Percy, Earl of Northumberland, a priceless volume, lately in possession of Mr. George Browne of Troutbeck, Kendal. This prayer-book is referred to by Sander in the *De Visibili Monarchia Ecclesiæ*. As it has been fully described in the *Ushaw Magazine*, by the Rev. George Phillips, I need not do more than refer to it. I give an illustration of two pages.

Another relic of B. Thomas More is his rosary-ring, in possession of the Trappes family. This consists of a hoop with a bezel engraved with the I.H.S., and ten knobs whereon to count the *Aves*. A somewhat similar ring, said to have belonged to B. Edmund Campion, is at Farm Street. That of B. Thomas More is said to have come through Mother Mary More (the last survivor of the family), who was Superior of the English Convent, Bruges.

At Hendred House, Berks, the seat of the Eyston family, is, as before mentioned, the can or drinking-cup of B. Thomas More, and the walking-staff of B. John Fisher, which he carried to the scaffold.

Some very precious vestments used by martyrs are in the possession of Mr. Herbert, of Helmsley Hall, near York. They belonged to the

Thwing family, of which the late Mrs. Herbert was a member, and must have been used by the two martyrs of that family—V. Edward (Lancaster, July 26, 1600) and V. Thomas Thwing (York, October 23, 1680). One of the chasubles is an exceedingly beautiful Gothic vestment, 51 inches long and 37 inches wide, made of crimson velvet pile, with a cross and pillar of green satin, embroidered on the back with the Assumption of Our Lady and Seraphs. The other is of woollen brocade, woven in crimson, green and white ; evidently in order that it might be used for any of these colours. It is also Gothic in shape. The *palla* preserved with these vestments possesses a special interest, having still attached to it by small solid-headed pins the linen pall, as used by the martyrs. These vestments were lent to the convent at York, and exhibited at the Ransomers' pilgrimage there at Whitsuntide.

At Farm Street are a quantity of relics collected by the late Father Morris, but they are mostly quite small ones, as the larger ones he placed at Roehampton. Others are portions of larger ones at Stonyhurst and elsewhere. I therefore pass them over. The relics belonging to the Huddlestone family, of Sawston Hall, near Cambridge, are also very small, but are exceedingly interesting as some of them are very rare. They are chiefly of the martyrs of the time of the Oates plot. Two seem to be unique, those of V. John Grove and V. John Lloyd. There is also some straw with a very puzzling inscription, apparently in Portuguese, which is almost indecipherable. It apparently reads : " Da esteira em que forao martyrisados il noster geroues [Grove ?] e noster ? Lomda " [Ireland ?]—*i.e.*" From the straw on which were martyred our (?) and our (?) " (or perhaps, " in London "). But almost every word has to be guessed at, and I have no idea what martyrs can be meant.

The spelling of the inscriptions attached to these relics is remarkable. Thus, Archbishop Plunket becomes " the holy B : plompin " ; V. John Grove is " Mr. Growfe " ; V. John Lloyd, " F. Flouid " ; and straw is spelt " stray."

The Carmelites at Chichester have some interesting relics, fifty-four in all, of twenty-eight English martyrs. They (like those of Colwich) have been lost sight of for many years and were only found again in 1906. Among the rarer relics are the following : " Of the Bloud & of the haire girdle of the Venerable M. Father William Harcourt." This is a large mass of horse-hair, as a relic it is unique. Another is inscribed : " Un peu du cœur propre du perre irlandt [Fr. Ireland] con a tiré hor du feu un de la premier Exsecutte."

Most of these relics are of the Oates plot martyrs.

We now come to the great relics at Stonyhurst, which, indeed, in regard to their importance, ought almost to have had the first place.

376

THE CLAUGHTON ALTAR CLOSED
*The Pre-Reformation crucifix is also from Mains Hall.
The small carved oak box was used by the V. Thomas
Whitaker for the reservation of the Blessed Sacrament.
Photo by the author*

To face page 376

THE ALTAR FROM MAINS HALL (NOW AT
CLAUGHTON HALL) OPENED FOR MASS
*Photo by the author*

# RELICS OF THE ENGLISH MARTYRS

The relics of the *Beati* were contained in four mahogany boxes, lined with crimson velvet.* The inscriptions are in red ink in a very early hand. One of the most touching is the rope of B. Edmund Campion. It seems to be nearly twelve feet long. There are in the same case relics of BB. John Fisher, Thomas Ford, William Filby, Ralph Sherwin (a knuckle-bone), Luke Kirby (a phalanx of foot), and Edmund Campion (blood-stained linen). In another case is a most precious corporal, on which five martyrs said Mass when imprisoned in the Tower. Their names are embroidered in red silk on the linen (BB. Luke Kirby, Robert Johnson, Alexander Briant, S.J., John Shert, and Thomas Cottam, S.J.). But the most intrinsically precious, as well as the most interesting, are, of course, the famous More relics. As these have been described in Father Bridget's " Life of B. Thomas More " (Appendix), I need not do more than refer to them. They consist of the " George," a most splendid jewel of priceless value ; two crucifixes (one of which contained a relic of St. Thomas the Apostle), the martyr's seal (as Sub-Treasurer of England), a cameo with the head of Our Lady, a crystal and silver reliquary containing one of the martyr's teeth and a piece of thick bone; and a shell (tiger cowrie) made into a pouncet-box. In another case are Sir Thomas's curiously embroidered cap and his hat. I give an illustration of the " George."

Other relics of B. Thomas More, consisting of a sword, a small clock, &c., are in the possession of Mrs. Forman, who is descended from the martyr in the female line.

There is also at Stonyhurst an old reliquary, containing a thumb of V. Robert Sutton (Stafford, July 27, 1587), which was given to F. John Gerard, S.J., by the martyr's brother, and by him enclosed in this reliquary, as he tells us in his autobiography. Besides this, there are some large bones of one of the Durham martyrs, an eye of V. Edward Oldcorne, S.J., and a very elaborate silver spoon, parcel gilt, in a curious case, which is said to have belonged to B. Richard Whiting, O.S.B., last Abbot of Glastonbury. This spoon is dated 1500. The handle terminates in a female bust growing from a vine-stock, doubled and twisted, and bearing leaves. It closes up, to fit into a case. When open, a ferule slips over the hinge and keeps the handle in position ; on the front of this ferule is engraved a human head. The case is made of parchment which has been moulded into its present shape while wet, and is covered with thin black skin, probably moleskin, the joint down the side being so delicate as to be hardly perceptible. The history of this relic

---

* Quite recently they have been translated into reliquaries of crystal and silver gilt, which can be exposed on the altar. I give illustrations of two of these, from photographs kindly supplied by the Very Rev. Father Rector of Stonyhurst.

is, unfortunately, at present forgotten, and it is not known how it came to Stonyhurst. Besides these great relics, there are quantities of small relics of various martyrs which it would be tedious to enumerate here.

In the sacristy of St. Joseph's Church, Roehampton, is a large case of relics, collected and arranged by Father John Morris, S.J. Besides the relics of B. Thomas More already mentioned, there are about thirty-eight other relics. There are, for instance, large bones of VV. John Lockwood, Edmund Catherick (from Augsburg), Robert Southwell, S.J., and of two Douay martyrs whose names are unknown. There are also pieces of linen dipped in the blood of VV. Thomas Thwing, William Plessington (Chester, July 19, 1679), John Wall, O.S.F., Thomas Garnet, S.J., John Almond, John Southworth, &c. Two of the most interesting are a bone of B. Edmund Campion, being half of the relic preserved at the Gesù (and which is, in all probability, the martyr's thumb), and a piece of the hat which he wore when paraded through the streets in mockery. On it was fastened a paper bearing the inscription: "Campion, the seditious Jesuit." There is also a large piece of the rope with which V. David Henry Lewis, S.J. (*alias* Charles Baker), was hung at Usk (August 27, 1679), and a tooth of V. Thomas Whitbread, S.J. (from Taunton); also a piece of blood-stained linen in a paper bearing the inscription: "*The keeper of the preson said cirtanly he was a St. all that saw him die thought no less pay [pray] prize this.*" We do not know to what martyr this refers. There are also two relics of V. Richard White (Wrexham, October 17, 1584), which are the only ones existing, as far as I know.

At Manresa House is preserved a copy of the Summa of St. Thomas Aquinas, which belonged to B. Edmund Campion, and contains many notes in his own hand. Another book that apparently once belonged to a Jesuit martyr, is a missal in possession of the Lady Catherine Berkeley, which bears the curious inscription: "*Alexandro Brianto Alexander Farnesius.*" This certainly suggests the idea that the famous Duke of Parma gave the book to B. Alexander Briant, who may have come under his notice when a student at Douay. At the end of the books are some prayers written in the same hand.

At Erdington Abbey there are relics of about forty martyrs, the most important of which are a finger of V. John Roberts, O.S.B.; a bone, about three inches long and also part of a rib, of V. Ambrose Barlow, O.S.B.; the *palla* used by V. Martin Woodcock, O.S.F., at his last Mass; and a large piece of the hat of B. Edmund Campion. This last relic is doubly interesting, as the hat in question belonged first to S. Francis Borgia, S.J., who gave it to B. Edmund when he was leaving Rome. It is now kept at the old Jesuit College (now the Episcopal

378

THE CLAUGHTON CHALICE FROM
MAINS HALL
*Probably used by Blessed Edmund Campion*

*To face page* 378

Seminary) at Prague. It is made of black felt. There are also some large pieces of linen soaked in the blood of V. David Lewis, S.J., V. Oliver Plunket, V. Henry Heath, and V. John Wall. The *palla* already referred to is covered on the upper side with light blue diapered silk. In the centre is a broad Greek cross of light gold-coloured silk, which is outlined with a twisted silk lace of a brighter yellow. The same lace is used to border the *palla*.

At Claughton-on-Brock, in Lancashire, are two interesting relics of V. Thomas Whitaker, who once served this district. The one is a plain oak desk in which the martyr stored his vestments and other things necessary for holy Mass ; and the other a box, about seven inches square, in which he used to keep the Blessed Sacrament. This is elaborately carved on the panels. These relics came through the Midgeall family, with whom the martyr lived.

We give an illustration of the latter placed on an old missionary altar which belongs to Mr. Fitzherbert Brockholes of Claughton Hall. The Pre-Reformation crucifix, like the altar itself, comes from Mains (or Monks') Hall, the ancient seat of the Hesketh family, which was visited by Blessed Edward Campion on his missionary journey in Lancashire in 1581. I think the altar (which, as it will be seen, is of the bureau type) cannot be older than the early part of the eighteenth century, but the crucifix is a beautiful specimen of a mediæval processional cross. A still greater treasure at Claughton is the magnificent Pre-Reformation chalice, which also comes from Mains, and which was used, there can be very little doubt, by the Blessed Edmund himself when he said Mass at Mains.

By Mr. Fitzherbert Brockholes's kindness I am able to give an illustration of this beautiful relic. It closely resembles that preserved in the Catholic church at Hornby in the same county, but the Claughton one is, perhaps, the more beautiful and elaborate of the two.

Its date is the latter half of the fifteenth century, or perhaps the first decade of the sixteenth. The kind of *calix* at the base of the bowl is, however, a modern addition. The knot, formed with six lobes, is extremely beautiful. Between the lobes above and below are pierced and traceried compartments. The foot is mullet-shaped, five of its compartments being filled with I H C and X P C alternately, while the sixth has the crucifix.

Small knobs are attached to the points of the mullet foot in the manner of toes, and these add greatly to the artistic effect of the whole.*

Beautiful and precious as this chalice is, the thought that it was probably used at the Holy Sacrifice of the Mass by one of the greatest

* See *English Mediæval Chalices and Patens*, by W. H. St. John Hope and T. M. Fallow, in the *Archæological Journal*, vol. xliii. p. 147.

of all our martyrs, adds immeasurably to its value, and it is a joy to think that it still remains in Catholic hands. The present writer has himself had the privilege of using it.

At St. Scholastica's Abbey, Teignmouth, is preserved a very interesting and beautiful old reliquary crucifix of which we give an illustration.

The tradition about this precious cross is that it was dug up at Fountains Abbey, and it is supposed to have been the pectoral cross of one of the Abbots of that great Cistercian house. It is silver, and the cross is circular in section, and grooved to resemble the bark of a tree. In the back, at the centre, is fixed a tooth. Three ends of the cross (*i.e.*, the top and the two arms) also contain relics, and on the silver ends are engraved initials as follows: At the top R.B., at the right arm M.C., and at the left, T.H. There has also been an inscription at the bottom, but it is so much battered (and there is moreover a hole through the letters) that it is impossible to do more than guess what it was, though it looks like H.P. We can give no conjecture as to the names represented by these initials.

Reliquary Cross at St Scholastica's Abbey, Teignmouth

The Martyr's tooth set in back of Cross.

Curiously enough, there is a precisely similar crucifix at the Franciscan Convent, Taunton. If the Teignmouth one was really dug up at Fountains Abbey, this must be a copy of it. The only distinction between them is that there are no relics at the ends, nor initials. But a tooth is inserted in the back, exactly as in the Teignmouth one. The nuns do not seem to have any notion as to how or from whom they received the cross; there is, however, a tradition that it is a tooth of V. John Wall, O.S.F., the martyr of Harvington Hall.

The Teignmouth nuns have no tradition as to the relics in their cross, but they think that the cross was brought to them by Lady Abbess Messenger, of the Benedictine Monastery at Pontoise, who was a relation of the owners of Fountains Abbey, and who joined their community with three others when the Pontoise nuns, owing to their extreme poverty, were obliged to disperse. If the cross were dug up at Fountains in its present state the relics cannot be those of English martyrs, nor do all the initials correspond with the names of martyrs known to us. However, the relics may have been added later. Personally,

380

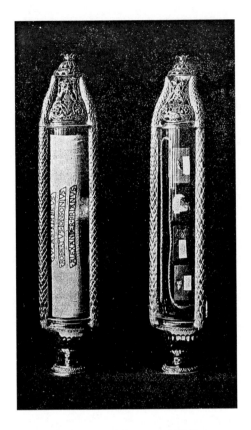

RELICS OF THE BLESSED
ENGLISH MARTYRS FROM
STONYHURST COLLEGE
*The corporal on which five Beati saia
Mass in the Tower*
*The rope with which Blessed Edmuna
Campion was bound, and other relics
of the Beati*

THE THUMB OF THE
VENERABLE ROBERT
SUTTON
*In the original reliquary given
by Fr. John Gerard, S.J., now
preserved at Stonyhurst College*

*To face page* 380

however, we are inclined to suspect that the crucifix is not of such an early date as the tradition of its origin would suggest.

Some mention must be made of the relics of the last Englishman who suffered during the persecution. V. William Howard, Viscount Stafford, was beheaded on the Feast of St. Thomas of Canterbury, December 29, 1680. Many secondary relics of this glorious martyr are preserved by his descendants; for instance, the shirt in which he suffered, and the furniture of his Chapel are in the possession of Mr. Howard of Corby. The two relics figured here, are the martyr's watch, with its curious old silver case, and the diamond pendant which he wore on the scaffold. The former is in possession of the Lady Stafford, and the latter belongs to Lord Stafford and is preserved at Costessy. I owe the photograph from which the drawing of the pendant is taken to the kindness of Mr. Stafford H. Jerningham. The jewel is exceedingly brilliant and beautiful, and is composed of large diamonds. The drawing gives but an imperfect idea of its beauty. The pendant was recently shown at the very interesting Art Exhibition held in connection with the first National Congress at Leeds in August 1910, where it excited great admiration.

LORD STAFFORD'S
DIAMOND PENDANT

With this splendid treasure, this account of our martyrs' relics may come to a close here. It is necessarily very brief and incomplete, but I think most of the more important relics have been mentioned.* If this account of them elicits information as to further treasures as yet unknown to me, I shall be amply repaid for the trouble of writing it. I must acknowledge my obligations to Father John Pollen, S.J., who has kindly placed at my disposal the papers of the late Father Morris, and to many other friends who have most kindly assisted me in my inquiries.

* I find that I have notes of relics of about 107 different martyrs, besides several anonymous relics. Of the following I only know of one relic: B. Thomas Beche, Abbot of Colchester (pectoral cross belonging to Lord Clifford); V. Roger Cadwallader (bone, Stonyhurst), V. John Carey (finger, Bruges), V. Roger Filcock, S.J. (Stonyhurst), V. Matthew Flathers (Bruges), V. John Grove (Sawston), B. Everard Hanse (blood, Westminster), V. William Harrington (Colwich), Lawrence Hill (Colwich), V. Francis Ingelby (hand, Taunton), B. Robert Johnson and B. John Short (corporal, Stonyhurst), V. Richard Langhorne (Colwich, part now at Downside), V. John Lloyd, S.J. (Sawston), V. Francis Page, S.J. (Stonyhurst), B. Thomas Percy, V. John Robinson (Stonyhurst), B. Richard Thirkeld (Colwich), V. Margaret Ward (Colwich), V. Richard White (Roehampton), (?) Wilks, (?) Confessor Priest (York). There are none at all of most of Henry VIII.'s victims.

# APPENDIX A

[*See page* 35]

LETTERS PATENT OF QUEEN ELIZABETH, NOMINATING SIR WALTER ASTON, KNIGHT, RICHARD BAGOTT, THOMAS TRENTHAM, AND JOHN VERNON, ESQUIRES, ARBITRATORS IN THE DISPUTE BETWEEN SIR THOMAS FITZHERBERT AND HIS NEPHEW, THOMAS FITZHERBERT, ESQUIRE

IF THEY CANNOT COME TO A FINAL DECISION THEY ARE TO REFER THE MATTER TO THE ROYAL CHANCERY BEFORE THE MORROW OF CANDLEMAS FOLLOWING

DATED DECEMBER 5, 29 ELIZABETH, 1586

[*No. 30 of the Norbury deeds at Swynnerton*]

**Elizabeth** dei gratia Anglie ffrancie & hibernie Regina fidei defensor, &c. **Dilecto** et fideli suo Waltero Aston militi ac dilectis sibi Ricardo Bagott Armigero Thome Trentham Armigero & Johanni Vernon Armigero salutem. **Cum** varie lites & controversie nuper orte et mote sint inter Thomam ffitzherbert militem ex una parte et Thomam ffitzherbert Armigerum ex altera parte Ac ipsi ex eorum mutuo assensu et consensu easdem materias per vos finaliter determinandas vestro arbitrio comisere vestroque in premissis iudicio stare decreverunt **Sciatis** igitur quod nos de fidelitatibus & providis circumspectionibus vestris plurimum confidentes assignavimus vos ac tenore presentium damus vobis vel tribus vestrum potestatem & auctoritatem materias predictas audiendi et examinandi & finaliter si poteritis determinandi. **Et ideo** vobis vel tribus vestrum mandamus quod ad cunctos dies et loca quos ad hoc provideritis tam partes predictas quam testes quoscunque quos maxime pro testificatione veritatis in hac parte fore videritis necessarios & oportunos coram vobis vel tribus vestrum venire faciatis & evocetis. Ac ipsos testes & eorum quemlibet per se separatim tunc ibidem de & super quibusdam Interrogatoriis per partes predictas seu earundem partem alteram vobis vel tribus vestrum deliberandi super sacramenta sua coram vobis vel tribus vestrum per sancta dei evangelia corporaliter prestanda diligenter examinetis examinationesque suas recipiatis et in scriptis redigatis de materia & probationibus in eisdem per vos plenius intellectis & animadversis auditisque hinc inde partium predictarum rationibus et invicem propositis et proponendis allegationibus intellectaque totius rei veritate easdem materias omnibus viis modis et mediis quibus melius sciveritis aut poteritis iuxta sanas discretiones & consciencias vestras finaliter ut predictum est si poteritis determinetis. Ac si materias predictas finaliter ut predictum est

383

# APPENDIX A

determinare non poteritis, nos cujus defectu id exequi non poteritis ac de toto facto et iudicio vestro in premissis in Cancellariam nostram in crastino Purificationis beate Marie proxime futuro ubicunque tunc fuerit sub sigillis vestris vel trium vestrum distincte et apte reddatis certiores hoc breve nobis remittentes ut ulterius inde fieri faciamus quod de iure fuerit faciendum. Teste me ipsa apud Westmonasterium quinto die decembris anno regni nostri vicesimo nono.

P. GERRARD

# APPENDIX B

[*See page* 61 *supra*]

## ARTICLES AGAINST WILLIAM BASSETT *

[*Note : the passages in italics are underlined in the original MS.*]

34 ELIZ.—Articles against William Bassett Esquire now Sheriff of Derbyshire, preferred by Thomas Fitzherbert her Majesty's sworn servant under his hand & seal in her Majesty's hand.

A brief of such articles as be delivered to the Queens most excellent Majesty from Thomas Fitzherbert Esq^re her highness' sworn servant under his hand sealed against William Bassett of Langlays & Blore in Derbyshire Esquire.

1. William Bassett was brought up in his uncle Sir Thomas Fitzherberts house under these many popish priests and schoolmasters, to wit, Robert Gray, Robert Hyll, John Morryn, Thos. Collier, William Batersby, Rich. Gray, all priests and Martin Audlaye a civilian, all traitorous affected persons as Sir Thomas Fitzherbert himself was. And so were his cousin Germayne, Thomas now here and George at Rome a Jesuit, Nicholas servant unto Cardinal Allen as his secretary, francis a barefooted friar, Anthony that hath received seminary priests, Thomas Fitzherbert of Swynnerton a notorious traitor and pensioner of the King of Spain and of ye Scott. Queen while she lived and divers others little better.

*He will not deny that he was so brought up ; and It appears in Martyn Audlay's examination, pag :*

2. William Bassett hath been affected to bad persons in allegiance as to the *Lord Paget* the traitor. So as he *commanded* William Copwood by a letter which he sent from London (when the Lord Paget fled) *to rid his two houses* Langley and Blore and to make away all letters and other matters that concerned the Lord Paget. So did Copwood and one Richard Dakyn then help him as he can tell by good tokens.

Richard Dakyn

Wm. Copwood

3. William Bassett *keepeth* in his house and park at Langlay one Thomas Thomson and his wife recusants and the husband long was in prison and *outlawed for recusancy*, the wife is his launderer and he calleth her his noone [?]

* Harl. 6998, f. 248

3 c

385

4. W<sup>m</sup> Bassett in a° 1588 *received a letter from Thomas Fitzherbert* of Swynnerton his dearest darling and *Spanish traitor* by his man John Britel-bank wherein Thomas writes for money and did promise repayment *when the fleet should come shortly* whereupon *Bassett commanded Richard Dakyn* then keeper of his money to deliver £10 to George Raworthe another servant to go to hunt the hare and Brytelbank should see Raworth throw down that bag of £10 into a bush and take it up for his master Thomas Fitzherbert of Swynnerton & carry it to him & Brittelbank was asked by Dakyn if he had not found the hare whereunto Brittelbank answered 'Yea I have her here' and Bassett clapped him on the breast and said they would be here shortly.

John Britelbank himself to be had

George Raworth.

Ric Dakyn and his book of Accounts Extant of £5000 reckoning he being and dakyn is a plain simple man

And he called for Dakyn's book wherein he had entered nothing of his own handwriting before, Bassett did then write, Received by my self £10 and for fear of suspicion and to remember to whom it was sent or given, he did write over these words (myself) vide<sup>ct</sup> *Bruse bone* or *Boane Brewse.*

5. William Bassett did know assuredly that one Todd was a massing priest taken with two other Seminary priests Bodlam [*sic*] & Garlick executed as traitors at Derby. Todd continuing in the Gaol at Derby, when Bassett's cousin Mr. Dethick was sheriff he did send for Todd out of prison to his house Langlay and *kept him in his house there a month* or 6 weeks in anno 1591. So hath he *received Sir Walter Barlow a priest out of the gaol at Stafford* when himself was sheriff of that shire & by that priest's labour granted a Gaolership unto harby there in anno [blank in MS.]. And in that year Robert Sutton the Lord Paget's traitorous priest being condemned for treason, Bassett dealt secretly with him, Sutton desiring that he might live but to reveal matters of great importance and treason touching England and her Majesty, but Bassett would not stay execution which he might have done, lest the priest had discovered more matters than Bassett would have liked (as men judge) & Dakyn Bassett's cook did make the priest Caudles and about that time when letters were sent down to the old Earl of Shrewsbury to apprehend Richard Fitzherbert & Martin Audlay

*John Bamford*
Rich : Dakyn
*Ralf Maison, Gaoll<sup>r</sup> of Darby*

Harby Gaoller of Staff.

386

and Seminary priests at Norbury Sir Thomas Fitzherbert's house, Bassett did send Randall Swynnerton to give warning to Richard Fitzherbert to fly away.

Ric Cotton
Ric Dakyn
Randall Swynnerton

6. *W^m Bassett did send for Rich : Gray a traitorous priest* from Buxtons or from Langford to Langlay his own house & there entertained him gave him venison & *desired him to go & make a concorde betwixt his cousin Henry Sacheverell and his wife which Gray did* & since Michælmas last *Bassett received a Seminary* priest, as Mr. P—— sayth.

Ric Dakyn
John Bamford

7. W^m Bassett practised upon his uncle Sir Thomas Fitzherbert committing [*sic*] for Treason to Lambeth house with one John Sherrat that he should *steal away a casket locked of Sir Tho : Fitzherbert's* where it was hidden with other traitorous matter, & *after Bassett had it in his hands he did break it open & found* therein both assurance of Lands of the said Traitor's Thomas of Swynnerton his said darling and *letters of importance* sent from the one of those traitors to another. A disloyal presumption & offence & he dispersed other caskets locked full of other writings at his pleasure which were that arch traitor's Sir Thos. Fitzherbert his uncle's to the great hindrance of her Majesty's Service, he having warning to the contrary.

Jhon Sherratt's examination extant

*Jhon Bamford*
Rich. Topcliff

8. W^m Bassett hath conversed with & *entertained at his houses Nigromancers* as Thomas Allen of Oxford being together at Langlay 12 or 13 years past sent Richard Johnson for a smith's steddy & hammer. They did all watch when the sun should come to the noon stead & the very prick of noon and then if the sun did shine the hammer should strike upon the stethy * 3 times together. After W^m Bassett should have answer truly made to such questions as he should demand by a voice or vision. But so it chanced that the sun did not shine nor they could discern the true hour & thereupon Allen said that a year's labour was lost. As John being one of the 3 told Richard Dakyn.

Ric. Dakyn
Ric. Johnson
A Smith at Langlay

9. W^m Bassett hath long since and lately had great trust in Nigromancers and Astrologers, &

* Steady or stithy : a blacksmith's anvil.

387

hath said that one of his own house should put him
in danger & be betrayed and perceived the same
by his owne nativity that was cast & was written
in a reddish gilded book covered with leather &
gilded leaves about 2 fingers thick, in which many
things he blotted out for fear and this he did speak
one time when W^m Copwood & he fell out
being his man.   As Dakyn heard.                    Ric Dakyn

He and his master's men did call it *the book of
their master's fortune.*

And by that means Bassett would often speake
of his own marriage.

10. W^m Bassett about *Michaelmas last* had at
Langlay one M^r Davis a setter of figures & Allen
also ; At which time Bassett did speak this or     John Bamford
like words to Randall Swynnerton v^t what a world   Randall Swynnerton
is this Randall *if a man should be sheriff at the death
of a prince, what wonders might a sheriff then do &
work at that time, & about Lenten now 2 years past
Davis was at Langlay* with a trunk full of books
& he did give Davis a horse and an armour
valued at £100, the horse called Bay Lewcye.

11. W^m Bassett hath used to say before his       Ric Dakyn and most of
servants sometimes secretly sometimes more openly  his men.
that *he should be as great a man ere he died as any
was in his country* and thereof he was sure.
W^m Bassett since he had his cousin Thomas
Fitzherbert in his house prisonner, *one reported* part
of the Lord *Keeper's oration or speech* before the   Ric Cotton
Queen's Majesty in the Parliament House of the      John Bamford
preparing of the Spaniard for a new invasion into   S^rceant Fowller
England by Scotland.   Then in a bravery W^m        Thos. Fitzherbert himself
Bassett said *Well I shall be as great a man in Spain
as any is in my Country* & further *threatened Thomas
Fitzherbert that he would be revenged of him* (being
his prisoner) *for the death of his good uncle Sir Thomas
Fitzherbert* & either break Thomas Fitzherbert's
back or his own.   And so hath Bassett often
threatened his cousin Thos Fitzherbert, Bassett
having knowledge and sight of Sir Thomas Fitz-
herbert his uncle's treasons.   When Mr. Top-        Ric. Topcliffe
cliffe was sent down to Norbury Sir Thomas' house
to search for his traitorous matter hidden.   At
which time Mr. Bassett walked up & down by
the table when a foul spider was found by Mr.
Topcliffe in his milk prepared for his breakfast by
388

# APPENDIX B

2 or 3 women in the house whose husbands fathers and friends had been lately committed to prison in London, for Sir Thomas's and their own treasons &c.

Bassett would needs persuade Topcliffe that it was not a spider but a humble bee. But Topcliffe told Bassett that he did find the leggs & if Bassett would find the wings then he would believe Bassett that it was a humble bee.

W^m Bassett being in the Lowe Countries with the Earl of Leicester was desirous to return. W^m Bassett devised that Randall Swynnerton should counterfeit a letter in the name of some person in England signifying Bassett that it were convenient for him to come over for suits touching his cousin Langford. W^m Bassett by that device returned over and after lodging at Skinner's, Bassett and Francis Leake fell foully out, and Randall Swynnerton thereupon persuading W^m Bassett to fight with Francis Leake. W^m Bassett did answer Swynnerton to this effect. Sir Randall let me alone. By the death of God (& clapped his hand upon his breast said) *When the Queen shall die I will burn Francis Leake his house and him therein & all his family, for the Queen grows to be old* and cannot long live & in the 57^th year of her age and [*sic*] 63^rd year of her age the Queen shall die for that those years were most dangerous and he termed those years Annos Climaticos or such like.

And divers times William Bassett hath spoken to the like effect, &c.

W^m Bassett and Randall Swynnerton riding to a town Gryndon (being W^m Bassett's) Bassett did devise a plat of ground whereon he said to Swynnerton, *Here about this toun will I make a skonce wherein if my tenants can hold their cattle but 2 or 3 days within a trensh at the death of the Queen* and the time of alteration then can I relieve my tenants and bring a number of men with me and then there will be such a stir as that a thousand pounds in money will be worth a thousand pounds Land and thou shalt live to see that day come very shortly, and to the like effect hath W^m Bassett spoken divers times and in divers places.

Randall Swynnerton

Randall Swynnerton

389

# APPENDIX C

[*See page* 60 *supra*]

## TOPCLIFFE'S LETTERS TO THE COUNCIL AND TO QUEEN ELIZABETH FROM THE MARSHALSEA PRISON, APRIL 1595

[*British Museum. Harleian MSS. No.* 6998, *f.* 184 *et sqq.*]

MAY it please your LL<sup>s</sup> and the residue, I remaining as I do here in this prison of the Marshalsea committed by the Q's Ma<sup>tys</sup> commandment, by the mouth of my Lord Treasurer for all your Honours, Being so her Ma<sup>ty's</sup> prisoner I did think my chief duty to explain my innocency about her Ma<sup>tys</sup> sacred person by two letters & my meaning for any offence that I was guilty of.

Although by words passed from me in answer to questions asked of me, an offence was conceived of my speech for two several grounds of offence given (as they were taken)

1. First, that I should mean that your Lordship the Lord Keeper had not done me ordinary justice.

2. Secondly, that I should mean that I could charge some of your honours with taking gifts of £10,000 value—— To both which I must (while I live) protest upon the peril of my soul that I neither meant an ill thought or word to the Lord Keeper, nor to the person or doings of any of you of that honourable table. And as I have in those two letters explained my grief chiefly that her Ma<sup>ty</sup> hath conceived I have done undutifully at this yeare of 63, and never before frowned of or called to question, so have I sent to your LL<sup>s</sup> & Honours hereinclosed a true copy of those two letters that I have written to her Ma<sup>ty</sup> to plead for me to every one of you for my mercy, not doubting but if the letters themselves obtain not grace at her Majesty's hands for me in as ample sort as my heart desireth in those two letters, yet that my service hereafter shall weigh against this offence, and so I doubt not but all your HHs will think yourselves        Most of whom have valued my services past far exceeding that which myself have weighed them at.

If any thing want in this that your HHs expect for, I beseech your LL<sup>s</sup> & your residue to lay this my humble letter & that which is contained in my said two copies of my letters to her Majesty together, and therewith I trust your honourable wisdoms and the Lord Keeper particularly will hold himself satisfied. Otherwise the length of time & loathsomeness of prison must make satisfaction for my answers unto questions (the answers mistaken) which questions drew me to make answer as I did pass through the Council chamber, and neither complaining myself nor I complained upon by any person nor any matter of state the ground of those questions nor of my fault.  Then I shall quietly endure seven years imprisonment if it be laid upon me, and yet do my best service to God my queen and country, if my avowed enemies here suffer me to live, where I am forced upon good grounds to become my own cook continually, seeing daily here walk before me a murderer of fresh [? French] Byrthe [*sic*], who (as 3 witnesses offered to justify) did come out of Ireland from priests to murder me, And yet he is not the

390

worst of the papists that daily front me with envious eyes from whose *crooks* God keep her Sacred Ma^ty and you all.

from the Marshalsea this Monday in Easter week 1595
the humble prisoner of her Majesty
RIC. TOPCLIFFE

A true copy of my first letter sent to the Queens most excellent Majesty and also of my second letter, I think both rejected, since I was committed.

My most gracious and only Sovereign, I have long since heard and lately believed that the indignation of a prince to a faithful subject is a kind of death. Myself hath lived in 3 or 4 of my KK^s and QQ^s days & have thought any of their frowns to be deeper wounds than any of any other degree, prince or subject, can cure ; But the same eyes, brows or speech that doth give the blow, I mean the delightful cheer of the Same my Sovereign, can only heal and cure.

Now find I the latter of those to grieve and the lesser over true, at 60 and 3 years of age, so far as when I was told at your Highness's Council table that your Majesty's sacred pleasure was upon unhappy Palm Sunday that I should be committed to prison for an offence growing through my own answer to questions asked me wherein (as the Almighty judge me) I never meant the matter as it was conceived nor meant the man as took the matter as meant to him (the Lord Keeper I mean) I did feel then that heavy doom oppress and wound me at the heart at one instant with sorrow, disgrace and undoing. So far, as my foes will grow now to be hardier to whet their swords, daggers & to provide bullets powder and poison to requite their malices against me : which enemies of mine did give out three days before I was committed that I was committed, some said to the Fleet, others said to the Gatehouse.

Therefore I wish that when I had unknown *poison given to me at Newgate at a dinner presently after I had given my sharp evidence against Bellamy's wife*, then judged, then that my tongue had lost power to speak for a year rather than I should have given to your princely conceit the least cause of offence, for any evil meaning of mine, that might be construed against the meanest councillor of your Majesty, for the Almighty God knoweth I have ever honoured your choice & themselves & the Lord Keeper particularly, as your Sacred Majesty doth know, to whom I have many times desired your Majesty to refer me above others, and his secret conscience doth know my true and plain affection to his Lordship. And my own conscience condemn me to hell if I meant any evil in these words, videlicet :

1. If *I may have ordinary justice I shall recover £3000 of Fitzherbert.*
I meaning as well when I shall have execution upon my judgment, as also in the Common pleas or in the King's Bench, when I shall sue for 40 marks land a year which Fitzherbert hath assured me, upon which mistaking of my words, I was told that I had spoken dishonestly & that I was a dishonest man, in which place it hath pleased your Majesty to say that I have not served your Majesty, but in a better degree.

2. Secondly, offence was taken when I was asked how I could deserve to have a bond of a prisoner of £3000. I answered that I had that bond & the other gifts three years before he the same Fitzherbert was a prisoner, and that I had deserved it *as well as some had done for whose favour £10,000 had been given*

391

and this was construed to be meant, that I said that some Counsellor of them had taken £10,000 which of my soul I meant not. But I offered to set down in writing by how many I meant it; And to your Majesty as to my goddess, I will explain it whensoever my service to come shall deserve that I may be admitted to your most joyful presence, and so most lowlily I cease

the 15 of April 1595

your Majesty's prisoner humbly in the Marshalsea

RIC. TOPCLIFFE

A true copy of a second letter that I presumed to write & send to her most excellent Majesty upon good friday next after, explaining also my fault and meaning.

Every prince's subjects, dear Queen, hath privilege (being wronged) to appeal to his supreme sovereign from any inferior party, although an inferior prince. Myself do not appeal for my judgment to prison because your honourable table said that it was your sacred pleasure which cannot err.

No more did my heart err, nor my words erred, but his Lordship that *wrested my well-meaning* words *to a wrong meaning of my own and construction* of words. He might be deceaved for he is but a man raised to the state of a god in your earth, in regard whereof I will still honour him so much that if your Majesty will say or command me that I shall say, I am in fault, because your honours did commit me, I will say so. *But to the God of heaven and to yourself my Goddess on earth*, I must say that my words & meaning was innocent & mistaken by his Lordship, then were it a sin to condemn & accuse myself.

*In my words their Lordships and I differ not. But in meaning we differ, and therefore there is error in their or in my meaning*, for which I wish that there lay a writ of execution or trial for my life with mine equal, or that I had lost my left hand, upon condition that your Majesty had heard me speak, my words were so clear from thought of evil or fault in my heart.

But when I said at that table, that it was given out abroad two or three days before I was committed, and wagers offered to be laid thereof in sundry places of note, then a Counsellor told me that it was a prophet that so gave out. But that prophet was not my judge, for if he had been or were, he would judge me from hence to Tyburn, to which place I have helped more traitors than all the noble men and gentlemen about your court, your Counsellors excepted. And now by this disgrace I am in fair way and made out to adventure my life every night to murderers, for since I was committed wine in Westminster hath been given for joy of that news, & in all prisons rejoicings. It is like that the fresh dead bones of father Southwell at Tyburn and father Walpole at York, executed both since Shrovetide will dance for joy. And now at Easter, instead of a Communion, many an Alleluia will be sung of priests and traitors in prisons and in ladies closets, for Topcliffe's soul and in farther kingdoms also.

My doating friends will lament, with whom I meant to have meat at my house in Lincolnshire, myself & some of them to have set a trap for . . . my cousin with whom I have had a familiar attending & upon his . . . this winter [blanks in MS]. My horses being brought up from thence for that purpose yesterday above 100 miles to my slaying, which was decreed in prisons before (as hath been told me) by these professors, wagers and rejoicings, and if it had not chanced as it did, I had been like to have taken a priest upon Palm Sunday at night.

If my disgrace, yea or my death, may avail this policy of this present time or state, I wish then both were ended, myself & all I have, no creatures living but Queen Elizabeth nor ever to be altered, as the mighty God knoweth, who preserve your Majesty ever.

At the Marshalsea this good or evil friday 1595

Only your Majesty's humble prisoner,

RICHARD TOPCLIFFE

# APPENDIX D

*[See page 37 supra, and the facsimile]*

## AN EXEMPLIFICATION OF A FINE GRANTED IN THE COURT OF COMMON PLEAS, TRINITY TERM, 32 ELIZABETH, 1590

## RICHARD TOPCLIFFE, ESQRE., PLAINTIFF, AND THOMAS FITZHERBERT, ESQRE., DEFORCIENT. OF THE MANORS OF OVER AND NETHER PADLEY SUPER DARWENT, COUNTY DERBY

TRANSCRIPT

*[The abbreviations have been written out in full]*

**Elizabeth** dei gratia Anglie ffrancie et hibernie Regina fidei defensor etc.

**Omnibus** ad quos presentes littere * . . . finis cum proclamationibus inde factis secundum formam statuti in huiusmodi casu nuper editi et provisi levata fuit in curia nostra coram tunc * . . . Westmonasterium termino Sancte Trinitatis anno regni nostri tricesimo secundo **Tenor cujus** sequitur in hec verba

**Derb. ss.** hec est finalis co[ncordia facta in curia] Domine Regine apud Westmonasterium in Octavis Sancte Trinitatis anno regnorum [*sic*] Elizabeth dei gratia Anglie ffrancie et hibernie Regine fidei defensoris etc. a con[questu tricesimo] secundo coram Eduardo Anderson ffrancisco Wyndam Willelmo Poryam et Thoma Walmysley Justiciariis et aliis domine Regine fidelibus tunc ibi presentibus

**Inter** Ricardum Topclyffe Armigerum questorem

**Et** Thomam ffitzherbert armigerum deforcientem de maneriis de Over padley et Nether padley super Darwent cum pertinentiis ac de sex mesuagiis duobus cotagiis decem gardinis decem pomariis mille acris terre quingentis acris prati sexcentis acris pasture trescentis acris bosci mille acris jampnorum et bruere et viginti solidatis redditus cum pertinentiis in Over padley Nether padley Gryndleforde alias Grindelforde et Lyam alias Lyham in parochia de Hathersedge alias Hadersytche **Unde placitum** convencionis summonitum fuit inter eos in eadem curia

**Scilicet quod** predictus Thomas recognovit predicta maneria et tenementa cum pertinentiis suis esse jus ipsius Ricardi

**Ut illa** que idem Ricardus habet de dono predicti Thome

**Et illa** remisit & quiet'clamavit de se et heredibus suis predicto Ricardo et heredibus suis imperpetuum

**Et preterea** idem Thomas concessit pro se et heredibus suis quod ipse warrantavit predicto Ricardo & heredibus suis predicta maneria & tenementa cum pertinentiis suis contra omnes homines imperpetuum

**Et pro hac** recognitione remissione quiet'clamatione warranta fine et concordia idem Ricardus dedit predicto Thome octingentas marcas argenti

**Tenor** proclamationum hujus finis sequitur in hec verba secundum formam statuti

* A corner of the deed having been cut off at some time, a few words are missing.

# APPENDIX D

**Prima** proclamatio facta fuit octavo die Julii termino Sc̄e Trinitatis anno tricesimo secundo Regine infrascripte

**Secunda** proclamatio facta fuit vicesimo die Octobris termino Sc̄i Michaelis anno tricesimo secundo Regine infrascripte

**Tertia** proclamatio facta fuit vicesimo octavo die Januarii Termino Sc̄i Hillarii anno tricesimo tercio Regine infrascripte

**Quarta** proclamatio facta fuit vicesimo quarto die Aprilis termino pasche anno tricesimo tercio Regine infrascripte

**In Cujus** rei testimonium sigillum nostrum ad Brevia in Banco predicto sigillandum deputative presentibus apponi fecimus

**Teste** E. Anderson apud villam Sancti Albani Sexto die Novembris anno regni nostri tricesimo quinto

CROMPTON

ENDORSED BY TOPCLIFFE. — AN EXEMPLIFICATION OF A FYNE LEVYED FROME THOMAS FITZHARBERT ESQUYER, TO MEE, OF THE MANER OF PADLAYE &c. IN OCTAVIS SCTI TRINITAT A RREG. ELYZABETH 32 :

[*See facsimile supra, facing page 58*]

## TRANSLATION

Elizabeth by the grace of God Queen of England, France and Ireland, Defender of the faith etc.

To all to whom the present letters shall come . . .

A fine, with the proclamations made thereof, according to the form of the statute lately passed and provided in such cases, was levied in our Court before . . . . . . at Westminster in Trinity term in the 32$^{nd}$ year of our reign, whose purport followeth in these words :

**Derby : to wit.**—This is the final concord made in the Court of the Lady Queen at Westminster in the Octave of the Holy Trinity in the 32$^{nd}$ year of the reign of Elizabeth &c, in the presence of Edward Anderson, Francis Wyndham, William Poryam and Thomas Walmesley Justices, and other lieges of the Lady Queen there present.

Between Richard Topcliffe Esq$^{re}$ plaintiff and Thomas Fitzherbert Esquire deforcient, of the manors of Over and Nether Padley on Derwent with the appurtenances, and of six messuages, two cottages, ten gardens, ten orchards, a thousand acres of land, five hundred acres of meadow, six hundred acres of pasture, three hundred acres of wood, a thousand acres of furze and heath and twenty shillings of rent with the appurtenances, in Over Padley, Nether Padley, Grindel ford and Lyham in the parish of Hathersage. Therefore a plea of covenant was declared between them in the same court, namely that the said Thomas recognised the said manors and tenements with their appurtenances as the right of this Richard

As being those which the same Richard holds by gift of the said Thomas.

And these he renounced and quitted claim of for himself and his heirs to the said Richard and his heirs for ever.

And moreover the same Thomas granted for himself and his heirs that he has warranted to the said Richard and his heirs the said manors etc. against all men for ever.

And for this recognition, remission, quit claim, warranty, fine and concord, the same Richard gave to the said Thomas eight hundred marks of silver.

The order of the proclamations follows according to the form of the statute.

The first was made July 8, 1590, the second October 20th 1590, the third January 28, 1590–1, the fourth April 24th 1591.

In witness of which, we have caused our seal for Briefs in the said Bench to be affixed by deputy to these presents.

The Judge, Edward Anderson was witness [that the money was paid at the court] at the town of St. Albans, on November 6, in the 35th year of our reign [1593].

CROMPTON

(*Signed*)     TOPCLIFFE

# APPENDIX E

[See page 68 supra, and the facsimile]

## QUIETUS GRANTED TO ANTHONY FITZHERBERT FOR PENALTIES INCURRED BY HIM FOR HIS RECUSANCY, AMOUNTING TO £120

### DATED EASTER TERM, 3 JAC. I., 1606

[No. 40 of the Norbury deeds at Swynnerton]

## IN ROTULO EXONERATIONUM RECUSAÑ IN DERB.

**Derb.** Anthonius Fitzherbert nuper de Padley in parochia de Hethersedge in com. predicto generosus debet cxx. li. videlicit lx. li. inde virtute cuiusdam actus parliamenti apud Westm. xxix$^{no}$ die Octobr. Anno XXVIII$^{vo}$ Regine Elizabeth inde nuper editi et provisi intitulat 'an act for the more speedy and dewe execucion of certen branches of the statute mayd in the XX$^{th}$ yeare of the Queenes Ma$^{ts}$ raigne Intituled an act to retayne the Quenes Ma$^{ts}$ subiects in ther due obedience.' Eo quod ipse non accessit ecclie parochiali de hethersedge predicte nec alicui ali ecclie capelle aut usuali ali loco co'is precat. infra spatium trium mensium proxime sequen[tium] XX$^{m}$ diem Decembr. Anno XXX$^{mo}$ eiusdem Regine Et lx. li res[iduas]virtute actus predicti Aquarto die Julii Anno XXXI$^{mo}$. eiusdem Regine quo die convictus fuit usque XXVI$^{m}$ diem Septembris tunc proxime sequentis Scilicet pro tribus mens. Eo quod ipse non fecit submissionem et devenit confirmabilis [sic] secundum veram Intentionem Actus parliamenti predicti. S[equit]ur Exon[er]at$^{io}$ de cxxli. predictis per consensum Baronum annotat. in memor$^{d}$ ex parte Remem. Thes. de Anno Tertio R. nunc Jacobi viz. inter record. de termino pasche Rotlo [blank].

M : N$^{D}$

quietus est
H. PALMER

Exoneratio pro Pasc. ter. Record.
A$^{o}$tertio Rs. Ja :
   Ex parte Rem. Thes.
      He : SPYLLER

## TRANSLATION

Derbyshire. Anthony Fitzherbert, lately of Padley, in the parish of Hathersage in the aforesaid county, gentleman, owes £120: namely, £60 in virtue of a certain act of parliament at Westminster, October 29, in the 28th year of Queen Elizabeth, then lately published and provided, entitled 'An act for the more speedy and due execution of the statute made in the 20th year of the Queen's Majesty's reign, entitled An act to retain the Queen's Majesty's subjects in their due obedience': inasmuch as he has not attended the parish church of Hathersage aforesaid nor any other church, chapel or other usual place of common prayer, within the space of three months next following the 20th day of December in the 30th year of the same Queen : and the remaining £60 in virtue of the said act from the 4th day of July in the 31st year of the same Queen, on which day he was convicted, unto the 26th day of September then next following, namely for three months ; Inasmuch as he did not make submission and became conformable according to the true intention of the aforesaid act of parliament Followeth the Exoneration (or final discharge) of the aforesaid £120 noted by the consent of the Barons in the Memoranda Rolls of the Treasurer's Remembrancer in the third year of the present King James, namely among the records of Easter Term in the Roll—

It is discharged<br>H. PALMER

NOTE.—It is not clear why Anthony Fitzherbert owed for these periods only, or why they were exacted so late. Possibly it was an attempt to make him take the Oath of Allegiance. Each of the periods mentioned is one of three lunar months—*i.e.* of twelve weeks only. The first includes the time of Anthony's arrest (December 20 to March 14, 1587–8 ; he was arrested February 2 of that year), and the other covers three months of his imprisonment in Derby Gaol (from July 4, when he was convicted, to September 26, 1589). He did not promise to conform till May 1591. I must leave the puzzle to be cleared up by more learned searchers.

It should be noted that this document is an " office copy " of the entry in the *L.T.R.* [*i.e.* Lord Treasurer's Remembrancer] *Memoranda Rolls.*

The Acts referred to will be found in Coke's *Statutes at Large*, vol. ii. The Act of the 28th Elizabeth is mainly concerned with the levying of the arrears owed to the Crown by Recusants.

# PART OF THE PEDIGREE OF THE FITZHERBERTS OF NORBURY AND SWYNNERTON

Arms : Arg. a chief vairée or and gules, over all a bend sable

NOTE:—This pedigree, as far as Sir Thomas Fitzherbert, is based on a document preserved at Swynnerton (Norbury Deeds, No. 25), Exemplification of Record of Pleadings in the Court of Arches relating to the tithes claimed by Nicholas Browne for the lands of Norbury. Sir Thomas proved his case (23 Elizabeth, 1580). However, Nicholas Fitzherbert, armiger, sued John Bothe, arm., for the manor of Ashe (Plea Rolls de Banco, Mich., 31 Henry VI. 1452— Salt Library, Stafford, ii.3, 205) which he claimed that Thomas Fitzherbert of Somersall had given to Sir William Fitzherbert, Fifth Lord of Norbury, and Ededra his wife, and to their heirs, and he gave the following descent: William, Henry, William, John, William, William, Henry, Nicholas. (John Bothe admitted claim.) But there are many authorities who say that Sir John was son of Henry, and not of William. The most decisive is to be found in Placita de Quo Warranto of 4. Edw. III. Sir John was summonded to prove his right of free warren. He stated that King Henry III. had granted free warren to William Fitzherbert of Norbury, his grandfather, and to his heirs for ever, and from William the right descended to Henry as son and heir, and from Henry to himself as son and heir. The original grant of free warren is dated 4 Sept. 36 Henry III. and included Ashe.

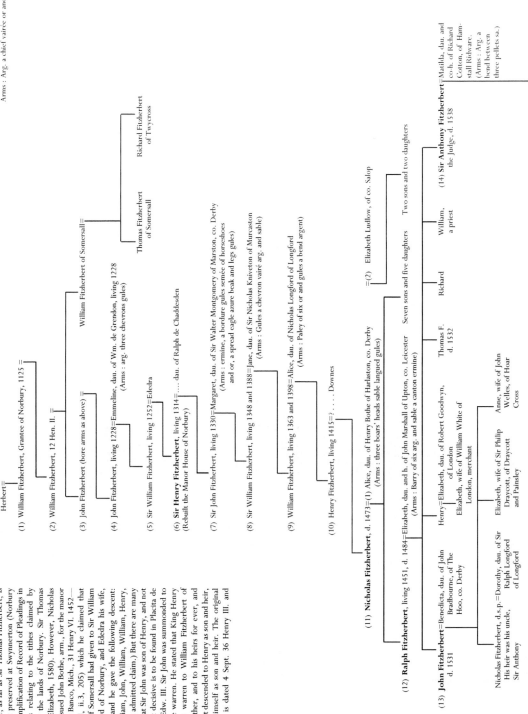

Herbert=

(1) William Fitzherbert, Grantee of Norbury, 1125 =

(2) William Fitzherbert, 12 Hen. II. =

(3) John Fitzherbert (bore arms as above) =          William Fitzherbert of Somersall=

(4) John Fitzherbert, living 1228=Emmeline, dau. of Wm. de Grendon, living 1228
(Arms : arg. three chevrons gules)

(5) Sir William Fitzherbert, living 1252=Ededra          Thomas Fitzherbert of Somersall=

(6) Sir Henry Fitzherbert, living 1314=.... dau. of Ralph de Chaddesden          Richard Fitzherbert of Twycross
(Rebuilt the Manor House of Norbury)

(7) Sir John Fitzherbert, living 1330=Margaret, dau. of Sir Walter Montgomery of Marston, co. Derby
(Arms : ermine, a bordure gules semée of horseshoes and or, a spread eagle azure beak and legs gules)

(8) Sir William Fitzherbert, living 1348 and 1388=Jane, dau. of Sir Nicholas Kniveton of Murcaston
(Arms : Gules a chevron vairé arg. and sable)

(9) William Fitzherbert, living 1363 and 1398=Alice, dau. of Nicholas Longford of Longford
(Arms : Paley of six or and gules a bend argent)

(10) Henry Fitzherbert, living 1415=? . . . . Downes

(11) Nicholas Fitzherbert, d. 1473=(1) Alice, dau. of Henry Bothe of Harlaston, co. Derby
(Arms : three boars' heads sable langued gules)
=(2)  Elizabeth Ludlow, of co. Salop

(12) Ralph Fitzherbert, living 1451, d. 1484=Elizabeth, dau. and h. of John Marshall of Upton, co. Leicester          Seven sons and five daughters          Two sons and two daughters
(Arms : Barry of six arg. and sable a canton ermine)

(13) John Fitzherbert=Benedicta, dau. of John Bradbourne, of The Hoo, co. Derby    Henry=Elizabeth, dau. of Robert Goodwyn, of London          Thomas F. d. 1532    Richard    William, a priest    (14) Sir Anthony Fitzherbert=Matilda, dau. and
d. 1531                                                       Elizabeth, wife of William White of London, merchant                                                                 the judge, d. 1538    co-h. of Richard Cotton, of Ham-stall Ridware.
(Arms : Arg. a bend between three pellets sa.)

Nicholas Fitzherbert, d.s.p.=Dorothy, dau. of Sir    Elizabeth, wife of Sir Philip    Anne, wife of John
His heir was his uncle,    Ralph Longford    Draycott, of Draycott    Welles, of Hoar
Sir Anthony    of Longford    and Painsley    Cross

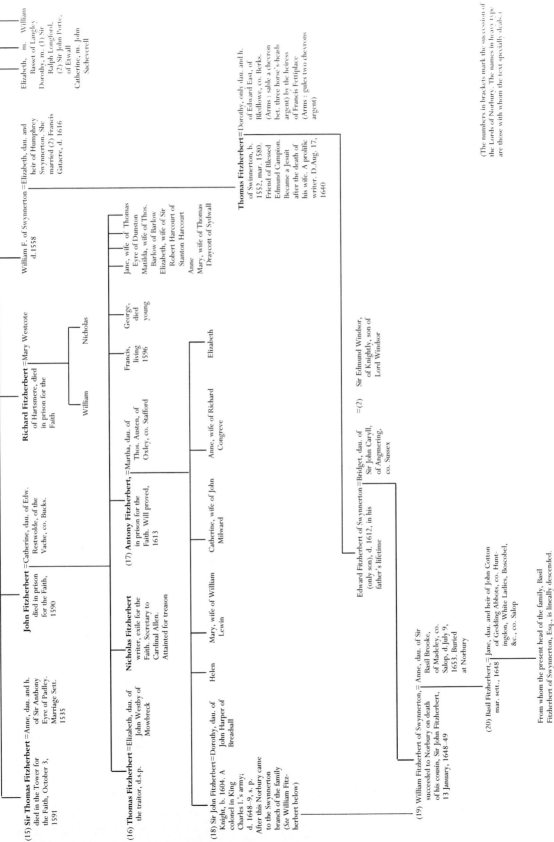

(15) **Sir Thomas Fitzherbert** = Anne, dau. and h. of Sir Anthony Eyre of Padley. Marriage Sett. 1535
died in the Tower for the Faith, October 3, 1591

**John Fitzherbert**
died in prison for the Faith, 1590

**Richard Fitzherbert** = Mary Westcote
of Hartsmere, died in prison for the Faith

William F. of Swynnerton = Elizabeth, dau. and
d. 1558
heir of Humphrey Swynnerton. She married (2) Francis Gatacre, d. 1616

Elizabeth, m. William Basset of Langley
Dorothy, m. (1) Sir Ralph Longford, (2) Sir John Porte, of Etwall
Catherine, m. John Sacheverell

William

Nicholas

(16) **Thomas Fitzherbert** = Elizabeth, dau. of John Westby of Mowbreck
the traitor, d.s.p.

**Nicholas Fitzherbert**
writer, exile for the Faith. Secretary to Cardinal Allen. Attainted for treason

(17) **Antony Fitzherbert**, = Martha, dau. of Thos. Austen, of Oxley, co. Stafford
in prison for the Faith. Will proved, 1613

Francis, living 1596

George, died young

Jane, wife of Thomas Eyre of Dunston
Matilda, wife of Thos. Barlow of Barlow
Elizabeth, wife of Sir Robert Harcourt of Stanton Harcourt
Anne
Mary, wife of Thomas Draycott of Sydwall

**Thomas Fitzherbert** = Dorothy, only dau. and h.
of Swynnerton, b. 1552, mar. 1580. Friend of Blessed Edmund Campion. Became a Jesuit after the death of his wife. A prolific writer. D. Aug. 17, 1640
of Edward East, of Bledlowe, co. Berks. (Arms : sable a chevron bet. three horse's-heads argent) by the heiress of Francis Fettiplace (Arms : gules two chevrons argent)

(18) **Sir John Fitzherbert** = Dorothy, dau. of John Harper of Breadsall
Knight, b. 1604. A colonel in King Charles I.'s army; d. 1648-9, s. p. After this Norbury came to the Swynnerton branch of the family (See William Fitzherbert below)

Helen

Mary, wife of William Lewin

Catherine, wife of John Milward

Anne, wife of Richard Congreve

Elizabeth

Edward Fitzherbert of Swynnerton = Bridget, dau. of Sir John Caryll, of Angmering, co. Sussex
(only son), d. 1612, in his father's lifetime

= (2) Sir Edmund Windsor, of Knightly, son of Lord Windsor

(19) **William Fitzherbert of Swynnerton,** = Anne, dau. of Sir Basil Brooke, of Madeley, co. Salop, d. July 9, 1653. Buried at Norbury
succeeded to Norbury on death of his cousin, Sir John Fitzherbert, 13 January, 1648-49

(20) **Basil Fitzherbert,** = Jane, dau. and heir of John Cotton of Gedding Abbots, co. Huntingdon, White Ladies, Boscobel, &c., co. Salop
mar. sett., 1648

From whom the present head of the family, Basil Fitzherbert of Swynnerton, Esq., is lineally descended.

(The numbers in brackets mark the succession of the Lords of Norbury. The names in heavy type are those with whom the text specially deals.)

# INDEX

399

# INDEX

# INDEX

3 F

# INDEX

# INDEX

**Nibil Obstat.**

F. OSMUND COONEY, O.F.M.

*Provincial*


**Imprimatur:**

EDM : CANONICUS SURMONT

*Vicarius Generalis*


WESTMONASTERII,

*die 25 Augusti* 1910